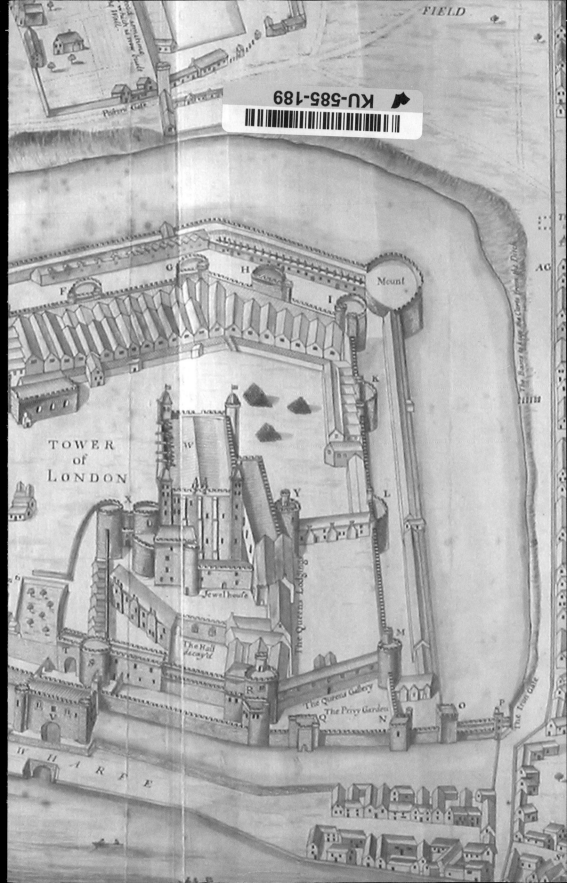

Jane Boleyn

THE INFAMOUS
LADY ROCHFORD

JULIA FOX

Weidenfeld & Nicolson
LONDON

First published in Great Britain in 2007
by Weidenfeld & Nicolson

1 3 5 7 9 10 8 6 4 2

A CIP catalogue record for this book
is available from the British Library.

ISBN 978 0 297 85081 6

Typeset by Input Data Services Ltd, Frome

Printed and bound by Butler and Tanner Ltd,
Frome and London

The Orion Publishing Group's policy is to use papers that
are natural, renewable and recyclable products and made
from wood grown in sustainable forests. The logging and
manufacturing processes are expected to conform to the
environmental regulations of the country of origin.

Weidenfeld & Nicolson

The Orion Publishing Group Ltd
Orion House
5 Upper Saint Martin's Lane
London, WC2H 9EA

www.orionbooks.co.uk

IN MEMORY OF MY PARENTS

Contents

A WOMAN OF IMPORTANCE

THE WINDS OF CHANGE

CARVING A CAREER

THE PATH TO THE BLOCK

Acknowledgements

I'm not sure quite how Jane Boleyn came into my life. She simply did. One moment I was considering a book on Henry VIII's queens and the next those beguiling ladies were totally sidelined in favour of this woman, a pariah of Tudor history, whom no one had really considered before. I was hooked instantly. And the more I dug through the records, many ignored for centuries, the more obvious it was that Jane Boleyn's story was not only just as gripping as those of the queens she had served but that she had been thoroughly maligned. She was no fairy godmother, but she was no wicked witch either. Forced to look out for herself in a man's world, she so nearly succeeded.

No book of this type, however, is a solo effort. I could never have even started without access to the finest scholarship currently available on the reign of Henry VIII. Amongst that of the many giants of Tudor history, the work of Professor Eric Ives and Dr David Starkey, has proved invaluable. To them, in particular, I owe an immense debt. I also thank the Hon. Auriol Pakington for generous permission to cite family documents deposited in Worcester Record Office and Thomas Campbell of the Metropolitan Museum of Art in New York for so kindly allowing me to read in typescript his excellent book on tapestries and cite his research. Christine Reynolds, Assistant Keeper of the Muniments in the Library, Westminster Abbey, showed considerable patience in answering my many requests for information concerning the Abbey layout in Tudor times and I am grateful to her. Thanks are also due to the staff of the London Library, the British Library and the National Archives for their efficiency and expertise and to the archivists of the Essex Record Office for their exemplary courtesy and helpfulnes.

And the list cannot stop there. Peter Robinson, my agent, supported my desire to tell Jane's story and gave me the confidence to attempt to do so. My editors, Alan Samson and Francine Brody, were unstinting with their time and advice, and I am grateful for their painstaking efforts to iron out so many crinkles in my manuscript. I must take full responsibility for those that remain. To Richard Guy, who laboured so hard to produce the family trees from my rough drafts, to Audrey Kimberley who read the finished work with an eagle eye, to Jessica Sharkey who so willingly translated pages and pages of Latin text for me, and to so many of my long-suffering friends who endured hours of discussion about Jane and her dilemmas, I offer my sincerest gratitude. The involvement and interest shown by my brother and sister-in-law went far beyond the call of family duty and I thank them both. But it is to my husband that I am most indebted. His assistance with the Notes and Bibliography has been crucial and, if I have gone any way towards redressing the balance, and removing any of the stigma attached to Jane's name, it is because of his constant love, encouragement and acceptance of her right to be a constant presence in our lives for over three years.

List of Illustrations

(*BETWEEN PAGES 270–271*)

Anne Boleyn by an unknown artist. *Hever Castle, Kent/The Bridgeman Art Library.*

Letter written by King Henry VIII to Anne Boleyn. *Weidenfeld & Nicolson Archive/ Biblioteca Apostolica Vaticana.*

Hever Castle, Kent. *The Bridgeman Art Library.*

Sir Thomas Wyatt by Hans Holbein the Younger. *The Royal Collection © 2007 Her Majesty Queen Elizabeth II, The Royal Library, Windsor.*

Brass of Sir Thomas Boleyn over his tomb in St. Peter's Church, Hever. *Courtesy of St Peter's Church, Hever.*

Sir Thomas Cromwell by Hans Holbein the Younger. *The Frick Collection, New York.*

The seating plan for Anne Boleyn's coronation. *The British Library, London.*

Hans Holbein the Younger's design for Mount Parnassus, a tableau on the route of Anne Boleyn's coronation procession. *Weidenfeld & Nicolson Archive/BPK Berlin/Kupferstichkabinett.*

An illustration from George Cavendish's *Life of Cardinal Wolsey. The Bodleian Library, Oxford.*

A map of the Tower of London, 1597. *The Society of Antiquaries, London.*

The Duke of Norfolk by Hans Holbein the Younger. *© Castle Howard, North Yorkshire, UK/The Bridgeman Art Library.*

Jane Seymour by Hans Holbein the Younger. *Kunsthistorisches Museum, Vienna/The Bridgeman Art Library.*

Anne of Cleves by Hans Holbein the Younger. *Victoria and Albert Museum, London.*

Catherine Howard by Hans Holbein the Younger. *The Royal Collection © 2007 Her Majesty Queen Elizabeth II.*

Charles Brandon, Duke of Suffolk and his wife Mary Tudor, the French Queen, by an unknown artist. *By kind permission of His Grace the Duke of Bedford and the Trustees of the Bedford Estates.*

Henry Fitzroy, Duke of Richmond, by Lucas Hornebolte. *The Royal Collection © 2007 Her Majesty Queen Elizabeth II.*

Mary Tudor by Master John. *The National Portrait Gallery, London.*

The young Elizabeth by an unknown artist. *The Royal Collection © 2007 Her Majesty Queen Elizabeth II.*

Edward VI by Hans Holbein the Younger. *AKG-Images/ National Gallery of Art, Washington, Andrew W. Mellon Collection.*

Portrait of John Russell 1st Earl of Bedford (1485–1555) engraved by Francesco Bartolozzi (1727–1815) (engraving) by Holbein, Hans the Younger (1497/8–1543) (after) *© Private Collection/The Stapleton Collection/The Bridgeman Art Library.*

Two designs for pendants by Hans Holbein the Younger. *The British Museum, London.*

A costume design by Hans Holbein the Younger. *The British Museum, London.*

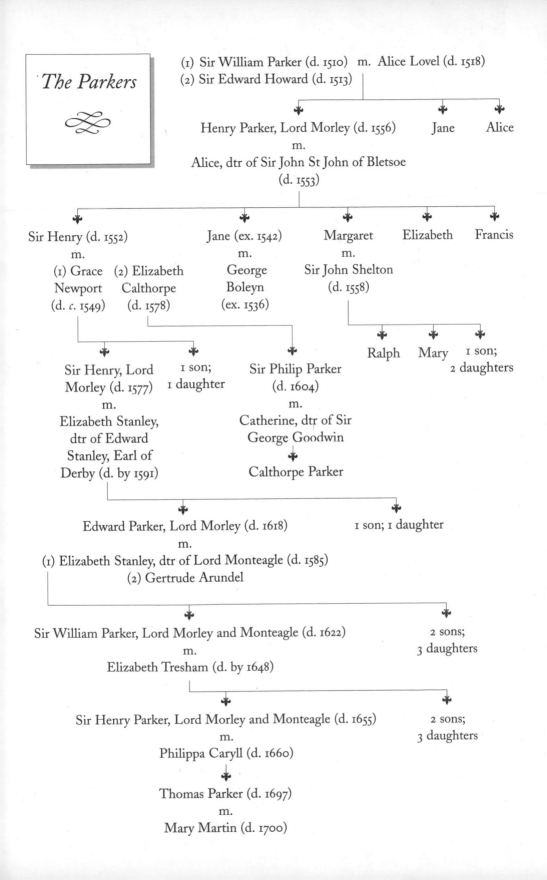

The Parkers

(1) Sir William Parker (d. 1510) m. Alice Lovel (d. 1518)
(2) Sir Edward Howard (d. 1513)

Henry Parker, Lord Morley (d. 1556)　　Jane　　Alice
m.
Alice, dtr of Sir John St John of Bletsoe
(d. 1553)

Sir Henry (d. 1552)　　　Jane (ex. 1542)　　　Margaret　　Elizabeth　　Francis
m.　　　　　　　　　　　m.　　　　　　　　　m.
(1) Grace (2) Elizabeth　　George　　　Sir John Shelton
Newport　　Calthorpe　　Boleyn　　　　(d. 1558)
(d. c. 1549)　(d. 1578)　(ex. 1536)

Ralph　　Mary　　1 son;
　　　　　　　　　　　　　　　　　　　　　　　　　2 daughters

Sir Henry, Lord　　1 son;　　　Sir Philip Parker
Morley (d. 1577)　1 daughter　　(d. 1604)
m.　　　　　　　　　　　　　　　m.
Elizabeth Stanley,　　　　　Catherine, dtr of Sir
dtr of Edward　　　　　　　George Goodwin
Stanley, Earl of
Derby (d. by 1591)　　　　　Calthorpe Parker

Edward Parker, Lord Morley (d. 1618)　　　1 son; 1 daughter
m.
(1) Elizabeth Stanley, dtr of Lord Monteagle (d. 1585)
(2) Gertrude Arundel

Sir William Parker, Lord Morley and Monteagle (d. 1622)　　2 sons;
m.　　　　　　　　　　　　　　　　　　　　　　　　3 daughters
Elizabeth Tresham (d. by 1648)

Sir Henry Parker, Lord Morley and Monteagle (d. 1655)　　2 sons;
m.　　　　　　　　　　　　　　　　　　　　　　　　3 daughters
Philippa Caryll (d. 1660)

Thomas Parker (d. 1697)
m.
Mary Martin (d. 1700)

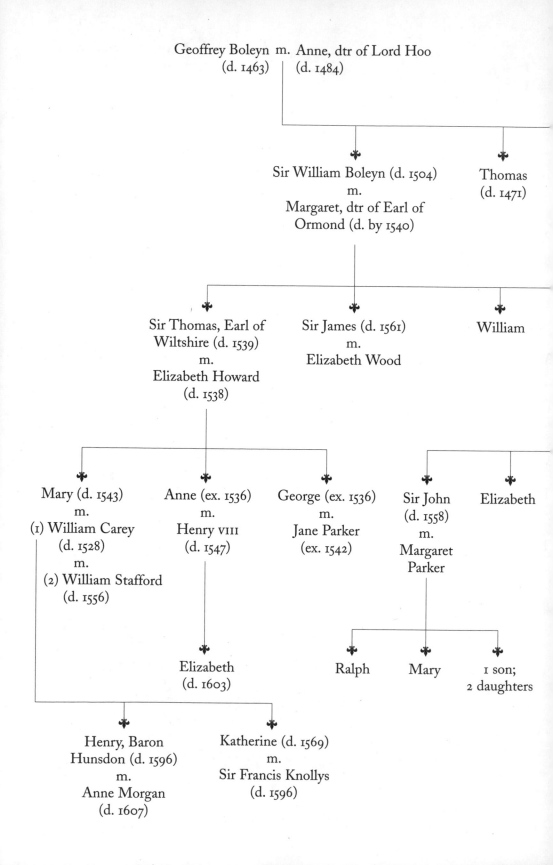

Geoffrey Boleyn m. Anne, dtr of Lord Hoo
(d. 1463)   (d. 1484)

Sir William Boleyn (d. 1504)
m.
Margaret, dtr of Earl of
Ormond (d. by 1540)

Thomas
(d. 1471)

Sir Thomas, Earl of
Wiltshire (d. 1539)
m.
Elizabeth Howard
(d. 1538)

Sir James (d. 1561)
m.
Elizabeth Wood

William

Mary (d. 1543)
m.
(1) William Carey
(d. 1528)
m.
(2) William Stafford
(d. 1556)

Anne (ex. 1536)
m.
Henry VIII
(d. 1547)

George (ex. 1536)
m.
Jane Parker
(ex. 1542)

Sir John
(d. 1558)
m.
Margaret
Parker

Elizabeth

Elizabeth
(d. 1603)

Ralph

Mary

1 son;
2 daughters

Henry, Baron
Hunsdon (d. 1596)
m.
Anne Morgan
(d. 1607)

Katherine (d. 1569)
m.
Sir Francis Knollys
(d. 1596)

The Boleyns

3 daughters

Sir Edward
m.
Anne Tempest

4 daughters

Mary (d. 1570)
m.
Sir John
Heveningham

Anne (d. 1555)
m.
Sir John Shelton
(d. 1539)

Margaret

Alice (d. 1539)
m.
Sir Robert Clere
(d. 1531)

Margaret
m.
John Sackville
(d. 1557)

Richard   3 daughters
Christopher   John

Sir John (d. 1557)
m.
Anne Tyrell

2 sons

Edward (d. 1606)
m.
Frances, dtr
of Sir Richard
Fulmerstone

2 sons;
2 daughters

The Howards

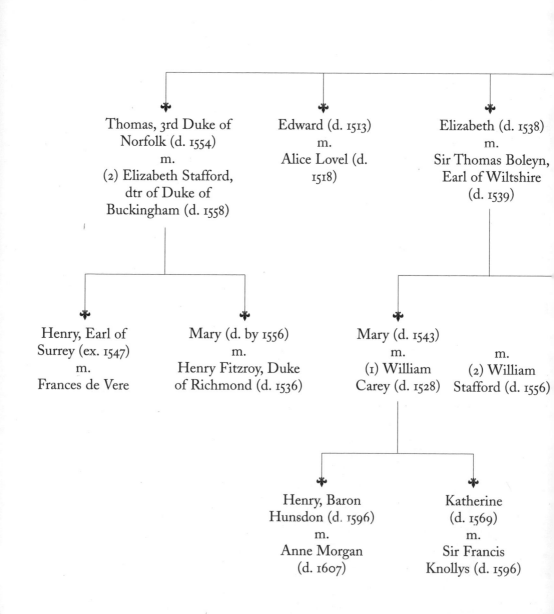

Thomas, 3rd Duke of
Norfolk (d. 1554)
m.
(2) Elizabeth Stafford,
dtr of Duke of
Buckingham (d. 1558)

Edward (d. 1513)
m.
Alice Lovel (d.
1518)

Elizabeth (d. 1538)
m.
Sir Thomas Boleyn,
Earl of Wiltshire
(d. 1539)

Henry, Earl of
Surrey (ex. 1547)
m.
Frances de Vere

Mary (d. by 1556)
m.
Henry Fitzroy, Duke
of Richmond (d. 1536)

Mary (d. 1543)
m.   m.
(1) William   (2) William
Carey (d. 1528)   Stafford (d. 1556)

Henry, Baron
Hunsdon (d. 1596)
m.
Anne Morgan
(d. 1607)

Katherine
(d. 1569)
m.
Sir Francis
Knollys (d. 1596)

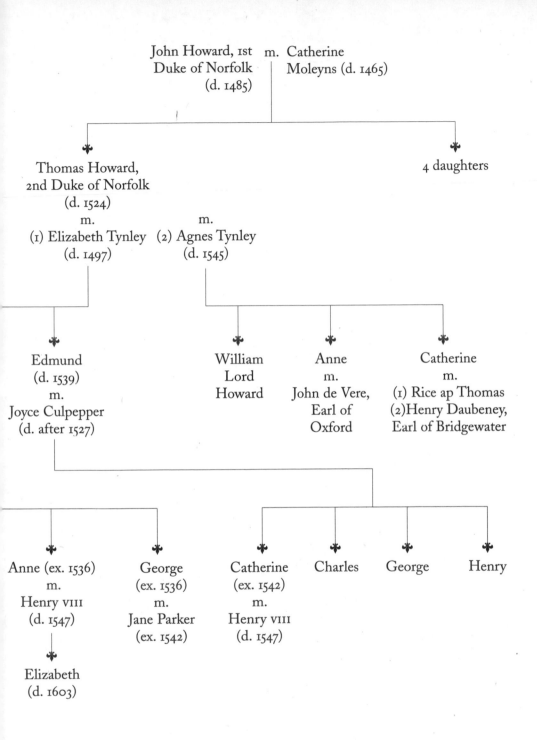

John Howard, 1st m. Catherine
Duke of Norfolk   Moleyns (d. 1465)
(d. 1485)

Thomas Howard,   4 daughters
2nd Duke of Norfolk
(d. 1524)
m.   m.
(1) Elizabeth Tynley (2) Agnes Tynley
(d. 1497)   (d. 1545)

Edmund   William   Anne   Catherine
(d. 1539)   Lord   m.   m.
m.   Howard   John de Vere, (1) Rice ap Thomas
Joyce Culpepper   Earl of   (2) Henry Daubeney,
(d. after 1527)   Oxford   Earl of Bridgewater

Anne (ex. 1536)   George   Catherine   Charles   George   Henry
m.   (ex. 1536)   (ex. 1542)
Henry VIII   m.   m.
(d. 1547)   Jane Parker Henry VIII
                    (ex. 1542)   (d. 1547)

Elizabeth
(d. 1603)

Author's Notes

NOTE ON DATES

For the dates in this book, the Old Style has been retained, but the year is assumed to have begun on 1 January, and not on Lady Day, the feast of the Annunciation (i.e. 25 March), which was by custom the first day of the calendar year in France, Spain and Italy until 1582, in Scotland until 1600, and in England, Wales and Ireland until 1752.

NOTE ON CURRENCY

In citing units of currency, the old sterling denominations of pounds, shillings and pence have been retained. A hundred marks were worth £66 13s 4d.

NOTE ON TRANSCRIPTION

The spelling and orthography of primary sources in quotations are always given in modernised form. Modern punctuation and capitalisation are provided where there is none in the original manuscript.

The Hand of Fate

Their way lit by the flickering light from great wax torches, and to the soothing sound of chanted prayers, the mourners walked solemnly towards the three black-draped barges ready at the river's edge. Amongst them were the leading men of the land, entrusted with the sombre task of accompanying the tiny coffin containing the body of the infant prince to its resting place with his ancestors in the Abbey Church of St Peter's at Westminster just a few miles away. It was February and bitterly cold. The icy waters of the Thames lapped against the sides of the vessels, the leafless trees stood stark and sentinel as if to guard the baby on whom so many hopes had rested, the breath of the oarsmen was clearly visible as they watched the casket being gently brought aboard. The final journey had begun.

A tolling of the bells could be heard as the cortège made its way slowly from the royal palace of Richmond where the child had died so suddenly, to the Abbey where the monks waited patiently. All would be done according to strict protocol and tradition, every minute detail of the prescribed ceremonial observed. Eight royal officers – yeomen and grooms of the household – were stationed at the door of St Peter's to receive the tall funeral torches: thick wax and resin candles fixed into wooden holders, carried by the twenty appointed torch bearers. The choir, which faced the sanctuary, and the catafalque on which the coffin would be placed, were draped with over three hundred yards of black cloth, arranged under the meticulous supervision of Ralph Jenet, the yeoman of the Wardrobe of Beds. He could never have performed a more poignant task for the king his master. The air inside the church was heavy with the smell of the burning wax and the soft fragrance of the incense.

Light and colour abounded, for all was decorated for the glory of God. The walls were covered with paintings in vibrant reds and blues and greens and yellows, or with richly embroidered hangings, which glittered with gold and silver thread. Sculptures of stone angels smiled benignly down on the intricately carved friezes of birds, flowers and foliage adorning the tracery around the monuments or the niches encircling the painted and gilded statues of saints. Diffused light of every shade and hue flowed through the panes of the towering stained-glass windows. The dancing flames of hundreds of candles were everywhere. The shrine, shimmering with gold and precious stones, containing the remains of St Edward the Confessor, a founder of the Abbey, was housed in its own chapel together with sacred relics such as a thorn from the crown of thorns, the girdle of the Virgin Mary and a phial protecting a few drops of the blood of Christ. The chapel stood proudly in the heart of the church, just behind the high altar, itself a stunning testament to medieval skill, craftsmanship and faith. It was the perfect setting for the burial of a prince.

More than four hundred people were present at the interment. One hundred and eighty paupers held yet more torches as they walked in the procession. They took their role in the ceremony very seriously because the prayers of the poor would help those facing divine judgment. Five of the king's knights carried specially made funeral banners. Then came the elaborate hearse swathed in more than seven yards of black cloth of gold and decorated by painters who had worked day and night to complete it. Four knights reverently bore the coffin, covered with black cloth of gold and with a white cloth of gold cross upon it, over which there was a canopy held by four more knights. Four earls, a marquess, barons and yet more knights followed. Next came chaplains, preachers, those who were 'daily waiters upon the prince', even two knights whose job it was to ensure that the correct order of precedence was maintained amongst the congregation. Nothing was left to chance. The mourning robes themselves were graded in fabric and richness according to the rank of the wearers, the chief of whom wore hoods covering their heads.

The king had chosen the child's final resting place carefully. He was placed as near as possible to those previous kings whose ranks he could join only in death. Although he would never sit upon St Edward's Chair with the crown upon his head, he would lie on the left-hand side of the altar, close to the canopied tomb of Edmund Crouchback, the youngest son of Henry III, a few steps from the Chapel of St Edward.

The customary, consoling words of the Latin burial service began; the coffin was ritually sprinkled with holy water and censed at each of the four sides and, as the echo of the final prayers and the antiphons led by the king's composer and musician, Robert Fayrfax, faded away, everyone left the confines of the church. The monks could once again carry out their daily routines uninterrupted by the formalities of state. And the baby could sleep.

It was all so different from just seven weeks earlier when his birth was announced on New Year's Day, 1511. His parents were King Henry VIII of England and his queen, Katherine of Aragon. He was their first living child. They were still young – the king was not yet twenty, although Katherine was almost six years older – and both were delighted that the succession was now assured. The boy seemed healthy; there was every reason to believe that he would be joined by brothers and sisters in due course. Henry was so grateful that he rode to the shrine of Our Lady at Walsingham, in Norfolk, to give thanks, a journey of about two hundred miles. Bonfires were lit in the streets of London to celebrate the birth; free wine provided for some lucky revellers; the happy news proclaimed throughout the kingdom and to the royal courts of Europe. The child was christened Henry after his father and grandfather, the first Tudor monarch.

In the second week of February, Henry VIII and Katherine attended two days of magnificent jousts in the child's honour at the palace of Westminster. The queen presided over the tournament serenely, secure in the knowledge that she had fulfilled her primary function as consort by producing a son. On the second day, she presented the prizes to the victors, including one to her husband, for Henry joined the lists as the gallant 'Loyal Heart'. The chief nobles of the land were all there. No one imagined that the little prince would die just ten days later and would lie in a grave not far from the tiltyards.

Nor could anyone have known then that Henry and Katherine would become only too familiar with grief. The king at first tried to hide his sorrow and comfort the queen with thoughts of the family they would one day have but, despite her numerous pregnancies and many long hours spent in prayer, Katherine managed to give birth to only one child who lived to grow up. And that was a girl, Princess Mary. What use was she in a masculine age when prowess on the battlefield could decide the success or ruin of a dynasty?

Henry understood this only too well. There was little he would not do to gain the son he needed. In the process, his country was changed for ever and few of his subjects were untouched, although some were more affected than others. One of the knights who had jousted with the king on that carefree day, and who later helped carry the body of the tiny child, was Sir Thomas Boleyn, a courtier very much in favour with his sovereign. Thomas and his wife, Elizabeth Howard, had two daughters and a son. The girls' names were Anne and Mary and their brother was George. When the mourners entered Westminster Abbey on that raw February day, these children were playing with their attendants. So was a little girl, one Jane Parker, who would one day marry George Boleyn. They grew up blissfully unaware that the direction of their lives and even their ultimate fate would be so determined by the death of a prince they had never seen. Those four children were not to know that one would become a queen, one would eventually lead a life of relative obscurity, three would face the headsman's axe and Jane's reputation would become tarnished with tales of adultery, incest and betrayal.

THE EARLY YEARS

1

Childhood

It was time to go. The horses shifted and stamped restlessly. They always seemed to know when a long journey was imminent. The carts were laden with fashionable clothes, domestic items, everything needed to make life comfortable. Servants and escorts stood ready too. For Lord Morley's daughter, Jane Parker, a new life was about to begin. She rode out towards London, leaving behind her family home at Great Hallingbury.

Until now, the Tudor mansion, built by Lord Morley, had been her world. The solid, red-bricked house replaced an earlier Morley dwelling that had nestled in the same Essex village for over three hundred years. It was huge, a magical place for giggling children to hide and play. Scattered amongst the richly carved oak furniture and plate inside the building were many reminders of Lord Morley's mother, Alice Lovel. When she died in 1518, Alice made generous bequests to her son. Lord Morley could sleep in the bed of cloth of gold and tawny velvet that she left him. He could sit in her 'best chair', which probably stood in the long gallery, now equipped by Lord Morley with expensive linenfold panelling and tall, graceful windows. Alice's gilt bowl, emblazoned with her own coat of arms as well as that of her first husband, was on display for all to see. Also on view was an even older and more precious heirloom, the special cup with its gilt cover that Alice said was 'gotten' by her ancestors. One of the exquisitely embroidered wall hangings also came from her. Lord Morley had been allowed to choose whichever one he wanted from her estate. Everything fitted perfectly into his newly constructed home, which was one of the finest in the county. Its grounds were impressive too. If the weather was fine, Jane roamed happily outside in the carefully tended gardens, which stretched for over two acres. There was an orchard, to provide apples, pears and quinces for the quince marmalade that everyone loved. There was a pond, surrounded by trees and stocked with fish. There was a long brick stable block and hay loft, so necessary for the Morley horses, surmounted by tall red Tudor chimneys. Whether Great Hallingbury, or Hallingbury Morley as her father preferred to call it, was snuggling under thick snow or basking in the warm sunshine of a summer's afternoon, the setting was idyllic, especially during those few precious years of childhood when the years pass slowly and growing up seems so far away.

Just a short walk across the fields from the house was the parish church of St Giles. It is still standing. Built largely of flint and limestone, with a square bell tower, it is small and intimate. The nave, forty-five feet long, with circular windows set deeply into the walls, led into the chancel through a round arch constructed of Roman bricks, for there had once been a Roman site here. It was probably in this pretty church, so much the heart of the village, that Jane was baptised. About the year 1505, the tiny girl was carried to the porch of St Giles by her mother's midwife. Lady Morley was not present as it was customary for mothers not to re-enter society until they had been churched, or purified, about forty days after giving birth. With Jane's godparents at her side, the midwife gently took her inside for the baptism itself. There, at the stone font, before the richly carved rood screen and amidst the painted walls and brightly coloured statues of saints, the baby was welcomed into the great Catholic fold. Lord and Lady Morley knew how important it was that babies be received into the protection of the Church as quickly as possible after their birth. Life was unpredictable and diseases often struck without warning; they did not want their little daughter to fall into limbo, the dreadful nothingness that awaited the souls of unbaptised children. Everything, therefore, was correctly done. The priest blessed Jane with holy oil on her shoulders and chest, on her right hand and on her forehead. Salt was placed into her mouth so that she would be 'freed from all uncleanness, and from all assault of spiritual wickedness'. She was dipped three times into the sacred water in the font. She was anointed with holy chrism.

The godparents, whose names are lost to us, vowed to ensure that Jane's mother and father kept her 'from fire and water and other perils' and to make certain that she knew 'the Pater noster, Ave and Creed, after the law of all holy church'. They told the priest the name chosen for her: she was christened Jane, possibly after her father's sister, another Jane Parker. Family ties were always important.

As she rode away from these familiar surroundings, Jane knew how important those ties were. She had every reason to feel pride in her lineage. Her father, Sir Henry Parker, Lord Morley, was a peer of the realm, owning lands in Norfolk, Buckinghamshire and Herefordshire as well as in Essex. He came from ancient stock. His ancestors had played their part in tumultuous events over the centuries, helping to quell the Peasants' Revolt and fighting for king and country in the Hundred Years War against England's traditional enemy, France. Yes, Jane could feel proud.

She knew, of course, that it could all have been otherwise. The family lands and title came through Jane's grandmother, Alice Lovel. Alice's brother, a previous Lord Morley, died in Flanders fighting for Edward IV. However, although he had died a hero, he also died without children so his entire estate went to Alice. Girls sometimes had their uses. But Alice's first marriage, to Sir William Parker, Jane's grandfather, had brought the family close to disaster: Sir William Parker had fought on the wrong side at the Battle of Bosworth. He supported the doomed Richard III against Henry Tudor, the victorious Henry VII. Sir William survived the battle but the new king never really trusted him. His son, the young Henry Parker, the future Lord Morley and Jane's father, was fortunate to have been brought up in the household of Lady Margaret Beaufort, Henry VII's mother.

Stern and formidable she might be, but Lady Margaret was loyal to those she took under her wing. She was particularly concerned that the little boy should receive what she felt was his due, especially when his mother remarried after Sir William's death. Lady Margaret paid 500 marks to Alice's new husband, Sir Edward Howard, to make sure that young Henry Parker kept some family land, presumably at Great Hallingbury. Sir Edward adhered to the bargain and also remembered his stepson in his will of 1512. He bequeathed the manor of Morley Hall in Norfolk to his wife, Alice, for her lifetime after which it would pass to Jane's father. The legacy did not come without conditions, however. In exchange, Morley was required to give land worth 10 marks a year to the prior and convent of Ingham in Norfolk or forfeit Morley Hall to them. Morley was lucky that Alice and Sir Edward had no children to complicate the situation further. Sir Edward had sired two bastards for whom he did his best to provide: he asked the king to choose one, the other being allocated to Charles Brandon, Duke of Suffolk. Howard hoped their new guardians would be 'good' lords to his sons but, as an extra safeguard, he left the boys money to help them set 'forth in the world'.

This did not, of course, affect Lord Morley or his inheritance. In fact, as far as Jane's father was concerned, the Howard marriage, which might have proved so awkward, brought him both land and valuable connections at court. The Howards were a very influential family. Sir Edward's father was the Duke of Norfolk, one of the leading men in the land, and Sir Edward's sister, Elizabeth, had married Sir Thomas Boleyn. Sir Thomas was a rising star, an ideal companion to the gregarious Henry VIII, certainly a man it was advantageous to know. And he was a neighbour, for, like the Morleys, the Boleyns owned lands in Essex and Norfolk. Being linked to the Boleyns created more associations since Thomas had sisters who married into other Norfolk or Essex families. His sister Anne, for example, married Sir John Shelton, Alice married Sir Robert Clere and Margaret married Sir John Sackville. Although the inter-relationships were complicated, Lord Morley had every reason to believe that he and his family would gain from them. And Sir Thomas Boleyn had a son, George, who was more or less Jane's age. Who knew what time might bring?

Certainly, as she rode to London, Jane understood that her destiny lay outside the confines of Great Hallingbury. Even while she enjoyed those brief years of childhood, Jane realised that they were but a preparation for the future – hers. Lord and Lady Morley took the upbringing of their children very seriously. It was their duty. Both boys and girls must be taught all that society demanded if they were to take their rightful place when the time came. Lord Morley had a love of learning that lasted his whole life. Educated at Oxford himself, he wanted a stimulating and rigorous education for his son and heir, Henry. Expertise in the classics, however, was not something to encourage in his daughters. No husband would want a wife who was more knowledgeable than himself. Jane's schooling was therefore designed to fit her for the role of a wife and mother. She stayed at home in those early years, learning how to read and write, how to supervise servants and run a large household, and how to harness the healing properties of common herbs so that she could treat everyday ailments. Then, of course, there was needlework. Jane spent hours quietly sewing and perfecting convoluted yet delicate stitches. In this she was not alone, as most wealthy women excelled in this pastime. Even Queen Katherine made shirts for her husband and thought nothing of mending them herself as a sign of her love. And, perhaps Jane's greatest pleasure, she learnt the rudiments of dancing and music. A talented musician himself, the king delighted in everything musical. He revelled in the highly choreographed and glittering masques performed after supper at court. In these spectacular entertainments, favourite gentlemen strutted about in elaborate costumes, playing the roles of holy pilgrims, mysterious strangers or brave knights ready to rescue damsels in distress. The prettiest and most accomplished of the ladies always got the best parts. For Jane, it was as well to be ready. Opportunities to be on show before the entire court did not come easily, even for the daughter of a peer. Chances had to be seized.

That is, naturally, if God willed it so. Religion underpinned everything. While still a child, Jane was instructed with the underlying beliefs of Catholicism. She learnt about the sacrifice of Christ and the sacrament of the mass. She took comfort in the gentle goodness of the Virgin Mary who, along with the saints, could intercede for her with God. She prayed for the pope in Rome and she prayed for the king and queen. With her rosary beads in her hands, Jane recited the prayers she was taught, attending the services that were conducted in the Morleys' private chapel within the house itself. The Latin words of the mass became familiar to her as she knelt with her relatives and servants before the altar and watched the priest use the chalice and other religious ornaments given by the late Alice Lovel. Before her were the terrifyingly vivid doom pictures painted on the church walls, which showed the souls of the righteous led into heaven by saints, martyrs and winged angels while the damned were dragged away to eternal torment by laughing devils and monsters. She was thankful that the Catholic Church stood between herself and the horrors of hell, for the Church was invincible.

It also preserved the fabric of society and the established hierarchy. For Jane, this meant that, next to the king, her father was the most revered person in her life. He was head of the family and took all the major decisions. One day he would arrange her betrothal and she would be expected to conform to his wishes. Every family chose their children's spouses with infinite care. Marriage was, after all, a contract. It brought material and social advantages to both sides. It was not something to be entered into lightly. It was what she was being trained for and one day it would happen.

Of course, it would also bring responsibilities. Jane had only to watch her own mother to appreciate the complexities of the life that awaited her. Alice St John was the daughter of Sir John St John, a prosperous and respected Bedfordshire landowner. Her wedding to Lord Morley was brokered by Lady Margaret Beaufort, Morley's patroness and a relative of the St Johns. Jane saw how well the match worked. Alice gave birth to at least five children: Jane herself, her sister Margaret, presumably named after Lady Margaret, who helped pay the christening expenses for the Morley progeny, another sister Elizabeth, and two sons, Henry, the heir, and his brother Francis. Childbirth was both painful and hazardous but it did not interfere very much with a noblewoman's other duties. Although the bond between mother and baby could be as strong then as it is now, Lady Morley was not required to care for any of her offspring herself; wet-nurses and servants did that. She supervised their upbringing only in the most general of terms. In fact, Jane rarely saw her mother when she was very young for, like so many women of her station, Lady Morley accompanied her husband on his visits to court, sometimes staying away from the family houses for long periods. As a peer, Lord Morley had to play his part in the affairs of state. For most nobles, this meant engaging in the dangerous jousting that the king so enjoyed and fighting in the wars against France. Morley, however, was no soldier. Eventually, he served Henry with his pen, as a writer and translator of classical texts but, in the meantime, attendance at court was a painless way of proving his loyalty and doing his duty. Naturally, Lady Morley went with him, as, once she was old enough, did Jane.

Unsurprisingly, since her true importance still lay in the future, much of Jane's early life is undocumented. There was nothing unusual or noteworthy in the way in which she was brought up. As a way of widening experience, it was customary for young girls of her class, while in their early teens, to be sent away from home to serve in the households of other rich noblewomen. Sir Thomas Boleyn sent his two daughters abroad; little Catherine Howard, another relation of Jane's through marriage, spent her formative years with the Duchess of Norfolk. For the Morleys, the crucial decision was not whether or not to let Jane go, it was her destination. The most envied situation of all for a girl was admittance to the royal court in the train of a great lady. The greatest lady of all was the queen. Mothers schemed and plotted furiously to place their daughters with her. And very possibly, this is what happened to Jane. In his series of poems, 'Metrical Visions', George Cavendish, who knew her personally, wrote that Jane was 'brought up at court' all of her 'young age'. Certainly, when Jane departed from Great Hallingbury and left childhood behind, she travelled to a new life, a life that was centred on the court of Henry VIII with all its intrigue, jealousies and sheer exuberant luxury. It was an environment that she would never really leave.

2

All that Glisters

From the moment that she walked into Henry's court, Jane entered another world. It was a world of complete opulence, a world in which everything that could make life more comfortable and more pleasurable was abundantly provided. The king demanded only the best. His palaces were richly furnished; his plate was silver, gilt or even gold. At night, the twinkling flames from hundreds of candles, firmly secured into the branches of gilt candelabra, glowed against the wooden panelling or brought alive the deep colours of the priceless tapestries that adorned so many walls. The evening suppers comprised course after course. Venison, veal, lamb, peacock, quail, heron, pigeon, turbot, salmon, bream – anything could appear, perhaps flavoured with exotic spices like pepper, mace, nutmeg or saffron. By day, there could be hunting, jousting, tournaments; after supper, the haunting melodies of Henry's musicians could fill the air or there could be dancing or even a masque or pageant to delight the eye. Amidst this moved the rich, the famous, the glamorous, resplendent in bright, stylish garments glinting with precious stones. Jane did not see the king or queen every day, as they would often retire to their private or privy apartments to be served only by the select few who were allowed admittance, and there were plenty of hours to be whiled away in quiet sewing, but for a girl fresh from the calm tranquillity of rural Essex, the sights and sounds of those first days were almost unbelievable.

Jane was barely given time to take it all in before she was on the move. This was not unusual, as the court was not fixed in one place. Its personnel followed Henry from palace to palace and he moved frequently so that each building could be thoroughly cleaned to reduce the threat of disease. In fact, he had such a dread of infection that he refused to be in any city where there was a hint of contagion. This move, however, was entirely different: it meant crossing the Channel to the English port of Calais. Near there, in June 1520, Henry met the French king, Francis, for a series of discussions arranged by Henry's principal minister, Cardinal Thomas Wolsey, in the glittering extravaganza that came to be known as the Field of Cloth of Gold. And Jane travelled there with her king.

She was, of course, not alone. Since they were bitter rivals, neither Henry nor Francis wanted to be upstaged by the other. Thus, they were accompanied by their queens, by the most important people of their kingdoms and by an army of servants and attendants. The names of many of those who embarked at Dover with the king are known. They range from the great Dukes of Buckingham and Suffolk, to knights of the shires, to gentlemen such as Thomas More, down to hirelings like Thomas Wilson, a farrier. Then, amongst the list of Katherine's gentlewomen, we find the name of Mistress Parker, the form of address that was commonly used for Jane as the daughter of Sir Henry Parker, Lord Morley. In fact, almost six thousand men and women were assembled from each side. The sheer logistics of transporting them, let alone housing and feeding them, were a nightmare. Fortunately for Henry, Wolsey was the perfect man for the job. Indeed, Wolsey seemed capable of anything. He oversaw absolutely every detail connected with the meeting, although even he was forced to delegate some of the arrangements. A central figure in this was Sir Richard Wingfield, the resident ambassador in France, whose sterling efforts in liaising with the French court ensured that both sides did exactly the same thing and arrived with exactly the same numbers in their entourage. For the French to flaunt their superior wealth would never do. However, as an experienced diplomat in his own right, Wingfield was astute enough to be punctilious in consulting Wolsey on every detail that cropped up, no matter how trivial. And it was Wolsey who had engineered the talks in the first place.

This was no mean feat. The English nobles were never happier than when fighting their traditional enemy; Henry shared their enthusiasm. Since he always believed himself the rightful King of France, and felt fully justified in using the title even though the only French land that England possessed was the port of Calais and the area around it, persuading him to these talks required all of Wolsey's 'filed tongue and ornate eloquence'. Now that everyone had braved the Channel crossing, though, the fashionable humanist concept of peace and harmony captured their imaginations, especially since the celebrations themselves were so bewitching. In any case, war was a cripplingly expensive pastime and no one wanted Wolsey to concentrate on the vexatious question of increased taxation. No, supporting their king in a face-to-face meeting, designed to bring about peace in Europe, was acceptable, even exciting. There was bound to be a good joust or two to look forward to; they would provide a welcome excuse to parade English military prowess. And Henry was determined to put on a first-rate show. His England might be the smallest of the big three powers compared to the dominions of Francis and Katherine's nephew, Charles V, King of Spain and Holy Roman Emperor, but it was civilised, cultured and sophisticated. He would prove it.

So it was that Jane and the rest of the court sailed across the Channel with their king. Her first sight of Calais was its stout walls as they became distinctly visible in the distance; it was a sight that she was destined to see again in very different circumstances. A few days after landing at Calais, Henry and his party moved on to the town of Guisnes, where a temporary palace had been erected for him. According to the chronicler Edward Hall, it was 'the most noble and royal lodging before seen'. It was connected to the castle of Guisnes by a special gallery 'for the secret passage of the king's person into a secret lodging within the same castle the more for the king's ease'. The building itself was 'sumptuous'. It had stone foundations with walls partly of brick and partly of wood, in which tall glass windows were set, clearly a miracle of Tudor engineering. There were two pillars at the entrance with statues of Bacchus and Cupid 'from which flowed streams of malmsey and claret into silver cups'. The interior was just as breathtaking. Apartments were prepared for Henry, for Katherine, for Henry's sister, Mary, the Dowager Queen of France (a title she retained until her death) and now the wife of the Duke of Suffolk, and, significantly, for the cardinal also.

Preparations for the king s reception had been under way for weeks. The Lord Chamberlain and officers of the Wardrobe had been sent over to France to get everything ready for him forty days before he was due to arrive. They carefully draped the ceilings of the rooms with silk. Cloth of gold or silver was bought by the yard and used lavishly, as were silver damask and black, yellow and crimson velvets. The Great Hall provided the ideal gallery in which to show his tapestry collection to perfection. These hangings were crafted in vibrant colours, in threads of gold and silver, with subjects taken from many Biblical stories. One of particular beauty portrayed a scene in which King David coveted Bathsheba. It is hardly surprising that all who saw them marvelled. For Henry, expense was a minor issue; visible magnificence was paramount, and that applied to every single part of the edifice. With cloth of gold hangings on the walls, some set with pearls, and gold candlesticks, crosses and other religious ornaments gleaming on the altar, the chapel within the palace was particularly dazzling. Vestments given by Henry VII to Westminster Abbey had been borrowed and packed reverently for use within it. Like their king, no English courtier wanted to be eclipsed by the French. All took pride in this display of English wealth and craftsmanship. That the stunning French pavilion, a patently fragile structure of gold brocade, its ceiling decorated with stars of gold foil, had to be dismantled after four days because of the wind and rain was especially gratifying to the chauvinistic English. Their palace stayed up despite the weather. Wolsey's careful preparations had paid off.

Never one to waste an opportunity, Wolsey managed to find time to talk with French clergy and ambassadors while Henry and Francis resolutely threw themselves into the serious business of entertaining each other during the two and a half weeks or so that the meeting lasted. They jousted, banqueted, performed in astonishingly costumed masques and once had an ostensibly playful wrestle which, to Henry's chagrin, Francis won. They even managed to squeeze in a discussion on joint policy, talking, inevitably, in a golden tent. The jousts were a particular favourite for the crowds of spectators, who revelled in Henry's exploits as, with his horse draped in cloth of gold, he broke spears time and time again until 'he finished his courses right nobly and like a prince of most valiance'. These bouts were fought before a remarkable tree of honour with leaves of green damask and cloth of gold. Jane's senses reeled from being a part, even an unimportant part, of what was being thought of as a wonder of the world. She also had fun. At one banquet, given by Katherine for Francis while Henry was feasted by the French queen, Claude, Francis insisted on kissing all of Katherine's ladies except for four or five whom he considered 'old and not fair'. So Jane, who was neither, was kissed by a king.

Then, on Saturday 23 June, came the climax of the entire event, a great mass. Jane took her seat in the stands just before ten in the morning. Dressed in scarlet, the cardinals and legates of England and France made their way on to the platform. The French bishops and archbishops, who sat close to the altar, came next. They were followed by the English bishops whose task that day was to serve as deacons and subdeacons, usually too lowly a duty for them. Once all were ready, the joyous notes of Henry's musicians of the Chapel Royal rose to the heavens. Some of these were young boys with clear, pure, unbroken voices but there were adult singers too. Amongst them was Robert Fayrfax, who had performed so movingly at the funeral of Henry's baby son a few years earlier.

Jane sat with the other ladies of Katherine's entourage in the same stands from which they had watched the jousts. The service was sung from a wooden chapel built overnight in those very tiltyards. Everyone who was anyone was there on that day, from the king's sister, Mary, to various young gentlemen of the privy chamber such as William Carey and Henry Norris. Jane's mother, Lady Morley, whose name, along with that of her husband, appears on the roll of those who were to be in Katherine's retinue, sat close to her daughter. The Boleyns, Sir Thomas and his wife, Elizabeth, were near by, as was their daughter, Mary, still a newlywed as she had married William Carey a few months previously. Mary Carey and Jane, both listed as 'gentlewomen', had time to become acquainted. No doubt Thomas and Elizabeth enjoyed chatting and reminiscing to Bridget, the wife of Sir Richard Wingfield, who had grown up in Stone

Castle in Kent, a few miles from the Boleyn estate at Hever. Her father still lived there. For the Boleyns, the event probably provided the chance of a family reunion. Their second daughter, Anne, was a member of Queen Claude's household. While Anne is not mentioned in the roll of names on the English side, it is likely that she was present with her royal mistress. Perhaps Jane was able to meet, for the first time, the woman who was to become both her queen and her sister-in-law. It is also possible that Jane's future husband, George Boleyn, was there, for knights were allowed to bring attendants and Sir Thomas may well have decided to offer his only son the experience of a lifetime.

But the real star of the event was Cardinal Wolsey. Wearing jewelled vestments, brimming with confidence and totally in charge, he dominated the proceedings just as he dominated Henry's government. Everyone knew his story. The son of an Ipswich butcher and himself an Oxford graduate, Thomas Wolsey had been chaplain to several officials before entering royal service as chaplain to Henry VII. From the employ of the father, he passed smoothly to that of the son. Once made a member of the Royal Council in 1510, he never looked back. He greedily collected Church benefices, including the archbishopric of York, becoming a cardinal and then a papal legate, an office that made every other churchman in England subject to his authority. Despite being a newcomer to Henry's court, even Jane was fully aware that Wolsey's hold over the Church was mirrored by his grip on the state. He 'ruled all under the king'. Nothing was beneath his notice nor outside his sphere of influence. As Lord Chancellor, he controlled the legal system; as the king's chief minister, he controlled everything else. In the process, he became incredibly rich, with a palatial lifestyle similar to that of the king his master. He epitomised magnificence on a major scale. His London residence of York Place, his by right as Archbishop of York, was transformed by massive building works to make it a more suitable setting for the man who had become a prince of the Church. His pride and joy was Hampton Court by the River Thames.

Jane knew from court gossip how Wolsey lived. She heard that in just one room at Hampton Court, he displayed astonishing quantities of plate of gilt, plate of pure gold, silver and gilt candlesticks, and allowed candle lights to burn in dishes of silver and gilt. When he dined, he sat in solitary splendour under a cloth of estate. When he rode his mule in public, the animal's trappings were of crimson velvet, its stirrups were gold, and the cardinal was preceded by a procession of attendants and footmen, some of whom carried crosses of gold or silver. A nobleman 'or some worthy gentleman' was required to carry before him the great seal and his cardinal's hat. All for the son of a butcher. Indeed, no matter how far back any aristocrat could trace his ancestry, he would have to take second place to the cardinal who now 'ruled all them that before ruled him'. Stories abounded of how this so affronted the proud Duke of Buckingham that he had not been able to conceal his anger but, while it might rankle, as long as Wolsey remained in Henry's 'especial grace and favour', no one dared to criticise him. On that June day in 1520, Wolsey basked in his own importance.

As he began the high mass at noon, all eyes were upon the area around the altar. In front of the cardinal were the two kings and their queens. Jane, like the rest of the English contingent, looked with pride upon her sovereign. At roughly six feet tall, Francis did indeed match Henry for height, both men towering over most of their contemporaries; it was also true that Francis enjoyed a repu-tation as a poet and sportsman. But, for the English, no one could surpass Henry. Almost thirty, three years older than Francis, he was very much in his prime. His reddish hair shone in the sun like the gold that surrounded him and his muscular, athletic body, honed through physical sports, was still as impressive as when he had become king when not quite eighteen years of age.

Then, this beautiful young man, with his chivalrous demeanour, affability, approachability and love of learning, had appeared like a god to a country used to his avaricious father, Henry VII, who had given the impression of being born middle-aged and cunning. When he first tried to describe the new king, the chronicler Edward Hall was uncharacteristically lost for words. He felt unable to 'express the gifts of grace and of nature, that God hath endowed him with all'. There was nothing in which Henry did not excel. He danced, he sang, he played the lute, the virginals and possibly the harp, he composed. Clearly, he entranced the Venetian ambassador, Sebastian Giustinian. Watching Henry play tennis was 'the prettiest thing in the world', he wrote, with Henry's 'fair skin glowing through a shirt of the finest texture'. He spent hours in the saddle hunting, managing to 'tire eight or ten horses' stationed along his route; he took part in tournaments as the queen's loyal knight. And he combined these attributes with a deep and genuine interest in theology and devout religious observance, hearing mass several times a day.

At first, no one could believe their luck in having such a ruler and, even by 1520, nine years later, there was still no reason for anyone to think otherwise. Of course, it was true that Henry relied greatly on Cardinal Wolsey, whose wealth and flamboyance appeared to be growing with every day that passed, but, after all, the king was God's representative on earth and his wishes were supreme. It was common knowledge that Henry despised the dreary grind of mundane affairs of state and loathed those councillors who tried to persuade him to attend to them. He expected to be able to enjoy being king and 'loved nothing worse than to be constrained to do anything contrary to his royal will and pleasure'. It was hardly surprising that he felt 'affection and love' for Wolsey. The cardinal's tireless labour left the king freer to pursue his own interests, many of which, like hunting and jousting, were the interests of his nobles too. There were times when he and his favourite courtiers were simply all young men together. Provided his position was never forgotten, Henry could be both convivial and engaging.

Certainly the women of the court found him so. Who would not be flattered by the attentions of such a monarch? Jane was an adolescent, too immature for Henry. Once he started to register their existence, he realised that the court abounded with ladies only too willing to catch his eye and respond to his charms. He found a kindred spirit in the entrancing, vivacious Elizabeth Blount, one of his wife's maids of honour. Like him, she enjoyed music and dancing and was his partner in the New Year revels of 1514. The couple soon became partners in other areas too. Five years later, Elizabeth presented her royal lover with a son, Henry Fitzroy. Elizabeth was not present at the Field of Cloth of Gold, since by then the affair was over. Was the king perhaps ready to look elsewhere?

It was obvious, even to Jane, that Henry's attention was no

longer focused on his wife. Conjugal bliss had definitely ebbed. Jane watched as Katherine knelt with her husband at the start of the mass. The queen was much loved and respected for her virtue and piety but she was no longer the shy, delicately featured girl who had arrived from Spain to marry Henry's elder brother, Arthur, then Prince of Wales and Henry VII's heir. The marriage, designed to cement Anglo-Spanish amity, lasted only five months before Arthur died. His brother's premature demise meant that Henry had succeeded to his offices, titles and, eventually, to their father's throne. He had also replaced his brother in Katherine's bed, marrying the widowed princess within two months of his own accession. The idealistic young Henry had been a devoted husband who delighted in his attractive and accomplished bride, for Katherine was very well educated and was probably a better Latin scholar than Henry himself. He had trusted her judgement; he had confidently left her in charge of the country as regent while he went to fight the French. In those early years, Henry and Katherine had looked good together, Katherine's graceful figure a perfect foil to the ebullient, physical specimen that was her husband. But all of that was a long time ago. The Katherine who had so enchanted Henry was now portly, her soft prettiness a thing of the past. And the difference was noticed. Francis called her 'old and deformed' – by which he meant fat – in sharp contrast to Henry who was 'young and handsome'. A root cause of the change was her frequent pregnancies.

Katherine's gynaecological history was a nightmare. Every woman worshipping with her at the mass on that June day sympathised. The loss of little Prince Henry was not her only tragedy, nor was it her last. Her situation following the sudden death of Arthur had been difficult enough, as for several years it remained uncertain whether her marriage to his brother would actually take place. Once it did, she miscarried a daughter within months of the wedding. Then, after the anguish of losing the son they both wanted so badly, she lost in quick succession three more babies in miscarriages or stillbirths. Finally, in 1516, Princess Mary was born safely and, much to her parents' relief, survived. Katherine doted on the child, but no one could get away from the fact that the infant was a princess and not a prince. The queen's final pregnancy, a couple of years later, ended in the usual disaster with yet another dead daughter. Since then, despite Henry's best efforts and her own increasingly desperate prayers, she had failed to conceive. Nonetheless, miracles did happen; the Bible was littered with examples of post-menopausal women who, at God's will, became mothers. Henry might yet gain the heir he needed. Like all loyal English subjects, Jane hoped so.

Meanwhile, it was time for her to concentrate upon the ritual of the mass. Like everything else at the Field of Cloth of Gold, it was an example of Wolsey's immaculate planning at its very best. Although he officiated, it was important for reasons of prestige that both countries played an equal part in the ceremony. Thus, there were both French and English musicians, who took it in turns to sing the sacred words, each group accompanied by the organist of the other nationality. Then, suddenly, as Jane followed the familiar words of the liturgy, there was an enormous crash. At first, no one was sure what it was. Some feared it was a 'comet', or even a 'monster' but such was the underlying Anglo-French distrust that thoughts of treachery flashed through the minds of many spectators. But then Jane, like everyone else, looked upwards. A massive firework, in the shape of a dragon or perhaps the salamander that was Francis's emblem, streaked across the sky. It had come from the English encampment and had probably been intended to be let off later in the evening during the masques and entertainments. Although it is not clear what had gone wrong – we know only that a certain Thomas Wright was paid 20s 4d for the 'canvas for the dragon' – if the English had wanted to flaunt their superior expertise in firework manufacture by producing one to dumbfound the French, their wish was definitely granted. It was a display for all to remember. However, once the fuss had died down and the congregation was settled again, Wolsey calmly returned to the matter in hand and the service resumed. The pax, or gospel, was taken to the two kings to kiss by Cardinal de Bourbon. Slightly bemused as to the correct etiquette, Henry politely offered it to Francis first but he charmingly 'refused the offer'. When Cardinal de Bourbon moved on to Katherine and Claude, neither queen knew what to do either so, to great delight, 'kissed each other instead'. Finally, following a Latin discourse on the merits of peace proposed by William Pace, one of Henry's secretaries, a papal indulgence, useful for reducing the time that souls spent in purgatory, was proclaimed and all was over.

At least, it was over for the moment. There was just about enough time for Jane and the other courtiers to prepare for that night's frivolities. By now, she was becoming used to the 'rich attires' and 'sumptuous jewels' that she needed to wear in order to uphold her country's honour, as well as to the vast menus of delicacies, produced by the legions of cooks, to tempt even the poorest appetite. As she watched the bonfires and heard the gunfire that rounded off the final evening's entertainments, those years at Great Hallingbury seemed a lifetime away.

But this spectacle could not go on for ever. Tournament prizes were awarded to the bravest and best of the sportsmen; naturally, Henry and Francis were winners but so was Mary Boleyn's husband, William Carey, clearly an up-and-coming young man within the royal circle. Then, after an exchange of presents – Henry gave Francis a jewelled collar and received a bracelet of precious stones in return – promises of peace were made and affectionate farewells said. Jane, her parents and the members of the court had to return home. All had gone so well. Everything had glittered and gleamed. There was peace between the old enemies and England was safe and secure under the wise government of its most bountiful king. And, as the hordes of weary servants set about packing up and clearing away all that remained of the Field of Cloth of Gold, Jane's own chance to glitter and gleam was about to come.

3

Château Vert

Jane's first visit to Calais over, she returned to England with the rest of the royal entourage. By now, she was becoming more and more familiar with life at court. The wonders that it had held for her on her first arrival had subsided somewhat over time, but its addictive allure still held. The chance to mingle with the great and the good, and to be close to those whose decisions determined the fate of thousands, remained intoxicating. She knew that her parents would arrange her marriage eventually. It might mean a quiet, country lifestyle as a wife and mother with only rare and fleeting visits to the court. It might mean fewer trips to her husband's estates but a more permanent arrangement for herself within the queen's privy chamber while her spouse played his part in affairs of state. She was trained for both. Either would give her the status and security which were her birthright. However, until then, there was so much to bewitch and beguile. And, for a young and pretty girl surrounded by such interesting people, each moment was one to savour.

Every morning her maid helped her to dress. Lady Morley equipped her daughter with the very best and most fashionable of clothing: the jewel-set or embroidered sleeves, the slashed sleeves which allowed fine undersleeves to peep through, the Spanish farthingale to give the many skirts their shape, the tightly laced bodices, the silk stockings she needed for court entertainments, the soft leather, velvet or silk shoes, the jewellery. The list was endless but for Jane to hold her own, let alone to stand out, amongst those who were happy to parade their wealth on their backs, her parents accepted the outlay. Henry demanded no less from everyone around him. For

Jane, these were carefree days. She mixed with the other young girls and flirted happily with the equally beautifully dressed young men. Nothing, of course, would come of such harmless dalliance. She knew the rules: love was verbal, not physical. Still, it all added a delicious frisson to everyday life, and just occasionally that frisson was needed for, as she saw for herself, Henry's court was no make-believe world of cloudless skies and endless summer designed solely for hedonistic diversion.

Many of those who sauntered though the corridors and tapestry-covered walls of Henry's palaces, or stopped to chat and laugh, seemed permanent fixtures. Some, like Sir Thomas Boleyn or the Dukes of Suffolk and Norfolk, were members of Henry's Council. Although they had estates to run, their state responsibilities necessitated frequent attendance on the king. Others, like Jane's own father, Lord Morley, were less regular visitors. But since everyone depended on the king for their position, no one was invincible. Proof of just how vulnerable even the most mighty truly were was brought home forcefully in 1521.

In that year, Edward Stafford, Duke of Buckingham – undoubtedly eminent if unpopular, a man rich enough to pay 20d for a haircut, more than five times the daily wage of most of the king's servants – was executed for treason. No longer the open and approachable monarch of the early days, Henry had suddenly become so wary of the duke, and of other members of his court, that he had written a private letter to Wolsey in his own hand, in which he had ordered the cardinal 'to make good watch on the duke of Suffolk, on the duke of Buckingham, on my lord of Northumberland, on my lord of Derby, on my lord of Wiltshire and on others which you think suspect'. The result had been Buckingham's arrest.

Henry's mysterious undated letter leaves no clue about how the duke had aroused his distrust. Perhaps it was due to a seemingly throwaway remark of Wolsey's. Perhaps it was simply that the king's worry about the lack of a male heir was beginning to niggle for, as Buckingham was a descendant of Edward III, his impeccable pedigree was conceivably dangerous. A proud and arrogant man, not only did the duke never forget his royal blood, he allowed no one else to forget it either. After listening recklessly to a prophecy that he would reign when Henry died, he went one stage further by allegedly vowing to kill the king should he ever be arrested. Evidence to that effect was given against him by, amongst others, Charles Knyvett, recently dismissed from the duke's service. Whether the witnesses spoke the truth or were driven by a desire for revenge or concern for their own skins, their allegations were dynamite. Buckingham was doomed. It was common knowledge that it was treason merely to speculate on the king's death, let alone to do anything to hasten it. Nevertheless, the trial was sensational, and the condemnation of such a formidable member of the old nobility was bound to send shivers down many a spine. Jane might well have heard a first-hand account of the proceedings since her father was in court as a member of the panel of peers who tried the case. It would not be Lord Morley's only brush with treason trials.

Despite Buckingham's death, life at court, with its sparkling conversation, its amusements and its flirtations, continued much as before. However, the international scene was gradually changing from the heady days of the Field of Cloth of Gold. That meeting had been between Henry and Francis only. The Emperor Charles V, Katherine's nephew, had not been present. But although out of sight at the Field of Cloth of Gold, he was never out of mind. Physically, he was no match for either Henry or Francis, nor, by any obsequious stretch of the imagination, could he be called handsome, especially since he possessed the protruding jaw so characteristic of the Habsburgs. Yet he was, on paper, the most powerful man in Europe, controlling Spain, Burgundy and the Netherlands, parts of Italy, the Holy Roman Empire and much of the recently discovered New World, which promised riches beyond men's dreams. Any ruler or minister who ignored him did so at their peril, and Henry was no exception. It was as well, then, that England's relationship with Charles V was good. Indeed, Henry had discussions with the emperor both before and after his talks with Francis, delighting Katherine, who relished the rare opportunity to make personal contact with her sister's busy son.

Unfortunately, the peace, which Wolsey had laboured so hard to broker, was precarious. It was really only a matter of time before Charles and Francis, his only realistic rival, were at each other's throats. When that happened, Henry's role was crucial. The complex negotiations which had preceded the Field of Cloth of Gold involved a universal peace treaty by which any signatory attacked by another should be supported by the rest. Trouble presented itself when Charles, protesting that Francis had violated the agreements, demanded Henry's military and financial assistance. Although Wolsey resumed his diplomatic efforts to preserve the peace, it looked as though war was likely. Charles, anxious to press the king for help, sent ambassadors to England. His shrewd and wily resident representative, Bernardino De Mesa, a Dominican friar and bishop of Badajoz and Elne, was joined by Jacques de Caestres, a highly capable soldier, and Charles Poupet de Lachaulx, a man very much in the emperor's confidence.

Jane's chance to move into the spotlight came at an entertainment devised to impress these envoys. She was then about seventeen years old and good-looking or she would not have been on show, whether the daughter of a peer or not. The occasion was a pageant at the cardinal's palace of York Place on Shrove Tuesday, 4 March 1522. Led by Wolsey and the king after supper, the ambassadors entered a 'great chamber' lit by hundreds of candles, its walls lined with vibrantly coloured tapestries, some probably echoing the action about to be performed. It was like going into a theatre just before the curtain rises. Attention immediately focused on the end of the room where an amazing imitation castle, Château Vert, was installed. It had three towers and battlements gleaming with green foil, each tower surmounted by a different flag suggesting the power that women could have: one depicted three men's torn hearts, one a man's heart held in a woman's hand and the third showed a man's heart being turned around. The spectators soon realised that in the towers were eight brilliantly dressed court ladies. In their white satin gowns, with their hair encased in gold cauls and with golden bonnets dotted with jewels on their heads, they looked magnificent, shining out against the iridescent green foil. The name of each lady's character was picked out in yellow satin and sewn on to their costumes for the audience to see. The identity of the woman dressed as Pity is unknown, but we do know who the rest were. Mary, the French Queen, with recognisable typecasting, portrayed Beauty. Of the other six, five had been part of Katherine's entourage at the Field of Cloth of Gold. The Countess of Devonshire was Honour. Mistress Browne represented Bounty and Mistress Dannet Mercy. Of the remaining three, it was their real lives which were destined to be fatally entwined. Mary Carey was Kindness, Jane was Constancy and Perseverance was played by Mary's sister, Anne Boleyn, who had returned from the French court only recently and whose chic dress sense and cosmopolitan ways had already aroused male interest.

While these eight ladies epitomised agreeable female qualities, the castle was defended by eight more who represented contrary and unwanted attributes. They included Danger, Disdain, Jealousy, Unkindness, Scorn, Malbouche (slander or bad-mouthing) and Strangeness (remoteness or unapproachability). The name of the eighth is not recorded. They were, in fact, not women at all but children of Henry's Chapel Royal. Dressed 'like to women of India', they guarded the castle from the eight gentlemen who, decked in cloth of gold with blue satin cloaks, then appeared. They, too, had names: Amorous, Nobleness, Youth, Attendance, Loyalty, Pleasure, Gentleness and Liberty. One, but we do not know which, was Henry himself, always eager to join in the revels whenever he could. The suitors were led by Ardent Desire, spectacularly arrayed in crimson satin, who was perhaps William Cornish, master of the Chapel Royal.

When Ardent Desire playfully asked the women to come down to meet his companions, the fun really began. The eight desirable ladies were so attracted to these gorgeously apparelled men that they were prepared to give up their castle, but Scorn and Disdain encouraged their fellow defenders to hold out. In what was almost slapstick comedy, the assault consisted of mock gunfire and the throwing of 'dates and oranges and other fruits made for pleasure' by the gentlemen, with similar weapons (rosewater and sweets from the real women, and 'bows and balls' from those of the Chapel

Royal) being employed by those under attack. All who watched, enthralled, recognised this archetypical gentle method of defence; it surfaced in stories of romance and chivalry such as *Roman de la Rose*. At last the castle fell, and the less agreeable 'women' such as Scorn fled, leaving the gentlemen to escort Jane and the other ladies down from the turrets. Choreographed dancing took place to the gentle harmonies provided by hidden minstrels before everyone took off their masks so that all could see who they were. It was predictable perhaps, but magical to watch and even more magical for the performers. Despite her experiences at the Field of Cloth of Gold being vividly fresh in her mind, Jane could never before have spent such an evening. Henry might have taken the floor with his sister, Mary, but, equally, he might have chosen any one of the others. Perhaps he danced with the woman who was to be his 'sweetheart' and for whom he was to change his country for ever. We shall never know.

What we do know is that at a cost of £20 16s 4d, the whole event was not cheap. The ambassadors were regaled in some style. The green foil alone cost 3s and a barge with four rowers was hired to carry everything to York Place for a price of 13s 4d. Wherever possible garments were re-used but although this was true of the ladies' satin dresses, their cauls were bought for the fabulous sum of 8s each, and the price of the yellow satin for their names was also 8s. This time, however, the ladies were allowed to keep their cauls and possibly the other costumes. Maybe Jane, who came to relish evenings like that, gained a tangible reminder of what was far from an ordinary entertainment, one in which she was specifically selected to be Constancy.

For that is what is so interesting. No longer inconspicuous, Jane was given a starring role in a pageant carefully designed to amuse the envoys of Charles V. That involved some responsibility. Being Lord Morley's daughter would not alone confer such a degree of prominence unless it was combined with an attractive appearance, considerable dancing ability and a winning manner. Evidently, she had become an accepted gentlewoman of the court and could be trusted to be a credit to her king. However, time was passing. There was no disputing the fact that Jane Parker was of marriageable age. Pageants, dancing and silk stockings were all very well but the serious business of life was about to begin.

4

A Suitable Match

In 1524, Lord Morley began talks which were to determine the direction of Jane's life until the day she died: it was time for him to arrange her marriage. Wedlock was the most serious step any Tudor woman could take. Jane knew that once she left the safety of her own family, she would be dependent upon her husband for her status, her role in society, her financial security, her domicile, even for the clothes upon her back and the food she ate. Under the concept of coverture, her very identity would be subsumed in his: he was her lord and she was required by convention and religious duty to submit to his will. Her vows at the ceremony included her promise to be 'buxom at bed and board'. In reality, of course, marriage was not an appalling fate but a career. To be unmarried was unthinkable. Most couples rubbed along quite well but were clear that the purpose of their union was primarily a property settlement to the advantage of their families and the birth of children to continue the dynasty. This did not preclude comfortable companionship, affection, love, or even sexual attraction, but these were bonuses to be hoped for, not expected as a right.

Such serious matters were not meant to trouble the minds of adolescent girls. Jane relied upon her father to sort them out for her. Once the decision concerning who was going to marry whom was taken, the hard bargaining over the bride's settlement and jointure would begin in earnest. Mundane details such as organizing the banns, the church service and the bridal feast were easy in comparison. In fact, Lord Morley was becoming reasonably experienced in all things matrimonial. In 1521, he was concerned with a deed relating to the estates of his sister-in-law, Elizabeth Edgecombe, and then, more significantly, in May 1523, Henry Parker, his son and heir, was married to Grace Newport. This was, in every way, a most satisfying alliance. Grace was the daughter of John Newport, a landowner at Furneux Pelham and at Stapleford, both situated close to the border between Hertfordshire and Essex. Since these estates were within twelve or so miles of the Morley seat at Great Hallingbury, the two families were virtually neighbours – always an excellent reason for a marriage. Then, Grace was also Newport's only heir so she would bring his lands to the Morleys. As her father died within eight days of the ceremony, she brought them sooner than anticipated. Admittedly, the girl was only eight years old, but that was not an insuperable obstacle; it just meant that consummation would have to wait for a few years. In normal circumstances, Grace would have lived with her father until puberty, keeping in touch with her young spouse via the occasional social meeting but, as things stood, it is more likely that she grew up within the Parker household.

Having successfully settled his son's affairs, Lord Morley turned his attentions to those of his daughter, Jane. The first decision concerned the bridegroom. In this, Jane was lucky for she already knew him. Her father's choice was George Boleyn, Sir Thomas Boleyn's only son. Again, Lord Morley's selection made sound economic sense. By the 1520s, Thomas and his wife were affluent, influential at court and highly regarded by the king. Like the Newports, they were also near neighbours – so convenient.

The Boleyns began to be important in the fifteenth century when Geoffrey Boleyn, an astute and clever London merchant, made money as a mercer, trading in fine fabrics like velvet and silk. He was soon very prosperous indeed. Not only was he knighted, becoming Lord Mayor of London in 1457, he prudently invested in property, buying, amongst other lands, large country estates at Hever in Kent and at Blickling in Norfolk. He knew how his world worked: social standing and respect came only from the possession of land. But it was his wealth which made him sufficiently eligible to marry Anne, the daughter of Lord Hoo, as his second wife. The family fortunes continued to rise following the wedding of his heir, William, to Margaret, the daughter of Thomas Butler, Earl of

Ormond, an Anglo-Irish peer with substantial lands in England. What made this marriage potentially significant was that Ormond had two daughters, Margaret and her sister, Anne, Lady St Leger, but he had no legitimate son. Unless there was a surprise arrival in the Butler family, Margaret and Anne would one day share a fortune. Since the control of a woman's property was in the hands of her husband, all this boded well for the Boleyns.

The real beneficiary of this shrewd alliance was Sir Thomas Boleyn, the eldest son of Sir William and Margaret, Jane's future father-in-law. In 1511, four years before the Earl of Ormond's death, Thomas came to an arrangement with his by then widowed mother, Margaret. They agreed an indenture between them by which Thomas would have everything that would come to Margaret from the Ormonds in exchange for an annual annuity of 200 marks and some manors in Norfolk, including Blickling, as well as land in Buckinghamshire and Hertfordshire. The money was to be paid twice a year in the pretty parish church of Blickling between the hours of 8 a.m. and 11 a.m. The church is still there, altered by the Victorians, but not dissimilar to how it was when Thomas's agent doled out the coins. Margaret was certainly not left penniless and one must hope that she was able to keep the more personal bequests mentioned in Ormond's will. However, it was Thomas who gained by far the most. The wily Sir Geoffrey could be proud of his grandson. On the death of Ormond, his fabulous estate of New Hall in Essex was part of Thomas's haul, although he was swift to sell it to the king for a breathtaking £1,000.* Thomas retained other property in Essex, including the manor of Rochford with its comfortable house, as well as his vast acres in Norfolk, of course, counties in which the Morleys also owned land. A union between the two families would benefit both and provide admirably for Jane. No father could have done more for his daughter.

And George himself seemed an ideal match for Jane. The date of his birth is not recorded but he was probably about her own age. Here, too, luck was on Jane's side: she was not to be married to a man old enough to be her father, which was the destiny of many

---

* Henry changed the name of New Hall to Beaulieu.

women. Indeed, the king's own sister, Mary, the French Queen, gained her title from her political marriage to Louis XII of France. He was over thirty years her senior, had not worn well and could scarcely believe his eyes when he first saw his lovely young bride. Mary's response to her sacrifice was to exact a promise from her brother that, should she outlive Louis, her next husband would be one she had picked for herself, and she chose Suffolk, then a rather dashing man of action. At least Jane did not face that problem. To Lord Morley's gratification, she was also marrying into a family in which knowledge was valued. Thomas, while a competent soldier and good jouster, was keen to foster links with the humanist scholar Erasmus, and wrote to him frequently. Thomas's brother, Sir James Boleyn, had learnt Hebrew, a rare accomplishment for a man like himself who was involved in the law. Additionally, George's love of music and poetry, and his deep and genuine interest in theology, especially in the new religious ideas that were buzzing around Europe, combined with his undoubted skills in diplomacy, indicate that he, too, was well educated. Unfortunately, his physical characteristics elude us; there is no surviving portrait.

Like Jane, George was no stranger to Henry's court. While still a little boy, he played a part in a mummery at the Christmas revels and became a royal page. He obviously impressed the king as he was admitted to the privy chamber, although we cannot be sure precisely when. What we do know is that he shared in his father's rewards following the execution of Buckingham. Since the property of convicted traitors was subject to automatic and systematic confiscation, and the duke had been a very rich man with a yearly income in the region of £5,000, the king had plenty of lands to either redistribute or keep for himself. The Boleyns were given various offices centring around Tonbridge in Kent, so close to Hever. Then, significantly in 1524, George was granted the manor of Grimstone in Norfolk, in his own right. Another factor in his favour was that, as the only son, he was Thomas's sole heir. George's financial position was certainly most promising. Jane had nothing to complain of with her father's choice, nor had George with his. Jane's family may have fought on the losing side at Bosworth but they were loyal subjects now. George could marry the daughter of a respected peer, thus maintaining what was fast becoming a family tradition, without facing the daunting prospect of taking a stranger as his bride.

Once Lord Morley and Sir Thomas Boleyn agreed that their children should marry, they settled down to some determined haggling. A legal pre-nuptial contract was drawn up on 4 October 1524 to cover the financial aspects of the alliance. Jane's jointure, exactly what she was entitled to should George predecease her, was at the heart of it for estates passed to children, not to bereaved widows. Jane's parents did not want her to depend on whatever she might inherit from George's will; at best, that might be her clothes, her jewels, a few pieces of furniture and, if she was really loved, some silver or gilt plate. If she relied solely on his bounty, her outlook could be bleak. Her jointure would ensure that, in return for a fixed amount, paid in land or money by Lord Morley, Sir Thomas guaranteed to convey to her the rents of particular manors, or a specified annual sum, for the rest of her life. Neither she nor George were consulted about these delicate arrangements, although they may have been informed about them. What Jane did not know then was just how crucial the precise terms of her jointure would one day prove to be.

With his customary business acumen, Thomas secured a very profitable deal. Astonishingly, Jane came accompanied by 2,000 marks, over £1,300, more even than the price of New Hall. Lord Morley alone could not have raised so much. Indeed, there is a tantalising reference to tell us that Morley's servant paid Thomas £33 6s 8d for November and December 1525, which suggests that Morley was paying off a debt, possibly for the jointure, in instalments. What we do know is that the other contributor to Jane's jointure was no less a person than the king himself. This was not as unusual as it sounds. It does, though, indicate the regard in which Henry held Thomas and, perhaps, Lord Morley. That Thomas was a favoured courtier is undeniable. His prowess on the jousting field and his martial exploits in the wars against France at the beginning of Henry's reign endeared him to the king, but his excellent French also made him especially useful as an ambassador. Already treasurer of the royal household, he became a Knight of the Garter just before he began his talks with Jane's father. George's grant of Grimstone is further proof of royal approbation. Since he received it scarcely three months before the various legal papers were signed, it was conceivably a generous royal gesture, on the eve of his wedding, to a young man the king liked. Morley, too, was on good terms with Henry and perhaps he was on the king's mind. Like Thomas, Lord Morley had been an emissary on a diplomatic mission. In December 1523, he had been one of the English ambassadors sent to present the Order of the Garter to the Archduke Ferdinand of Austria, the younger brother of Charles V. Although somewhat perturbed at the unrest caused by the spread of Lutheranism, Morley had rather enjoyed his foreign trip, writing back to the king at least once and to Wolsey three times, giving vivid descriptions of where he had been and whom he had met.

With the figure agreed, Sir Thomas and Morley turned to the vexed question of exactly which lands would be designated for Jane's jointure. The couple were barely twenty; there was no reason to suspect that the transaction would come into full fruition for many years yet, if at all. Barring the constant threat of sudden illness, Jane was more likely to die in childbirth than to outlive her husband. Nevertheless, her father was keen to assure her future. It was decided that she and George would be given the manors of Aylesbury and Bierton in Buckinghamshire and various other manors in Norfolk, including West Laxham. The newlyweds would be allowed to access the proceeds immediately after their nuptials, a common practice. Should George die first, Jane would receive the specified manors or 100 marks (£66) a year. So far so good, except that the usual annuity for a widow was ten per cent of the original jointure price. Jane needed George alive rather than dead if she was to maintain herself in style.

What is immediately apparent is that much of this property was technically Margaret Boleyn's Ormond inheritance and that Thomas had already defined his mother's share. He actually divided up the same spoils twice. The final indenture accepted by Thomas and Lord Morley was indeed complex. But it was only complex if the natural order of things was disturbed. Providing George lived to a decent age, he would survive both Margaret, his grandmother, and Thomas, his father. He would then inherit all of the lands and there would be no problem. Should Jane die before her husband, there was no difficulty either as her jointure died with her and George would be free to marry again. But the seeds for discord were certainly sown. If the unthinkable happened, and George's life was cut short, then Jane would be free to demand her rights. Thomas would then face a major dilemma. Yet, as the ink dried on the contract, everyone was satisfied that the deal was reasonable for both parties. All minds were now focused on weddings not funerals.

5

For Better, for Worse

With the legal niceties out of the way, Jane and George awaited their wedding. There is no record of when Jane Parker became Jane Boleyn but discovering the date on which the jointure was signed, 4 October 1524, helps us pinpoint likely days with more confidence than has previously been possible. A second clue comes from Cardinal Wolsey. He was busily at work preparing changes to Henry's privy chamber personnel in the autumn months of 1525, which would take effect as the Eltham Ordinances in the following year. The document in which he set out his plans survives and is in his own hand. In it, he wrote that 'Young Boleyn' was 'to have twenty pounds yearly above the eighty pounds he hath gotten to him and his wife to live thereupon'. Only by examining his draft in its original and under ultraviolet light, unavailable to the diligent Victorians who transcribed it in the nineteenth century, can the £80 he mentions be deciphered. Clearly, the marriage took place sometime between the signing of the jointure document and the end of 1525, and Wolsey's note implies that while it was fairly recent, it had not only just happened.

Since the Church allowed marriages to occur only at certain fixed times within the religious calendar, and since there is no record of a special licence being granted to Lord Morley to ignore these restrictions, the wedding probably took place just before Epiphany in November 1524, or early in 1525; either would fit with Wolsey's comments. And the absence of a special licence, which would have been required had she married outside her parish, suggests that Jane married George in her local church of St Giles. Unfortunately, the records of baptisms, marriages and deaths there do not begin until after Jane was widowed and, while the churchwardens' accounts do start earlier, in 1526, there is no reference to the marriage or to a special gift to the church from the family.

What we certainly do know is that, for Jane, her wedding day was the most significant of her life, no matter what its date or venue. As her giggling maids slipped her chemise over her head and gently pulled on her fine stockings, she knew that everything for which she had been prepared was about to happen: she was to attain the status and respectability of a wife. When she left the confines of the church, she would be a different person. For a new life, she probably had new clothes. Lord Morley could afford to equip his daughter well; she was not of the same class as those women who simply wore their best garments. A mere handful of Tudor brides selected white for their weddings. It is true that both Katherine of Aragon and Prince Arthur had been clothed in white satin, and that Mary, the French Queen, shone in white cloth of silver when she married a dazzled Louis XII, but this was not the norm. Jane may have wanted white satin or richly embossed damask, but fabulously expensive cloth of gold or cloth of silver was beyond even her father's means, so her gown was probably velvet, and in deep crimson, the most fashionable choice of the moment, and the colour favoured by Eleanor of Austria, who became the second wife of Francis I about this time. Once her elaborate sleeves were in place and her full skirts neatly adjusted over her farthingale, Jane's maids fastened a jewelled girdle around her waist, perhaps eased a family chain or pendant over her head and then placed soft shoes on her feet. They combed her hair, leaving it unbound and flowing as was the custom, maybe threaded with small pearls or other precious stones, and almost certainly wreathed in flowers. All that was left was to drape a furred mantle lined with satin around her shoulders. Looking every inch Lord Morley's daughter, Jane was ready to leave girlhood behind.

Early that morning, for the solemnisation of matrimony was nearly always between 8 a.m. and noon, and accompanied by her bridesmaids, who may have had sprigs of rosemary fastened to their clothes or held bright garlands of flowers aloft, Jane went in a happy, lively procession to the church. She was glad to have her bridesmaids with her as she knew that these girls would help confuse the devil who, many maintained superstitiously, lay patiently in wait for vulnerable young brides. There were 'bridemen', too, who playfully guarded her and there was music and song so that all could share in the festivities along the way. Her parents came with her, to perform what was almost their last service for their daughter, for soon she was to be part of a new family and no longer their responsibility.

The young couple met at the door of the church for the ceremony. Like Jane, George was accompanied by his mother and father, and possibly by his sisters, Mary Carey and Anne, and perhaps his uncle, Sir James Boleyn, with his wife Elizabeth. Maybe the jointure trustees were there too. One of them, Sir John Shelton,* was intimately connected with the Boleyns, since his wife, Anne, was George's aunt. Boleyn honour required that George looked splendid. The wedding party were just as eager to see and comment upon his finery as upon Jane's. Sometimes, as with Katherine and Arthur, a bridegroom wore an outfit that complemented and matched that of his bride and carried flowers similar to hers. However they were dressed, Jane and George made an impressive couple, both young and well connected, with, as it seemed, a glittering life ahead. She stood on his left to remind everyone that woman 'was formed out of a rib in the left side of Adam'. Once the guests were ready, perhaps joined at a distance by some of Lord Morley's no doubt respectful tenants, who had come to share in the joy of their betters, together with the lucky few chosen to receive the customary largesse afterwards, the priest began the service. Convention demanded that much of it was conducted at the church door; the rituals must be properly witnessed.

All were there, the priest explained, 'to join together two bodies' into 'one body'. Then, once he had enquired 'about the dower of the woman', for no one forgot that this was an economic union as well as a spiritual one, he turned to George. In words that still echo down the centuries, he was asked whether he would take Jane as his 'wedded wife' to 'love her, and honour her, keep her and guard her, in health and in sickness ... forsaking all others ... for as long as ye both shall live'. More or less the same question was put to Jane,

---

* Shelton's son, also called John, later married Jane's sister Margaret.

except that while George was to 'guard' her, she was to 'obey' and 'serve' him.

Lord Morley stepped forward to give away his daughter and, with her hand in that of George, now the most important man in her life, Jane made her vows. 'I, Jane,' she repeated after the priest, 'take thee, George, to my wedded husband to have and to hold from this day forward, for better, for worse, for richer, for poorer, in sickness and in health, to be bonny and buxom in bed and at board, till death us do part.' Once the ring, its round, unending shape representing the eternal nature of their love, had been blessed and sprinkled with holy water, George slid it on to the fourth finger of her left hand, the finger from which it was believed that a vein ran directly to the heart.

After further prayers, the families and honoured guests went through the thick wooden door into the main body of the colourful little church, itself fragrant with the heady perfume of flowers and incense. To the sound of familiar psalms sung by the priest and his helpers, Jane and George processed along the nave, passing the gilded alabaster statues of the saints with their shining halos and the small round windows letting in shafts of light. When they reached the altar steps, her bridesmaids carefully arranged Jane's skirts as she knelt with her husband. The congregation of family and friends prayed for them both, asking God to bring them peace, strength, prosperity, children, and to join them 'in the union and love of true affection'. As the prayers faded away, the young couple were led into the presbytery, with Jane standing to George's right, for the start of the glorious, inspirational nuptial mass.

The holiest part of this came when they both prostrated themselves before the altar to pray. Four clerks 'in surplices' stepped forward, each supporting the corner of an embroidered canopy, which some believed was there to protect bride and groom from the evil that lurked everywhere. The clerks held it directly over Jane and George while they, and their union, were reverently blessed. They were man and wife, 'for better, for worse'. But here again the different demands made of men and of women were emphasised as, just before the couple left the church for their wedding feast, Jane was reminded of what was expected of her. With God's grace and help, she should be 'faithful and chaste ... amiable to her husband ... wise ... bashful and grave, reverential and modest ... [and] fruitful'. The priest gave no advice whatsoever to George about his conduct towards Jane.

To the delight of their families, Jane and George left St Giles as a married couple. The ring on Jane's finger proved it to the world. All the bargaining, the tense negotiations and the planning were over. With the business side of the arrangement completed and the Church having fulfilled its role, at least for the moment, the Boleyns and the Morleys could relax and enjoy themselves as the wedding feast began. There was eating and drinking, there were tired and harassed servants running to and fro, filling plates and pouring wine, there was plenty of ribald joking, there was music and there was dancing. The bridecake took pride of place on the high table where the most honoured of the guests sat. The bridecup, filled with spiced wine, was passed round. The celebrations could go on for hours.

But they could not go on for ever. Marriages needed to be consummated. However, there was no question of Jane and George being allowed to simply slip away quietly together and be alone. The great spectator sport of bedding the bride began when Jane's garters were pulled off by the 'bridemen' and fastened to their hats. Only then was she taken into the candlelit bedchamber to be undressed by her excited bridesmaids, themselves showing a vicarious delight in what was about to happen. Since Lady Morley and the other women guests had crowded into the room when Jane was tucked up amongst the clean pillows and crisp linen of the huge, flower- and ribbon-strewn bridal bed, there was little room for George at first. Undressed by his friends, he squeezed in next to her, much to the amusement of all who were watching. Both he and Jane knew precisely what to expect next: the laughing bridesmaids collected his stockings while the 'bridemen' grabbed hers, crouched down at the bottom of the bed and then threw the stockings at the newlyweds. Anyone who managed to hit the young couple on the head, providing that Jane was hit by George's stocking and vice versa, was predicted to marry soon afterwards. Yet Jane and George were still not left to themselves. With a cup of spiced wine and milk to fortify them for the ordeal ahead, they waited for the next arrival: the priest.

It was his duty to bless them yet again and to bless their bed-chamber. He first blessed the bed, asking God to protect 'thy servants who rest' in it from 'phantasies and illusions of devils' so that they might always think of their maker and be safe. He then blessed both Jane and George themselves as he prayed, 'May the hand of the Lord be over you; and may he send his holy angel to guard and tend you all the days of your life.' The *Sarum Missal* tells us that the priest 'shall sprinkle them with holy water and, dismissing them in peace', should 'depart'.

At last. The flickering candle flames were extinguished, 'two bodies' could become 'one body'. Jane and George were finally husband and wife, for better or for worse.

WOMAN IN THE SHADOWS

6

Kindness Captures a King

With George's ring gleaming upon her finger, Jane Boleyn re-entered society as a wife. Her role and her status were dramatically altered. Now considered grown up, she was treated accordingly. A respectable matron, she no longer sat amongst the maidens in church; she could be included in the female activities connected with the mysteries of childbirth. She even looked different, now that her servant arranged her hair underneath a coif in the accepted manner of a married woman. And her future lay with the Boleyns, not the Parkers. She stayed in one of their houses, perhaps at Rochford in Essex near her own parents at Great Hallingbury, or at Hever, or at Blickling, estates she had every reason to believe would one day belong to her husband and over which she would preside as mistress. She did not expect to run any of them yet. A young bride would normally remain with her in-laws for some time, to see at first-hand how the household was governed and gradually to acquire the furniture and goods she needed before the couple could set up on their own.

There is no record of exactly what wedding gifts Jane and George received, but included in their property, which later passed to the king, is a vast quantity of silver. Amongst this there were six silver dishes, five of which are engraved with the letter I (which doubled for J) and one with a B, as well as another four, presumably of a different pattern or style, with a B upon them. Conceivably, these were given at the time of their marriage. One guest probably had a rather dry sense of humour, for one book that George owned was a fifteenth-century manuscript, which we know that he acquired about this time and later passed on to his musician friend, Mark Smeaton. It was a copy of a satire on marriage.

Country life was not to last for George and Jane, however. Jane was quickly back amidst the surroundings and people she knew so well, although this time she went to court as Mistress Boleyn whose husband was a gentleman of the privy chamber, for the moment at least. As such, George was required to be available to serve the king on demand. After a whole month at Windsor, Henry spent much of the summer and autumn of 1525 hunting, going to and from palaces and houses in the South-East, rarely staying at any of them for very long. Some were very recently acquired and Henry was quick to make use of them, sizing up the building works he would order to bring them up to his exacting standards. Ampthill, for example, was bought in 1524 for the pleasures of the chase, and Hunsdon in 1525, from George's uncle, the Duke of Norfolk, for similar reasons.

Occasionally, the king was a guest at various monastic houses such as Reading and Dunstable. Sometimes he returned to the more luxurious surroundings of Windsor or Greenwich. Wherever he went, his ministers followed; pressing matters of state business never stopped. Since Henry expected his every comfort to be catered for at any hour, he needed servants and attendants on call at all times. Thus, there were always favourites from his privy chamber close at hand, men like William Carey, Mary Boleyn's husband, or Henry Norris, fast becoming a key figure around the king. And of course there was George.

The early months of Jane's marriage were, therefore, far from dull. Visits to the Boleyn residences, as the wife of Thomas's heir, were interspersed with joining George when it was his turn to attend the king. She had it all, a young and dashing husband and the security of the Boleyn estates combined with proximity to the monarch, the source of fortune and advancement for George. Lord Morley could not have chosen better for his daughter. And she was now a member of a family already reaping rewards from their benevolent sovereign.

For she and George were not the only Boleyns at court. Still a respected diplomat with his ever-useful French, in his post as treasurer of the household Thomas was a frequent presence around the king, busily gathering lands, offices and titles. Already a Knight of the Garter, he was made Viscount Rochford, a title which George would eventually inherit. In fact, the day on which Thomas became Viscount Rochford was also highly significant for the king for it was then that his illegitimate son, Henry Fitzroy, was granted the earldom of Nottingham and a dukedom. The title bestowed upon him, Duke of Richmond and Somerset, was portentous, because it had been held by Henry VII before his victory at Bosworth had elevated him to the throne, and an earlier Duke of Somerset had been a royal bastard who was later made legitimate. The boy's investiture, at Henry's palace of Bridewell, was lavish. Dressed as an earl, he was led into the chamber between the Earls of Arundel and Oxford to kneel at his father's feet. Sir Thomas More read aloud the patent granting the child his earldom. No sooner had he received it than he left the room, only to return in the robes of a duke, this time escorted by the Dukes of Suffolk and Norfolk. Once the additional grant was announced to the assembled company, a gold circlet was placed upon Fitzroy's head, and a golden rod and other accoutrements of his new rank were handed to him. It is not surprising that Katherine, concerned for the future of her daughter Mary, was alleged to be dismayed, or that this was the year she commissioned a treatise on the obligations of marriage from Erasmus; rumours abounded that Henry intended to groom the child, whom he was said to love 'like his own soul', for kingship. Jane knew every detail of that day's events, either because she was present or from a first-hand account from Thomas. Not only was he there to collect his own honour, he is recorded as one of the witnesses to Fitzroy's elevation No doubt, Jane's sister-in-law, Anne, too, also received a full account. If so, the time was coming when she would mull over it as she made a decision affecting her own future.

Despite his new title, however, Thomas was not in the privy chamber. William Carey was. There was every reason for Thomas to feel as pleased with his choice of son-in-law as Lord Morley was with his. While not of the highest rank, William came from a solid Wiltshire family and, through his mother, Eleanor Beaufort, was distantly related to the king. He was a pleasant young man, a sensible, pragmatic husband, willing to be accommodating to the ways of the world. A skilful jouster, a tennis player, a ready participant in the revels, Carey was a man after the king's own heart. And, as the Boleyns realised, it was the king's heart which they had to thank for bringing about advances in their circumstances: for Mary Carey became Henry's mistress.

Quite when the king first focused his attention on Jane's sister-in-law is uncertain. By the time of the Field of Cloth of Gold, Henry was certainly no longer sleeping with Elizabeth Blount. Indeed, it seemed as though he had stopped doing so round about the time that she became pregnant with his son, Henry Fitzroy. Once the delectable Elizabeth was safely married to Gilbert Tailboys, Henry's eye probably lighted upon Mary. As a young girl, Mary had gone to France with Henry's sister 'to do service' for her when she married King Louis XII, presumably coming home with her when Louis died. According to Francis, Mary 'did service' to male members of the court too, so much so that she earned herself a tarnished reputation as *'una grandissima ribalda et infame sopre tutte'*.* Whatever the truth about her morals, Henry was happy to be an honoured guest at Mary's wedding to William at Greenwich, giving a church offering of 6s 8d, and it was as a respectably married woman that she had sat with Jane in the stands watching the tournaments at the Field of Cloth of Gold.

By the time Mary and Jane had performed together at Château Vert, if not before, her affair with Henry was under way. Mary took her role of Kindness very literally. Although she was quite young at that stage, it is difficult to imagine that Jane was unaware of what was going on. In the claustrophobic Tudor court, where people lived in such close proximity, gossip flourished and keeping secrets was well nigh impossible. Jane had been brought up to guard her virtue, but to deny the king was an altogether different proposition. And she could see at first hand what benefits such a

---

* 'A very great bawd and infamous above all'.

liaison brought. The compliant William was the recipient of royal grant after royal grant. The annuity of 50 marks a year that he had been awarded earlier, no mean sum, paled into insignificance in the light of the manors and offices showered upon him by a grateful and contented monarch. Ironically, his haul included the keepership of Beaulieu, the former Boleyn property, where he was entrusted with the king's wardrobe, as well as several other manors in the same area. Beaulieu was a perquisite worth having. While the keepers of some houses were allotted designated rooms within them and a house in the grounds, the keeper of Beaulieu was allowed to live in it as if they owned it. And Henry's gifts did not stop there. William and one of Henry's pages, William West, were even given the joint wardship,* always a highly coveted and lucrative prize, of Thomas Sharpe, an 'idiot' in Canterbury. The pair were also allocated custody of Sharpe's lands. All of this mounted up most gratifyingly. Indeed, when William was assessed for a tax payment, the assessment was for one third more than that of Jane's father and almost half that of Thomas Boleyn. William, no less ready to sacrifice his wife than Thomas was his daughter, had duly earned remuneration.

But things rarely stay the same for long. The Eltham Ordinances, Wolsey's efforts at reform within the privy chamber, came to fruition and George lost his place. While William survived, as did Henry Norris, George was not named as one of the fifteen able to remain. The grooms included William Brereton, and Francis Weston became the king's page. George and Jane were acquainted with all these men. It is not known why George was removed; perhaps Wolsey preferred to cut down the number of Boleyns in intimate, daily contact with Henry. However, George was still close enough. Amongst the list of names of those 'assigned to have lodging in the

---

* Should a man die while his children were still minors, feudal law decreed that they became legal wards of the king. However, the sovereign usually allocated their wardship to a leading courtier, either as a present or for a price. It was lucrative to obtain a wardship as it meant that the new guardian could administer lands and arrange marriages for his charges, both highly profitable enterprises.

king's house when they repair to it' is 'Mr Boleyn' and his wife. Wolsey meticulously checked this register, ticking the names of those receiving this entitlement. George's name is ticked in the cardinal's hand. This is the same document in which George was allowed £20 a year, in addition to his own £80, as a salary for his new post: he was appointed as 'one of the king's cupbearers when the king dineth out'.

While it was a pity that George was no longer one of the priv-ileged few with virtually unrestricted access to the king, it did not affect the lifestyle to which Jane was fast becoming accustomed. The Ordinances were highly specific concerning the newly wedded pair. Jane and George were assured of a palace room 'on the king's side' in which to sleep and were probably fed at royal expense. William and Mary Carey were awarded the same perquisite, again, hardly surprisingly, on the 'king's side'. And, as 'dineth out' meant every occasion on which Henry ate in state anywhere other than in his privy chamber, George retained a position of prominence. An annual income of £100, more than twice what Thomas Boleyn had once had to keep himself and his rapidly growing family, ensured relative affluence. With the king meeting most of their everyday expenditure, Jane and her husband could continue to indulge themselves in a few luxuries, and enjoy the entertainments and exhilaration of life at the apex of society.

However, changes in the personnel of the privy chamber were matched by another change. Just as we do not know when Mary's affair with Henry started, we do not know exactly when it ended, although it is certain that Mary became pregnant and gave birth to a son, Henry Carey. Whether the child's father was the king or William remains a mystery. There were certainly rumours about his parentage. It is also true that much later he was treated generously by his cousin, Queen Elizabeth, who ennobled him as Lord Hunsdon, and that his grand tomb in Westminster Abbey – not far from the Sanctuary, lavishly decorated in black, white and gold and embellished with the Boleyn emblems of bulls and falcons – is fit for a prince. Wisely, Henry Carey always stayed silent on the matter. The king continued to hold Mary in some affection after the birth, but he desired her no more. So, as Thomas and Elizabeth gazed upon their first grandchild, and Jane and George upon their nephew, it seemed as though further Boleyn advances would have to come through their own efforts, as they had done before Mary had so conveniently slipped between the sheets of the king's bed.

But Thomas had another daughter, and George another sister: Anne.

7

The Falcon's Rise

It was Shrove Tuesday, 1526, when the Boleyns, Jane's new family, witnessed a tangible hint of what might be to come. Henry's Christmas celebrations had been so muted that the season was called the 'still' Christmas. When plague broke out in London, the king, in line with his usual terror of sickness, retreated to the seclusion and comparative safety of Eltham for almost five weeks, accompanied by just a 'small number' of 'such as were appointed by name'. Only when the worst of the sickness was over did a cautious Henry venture out, eager to start living again. Since, for him, there were few things more exhilarating than jousting, especially before an admiring audience, Shrove Tuesday provided the perfect opportunity to indulge in diversion and pleasure. This particular occasion, though, was unique: amidst the fun and frivolity, for those shrewd enough to realise it, was a glimpse of the future. For Jane, who had every right to attend the festivities, there were echoes of another Shrove Tuesday event four years earlier when she had played Constancy on the mock battlements of Château Vert. Two of her fellow performers were by now her sisters-in-law. If, in the intervening period, Mary had epitomised Kindness in reality as well as in jest, so Perseverance was soon to become Anne's middle name.

As the court cheered and clapped, their king entered the lists. Thoroughly enjoying himself, and revelling in the acclaim, he gave a spirited performance at the head of his band of eleven other jousters. He looked stunning. Henry and his men shone in cloth of gold and silver, with their horses draped in similar fabric. His emblem, a man's heart gripped inside a press and surrounded by flames, was significant, but it was his motto that resonated with meaning. Embroidered in French, it can be translated as 'Declare, I dare not.' Arrayed in costumes of green velvet and crimson satin, the Marquess of Exeter's company opposed the king. Their emblem, burning hearts upon which silver droplets of water trickled from containers held by ladies' hands descending from clouds, was a perfect example of romance and chivalric values. Unfortunately, the day was almost spoilt by a freak but grisly accident. To the horror of the spectators, a spear shattered as it hit Sir Francis Bryan, who lost an eye. Never one to be perturbed by the sufferings of others, however, Henry, carefree and intact, rounded off the evening with a banquet, himself waiting upon Katherine and her ladies.

The precise moment when Henry fell in love with the woman who was to mesmerise and unsettle him for so many years is hotly disputed but for Jane and the other Boleyns the date was immaterial. The important thing was that fall in love he did. Completely. Henry's enigmatic motto on that Shrove Tuesday said it all. Having dropped one sister, he yearned for the other, even if he was not yet ready to proclaim it to the world. And Anne was unmarried and available.

Whether she would stay so for long was another matter. Jane had come into very close contact with her when they had rehearsed the complicated choreography needed for the Château Vert pageant. Even then, Anne had been no retiring wallflower. Her looks were unconventional: a natural brunette with an unremarkable figure, she lacked the pale, translucent, fragile beauty then in vogue. The Venetian ambassador wrote scathingly, 'Madam Anne is not one of the handsomest women in the world; she is of middling stature, swarthy complexion, long neck, wide mouth, bosom not much raised.' But there was more to her than that. Her intelligence, her wit, her repartee, her sheer vivacity, her ability to light up a room, together with the charm and polish gained through her years at the Renaissance court of Charles V's aunt, the regent Margaret, as well as her time in France with Mary Tudor and Queen Claude, all combined to make Anne highly noticeable. And they made her different. Even the Venetian ambassador appreciated her most obvious asset – the dark, flashing eyes, which, he said, were 'black and beautiful' and which she so clearly used to advantage for they took 'great effect on those who served the Queen when she was on the throne'. Such a woman soon attracted admirers.

Long before Jane's wedding, Thomas Boleyn had considered suggestions for a marriage for his second daughter. Never a man to be fastidious or squeamish where property was concerned, he had pondered using Anne to settle problems over his Ormond inheritance. While he had acquired his father-in-law's English lands without too much trouble, he had not gained his title, and Thomas's claims in Ireland were contested by Piers Butler, Ormond's cousin. To marry Anne to Piers's son, James, was ostensibly an ideal solution to the rather messy dispute. Wolsey thought it such an excellent plan that he wrote of it to the king but, although talks dragged on for some time, they finally petered out. Jane heard about the scheme, though, for it was still festering away when she joined the Boleyn family. She certainly knew about Anne's other swains, the poet, Thomas Wyatt, and Henry Percy, the son of the Earl of Northumberland. Both were probably on the scene when the king first experienced what he was later to call 'the dart of love' and which he was to intimate at the Shrove Tuesday joust.

The problem with Wyatt was that he was already married, albeit miserably, to an equally unhappy Elizabeth Brooke, and the couple had two children. Handsome and cultured though he was, and Anne was no doubt flattered and excited by his attentions, all he could offer was an affair and perhaps the prospect of immortality through poetry. For the ambitious Anne, such enticements were simply not enough. Henry Percy was a much more realistic proposition. Heir to the vast Percy estates, he was about Anne's age and, to Anne at least, personable. They met at court when Percy resorted 'for his pastime unto the queen's chamber' where he fell 'in dalliance among the queen's maidens'. Soon he dallied with one maiden in particular. 'Being at the last more conversant with Mistress Anne Boleyn', the pair decided to marry when 'a secret love' developed between them. Or so we are told by George Cavendish.

What Anne divulged about how far her 'secret love' had progressed goes unrecorded, but it is inconceivable that her family knew nothing at all of what was going on. If she confided in anyone, it was most probably her 'sweet brother' for she and George were always close. There is no evidence of that practised negotiator, Thomas Boleyn, entering into tentative discussions with Percy's father so any family concerns did not translate into action. In fact, Northumberland decided that his son should marry Mary Talbot, daughter of the Earl of Shrewsbury, who would be a much better match for him than Anne. Her hopes, if hopes there were, were dashed and, according to Cavendish, they were dashed in spectacular fashion. He asserts that the relationship between Anne and Henry Percy was broken up by the cardinal himself, acting upon the king's personal order. Henry, Cavendish writes, was 'much offended' by Anne's relationship because he already had a 'secret affection' for her himself, which he was forced to 'reveal' to Wolsey. Having soundly berated Percy, Wolsey is alleged to have sent for the formidable Northumberland, who did the same. The earl then attended to the final details for the wedding to Mary Talbot. The result, Cavendish firmly declares, was Anne's lasting hatred for Wolsey. She was determined that 'if it ever lay in her power, she would work the cardinal as much displeasure'. Whatever the truth, Anne was sent back to Hever, out of harm's way, to come to terms with her disappointment or, maybe, to plot her revenge.

For Jane and the other Boleyns, court life continued much as usual despite the complexities of Anne's emotional upheavals with Wyatt and Percy. George waited upon the king when he dined in state, William Carey served him within the confines of the privy chamber, and Thomas remained close at hand. But with Anne's two suitors eliminated and the marriage negotiations with Butler running into difficulties, the way lay open for the king. He did something he normally detested: he took up his pen.

Thus began a courtship which changed not only Anne's life but the life of everyone around her. At first, no one, probably not even Anne herself, appreciated just how far Henry would go to gain the object of his desire. Until now, he had been denied nothing. Yet, to his bewilderment, Anne not only resisted him, she did so with consummate ease. In the seventeen letters that are extant in the Vatican archives, the king poured out his innermost feelings, his devotion and his love to the woman he thought of as his 'own sweetheart'. The letters are tender, filled with concern for her, revealing the torment of a man whose heart really was gripped by passion and yearning. For a Tudor daughter, even one as high-spirited and independent as Anne, to have concealed such missives is unthinkable. And, like the rest of the family, Jane was there from the beginning, as Anne's dark eyes focused on the pleadings of the king.

And pleadings they were. Jane was at court with George when, in an ironic role reversal, Henry cast himself as Anne's 'true servant', appealing for news of her 'health' and 'welfare'. He gently chided her for not contacting him as she had promised for, he wrote, 'it has not pleased you to remember the promise you made me when I was last with you – that is, to hear good news from you'. He sent her a present of a buck he had killed himself, 'hoping that when you eat of it you may think of the hunter'. Having George at his side was all very well but Anne was to know that the king 'very often wishes for you instead of your brother'. Another present, much more costly, was certainly not one that Anne could keep secret from her family. With the 'pain of absence ... too great' and knowing that he could not be 'personally present', Henry sent her the 'nearest thing' to himself, his 'picture set in bracelets' and with a 'device' which he knew she would understand. Totally confident in her ability to decipher cryptic messages, he placed another, simply a string of letters, at the bottom of a further communication.

Decode the puzzle Anne did. But she continued to refuse to submit to Henry's demands. Indeed, he began to wonder whether any hints that she might eventually succumb to his entreaties were groundless. 'Since my parting from you', he then wrote, 'I have been told that the opinion in which I left you is totally changed, and that you would not come to court either with your mother, if you could, or in any other manner.' This, he felt, was 'a very poor return for the great love' he had for her. He could not understand why, if she loved him, it was not 'a little irksome' to be apart. This letter went further. Anne truly did have to make up her mind. If she 'voluntarily desired' their separation, he 'could do no other than mourn my ill-fortune, and by degrees abate my great folly'. Even Henry's patience was not inexhaustible.

Although all of Anne's replies have since been lost, she certainly did not yield. So Henry tried once more. He had been, he said, 'for above a whole year stricken with the dart of love' and still did not know where he stood. Did she love him 'with an ordinary love' or a 'singular one'? He was desperate to 'know expressly' what she really felt 'as to the love between us two'. Then came what for him was the supreme offer. If Anne would surrender both her 'body and heart', she would be his 'only mistress'; he would think of no one else and 'serve' her alone. So desperate was he for her answer that if she did not want to reply in writing, he was ready to go wherever she wanted to 'have it by word of mouth'.

To have the king so besotted with Anne presented the Boleyns with an acute dilemma. Henry's lust for Mary had brought rich pickings for all of them but his craving for Anne, which had already lasted unrequited for over a year, was of an entirely different order. While the potential rewards were massive, so was the danger. Katherine had serenely ignored her husband's extramarital entanglements but, so far, they had amounted to little, and if they had, the well-loved, universally respected queen had powerful friends to support her. Wolsey could not be disregarded either; he would not easily relinquish his intimate influence with his royal master, either to Anne or to her potentially grasping relations. To cross him was unwise. Rumour had it that he had played a shadowy part in engineering the execution of Buckingham, who had once insulted him. Neither Thomas nor George wanted to count him an enemy, despite Anne's alleged bravado. More crucially, Henry remained a married man. An affair, even an exclusive one, would not last for ever. Henry was surrounded by young and pretty women. Both Elizabeth Blount and Mary Boleyn were living examples of Henry's fickle nature. The intelligent Anne understood the situation: once she lost his affection, she would be married off to an obliging courtier. For Elizabeth Blount the pay-off had been good, because she married Gilbert Tailboys, whose family owned lands in six counties, but, equally, there was a risk that Anne might be offered a minor noble and then sink into comparative obscurity.

And, whereas Mary had settled back into court life quite contentedly as Carey's wife, Anne would have found the status of discarded mistress intolerable. Yet to refuse the king for ever could be to give up the chance of a lifetime, not only for herself but also for Thomas and George. It was not a decision to be made lightly, nor was it one to be made alone. A free spirit in many ways, Anne, like Jane, was still a woman in a patriarchal society. She would be foolish not to ask the advice of her parents and, since she loved him, her brother. Finally, after countless hours of thought and, doubtless, family discussion, Anne made her choice. She gave in.

She did so in style and she did so symbolically. When she responded to the king, she gave him a token, one which required planning, thought, and some expense as it needed to be specially crafted. Since she possessed no lands in her own right, Thomas must have agreed to purchase this gift for her. The Boleyns were with her all the way. Intriguingly, there is a payment, which could be significant, listed amongst Thomas's accounts 'to Cornelys [Cornelius Hayes], the king's goldsmith, £4'. Four pounds was probably too small a sum to buy the whole present, but it might well have been an instalment.

Henry's response was ecstatic. 'For a present so beautiful,' he wrote, 'I thank you most cordially.' The gift was a jewel, a 'fine diamond' complete with a ship in which a 'solitary damsel is tossed about'. Anne's gift was shrewdly chosen. Henry understood its 'fine interpretation': Anne, the damsel, was safe in the ship just as she was safe in his arms. She entrusted herself to him. Henry promised everlasting love in return. He felt obliged, he said, 'for ever to honour, love and serve you sincerely', pledging 'loyalty of heart and a desire to please'. But he also fretted that Anne was still not prepared to sleep with him. His heart was hers, but 'I wish my person was too', he lamented. For, as Jane knew, Anne's surrender was only partial.

In fact, Anne and Henry had come to a breathtaking agreement. Anne would not be Henry's mistress; she would be his wife and his queen. With Katherine past the menopause, Henry's last hopes of a son by her had faded. Anne vowed to do better than the woman she intended to supplant: she would give birth to a male heir. Unlike Fitzroy, her child would be legitimate in the eyes of the world because she and Henry would marry. Audacious perhaps, but, if the plan was successful, the Boleyns really were there to stay.

8

Lady-in-Waiting

When Jane Parker became Jane Boleyn, she envisaged a life similar to that of her mother. There would be time on the Boleyn estates, coupled with visits to court with her husband and journeys back home to Great Hallingbury as a married woman to see her own family. She had not expected to become entangled in the events of the most significant love affair of her age. But, as the Boleyns embarked on their great gamble, that is what happened.

Secure in Anne's love, Henry could hardly bear to be apart from her. In yet another adoring letter to her 'whose absence has grieved my heart more than either words or writing can express', he begged her to come back to court for their 'meeting is more desired by me than anything in this world'. There was no joy 'greater upon earth than to have the company of her who is dearest' to him. Neither was ready to tell the world about their 'secret matter' just yet, of course, but, for one glorious evening after her return, Anne was in his arms in front of everyone. That included his wife.

When the French ambassadors arrived to discuss marriage plans for Princess Mary, the king provided for them the usual joust followed by a banquet and an elaborate entertainment in his hugely impressive, recently constructed building at the side of the tiltyards at Greenwich. With her husband as Henry's cupbearer that evening, Jane had every right to be there. Those who entered the great chamber of the new edifice did not know where to look first. Straight ahead was a huge arch painted with serpents and gargoyles, emblazoned with arms and emblems, and with a gallery above in which a group of musicians played softly. Above them the ceiling was covered with purple *brocatelle* embellished with representations of roses and pomegranates. The walls were adorned with Henry's fabulously expensive tapestries of King David. Amber-coloured candlesticks holding white wax candles which gave out their flickering light stood beneath the windows, and everywhere there was the gleam of gold. Golden vessels were stacked for display and the guests were served from gold or gilt containers that weighed so much that they 'troubled sore the bearers'. George's task was a little more onerous that evening too: the lords, entrusted with carrying the heavy wine cups, 'grudged to bear them'. Henry sat with Katherine and his sister under a cloth of estate as dish after dish was served to the assembled company. When the meal was over, the courtiers progressed underneath the vast arch into the second room for the entertainment, walking over a floor strewn with silk embroidered with lilies and beneath a magical ceiling decorated with a map of the world and the signs of the zodiac. Feasting his eyes on the ladies who sat together in the galleried seating around the side, the Venetian secretary was so overcome with their splendour and beauty that he compared them to a 'choir of angels'. There were many different diversions performed that evening but, for the Boleyns, it was the finale alone that counted.

Sparkling in cloth of gold and purple satin, with his face shielded by a golden beard and with his feet encased in black velvet slippers, Henry and his fellow maskers danced with ladies from amongst the spectators. The only woman whose name is recorded is Anne. And she danced with the king. No one took any particular notice. Anne spoke French, after all, and the whole event had been arranged for the French ambassadors. But, as Katherine watched fondly while an excited Princess Mary partnered Turenne, the most important French envoy, Anne and Henry were a couple. The moment passed. Henry returned to his duties as host and Anne to the company of the other women. She was not his wife yet. For Jane's sister-in-law to become queen, Henry had to end his marriage to Katherine. Neither he nor Anne thought that this would prove difficult.

On their departure from the building at Greenwich that evening, the guests walked past the King David tapestries. When she had attended the Field of Cloth of Gold, Jane had wandered through the great hall of Henry's temporary palace at Guisnes, spellbound by what she had seen. One of the wonders on show then was a magnificent example of the weaver's art: a tapestry, glinting with gold and silver thread, showing King David and Bathsheba. It hung on the wall again that night at Greenwich. And therein lay the clue. It was only when Henry had committed himself to Anne that Jane could really understand its significance. The king was deeply interested in David, the Old Testament hero who slew Goliath. David had a close relationship with his god and led his people to great victories against their enemies. For a devout king committed to the glory of war, the link was clear, but there was far more to it than that. David had suffered a serious setback. He so desired the lovely Bathsheba that he had been prepared to send her husband, Uriah, to die in battle so that he could possess her. This had earned him divine retribution: the death of his son by Bathsheba. A deeply religious man, Henry saw a direct parallel in his own life, for a verse in Leviticus (20: 21) threatened childlessness to a man who married his brother's widow. That was what he had done. In marrying Katherine he had sinned and had been punished. After all, little Prince Henry had been taken from him when only a few weeks old and his long years with Katherine had produced only a string of disappointments and one live daughter. This was the proof of God's displeasure. His conscience was troubling him 'daily and hourly'. Only by repudiating Katherine and finding a new wife could he hope to have a son and make his peace with God. He was convinced of the justice of his case, as, of course, were the Boleyns. And they were determined to help him.

Once Anne had agreed to marry him, Henry set about making it happen. As Wolsey had so far managed everything for him, it was Wolsey upon whom he relied to achieve his 'secret matter'. A worried cardinal begged the king not to proceed but his entreaties fell on deaf ears; for Anne's sake, Henry recklessly banished all caution. Banished, too, from his mind and Anne's was a realistic assessment of the difficulties ahead. The Leviticus text had been pored over at the Vatican more than twenty years ago when Pope Julius II had granted a dispensation to allow Henry and Katherine to go to the altar, an act which Henry now maintained exceeded the pope's powers. Henry's solution to the dilemma was ingeniously simple. Since Wolsey was a papal legate, all he needed to do was to pronounce Henry in the wrong for living with Katherine as her husband, require a penitent, remorseful king to leave her, inevitably with a show of reluctance and regret, and then induce the current pope, Clement VII, to accept this. In so doing, Clement would remedy his predecessor's mistake. Nothing could be more straightforward.

So on 17 May 1527, Jane's new family waited anxiously but confidently to hear what progress had been made. On that day, Wolsey opened the first session of a court at York Place specifically established to look into the legality of the king's marriage. Henry sat at the cardinal's right hand as he was accused by Dr Richard Wolman, in reality his own counsel, of living unlawfully with his brother's wife. At this stage, neither the king nor the Boleyns wanted Anne in public view. For Henry to admit his love for her would have weakened his case; he had to dissemble and protest that his sole purpose was to put his mind at rest concerning his marital situation. Indeed, he was later to declare that if his marriage to Katherine was lawful and he could stay with her, 'there was never thing more pleasant nor more acceptable' to him. Were it only possible, he 'would surely choose her above all women'. His love and respect, however, only went so far; he decided not to tell Katherine of his internal torment, nor of the existence of the legatine court. Instead, he prepared his arguments and relied on Wolman and Wolsey. For Anne and her relatives there was every reason for optimism.

Then came the first in what was to become a catalogue of disappointments. On the very day when the Boleyns hoped for the news that meant preparing for another wedding, Wolsey announced that the case was too complex for him and had to be referred to the pope. The issue had never been as clear-cut as the newly engaged pair asserted. Wolsey had always known it. Leviticus was not entirely helpful. The verse specified a lack of children, but Princess Mary was alive and well. The trouble was compounded because there was a conflicting Biblical text in Deuteronomy (25: 5), which appeared to require a living brother to marry his dead brother's wife if they had no children. That, of course, was precisely Katherine's situation. To make matters worse, she vowed that her union with Arthur had been unconsummated, meaning that she had never really been his wife and thus there was no impediment at all to her marriage to

Henry. It would seem that the papal dispensation, which had weighed up the crucial verses in both Leviticus and Deuteronomy with due care, was correct and the issue certainly was within the pope's jurisdiction.

This was the opinion of John Fisher, Bishop of Rochester and a highly respected theologian, whom Wolsey had consulted. After considerable research and reflection, Fisher pronounced that he could not 'see any sound reason to show that it is prohibited by divine law for a brother to marry the wife of a brother who has died without children'. Indeed, thought Fisher, now very much into his stride, 'considering the fulness of authority given by our Lord to the Pope, who can deny that the latter may give a dispensation to that effect, for any serious cause?' Unfortunately, Fisher's analysis was shared by other experts. Thomas More later said how astonished he had been when the king had first broached the subject as they were walking in the gallery at Hampton Court. Henry opened the Bible and pointed out the words that he felt backed up his case against his marriage. The king suggested that More should research the subject and discuss it with Edward Foxe, a Cambridge scholar and an able diplomat whose help had been enlisted. Although More was careful not to commit himself against his monarch, he never spoke out in favour of the divorce either. There was no way out of the impasse: for Henry to proceed further, he must petition Pope Clement.

That did not in itself mean disaster. Provided Anne's name was kept out of the proceedings, there was, in theory, no reason why Clement should not be amenable. The worldly and sophisticated papacy was usually accommodating to kings with political or succession problems. Henry had only to think back to his erstwhile brother-in-law, Louis XII, who had divorced his existing wife in order to make a dynastic marriage to Anne of Brittany. And annulments were even closer to home than that: the king's current brother-in-law, the Duke of Suffolk, had obtained permission from Clement himself to end his first marriage. Unfortunately, Katherine was neither as obliging nor as friendless as Jeanne of France or Margaret Mortimer. She 'intended to live and die in the estate of matrimony, into which God had called her' and was positive that her nephew,

Charles V, would help her. So, she thought, would the pope. Charles was indeed on her side. Affronted by what he called 'so scandalous a proceeding', he promised 'to do everything in his power on her behalf'. Thus, as Jane watched from within the Boleyn camp, the battle lines were drawn.

Battle it would be, for Clement was not an entirely free agent. Charles had an army in Italy. No matter how willing the pragmatic Clement was to assist Henry in his hour of need, especially at a time when he was only too aware that many were falling under the spell of the new doctrines promulgated by Martin Luther, the pope dared not antagonise Charles. Then the unthinkable happened. Charles's unruly and unpaid troops sacked the city of Rome itself. Harrowing tales reached England. The imperial soldiers had murdered the citizens, raped nuns, burnt down churches and used religious images for target practice. As the carnage began, Clement fled to his strong-hold, Castel Sant'Angelo. Jane was as horrified as the rest of the court by these outrages but, for her sister-in-law's cause, there was a silver lining. With the pope a prisoner, not only was he unable to pronounce in Henry's favour, he could not really pronounce at all. The solution was obvious: Wolsey, as papal legate, could give the verdict for him, and, as long as he could be trusted to labour on their behalf, the Boleyns, every one of them, were right behind him.

Here, too, they were thwarted. While Wolsey and Thomas More were in Amiens, negotiating with the French for joint action over the beleaguered pope, Clement was allowed to escape, which altered the whole situation yet again. A different plan of attack was required. As Jane quickly realised following her own wedding, George and his father were not only intelligent, well-read and thoughtful men, both were fascinated by theology. Involvement in religious debate was very much a family trait for George's uncle, James Boleyn, found such discussions just as thrilling as his brother and nephew. They were entirely equal to assessing the doctrinal and international impli-cations of Anne's 'secret matter' and to working behind the scenes to bring about the desired result. Jane watched as the Boleyn family machine swung into action.

What was needed was irrefutable material to reinforce Henry's cause if scholars like John Fisher were to be rebutted. A cast-iron case must be presented to Clement. Fortunately, the Boleyns knew the very man who could help: Robert Wakefield, the foremost Hebrew expert of the day, who believed that only a thorough knowledge of the early tongues allowed accurate interpretation of scripture. The acquaintance came through James Boleyn, once his pupil. And in 1527, Wakefield came to Henry's notice. The king's former personal secretary, Richard Pace, then recuperating at Syon from a fresh bout of a recurring illness, wrote to his master, enclosing the Hebrew alphabet to be delivered to Edward Foxe, together with a book by Robert Wakefield, a man of 'excellent learning and wonderful knowledge'. Pace went on to say that Wakefield offered to 'show unto your Highness such things as no man within your realm can attain unto or show the like, and as well for you as against you'. Pace's letter was followed by one to the king from Wakefield himself. He suggested defending 'Henry's cause in all the universities of Christendom', promising that he could 'in such manner answer the bishop of Rochester's book that I trust he shall be ashamed to wade or meddle any further in the matter'. Jane knew that for Wakefield to be so confident of helping the king, the scholar's interest in the annulment, which Henry and the Boleyns laboured so hard to keep secret, must have been kindled even before he wrote to Henry or spoke to Pace. Priming him about what was happening might well have been the job of George's uncle whom Wakefield remembered as a 'generous knight' and a 'learned' man. For James to contact an old friend for advice when in trouble was entirely natural, and placing Jane's sister-in-law on the throne of England would involve the efforts of the whole family.

Those efforts bore fruit. Wakefield's work was sensational, demolishing, at least in Henry's eyes, his opponents' arguments. His meticulous Hebrew translation suggested that the term 'childless' in Leviticus, a potent stumbling block, was wrongly gendered. It should refer only to a lack of sons, not children in general. Moreover, as Leviticus was part of Mosaic law, adherence to its restrictions was obligatory even for Christians. As for Deuteronomy, this applied to the Jews alone and was not binding upon Gentiles. Armed with such arguments, the chances of Henry and Anne achieving their desire were transformed. Fisher, who also derived his knowledge of

Hebrew from Wakefield, disagreed but even he admitted that Henry would be 'quite justified in submitting his difficulties to the pope', for it was his prerogative 'to clear ambiguous passages of Scripture, after hearing the opinions of the best divines', although the sceptical bishop went on to say that kings 'are apt to think that right which suits their pleasure'.

The waiting game went on. Thomas Boleyn, ever ready to help his king, and especially his daughter, did his part. Already part of the advisory circle nearest the king, he went on the first of many journeys to France to solicit support for their cause from Francis. George, an indefatigable ally of his sister, soon joined him. Henry's fellow monarch, delighted by the wedge developing between Henry and Charles, made appropriately soothing noises while continuing his own schemes to advance French interests in Italy and beyond. Wolsey, desperate to retain his own position, negotiated with Rome. Letters went thick and fast to Charles, from Henry, from Katherine, from the troubled Spanish ambassador. Henry collected more and more reasons to justify his cause and spent long hours writing about them in the various 'King's Books' that accumulated. Still the pope dithered.

Then, as a breakthrough suddenly looked more likely, Jane's husband fell desperately ill with a terrifying disease that could kill in less than a day. Worse still, he was not its only Boleyn victim.

9

The Sweat

The year 1528 had begun so well. Summoning up his courage, for he always hated direct confrontation, Henry had at last informed a tearful Katherine of his doubts over their marriage, confirming what in fact she had already been told by her growing band of supporters. Then, no doubt encouraged by Anne, he went one stage further, requesting Pope Clement to pronounce him free to marry again 'in case his marriage ... be pronounced unlawful'. Jane had only to hear of Henry's choice of words to be assured that his love for Anne was as strong as ever. He wanted every conceivable legal and religious pitfall removed in advance. Perhaps with Anne's friendship with Northumberland in mind, he asked the pope for permission to remarry even if his future bride had 'contracted marriage with another man, provided it be not consummated'. He went on to seek consent 'even if she be of the second degree of consanguinity or of the first degree of affinity', covering potential repercussions emanating from the king's affair with Anne's sister, a relationship that was the mirror opposite of Katherine's with his brother. No one wanted such uncertainty again; this union must be incontestable.

It was excellent news for the family. Jane's sister-in-law would be queen yet. She had a stunning emerald ring to prove it, not, of course, that it could be flaunted to those outside her immediate circle. With talk of the pope sending Cardinal Campeggio as his legate to try the case in England, there were fewer clouds on the horizon. But one remained, against which no papal dispensation could prevail.

At the beginning of June, Brian Tuke, a senior official in Henry's household, wrote to the Bishop of London informing him that he had just fled from his house in the city because one of his servants had become ill. This was no ordinary illness: a terrifying disease, the sweating sickness, was back. Henry and Anne, who was now so frequently at his side, were both at Greenwich when the epidemic struck, probably attended by both George and Jane. At first all seemed well, the royal party was untouched. The king had already decided to move on to Waltham Abbey when there was a scare: one of Anne's maidservants became ill. Henry, desperate to avoid coming into contact with the virus, hurriedly left for Waltham accompanied by George and some of his privy chamber, while Anne fled to the safety of Hever with her father. Whether Jane went with her husband or to Kent is not known. What we do know, though, is that on the very same day, George felt the first symptoms.

The disease could strike at any moment, and with incredible ferocity. Some victims even succumbed while riding. The sweat began with a headache, developing at frightening speed. The pain swiftly moved to the abdomen. Then there was vomiting and palpitations, sometimes paralysis, breathlessness, all accompanied by almost intolerable sweating. The first few hours were critical. Some died within four hours of the slightest trace of a headache, others within twelve. Those surviving for twenty-four hours normally lived. For Jane, the spectre of widowhood was beckoning.

Everyone was afraid. According to Tuke and the Venetian ambassador, the mere rumour that the sweat had returned caused some to collapse from fear. Lawyers alone were said to have gained. They 'had a fine time', said the French ambassador mockingly, since '100,000 wills have been made', amongst them one from an ever-vigilant Henry.

The onset of symptoms was so sudden that George's family did not hear that he was fighting for his life until later. Only if Jane had been with him would the devastating news have reached them, and then only as quickly as the fastest horse could gallop from Waltham to Hever. In any event, there was little that they could do. He received the best available treatment. Remedies abounded. The Dowager Duchess of Norfolk, the woman in whose household little Catherine Howard was to grow up, recommended 'treacle and water imperial'. John Caius, a 'doctour in phisicke', suggested other precautions, which were, of course, too late for George. What Caius and other authorities could state for certain was that the sweat must be allowed to flow freely to let the evil out of the body. So George lay in bed wrapped in quilts and fighting for his life, with meticulous care being taken to make sure he did not throw off the bedclothes in his delirium. Any exposure to the air was considered especially perilous, even potentially fatal, particularly if air touched the armpits. His chamber was kept warm, by lighting a fire if necessary, and his sweating was rigorously monitored. For those who did not sweat enough, Caius counselled gentle rubbing with a 'new and somewhat hard handkerchief, well-warmed but not hot' or cocktails of milk, vinegar and herbs.

Fortunately, George recovered and, for a while, it seemed as though the Boleyns might escape lightly. Henry, 'much troubled' by the pestilence, but anxious about Anne, was relieved to hear from Hever that she was well. 'The doubt I had of your health troubled me exceedingly,' he wrote, 'but since you have felt nothing, I hope it is with you as with us.' He was able to reassure her that George was 'now quite well', and tried to keep up her spirits by reminding her that 'few women have this illness'. Soon, however, one of those women was Anne. All the family's dreams hung in the balance as she hovered between life and death.

Henry was distraught. In a despairing letter to her, he described hearing of her plight as 'the most afflicting news possible', even protesting that he 'would willingly bear the half' of her sickness if it would cure her. This was from a man who was so fearful on his own behalf that he confessed his sins every day to a priest, compulsively moved from place to place, and was once found by Tuke 'in secret communication with his physician, Mr Chamber, in a tower, where he sometimes sups apart'. With Anne ill, however, Henry was practical. Desolate that the doctor he most trusted 'is at present absent', he sent her his 'second' best physician, Dr Butts, who duly hurried down to Hever. There he found Anne in great 'jeopardy . . . by the turning of the sweat before the time', always considered hazardous as the sweating had not done its work in ridding the body of all the 'venom'. Since by now Thomas Boleyn was as critically sick as his daughter, all of Dr Butts's best 'endeavour' and skill was needed to save them. But save them he did. No one could do the same for Mary Boleyn's husband, William Carey, who also caught the disease. He died, Henry hearing of his death as he went to bed. The first Boleyn widow was Mary, not Jane.

Thomas, never a man to be relied upon when there was trouble, gave little support to his grieving daughter. Insofar as Boleyn ambition was concerned, Mary was the past. The future had survived. It was in fact Anne who appears to have done the most for her sister. Her intervention with Henry prompted the king to contact Thomas, pointing out that 'it cannot so stand with his honour but that he must needs take her [should help her] his natural daughter now in her extreme necessity'. Anne's help did not stop there. While the customary scramble for Carey's offices was going on all around her, with its usual indecent haste, Anne prevailed on Henry to grant her the wardship of young Henry Carey, which was surely a great weight off Mary's mind. As the courtier Sir John Russell found to his cost when his pleas for the wardship of his wife's daughter fell on deaf ears, Henry could not be relied upon to allow such a lucrative perquisite to pass to relatives. If further proof of Henry's adoration was required, this gift certainly provided it. Unfortunately, Carey's death also exposed the underlying tension between the Boleyns and the cardinal.

Just before he died, Carey had been pressing for the appointment of his sister, Elinor, as abbess of a nunnery at Wilton in Wiltshire. Anne, too, supported Elinor against the other candidate, Isabel Jordan. When Henry heard that Elinor had led a scandalous life, even having two children by two priests, he maintained that he could not allow Anne to 'cloak' her conscience by promoting such an unworthy cause. A compromise abbess should be chosen instead. However, Wolsey went ahead without the king's permission and appointed Isabel Jordan. Henry's fury was no doubt matched by Anne's. He left the cardinal reeling from his anger, particularly because he thought Wolsey was trying to wriggle out of blame by saying that he did not know what Henry wanted. This, said the king, just made matters worse. As he wrote accusingly to Wolsey, 'You cloak your offence by ignorance, saying that you did not know my determination in this matter ... it is a double offence to do ill and colour it also.' Rarely had the great cardinal been faced with such naked antagonism from his 'loving sovereign lord and friend'. Only after humiliating and abject apologies from Wolsey was Henry pacified. For the Boleyns, Anne's hold over the king was emphasised yet again.

However, Wolsey had his uses. The cardinal's house at Tittenhanger provided Henry with what he hoped was a safe bolt-hole away from the ravages of the sweat and the king was content to stay there as long as he deemed necessary. Indeed, he felt sufficiently at home to make a few alterations to add to his comfort: a surprised Wolsey was informed that Henry had ordered his builder 'to make a new window in your closet, because it is so little'. More importantly, current Boleyn thinking was that working with Wolsey, rather than against him, remained the most sensible way to attain their objective, for the moment at least. Hiding her true feelings, Anne played her part. In a personal note, she thanked Wolsey for his letter, pledging 'to love and serve' him 'while breath' was in her body, and conveyed her relief that he had been spared the sweat. 'I thank God', she wrote, 'that those I desired and prayed for have escaped – namely the king and you.' But she was shrewd enough to remind the cardinal how close her relationship with his master actually was. In a letter in which ostensibly she thanked him abjectly for 'the great pains you take for me, both day and night' which 'are never likely to be recompensed', there is a telling postscript added jocularly by Henry. He guilelessly confessed to writing it because 'the writer of this would not cease till she had called me likewise to set my hand'. The cardinal was left uncomfortably aware that his own position was secure only if Anne and her family allowed it.

He was safe for the time being, for the breakthrough, cruelly interrupted by the sweat, materialised at last. An ecstatic Henry rushed to tell Anne, currently away from court, the good news. 'The Legate, which we most desire arrived at Paris on Sunday or Monday last post,' he wrote, 'so that I trust by the next Monday to hear of his arrival at Calais.' Not long after he set foot on English soil, Campeggio would, Henry and Anne believed, deliver the verdict for which they yearned. 'I trust within a while after to enjoy that which I have so longed for to God's pleasure and our both comfort,' she read. Her family would almost certainly have read it too. It looked as if their combined planning would bring them their reward: Jane's sister-in-law was about to become queen.

10

Fortune's Wheel

The court case that the Boleyns believed would change their
fortunes for ever began in the early summer of 1529. Cardinal
Lorenzo Campeggio had arrived some time before, having made his
will before setting off, as any journey then was perilous. He had then
had such an acute attack of gout that he was unable to walk and had
to be carried in a velvet chair for his first meeting with the king.
After a fruitless attempt to persuade Katherine to make things easy
for Henry and the Church by entering the seclusion of a convent,
Campeggio fulfilled the pope's reluctantly bestowed commission to
bring the case to trial. When Jane Parker married George Boleyn
and pledged to take him as her husband 'for better, for worse', the
prospect of a member of her new family replacing the respected and
established queen would never have crossed her mind, nor, probably,
theirs either. Since then, she had witnessed every stage of the burgeoning affair, as George and his father supported Anne while she
took those first tentative steps towards the throne. Now their hopes
were about to be realised, or so they thought.

There were still some lingering doubts, however, particularly
about the genuineness of Wolsey's professed commitment. Outwardly, the cardinal was tirelessly unremitting in his labours, so
much so that he delegated many routine tasks to his solicitor and
man of business, the shrewd and capable Thomas Cromwell, who
suddenly surfaces in the records. Cromwell received legions of
requests to convey information to his master or, increasingly, to help
secure favours for petitioners on his own account. Even Wolsey's
illegitimate son, Thomas Winter, manifestly thought that he was
more likely to get help from Cromwell at this time than from his

own busy father. Distrust of Wolsey's actions was spreading, however. Inigo de Mendoza, the Spanish ambassador, said as much to Charles V when he commented in a letter that Anne, 'the cause of all the disorder', suspected that the cardinal had deliberately placed 'impediments in her way, from a belief that if she were queen, his power would decline'. The Venetian ambassador, too, latched on to Wolsey's fears that Thomas Boleyn would 'deprive' him 'of his repute'. As indeed he would have. Even Francis I was alleged to have told the Duke of Suffolk that Henry should not 'put too much trust in any man, whereby he may be deceived'. The Boleyns had already assessed their own support in preparation for a potential confrontation with Wolsey. As a Howard, and an ambitious one, the Duke of Norfolk was on their side. With an acquisitive eye on Wolsey's confiscated property, the notoriously rapacious Suffolk, despite his wife's antipathy to Anne, was another ally. Both must be kept on board, which might not be easy. On the other hand, of course, should Wolsey prove true and remain useful, he was not the only problem. Charles V's response to the imminent proceedings was a deep concern. Despite his 'desire to oblige the king', it was anyone's guess whether Clement, hedged in by imperial forces, really would dare to antagonise the emperor by annulling the marriage. The pope's constant ill-health was a further worry. It was not going to be straightforward.

The unseasonable weather hardly lifted the spirits. Campeggio complained that he was forced to wear his winter clothes and have fires lit. There was anxiety that the sweat was about to make an unwelcome return. Yet, once the case began, Anne and Henry, as well as her entire family, anticipated victory rather than defeat. The king and queen returned to the capital from Hampton Court a couple of days beforehand in readiness for the proceedings. Henry was rowed to Greenwich, close to where Anne already had her own apartments and where she had spent Christmas. She obviously liked the general area for Henry later bought her a farm there.

George and Jane were probably in the same vicinity, for the king rented a house for them at Greenwich at about this time at a cost of £10 per annum. Unfortunately, the little-noticed reference gives us no details of what the house was like but the rent was sufficiently high for it to have been far more than merely comfortable. Jane was becoming used to the benefits of close association with royalty. Indeed, these advantages were coming thick and fast to the couple. Appointed Squire of the Body a few months earlier, with a salary of £65 6s 8d, George was also awarded an annuity of 50 marks (£33) a year to be paid 'by the chief butler of England, out of the issues of the prizes of wines' and in addition was given the office of Master of the Buckhounds. These hunting dogs were so dear to the king's heart that George was frequently allowed sums as huge as £3 or £4 to find them meat. Then he received the jackpot: in the list of grants authorised by the king for November 1528 is one that gave him the keepership of the old Ormond estate at New Hall, which Henry had transformed into his sumptuous palace of Beaulieu, together with a variety of other offices, once the perquisites of William Carey. This really was something worth having if only for the privilege of residing on the premises whenever he wanted. Although she and George did not move in immediately, Jane would soon have the chance to live like a queen herself. In fact, by now she was very much the established court lady. She received a gift from the king in her own right in the New Year's Gift lists of 1528 and 1529, the same years in which her servants were also given rewards by the king. She had come a long way since those early days at Great Hallingbury.

But, for the moment, much depended upon the outcome of the court case. It took place in the Parliament Chamber at Blackfriars, close to the river and to Henry's palace at Bridewell where he spent several nights during the trial, more or less alternating with Greenwich. Since it was not held in camera, there were plenty of spectators inside the hall and gawping crowds outside, straining to catch a glimpse of the main protagonists. For the pretence of her total non-involvement to be remotely credible Anne, of course, had to bow to decorum and stay away but Thomas and George were almost certainly present and there is no reason to suppose that Jane was not there as well. It was too important to miss. The room was carefully arranged. Campeggio and Wolsey sat on a dais at the far end with the officers of the court immediately in front of them. The king's chair was on the right underneath a gold brocade cloth of estate; a similar chair was placed for Katherine on the left, again

under a canopy, but at a slightly lower level than that of Henry.
Then there were judges, bishops, the Archbishop of Canterbury and
the counsels for the two parties. Henry and Katherine had their own
individual legal advisers, with the ascetic but formidable and highly
regarded Bishop Fisher foremost in the queen's camp. Both Henry
and Katherine were there in person, not just in proxy. Once the
pope's commission giving authority for the court to sit was read
aloud, the trial could begin.

Almost straightaway, Katherine reduced the hall to a stunned
silence. She heard Campeggio and Wolsey reject her request that
her cause be heard outside the kingdom, she listened impassively
while the king earnestly explained that all he wanted was to have
his scruples answered and his troubled conscience put at rest, and
then she struck. Ignoring the judges, ignoring everyone else in the
room, she concentrated on the man who, she maintained, was her
lawful husband. She rose from her chair, crossed to where Henry
sat and knelt at his feet. She was truly centre stage. She may have
been sidelined while Henry dallied with Anne but on that day
Katherine was regal dignity epitomised. Even the furious Boleyns
could hardly deny that she was magnificent as she fought for her
marriage and for the legitimacy of her daughter. Throwing herself
on the king's mercy as a woman and a foreigner, she appealed to him
directly. As she did so, the situation slid from bad to worse for the
amazed and disconcerted Henry. She vowed that she had been 'a
true humble and obedient wife', always 'conformable' to his 'will and
pleasure'. Referring to her many fruitless pregnancies, she touched
profoundly many of those who listened spellbound when she said
that 'by me ye have had divers children, although it hath pleased
God to call them out of this world, which hath been no default in
me'. Although her own colours were firmly nailed to the Boleyn
mast, the queen's childlessness would resonate with Jane, herself still
without issue after some years as George's wife. And Katherine was
not finished yet. With a tilt at Henry's assertion that her marriage
to Arthur was consummated, she vowed that she remained 'a true
maid without touch of man' at Arthur's death, as Henry's conscience
should tell him. With a final request that she be spared this trial
until she had more neutral counsellors, men who would risk the

king's displeasure as her current ones would not dare to do, she begged for time to seek further advice from her 'friends in Spain'. 'If ye will not extend to me so much indifferent favour,' she said to Henry, 'your pleasure then be fulfilled, and to God I commit my cause.' With that, she made a deep curtsey to the king and swept from the room, followed by many of the women. It was spine-tingling.

It also presaged disaster for the Boleyns. The trial continued in the queen's absence, of course, but hopes of a quick result were at an end. Bishop Fisher, exhibiting scant consideration for self-preservation despite Katherine's claims, fearlessly fought her corner against everything that came up. Nonetheless, Henry's argument was not finished yet. Evidence was given that Arthur and his bride had been of an age to consummate their union, that Arthur was often conducted to his wife's bedchamber 'in his nightgown', that they spent their nights together, that Arthur, who was of a 'good and sanguine complexion', was physically fit enough to do his duty. It all added up. The most vivid description of the morning after the wedding came from Sir Anthony Willoughby, who said that the prince demanded 'a cup of ale' for he had been 'this night in the midst of Spain'. A Mr St John, who also affirmed that Arthur had boasted about being 'in the midst of Spain', felt that such strenuous activity actually caused the prince's 'decay' as he 'was never so lusty in body and courage until his death'. The testimony was all to no avail. As Clement said to Wolsey, he could not give the king all he wanted 'without incurring manifest danger, and causing a scandal to Christendom'. So, on the pretence that the trial was dragging on into the months when all such cases were suspended in Rome, Campeggio adjourned it. And that was it. Although he said that it would be resumed in the autumn, Anne and the king were only too aware that this was a way of transferring the case to Rome, especially when the devastating news of Clement's accommodation with Charles reached them. Katherine had won this round.

But the battle was not conceded. As Jane and George repaired to the house at Greenwich, she watched the Boleyns regroup and re-plan. They knew precisely where to lay the blame. The court was buzzing with excitement and anticipation; even the queen, no friend of the cardinal, wrote to Mendoza that 'she perceives that all the king's anger at his ill success will be visited on Wolsey'. Jane, who had grown up during the years of his ascendancy, was about to see a furious Anne, together with George and Thomas, bring him down. Suffolk was quick to join them. 'It was never merry in England whilst we had cardinals among us,' he berated a shocked Wolsey, contemptuously brushing aside memories of the aid which he had once been so relieved to receive following his own clandestine marriage to the king's sister. There was no point in Wolsey counting on calling in past debts. Well might he call Cromwell his 'only refuge and aid' in the numerous notes with which he bombarded him.

It was really only a matter of time. Even for the once great cardinal, the odds stacked against him were too high. Not only had he failed the king, he had done so in the most spectacular fashion in the one area in which Henry would not accept defeat. And if it is true that Anne had vowed her revenge for the Percy incident all those years ago, as Cavendish asserted, her wish was granted in spades. His first loss was the chancellorship, but the fight had not quite gone out of him: when the Dukes of Suffolk and Norfolk arrived at his London house to demand that he yield the great seal, he refused to hand it over until they brought written orders directly from Henry. Such defiance merely postponed the inevitable, for they returned with such orders the following day, and Wolsey's resistance could not go on. When confronted with charges of praemunire* for his dealings with Rome, Wolsey pleaded guilty, knowing that he faced the penalty of permanent imprisonment and the confiscation of all the property and goods he had so painstakingly accumulated. After deliberating with his councillors, including Norfolk, Suffolk and Thomas Boleyn, the king sent the disgraced and ailing man to Esher and finally to York to take up the archiepiscopal duties he had neglected there. It was the end of an era.

But it was bonanza time again for the Boleyns. They soon secured a seat in Parliament for James, that dedicated Hebrew student, and a benefice in the diocese of Durham for George's second uncle,

---

* The criminal offence of introducing into the country, or acknowledging, foreign jurisdiction contrary to the king's prerogative and jurisdiction.

William, ordained as a young man. And on the principle of family solidarity, a third uncle, Edward, would secure the wardship of John Appleyard, the only son and heir of Roger Appleyard, a Norfolk gentleman. As the husband of wealthy heiress Anne Tempest, Edward tended to stay out of mainstream Boleyn affairs to concentrate on his Norfolk and Yorkshire lands, but it was as well to toss him something from the treasure trove. The king gave Anne's father the splendid Durham House, part of the assets of the bishopric of Durham, which Wolsey had lately exchanged for Winchester, adding to the profits Thomas was already raking in from other Durham lands. Sited close to the Strand, a stone's throw from Charing Cross and Covent Garden, the house had gardens stretching down to the banks of the Thames. Over three hundred years old, it had a hall of regal proportions supported by tall marble pillars. As a fine London mansion, it could not have been bettered. George and Jane had profited from Wolscy's troubles before. Realising his danger, the cardinal had hoped to win friends by arranging for George to receive an annuity of £200 from his lands as Bishop of Winchester and another of 200 marks (£133) from the Abbey of St Albans. This was very serious money. But once Wolsey's property was confiscated by Henry, things improved further for the Boleyns.

Not only did he lose everything, the new Spanish ambassador, Eustace Chapuys, informed Charles V, but as an additional humiliation Wolsey was forced to make lists of all his possessions down to the last kitchen pot. The extant records are certainly incredibly full and minutely detailed. Wolsey had denied himself nothing. His residences were awash with colour, beauty, and items of superb craftsmanship. There were countless embroidered wall hangings, many of which the cardinal had bought from the executors of various nobles; there were silk table carpets; there were magnificent arras tapestries with real gold and silver thread. All portrayed scenes and subjects of every type, from St George killing the dragon to a set of seven retelling the story of Samson, from the Virgin Mary with the baby Jesus on her lap to David and Goliath, from King Priam to a scene of woodcutters. His numerous beds and voluminous quantities of bedlinen, too, were of the very best quality. There were 56 pairs of blankets, pillowcases of black silk embossed with gold fleurs de lys, 88 down pillows, 157 mattresses. Of the many chairs, four 'were covered with black velvet, with a cardinal's hat and a double cross wrought in crimson satin and Venice gold'. The cushions included six in cloth of gold and blue velvet and two embroidered with a Tudor rose and a leopard's head. Amongst the multitude of plate, we hear of eighteen gilt trenchers, a gold salt adorned with pearls and precious stones and a gold bowl decorated with rubies, diamonds, pearls and a sapphire. It was worth a king's ransom. And, says Chapuys, the king could not wait to show it to the woman he wanted as his queen. When Henry apparently went to look at his spoils, finding them 'much greater than he expected', Anne and her mother, Elizabeth, accompanied him.

The rewards for the family went on and on. George, back in the privy chamber and sent on a diplomatic mission to France, was knighted in the autumn and was soon Viscount Rochford, making Jane a viscountess. He received this title because Thomas needed it no more: he became Earl of Wiltshire and, at last, Earl of Ormond, Piers Butler being bought off with the title of Earl of Ossory. The investiture ceremony, at which Jane was almost certainly an honoured guest, was lavish, as the largesse of £5 to the heralds-at-arms proves. Ironically, it occurred at Wolsey's former palace of York Place,* now in the king's possession, with the witnesses including the aged Archbishop of Canterbury, the Duke of Norfolk and the Duke of Suffolk, the latter shortly to acquire the cardinal's stable of mules. With every month that passed, the Boleyns were obviously becoming more and more comfortably entrenched at court and within the king's most intimate circle. Their leisure hours were often spent with him. It had been Henry, after all, who had once written the song, 'Pastime with good company', performing it to great acclaim while accompanying himself on the lute. Now he could do precisely that, for pass time they did, happily whiling it away in the open air or within the candlelit confines of the private apartments. They played bowls, they raced greyhounds, they competed at

---

* York Place was later known as Whitehall.

archery, they watched their coins spinning along in shovel-board. Each time they would bet on the result, with George winning sums as large as £45 and, once, £58. Jane's husband was particularly adept at cards, beating his sovereign at new and fashionable games like primero.

As for Anne herself, Jane could only watch with astonishment as the gifts came almost by the cartload. Nothing was too much for Henry's darling. Knowing her love of riding, the king sent her saddle after saddle, all of the finest workmanship and latest French fashion, with superb trimmings in black velvet fringed with silk and gold thread. Matching harnesses, reins, girths soon followed, together with the very best accoutrements for her litter. Henry's jeweller, Cornelius Hayes, was certainly kept busy. Again, Anne's family could only be overwhelmed for her as the most exquisite jewels were delivered. It was almost as if he wanted to adorn her entire body with gold and precious stones: a golden girdle, bracelets of pearls and diamonds, diamond rings, diamonds for her hair, gold borders studded with diamonds and pearls for her sleeves, gold buttons, diamond buttons, brooches – the list was endless. The sum of £20 was authorised for her to redeem a jewel once owned by her sister. He even arranged for some of her books to be decorated in silver and gilt. Her finery extended to her dress, where again costly materials, such as almost twenty yards of crimson satin at 16s per yard, were despatched for John Skut, her tailor, to turn into breathtaking gowns.

The trouble was, of course, that while he could shower gifts upon her, Anne was still Henry's sweetheart, not his wife. Wolsey had fallen, the Boleyns were becoming increasingly paramount at court, Anne and her family were growing richer and richer, but Katherine was still in place. So were her supporters, from Bishop Fisher to Charles V. For the king, another route must be devised, different experts consulted. Henry's relationship with Anne and the struggle for the divorce were about to move into a new phase and take a new direction.

11

Almost There

It was 1532 and October, not a good month for crossing the Channel. The winds, the storms, the mists were all unpredictable. A journey that could be as short as five hours in good weather could quickly become infinitely longer, with hours of debilitating seasickness only too common and fears of being driven into another port at best, or sinking at worst, being realised. No one would undertake such a voyage lightly, but Henry was determined to meet Francis again. For Jane, who had taken a similar trip back in 1520, this was an altogether different experience. Then she had been very young, immature and unimportant. Now one of the royal party that gathered at Dover ready to embark, she was not only a married woman with her husband beside her but a viscountess. She was also a member of the family that was influencing court politics and having such an impact on matters that back then she had thought firmly established. Times were changing.

A few moments' reflection would have revealed to Jane just how much had happened already. Her position, as the poised viscountess appreciated, had been immeasurably transformed, her status and responsibilities emphasised by her generous New Year's Gift to her king of two velvet and two satin caps, two of which were trimmed with gold buttons. Henry expected more than merely a token present from her, just as he did from Lord Morley who, typically, presented a book covered in purple satin, and from George and Thomas, whose offerings were more costly. No doubt after much deliberation, George gave two gilt 'hyngers' or daggers on velvet girdles, which Henry could hang around his slightly thickening waist, while Thomas's carefully chosen gift of a black velvet box with a gold stylus was yet more impressive, especially pleasing to a king who loved executive toys for his desk. This was the circle in which Jane now moved with ease. And her marriage to the favourite's brother enabled her to live in some style. George's position in the privy chamber and his rank assured them of good rooms at court but, with Thomas's acquisition of the impressive Durham House, there was also ample space for his son and daughter-in-law if they wished to stay there instead. With George such an active advocate of his sister's cause, both in England and in France, Durham House had proved very useful.

So had York Place, another of Wolsey's former residences. From the moment it had fallen into the king's hands at Wolsey's initial disgrace, Anne and Henry realised its practical value as a London palace and the king happily started to improve and extend it. Money was no object. Nearby houses were compulsorily purchased at a cost of over £1,000 so there was more space for the park, the gardens and the new buildings. Land was drained, trees felled, stone bought from Caen and Reigate, oyster shells (perhaps used as a form of cement) were purchased for masons to set the stones, and then there was glass and lead and oak rafters to be found. Seven pounds of candles were needed to provide light for those who laboured at night to try to get the work finished. The shopping list was endless. Wolsey's timber-framed gallery from Esher was transported wholesale as the nucleus of one of the new galleries which Henry ordered to be constructed, one of which he used to cross from the main palace into the park without getting wet. Then, of course, since Henry and Anne needed diversions, there were bowling alleys, tennis courts, a cockpit and a tiltyard. The privy pier was redone and every room was brought up to the standard the king demanded. What Jane saw as she wandered through the tapestry-hung rooms, or through the gallery painted with scenes from Henry's coronation, was grandeur on a massive scale. Chapuys mentions that Anne particularly liked York Place as there were no apartments for Katherine. There were, however, quarters for her family as well as herself. Anne's own panelled rooms were underneath the old library and therefore below those of the king. George's rooms were rather special, with a window, perhaps looking out over the park, set with 'a pair of garnets', presumably small panes of ruby-coloured glass. With such luxurious and convenient living space, it is no wonder that the house at Greenwich, which the king had rented for the Rochfords for the last two years, was redundant.

Yet, despite all the bustle and activity going on around her, Anne did not forget old friends. In a letter which is still extant, Jane's sister-in-law found the time to correspond with Lady Wingfield, a neighbour from Kent. Signing herself 'Anne Rocheford', she apologised for any past slight she might have unintentionally given. 'And, madam,' she wrote, 'though at all times I have not shewed the love that I bear you as much as it was indeed, yet now I trust that you shall well prove that I loved you a great deal more than I made fair for.' Indeed, other than her own mother, Anne knew of 'no woman alive that I love better'. Whether Jane was privy to the contents of this ostensibly generous and gracious note is unlikely. If she was, she could not have dreamt how important it was later to become.

As she waited on the landing stage at Dover, warmly wrapped up against the chill of that autumn morning, Jane knew that some of the people who had made that earlier visit would not be there this time. William Carey's loss had been a personal tragedy for the Boleyns, although, like Jane, Mary Carey was again one of the ladies accompanying Anne. Neither Mary nor William, however, had been major figures at the Field of Cloth of Gold. The dominant player then had been the great cardinal.

But, within thirteen months of his spectacular fall, Wolsey had died at Leicester Abbey on his way to London to face trial, for Henry had finally turned completely against the man who had once been his friend. For the Boleyns and their allies, Wolsey was decidedly unlamented. Like Norfolk and Suffolk, Thomas and George, not to mention Anne, had always been worried that he might somehow wriggle back into royal favour. His arrest on charges of treason, ironically delivered by Anne's former beau Henry Percy, now Earl of Northumberland, had dealt with that. Jane heard how ill the cardinal had been on the journey south, passing 'above fifty stools' in twenty-four hours, all of them 'wondrous black'. And Wolsey was not alone in being missing from the courtiers at Dover, ready for this latest voyage to Calais.

His successor as chancellor, Thomas More, was similarly missing, for he had resigned his post five months earlier to retire into what the Boleyns trusted would be obscurity. He would never be an ally but, with his sparkling wit, persuasive pen and the almost universal respect he aroused, they did not want him as an implacable foe. The queen was another absentee. On Jane's first visit to Calais, Katherine had been prominent in all the celebrations. Recently, however, she had been banished from court and separated from Princess Mary, her humiliation callously increased when Henry ordered her to return her jewels so that Anne could have them. His beloved wanted to look her best before Francis. Jane certainly saw the glittering stones. She may even have helped Anne fasten them around her neck or on her freshly designed gowns, or perhaps admired the priceless rings as Anne held up her hands to watch the jewels catch the light. Well might the discarded queen write to her nephew that the treatment she received was 'enough to shorten ten lives', not just hers.

Henry did not care, he wanted only Anne. He 'cannot be one hour away from her', said Chapuys scornfully. It was Anne who hunted with him, who sat next to him, who took precedence over even the proudest of court ladies, who listened while ministers reported to him and who was still being showered with gift after gift. Just as Jane became used to her own elevation, she had witnessed his latest offering, which saw her sister-in-law's status transformed as well: Anne had been created Marquess (the male title) of Pembroke in her own right, a singular honour for a woman. The lavish ceremony at Windsor Castle, in front of the most important figures of the land, including, significantly, the French ambassador, had been almost a dress rehearsal for the coronation that Henry could not yet give her. With her long dark hair flowing free, dressed in crimson velvet trimmed with ermine, her train carried by Norfolk's daughter, Anne had knelt at the king's feet for her investiture. She had arisen with a title which her sons, whether legitimate or not, could inherit and lands worth £1,000 per annum. She was not her father's daughter for nothing.

But, as Jane prepared to board, she did so with the Marquess of Pembroke, not with Queen Anne. In fact, the two women had become fairly close over time, as Anne's confidences later prove, so Jane had shared the frustration that Anne had felt at the failure of the Blackfriars court. As the days following Blackfriars had become weeks, then months and years, Jane had seen the king, once so affable, became more and more obdurate. He would get his way, at whatever cost, and was totally unwilling to countenance even the mildest opposition. Katherine understood this as she evaluated her own position. She wrote to Charles V that because her counsel were 'afraid to speak', she relied on Chapuys to promote her cause with Henry as she trusted that her nephew would do with the pope. When writing to Charles himself, the ambassador repeated the rumour that as there had just been repairs made to the Tower of London, Henry intended to confine Katherine there while he was at Calais. Chapuys dismissed such talk as 'highly improbable', but the queen was right to sense a change in Henry, who was no longer the idealistic young monarch who had wrestled with Francis twelve years earlier.

Always sure of himself, Henry had, if anything, grown even more confident. He had only to begin a sentence with the word 'Well' for the entire court to understand that his mind was made up and it was safer to obey. Wolsey had known exactly what sort of man he was dealing with when he had warned William Kingston, the Constable of the Tower, that while Henry was 'a prince of a royal courage' with 'a princely heart', he would risk half his kingdom 'rather than he will either miss or want any part of his will or appetite'. Despite the cardinal begging him on his knees to change his mind, he said, Henry would never do so. If ever Kingston became a member of the privy council, Wolsey had entreated, he should beware 'what matter ye put in his head, for ye shall never put it out again'. As even Jane, whose personal experience had been only with a gentle and bountiful Henry, could appreciate, the divorce had become his obsession.

Henry had been forced to move on from the trauma of Blackfriars as he and the Boleyns explored alternative routes to satisfy that obsession. Jane had often been without her husband for weeks on end during those years as he, like Thomas, put their case abroad, largely fruitlessly. In one key area, however, there had been a major breakthrough: the English clergy had been forced to accept that

Henry was the Head of the Church. The more he read, and the more others read for him, the more convinced the king had become that the pope had usurped authority that was rightfully his. If this was so, then the case could be decided at home, not in Rome, agreed by Convocation and ratified in Parliament. George had played his part in trying to convince Convocation to accept the official line. Henry had ordered him to go in person to present the clergy with various tracts which purported to debate even-handedly precisely where authority in Church and State lay. Old Testament kings such as Josiah, Convocation had been told, 'were princes temporal named yet they executed spiritual administration in setting forth the word of God, in depressing idolatry, and advancing God's only glory'. They had been informed that 'no impediment is known by scripture why that a temporal prince may not be a minister, yea a head over the Church, the spiritual kingdom of Christ'.

Memories of the struggle to get the Church to accept Henry's point of view were fresh and raw as Jane sailed to Calais with the rest of the Boleyn clan. George had done his best. Rather than the prelates succumbing to the force of the king's arguments, however, it had been fear of being indicted for praemunire that had worked like a charm. In exchange for £100,000, Henry had magnanimously pardoned his clergy for any wrongdoing and they, in turn, had accepted him as Supreme Head of the Church, albeit with the proviso that the title applied only as far as the law of Christ allowed. It was good enough as a start. When the Church reluctantly submitted to Henry's demands to control Church law, the Boleyns had been happier still. More's immediate resignation as chancellor had been grist to their relentless mill.

With all these deaths and resignations, there had been changes amongst the personnel of the court. Jane had become familiar with the new faces upon whom the Boleyns were relying. Thomas Cromwell was a particularly welcome ally. An astute operator, willing to work assiduously for whatever his king wanted, he was very much a man after Thomas's own heart. The Boleyns could do business with him. To have his loyal associate, Sir Thomas Audley, in line for the chancellorship was also encouraging. But most of all, the Boleyns had high hopes of the clever young Cambridge theologian

Thomas Cranmer, a man who shared their excitement at the new religious ideas springing up and who genuinely believed that the king's marriage was unlawful. With Edward Lee, Henry's almoner, and the scholar Edward Foxe, now Provost of King's College, Cranmer had proved tireless in his efforts to promote the king's cause. Then had come more good fortune for the family. Wolsey's demise had left the see of York vacant; Henry appointed Edward Lee. It could not have been better. Hopes that he might be able to give judgement on the divorce had floundered but the death of the elderly Warham of Canterbury brought fresh opportunities. As Jane set foot on dry land at Calais, the Boleyns knew whom they wanted: Cranmer.

As the royal party disembarked from Henry's ship, the *Swallow*, before the walls of Calais at about ten in the morning on Friday, 11 October after a mercifully tranquil voyage, and were met by Lord Berners, the Lord Deputy, and Thomas Tate, the mayor, the future looked much more encouraging. True, many of the English nobles thought the meeting a waste of time and money. It was also true that Francis's new queen, Eleanor, and the chief ladies of the French court would not be present, a rather pointed slight on the grounds of decorum, so Anne could not be officially greeted by the French. Wisely, the Boleyns pretended to ignore the snub, for Anne was still highly prominent. Indeed, a Venetian observer tells us that at Calais she lived 'like a queen' with the king accompanying her 'to mass and everywhere as if she was such'. And where Anne went, so did Jane. Their turn in the international spotlight, though, really came when Francis came to stay as a guest of his fellow monarch.

While both rulers had agreed that this encounter was to be far more modest than that of 1520, simple courtesy required the maintenance of royal etiquette. As the two kings rode into the town, Henry in his customary cloth of gold with diamonds and rubies flashing on his sleeves, they were greeted with a deafening gun salute. Henry conducted Francis to his sumptuously prepared quarters in the Staple Hall, staying himself at the Exchequer with Anne and a dozen or so of her ladies. Jane was probably lodged with her sister-in-law; it is most likely that George stayed with Henry rather than being billeted in nearby houses with the less important privy chamber attendants.

On the third night of his visit, Henry laid on a banquet for Francis in a chamber lined with silver cloth of gold, brilliantly lit by candles supported in silver and silver-gilt candelabra. Since Francis and his lords had dressed more extravagantly than their English counterparts, Henry's unstinting hospitality was a reassuring sop to national pride. Anne had not yet met Francis formally and was not at Henry's side during the banquet. Instead, with Jane, Mary Carey and four others, she was dressing and preparing for the entertainment that was to follow. As the guests finished their last dish, served on plates of solid gold, seven masked ladies suddenly entered to the gentle strains of Henry's musicians. Clad in cloth of gold, cloth of silver and crimson satin fringed with gold thread, and with all eyes upon them, the performers turned towards the spectators, then selected dancing partners. This was Anne's chance to take centre stage, as Henry had always planned, for her choice was Francis himself. After a couple of dances, a proud Henry removed the masks from the ladies' faces 'so that there their beauties were showed' and Francis could feign surprise at the identity of his companion. Anne's perfect French made conversation easy between them and they were, of course, old acquaintances from her years at the French court. As Henry watched proudly, the couple talked and danced for about an hour before Francis, with his perfect manners, politely said his goodbyes and left for the Staple Hall, escorted by an equally solicitous Henry.

Jane's partner is not recorded but he was definitely a man of some consequence since all those present were important lords and we know, for example, that the Countess of Derby danced with the King of Navarre. As Jane took to the floor, perhaps wearing her special masque stockings of silk trimmed with gold and with her face visible to everyone, her position as a woman of growing significance was apparent. The young girl from Great Hallingbury had come a long way since the Field of Cloth of Gold. George was certainly close to his sister but Jane had become so as well. She may well have shared the grapes and pears specially brought to Anne by a servant of Anne de Montmorency, Grand Master of France. There may have been no official French reception for Anne, but the shrewd and the wily were quick to ingratiate themselves with the woman who was likely to be queen. Indeed, Francis prudently sent her a gift of a fabulous diamond, which Jane would have seen.

When Francis had left Calais, after the usual round of present giving, Henry and his party prepared to return home. This time, however, the weather was unkind. Some of the first ships to leave were driven back by the wind, which became so fierce at one point that it was not possible to 'conveniently stir in the streets' of the town and the vessels in the harbour were tossed about so much that they were in danger of capsizing. Jane, with the rest of the royal party, was stranded. Maybe it was as he waited for the weather to lift that Henry lost 15s playing cards with Anne. She, like George, was a sharp card player to whom Henry frequently lost relatively large sums.

It was about a week before the king was willing to risk ordering his bed shipped back to England and a couple of days more before he ventured on the seas himself. The expressions of relief for his safe return were fulsome. The Council attended the *Te Deum* sung in St Paul's in thanksgiving. Sir Thomas Elyot, ambassador in Brussels, told Cromwell that the news was 'the most joyful thing that ever happened' to him; clearly, since he had professed himself 'bereft' of sleep when he heard that the king 'intended to pass the seas', this was no exaggeration, although we can afford to be slightly sceptical as the rest of the letter is largely about Elyot's debts, which he hoped Henry would settle.

If Calais was a success for Jane, it was a satisfying victory for Anne. Her place as Henry's consort was taken for granted. Those who muttered against it, like the Duke of Suffolk – who had proved a somewhat erratic ally once Wolsey was out of the way and whose wife's absence from the festivities had been noticed – were uncomfortably aware that Henry would not be moved. Indeed, there had been talk that Anne and Henry had intended to marry while on this trip but, as Jane was in a position to know, no wedding had taken place. Something else had: after years of calculated refusal, Anne at last allowed Henry to become her lover in deed as well as word. We will never know whether their first night together was spent in

Calais or whether they waited until they were once more on English soil.

Nor is there conclusive evidence of when she and Henry actually married, although we are sure that it was done secretly in front of very few witnesses. That Jane was one is remotely possible but speculative. That she knew about it is far more definite. Anne had come so far with the help of her entire family – it is inconceivable that she kept such a tumultuous event from them. Indeed, if Chapuys is to be believed, she was married 'in the presence of the father, mother, brother, and two of her favourites'. All were people she could trust. Henry, however, could not resist joking at the expense of those who were not privy to such insider knowledge. When dining with Anne in her apartments, he pointed to the costly tapestries and gold plate on display and asked the Dowager Duchess of Norfolk, who was sitting at a table with other members of the court, whether she thought Anne 'had a fine dowry and a rich marriage portion'. The duchess could not fail to understand that the only husband Anne contemplated was the king himself. What she did not know was that Anne was not only Henry's wife already, she was about three months pregnant.

Anne's pregnancy immediately raised the stakes. Suddenly her family and the king's advisers were plunged into a race against time so that the child, Henry's son and heir, would be legitimate. Calmly, Cromwell, such a useful man, drafted a parliamentary Act to prohibit appeals to Rome against verdicts given in England. With her hands comprehensively tied, Katherine could only hope that Charles or the pope would come to her aid when her title was stripped from her as her jewels had been. From now on, she was the Princess Dowager, a title she flatly refused to bear. Then, as a cowed Convocation declared in favour of the king, Anne's new rank was flaunted before the entire court as a fait accompli. Escorted by sixty female attendants, Anne processed in state to mass at Greenwich on Easter Saturday, 1533. She was, an outraged Chapuys wrote to Charles, 'loaded with jewels'. Dressed in cloth of gold and with Norfolk's daughter Mary again carrying her train, Anne received 'the solemnities, or even more' than those once given to Katherine. Worse, 'the preachers offered prayers for her by name'. The news that most of the congregation walked out when Anne was prayed for at St Paul's in London on the following day was gratifying to Anne's enemies but they would not be able to defy Henry with impunity again.

Cranmer, now appointed Archbishop of Canterbury, could be relied upon to deliver the *coup de grâce*. A month after Easter, he wrote to Henry from Dunstable reporting that he had pronounced 'sentence in your great and weighty matter'. After careful deliberation, he announced that Henry had never really been married to Katherine. Anne was, therefore, Henry's legal wife.

The Boleyns had won. Jane, who had been there from the very beginning of the great gamble, was there for its triumphant conclusion. It had never been a foregone conclusion. So much could have gone wrong but, after all those years of waiting and scheming, Jane's sister-in-law really was on the verge of becoming queen. Their marriage might have been conducted secretly, but both Anne and Henry were resolved that her coronation would be in full public view. No expense would be spared to make it an occasion to remember. It would be Anne's special day. And Jane would be with her every step of the way.

A WOMAN OF IMPORTANCE

12

Soaring with the Falcon

When Sir Stephen Peacock, a member of the Haberdashers' livery company, became Lord Mayor of London, he could never have foreseen himself escorting a former lady of the court into his city to become Queen of England. On the last Thursday morning of May 1533, however, that is what he prepared himself to do. He dressed with considerable care in his best scarlet robes, his chains of office shining around his neck and on his breast. All over the town, in so many of the comfortable timbered houses inhabited by wealthy merchants and aldermen, servants were helping their employers to do exactly the same. Everything had been arranged well in advance: oarsmen were waiting to row all the dignitaries in ostentatiously decorated vessels to Greenwich, where Anne would be waiting, and then conduct her respectfully to her recently refurbished apartments in the Tower. The planning had been punctilious; nothing could be allowed to go wrong.

The royal palace of Greenwich, a few miles along the river, was frantic with activity too as harassed attendants, most of whom had been up long before dawn, rushed around helping their masters and mistresses get ready. Since this was Anne's first public state appearance outside the court, she wanted her husband's subjects to see her at her most regal. Her ladies fastened her glittering jewels and assisted her into her dazzling gown of cloth of gold. Image mattered. She was to be accompanied on the journey by the leading figures of the land, including the Duke of Suffolk and the Earls of Derby, Worcester and Sussex. George was not there. He had already left for France with the Duke of Norfolk to meet Francis once again, the one ally Henry believed he could count upon. Otherwise, it was a family party. Thomas and Elizabeth Boleyn were all set to go with their daughter and bask in her success. And so was Jane. As she had shared in the years of frustration and suspense, so she was to share in the victory. Indeed, although the letter is no longer extant, we know that she wrote to George to tell him all that he had missed.

Anne and her ladies, together with most of the court, were to travel in their own private barges to the Tower. Anne's had once belonged to Katherine but Henry had requisitioned it for her supplanter. Anything on it that referred to the former queen had been removed, indecently so, according to Chapuys. He told Charles that when Katherine's arms had been taken off, they had been 'rather shamefully mutilated', an act for which he had 'rather roughly rebuked' Anne's chamberlain. Whether the barge would satisfy Anne, however, he remained unsure. 'God grant she may content herself with the said barge and the jewels and the husband of the Queen,' he wrote, only half ironically, 'without attempting anything ... against the persons of the Queen and Princess.' In fact, Anne and her family were only too conscious that the support both women continued to command could be dangerous. Katherine was particularly defiant. To Anne and Henry's fury, she flouted the order to be addressed as Princess Dowager and, according to Carlo Capello, the Venetian ambassador, had her staff 'arrayed entirely in new apparel, with letters signifying Henry and Katherine'. Clearly, something would have to be done. But not on that special Thursday.

Peacock and the rest of the entourage gathered at St Mary Hill in the ward of Billingsgate so that they could embark at 1 p.m. on to their appointed boat. There were fifty ships altogether, embellished with the arms of the various trading guilds, and flying pretty flags and pennants, all done 'after the best fashion'. Minstrels, who sang to the accompaniment of musicians playing trumpets, sackbuts, flutes and drums, were on board many of them. The procession was highly regimented and three easily manoeuvrable ships were assigned to ensure that the set order was maintained. Right at the front was a small vessel brimming with guns which acted as a mock wafter.* There was a mechanical dragon that moved and belched

---

* A wafter was a fully armed vessel used to ensure the safety of other ships.

fire on its decks, surrounded by men dressed as monsters or 'wild men' who terrified the excited crowds with their savage screams and cries.

The mayor's boat came next with the renowned Bachelor's Barge on his right. The latter's fame was well deserved. Festooned with cloth of gold, and with huge banners portraying the arms of both Henry and Anne, as well as the flags and emblems of the Haberdashers' livery company, and with myriads of tiny pennants on which hundreds of tinkling bells were attached, this barge really was an amazing sight. On Peacock's left was another ship, one specially designed to flatter and please Anne. Her chosen device, a white falcon, based on an Ormond symbol, was its theme. This falcon, though, was crowned. It stood on a golden tree root from which red and white roses grew, and was surrounded by young girls singing softly. More and more ships followed on, their colourful streamers fluttering in the wind and glinting in the sunlight, their image reflected in the ripples on the water. The companies faithfully obeyed the royal command to put on a wonderful display for Henry's beloved.

Once at Greenwich, the rowers skilfully turned the vessels round so that they could all leave in reverse order, with the mayor at the front once again. Now it was Anne's turn. With her most intimate attendants, she entered her barge, by now redesigned with her insignia and badges. Almost certainly, Jane was at her sister-in-law's side, a favoured confidante. Soon the 'whole river was covered' with brightly painted boats and the air was filled with the sounds of minstrels and music. 'He that saw it would not believe it,' or so the chronicler tells us. For those who lined the banks, keen to miss nothing, it was indeed a spectacle to remember, just as Henry hoped. So it was for Anne and her family. All those years of anxiety had been worth while. They had won.

The journey along the Thames took about half an hour. As the royal barge progressed towards the great walls of the Tower, on that day a welcoming rather than a fearsome sight, guns were fired in salute from craft waiting by the shore and then from the guns of the fortress itself. The noise was deafening. And then they were there. Anne, followed by Jane and her other ladies, stepped ashore. The first to greet Anne were Sir William Kingston, in his capacity as Constable of the Tower, a man with whom she was to become familiar in less happy circumstances, and the Lieutenant, Sir Edmund Walsingham. Then, after the Lord Chamberlain, Lord Sandys, had formally received Anne, an eager Henry came to meet her. He gently kissed her and she, mindful of her fresh rank, turned to thank the mayor and the other citizens courteously for the honour that they had given her. With the king, she entered the royal apartments, and the show was over. At least, it was over for the moment. There was still much more to come.

Anne spent Thursday evening and Friday settling into her lodgings in the Tower and resting. She was, after all, almost six months pregnant by now and the next couple of days would demand all her reserves of stamina and strength. Henry, still scarcely able to leave her for an instant, was there as well. For Jane, it was a chance to see Anne's beautifully appointed chambers for herself. She was not to know that the day would come when she would look on those imposing rooms in a very different light. It was also a chance to catch up with her own birth family, for both her mother and her father had travelled to London for the festivities. As a peer, Lord Morley was required to be present at Westminster when Anne was crowned, but before that there was another ceremony of more personal relevance: Jane's brother, Henry, was one of those young men chosen to be dubbed Knights of the Bath. To create these new knights had been part of coronation ritual for over two hundred years. Indeed, as Jane knew, George's father had become a Knight of the Bath when Henry himself had been crowned, so, in a sense, a family tradition was being preserved. It is possible that Henry Parker would have been selected anyway, of course, but Jane's influence cannot be discounted. Although now a fully fledged Boleyn, she had been schooled since childhood to appreciate her obligations to her wider family circle. Those soon to be knighted served the king water or a dish from the first course at dinner on Friday, 'in token that they shall never bear none after that day', so Jane watched as her brother performed his task. She knew what lay in store for him shortly afterwards when the solemn, age-old rites began.

Henry Parker and the other seventeen young men were taken to the separate, curtained compartments provided for them in the White Tower, where they were counselled and cared for by experienced governors, squires and existing knights, who were 'well nourished in courtesy and expert in the deeds of knighthood'. Once the postulants reached their chambers, the governors called for the barbers to prepare individual baths, with pieces of soap wrapped in clean white linen cloths. Carpets were placed on the stone floor 'for the cold of the night'. Then, after a barber had ceremonially cut young Parker's hair and shaved his beard, his governor, like those serving the other young men, went to ask the king for permission to proceed with the bath itself. The governors returned to their charges accompanied by squires of the household and the song of minstrels. The music faded away and in the silence, Jane's naked brother lowered himself into the bath where he took the oath of knighthood. After his special knight had taken some of the water in his hand and gently poured it upon Parker's shoulder, the young man stepped out of the bath and lay in his bed to dry. Squires rushed forward to dress him warmly and drape a fairly coarse black cloak with long sleeves and a hood 'in manner of a hermit' around him. A long vigil lay ahead.

To the soft melodies of the musicians, and his way lit by the flickering flames of tapers, Parker joined his fellow postulants as they walked slowly into the cold stone chapel to spend the hours of darkness in prayer and meditation. As dawn broke, they confessed their sins and participated in the sacred mass, removing their hoods briefly at the elevation of the host. Before taking the sacrament, they offered tapers, each of which had a small coin fastened to it, to the worship of God and in thanks to the king. Probably stiff with cold, they were led back to their beds for a few welcome hours of sleep.

Parker was awakened early and, with minstrels singing quietly in the background, was ceremonially dressed again by his squires. This was a slow process, as precedent dictated every move they made. They put on his shirt, breeches, doublet, gown and black silk hose, which had built-in shoes with leather soles, his sleeves, his white leather girdle, his red mantle and white gloves before taking him to where his horse stood ready. Even the horse's trappings were predetermined by ancient ritual. Preceded by his squire carrying his spurs and sword, Parker rode to the door of the room in which Henry was waiting. He dismounted and walked towards his king. The knights who had acted as his counsellors fastened his spurs on his ankles, while Henry buckled the sword around Parker's waist and smote the side of his neck. 'Be ye good knight,' the king ordered and then kissed him. Henry dined, while the new knights sat silently. Finally, after further prayers and, at last, refreshing food, Parker was arrayed in a blue robe, his former garb being given to the College of Arms. He was now Sir Henry Parker indeed. For Jane's family, this was a very proud moment, but it was also one in which the benefits of royal favour were openly revealed.

It is unlikely that Jane actually saw her brother's few minutes of glory. She was far too busy preparing to enter the limelight again herself; later on that Saturday, Anne was to be formally taken from the Tower, through the decorated streets, to Westminster and Jane was to go with her. Sir Stephen Peacock had another busy day for, like the river pageant, this was minutely organised and arranged according to tradition and prescribed protocol. Visitors had been arriving over the past few days, so the always bustling city was incredibly crowded. Indeed, as far as Henry's more influential subjects were concerned, it was wise to take the trouble to come, for the king demanded their attendance. Occasionally, Cromwell listened to and allowed excuses. One of those was from Sir William Courtenay who, in considerable pain after falling from his horse, could not face the long and arduous journey to London, so prudently wrote to the minister to explain his plight, knowing the risk of incurring Henry's displeasure on this most sensitive of issues.

The formalities concerned with the investiture completed, the procession started from the Tower in the late afternoon. Peacock, wearing crimson velvet, and with two footmen in red and white damask at his back, arrived to give the signal to begin. He was as sure as he could be that all was in order. It had taken hours to get the roads gravelled to prevent the horses slipping, the streets hung with velvet and cloth of gold, and to shepherd the officials to their designated places behind specially erected railings. There were hordes of ordinary citizens too, leaning out of windows along the route or pushing their way to the front of the thronged streets, hoping to get the best possible view of the new queen. Unpopular as Anne generally was, people were curious to see for themselves exactly what the woman who had bewitched their king really looked like. Since she was part of her sister-in-law's train, they would have gawped at Jane too.

Twelve French gentlemen in the service of the French ambassador were in the vanguard of the parade. In blue velvet, with yellow and blue sleeves, and mounted on horses draped with blue on which the white crosses of France were clearly visible, they looked superb. The spectators could only watch in wonder as the Frenchmen were followed by a long line of scarlet-robed judges, barons, important churchmen, earls and marquesses. Jane's family were well represented, for Lord Morley rode only a few hundred yards behind his son, now dressed in his knight's pristine blue gown with its furred hood. Archbishop Cranmer, who was to perform his sacred duties in the Abbey next day, was there, along with Edward Lee of York, and theirs were not the only famous faces. The Duke of Suffolk, resplendent as ever and Constable for the day, rode with William Howard, deputising as Earl Marshal for his brother, the Duke of Norfolk, who was still in France with George Boleyn.

At last it was the moment when the crowd might catch a glimpse of the woman they had all been straining to see. Preceded by some of her servants, Anne appeared in her litter. Quite simply, she shone. Her litter was covered in silver cloth of gold, the horses who drew it were swathed in silver damask. She was shielded by an embroidered silk canopy fringed with gold thread supported on gilded staves with silver bells, carried by four of the Lords of the Cinque Ports in their scarlet robes. Anne herself was a vision in white cloth of gold, with a similar cloak and a jewelled circlet gleaming on her beautiful dark hair, which cascaded freely about her shoulders.

Then, after Anne's chamberlain, Lord Burgh, and her Master of the Horse, William Coffin, who led her spare horse, which was also enveloped in fine cloth of gold, came Jane. She looked stunning, a tribute to the dressmakers' skills and the services of her own maidservants. She rode almost immediately behind Anne, her prominent place – even before Anne's own sister and far above that to which her rank entitled her – proving her close relationship with the new queen. She rode side-saddle with six other ladies, including Norfolk's daughter, Lady Mary Howard, and the Countesses of Derby, Worcester and Sussex. Her gown was sumptuous. Twelve yards of crimson velvet had been provided for each woman, along with one and a quarter yards of red cloth of gold for a border. Although Jane was accustomed to the opulence of the court by now and to the fancy costumes she enjoyed wearing to masques, she had never had a dress like this. Nor had she ever been involved in so phenomenal an event. The watching crowds, packed behind barriers, were not the only ones who would remember this day.

Two chariots came next: in the first, the Dowager Duchess of Norfolk, seated beside the widow of the Marquess of Dorset, and in the second, Anne's mother, with two countesses. Like the first group, they were allocated twelve yards of scarlet for their robes, much more than any of the other ladies who followed their new queen. After twelve ladies on horseback, amongst whom was Lady Baynton, the wife of Anne's vice-chamberlain, came a third chariot with six passengers. This completed the family party, for sitting with Lady Fitzwarren, Mistresses Mary Zouche and Margery Horsman, were Mary Carey, Jane's mother Alice and Lady Boleyn. They, however, were allowed a mere seven yards of scarlet for their gowns. Jane truly had a place of honour and esteem on that day.

And still the cavalcade continued. Madge Shelton and Kate Ashley were in the next chariot, and all of the ladies' female servants, sporting their red liveries, rode behind them. Anne's guard brought up the rear as the procession wound its way through the streets towards Westminster. Its progress was slow, since, in response to Henry's demands, the city dignitaries had prepared a series of pageants for Anne and her retinue to enjoy on the way.

An event was scheduled for every stop, most rich in symbolism, whose meaning would have been very clear to Anne. Sometimes children performed for her, as they did at Fenchurch Street when they read to her in English and in French, or at St Paul's where two hundred recited poetry, a performance which the pregnant Anne 'highly commended'. Sometimes the street fountains ran with wine rather than water, as at Cheapside and Fleet Street. Sometimes, she was entertained by music, as she was at St Martin's Church where the choir sang ballads in her praise. At the intricately carved Eleanor Cross, the city aldermen presented her with a gold purse containing well over £600, a sum large enough to satisfy even the king, and which Anne 'thankfully accepted with many goodly words'. And everywhere there were elaborately staged tableaux to amuse her. The merchants of the Steelyard outdid themselves with their 'costly and marvellous cunning pageant', designed by Holbein, which featured Mount Olympus complete with gods, muses and music, and a fountain from which wine flowed. Her falcon badge provided inspiration for the merchants at the Leadenhall. In their offering, an angel crowned a little white falcon with a golden crown, while St Anne watched with her children and grandchildren, one of whom made a pretty speech to the queen reminding her 'of the fruitfulness of St Anne and her generation, trusting that like fruit should come of her'. In another pageant, the goddesses Athena, Juno and Venus gave her the gifts of wisdom, wealth and happiness, and in yet another there were three 'ladies richly clothed' whose scroll referred to the joy she would bring to the people by bearing the king's son.

At last the long afternoon drew to its close as Anne reached Westminster Hall. She was carried in her litter towards the middle of the huge tapestry-hung chamber where her chair stood underneath a gold, silk-fringed cloth of estate similar in size to that of the king. Jane was with her as servants brought her wines and tempting spiced delicacies. Anne graciously passed them to her ladies, before thanking Peacock and the other officials for everything they had done to make the day so special. Only when they had been dismissed could she rest a little 'with a few ladies', one of whom was very probably Jane. In the privacy of Anne's apartments, they could discuss every detail of an extraordinary day.

For it had not all been perfect. The juxtaposing of Henry's and Anne's initials was unfortunate: the HA HA they formed was spotted by some of the more hostile elements of the crowd who literally burst out laughing. Then, Anne noticed those who refused to take off their caps as she passed, which she took as a blatant insult. Her woman fool made light of it. 'I think you have all scurvy heads, and dare not uncover,' she said, but it was a slight nonetheless. Clearly, not everyone was as delighted as the Boleyn family by

Anne's changed status. Then there were the absentees. Katherine's champion, Bishop Fisher, was, thankfully for the Boleyns, safely imprisoned. They did not want that particular spectre at the feast. A couple of others, however, should have been there. Henry's sister was gravely ill so she could be forgiven, but Sir Thomas More, who had no such reason, could not.

Even so, as night fell and Jane's servants helped her remove her magnificent gown, she knew that all had been worth waiting for. Anne was not the only person whose life had been transformed. And tomorrow was the coronation. Jane's future could only get better.

13

The Falcon Crowned

Jane's gentlewomen woke her early next morning. There was much to do if she was to be ready to accompany her sister-in-law to the ceremony that would form the culmination of all that the Boleyns had schemed for over so many years. In the river pageant, in the investiture of the new Knights of the Bath, in the entry into the city, Anne had been exhibited as Henry's wife and his queen, but it would be only after she had undergone the religious rituals of the coronation that Anne's status would be properly confirmed. Then, the falcon would be queen indeed. With the king's son growing in her womb and the crown of England upon her head, Anne would be impregnable. Or so the family hoped.

Jane's servants were not the only ones to be up and about at first light. All over London, officials and courtiers were roused by their attendants so that they, too, could take their places and honour Anne yet again. It was another busy day for Peacock. Once dressed in his crimson velvet robes and with his golden chain gleaming around his neck, he joined the aldermen and other city officials at 7 a.m. to be rowed by barge to Westminster Hall. The lofty stone building, its exterior adorned with the stone statues of ancient kings,* was the starting point for the short procession to St Peter's Church, the great Abbey of Westminster. There, close to the resting place of Henry's little son, Cranmer would crown Henry's wife. So, in the huge chamber, beneath the wonderful vaulted wooden ceiling and flying buttresses of carved angels, which are still there today, Peacock and his companions waited for Anne.

* These statues are now inside the hall but were outside in Jane's era.

She appeared over an hour later, her ladies with her. She wore deep purple and crimson velvet, her robes edged with ermine, her thick, dark hair confined under a jewelled coif, and on her head a circlet of precious stones. This time her train was carried by the Dowager Duchess of Norfolk. Jane was with Anne, in her own opulent crimson velvet gown, and she held her gold coronet in her hand. She followed as Anne walked to the middle of the hall and stood underneath her cloth of estate, while her entourage gradually gathered. Soon the hall teemed with people. The musicians of the King's Chapel, the monks of Westminster, and the abbots and bishops, were the first to arrive to escort her into the Abbey church and only when everyone was in their appointed position could the ceremony begin. The procession was led by the gentlemen, the esquires and the knights. They preceded the aldermen, the judges, and the Knights of the Bath, Jane's brother in their midst. Lord Morley and his fellow barons came next, with the viscounts, earls, marquesses and dukes behind them. Thomas strode purposefully amongst the other earls: it was a day for him to savour. In the next group came More's successor, Lord Audley, Peacock, a dozen or so abbots, Archbishop Lee, and the Bishops of London, Winchester, Lincoln, Bath and St Asaph's. Anne's entrance was the climax of the cavalcade. With her ladies behind her, Anne walked along the specially laid blue-striped carpet through the West Gate into St Peter's. As she did so, the monks and Henry's musicians sang solemnly. Her crown was carried reverently by the Earl of Oxford, the Earl of Arundel carried her rod and sceptre, and four Lords of the Cinque Ports held her canopy over her. Even had she been born royal, as Katherine had been, Henry could not have ordered anything grander than this.

Jane stood close by as Anne took her place on her throne between the choir and the altar. The brand-new chair – 'covered with rich cloth of tissue and fringed with gold', its pummels also gilded – was sited on a raised platform with steps draped in richly embroidered cloth. The new queen was in full view. Anne paused a little and then Cranmer led her to the altar. There she prostrated herself while the archbishop sang prayers over her in consecration. When she rose, a fine white linen coif on her head to prevent contact with her hair

Jane's father, Lord Morley, sketched by Dürer whilst in Germany in 1523.
Morley was one of the ambassadors sent by Henry to present the Order of the
Garter to Charles V's brother, Ferdinand.

The Lady Parker.

The portrait of Lady Parker, which one authority identified as Jane, but is probably Grace Newport, the first wife of Jane's brother, Sir Henry Parker.

Jane's signature on her letter to Cromwell seeking his help after George Boleyn's execution.

The letter in which Lord Morley tells Cromwell that he is sending him a greyhound. Morley signs the letter with a flourish, 'y[ou]r owne to c[omm]and, Harry Morley'.

(*Above*) 'Thys boke ys myn[e]' wrote George Boleyn in 1526. The book, which might have been a wedding gift, contained two French poems in manuscript form, including the satire on marriage.

(*Left*) Henry VIII's signature on the Act which settled Jane's jointure.

A design for tents which
may well have been
intended for the Field of
Cloth of Gold.

Henry VIII. A
portrait of power and
majesty, this image,
with its emphasis on
Henry's cod-piece, is
also a statement of
Henry's dynastic
intentions.

Francis I,
King of France.

Charles V,
King of Spain
and Holy
Roman
Emperor.

Henry VIII jousting. Katherine of Aragon is sitting in the stands watching.

Katherine of Aragon. The queen's youthful beauty, which had delighted Henry, has faded into staid, middle-aged corpulence.

Sir Thomas More.

The Challenge for Capturing a Castle. The court entertainments at Christmas, 1526, included this spectacular pageant.

Assembling the Riders, taken from the David and Bathsheba tapestry series still extant. Henry's tapestries were likely to have been very similar to the series from which this is taken.

Cardinal Wolsey.

Henry reading in his bedchamber. An illustration from the Latin psalter illuminated for the king by Jean Maillart, which contains Henry's marginalia claiming similarities between his own life and that of King David.

Henry dining in his privy chamber surrounded by his gentlemen. His cloth of estate is clearly visible.

(Overleaf) The Court of King's Bench, Westminster. The prisoners in the foreground await their fate.

from tainting the holy oil, Anne was anointed upon her forehead and upon her breast, and then was gently dried with a cotton cloth. All the while, an embellished canopy was held over her.

From the Boleyn perspective, the next part of the sacred ritual was the most significant, for Anne was crowned in nothing less than St Edward's Chair itself. It was not usual for a consort to sit upon the seat of kings and Anne may well have been the first woman to do so. She had already outdone her rival: Katherine had been crowned with Henry but she had sat on a small throne, not on the saint's chair. Nor had the former queen been crowned with St Edward's Crown, for this was worn only by ruling monarchs, not their wives. Uniquely, it was this glittering relic, which one day would grace her red-haired daughter, that Cranmer placed upon Anne's head. With the royal sceptre in her right hand and the ivory rod in her left, she was now every inch the queen. All eyes upon her, she sat while the choir's voices rose to the heavens in a glorious *Te Deum*.

Only then did Cranmer remove the heavy crown, replacing it with a much lighter one that had been specifically made for her. She returned to her throne for the holy mass. Jane, with the other ladies, knelt on Anne's right, the Dowager Duchess of Norfolk behind her, and the leading lords on the queen's left, as the familiar words began. Anne went back to the altar, gave an offering and, after further prayers, knelt again to receive the sacrament. She was allowed a few moments' rest and a little refreshment, and then Thomas stepped proudly forward to support his daughter's right hand while Lord Talbot took her left. Jane, now wearing her coronet, followed her sister-in-law as she processed back to Westminster Hall, a fanfare of trumpets bursting forth 'marvellously freshly' around her.

It had been a triumph. Every detail had gone according to plan, and in conformity with custom and tradition. Henry could not but be delighted. At one point, he had considered a double coronation with Anne, even rewriting the coronation oath to encompass his new ideas on his rights as Head of the Church, but nothing had come of it. Instead, the king having no wish to deflect glory from his beloved wife, it was all Anne's day. And it was not over yet. A richly decorated Westminster Hall was the venue for a magnificent banquet at which the new queen presided. Henry's musicians played softly by the windows as Jane took her seat in a position of honour at the table reserved solely for the ladies of the court. From there, she had an uninterrupted view of everything. As she probably knew, so did Henry. Having weathered so many storms to reach this point, he could not resist savouring every moment of his wife's success. With the ambassadors from France and Venice, he 'looked on from a little closet out of the cloister of St Stephen's'. Chapuys was not invited.

Anne, wearing her lighter crown, sat on Henry's marble throne quite apart from everyone else. Her cloth of estate was in place over her, as befitted an anointed queen. She was in the middle of the central table, with Cranmer, at a suitably respectful distance, on her right. The Countess of Worcester and the widowed Countess of Oxford stood on either side of her, ready to hold up a linen cloth to shield her should she want 'to spit or do otherwise at her pleasure'. Jane could have caught just a glimpse of the two gentlewomen whose task was to crouch under the table at the queen's feet ready to perform any other task for her, maintaining a convention that stretched back over the centuries. No one else was allowed anywhere near Anne, unless it was to serve her food and wine, although the current Earl of Oxford was deputed to stand behind her, between the archbishop and the widowed countess. The queen's dais, twelve steps high, was railed off from the hoi polloi below.

Jane's table, which was about eight yards long, was one of four set at right angles to the queen's platform. If she turned round, she could see Peacock, with his aldermen, city officials and wealthy merchants, happily ensconced at the table immediately behind hers, in front of the stone walls of the massive hall. Her mother was further down Jane's table, with the wives of other key nobles and courtiers. Again, it was a family occasion for Jane. Lord Morley, perhaps with a proud eye on his son, who was now Sir Henry and still wearing his robes as a Knight of the Bath, sat at the next table along, sharing it with judges like Sir John Spelman and leading churchmen. Near Archbishop Lee was Stephen Gardiner, Bishop of Winchester. Gardiner was well known to the Boleyns. Although an ally over the divorce, his presentation of Convocation's case, when the clergy were forced to submit to royal control, left a question mark in Boleyn minds over the depth of his allegiance. And even as Jane glanced along the serried rows of guests as they tucked into the thirty or so courses with which they were presented, she knew that many were there out of pragmatism rather than true loyalty to her sister-in-law's cause.

A quick look at the Duke of Suffolk would have reinforced that thought. In his role as high steward, he was in charge of much that was going on. He certainly looked the part. In embroidered crimson velvet robes, his doublet glistening with lustrous pearls, and with a tall white rod in his hand, he rode around the hall mounted on a charger draped in crimson velvet. He and Lord William Howard, also opulently clad and also on horseback, escorted in the first course with much flourish and 'rode oftentimes about the hall, cheering the lords, ladies, and the mayor and his brethren'. But how far Suffolk could be trusted was another matter. Getting rid of Wolsey was one thing; playing second fiddle to the Boleyns another. Suffolk's ambition and acquisitiveness were common knowledge. Anne's vice-chamberlain, Sir Edward Baynton, today resplendent in his new red robes, wrote as much to George. 'My lord of Suffolk', he said, 'is loth to let fall a noble unless he took up a royal* for it.' Already he had squabbled with Norfolk, his rival in East Anglia, and had been forced by the king to give up his office of Earl Marshal to him. There was no love lost there.

Nevertheless, Suffolk was performing well. There was no concrete reason to suspect him. The host of guests seemed to be enjoying the whole spectacle. Sir Edward Seymour, one of the king's esquires of the body, whose family came from Wiltshire, served Cranmer most competently. Jane could spot her cousin, Sir John St John, amongst those gentlemen who laughingly assisted with serving others in the hall. Young Sir Francis Weston, a recent recruit to the king's privy chamber who had just been invested with her brother, sat with his fellow Knights of the Bath as yet more and more dishes were brought forward by the army of attendants on duty that day,

---

* Nobles and royals were gold coins worth 108 and 120 pence sterling respectively in 1500.

every course announced triumphantly by the trumpeters and musicians.

Anne's resilience was admirable. She was on show the entire time and never faltered. As the feast drew to its close, the servants brought thin sweet wafers and spiced wine, and the queen rose. Jane and everyone else rose with her, standing silently while Anne washed her hands and dried them on special napkins. The Earl of Sussex handed her a final dish of sweetmeats, carefully arranged on a plate of solid gold. He was followed by Peacock, who presented her with a golden cup filled with wine, his last duty of the long day. Anne thanked him once more, before giving him the precious cup as was expected. With everyone still on their feet, she left the hall, her canopy again carried by the barons of the Cinque Ports. Her oarsmen waited, the waters of the Thames lapping against the side of her barge. They had one more task to undertake before they, too, could go home and relate the day's events to their families. Anne was helped aboard her vessel, perhaps with Jane at her side, for she needed her ladies with her. The queen was rowed the short distance along the river to where Henry was waiting: at Wolsey's York Place. The tiltyards were already being prepared for tourneys the following morning but, for a while, there was time for rest.

For Jane, too, it had been a very tiring few days. No doubt it had been good to catch up with Parker news and gossip, but Great Hallingbury was becoming more of a distant memory as the years passed. Jane's world was the court now, her horizons had expanded, her place was assured. Where the Boleyns went, so did she.

14

Long May We Reign

It was over. Ambassadors wrote copious accounts of what they had seen. Suffolk had the chance to hurry home to the bedside of his dying wife. Londoners carefully took down the banners and the hangings which they had used to decorate their streets. Peacock returned to his normal duties, as did the aldermen and merchants. They wanted to start making money again; coronations were expensive events and Henry had demanded substantial contributions from all of them. Subjects who had come to the city to become knights, or because the king had demanded their attendance, returned to their estates. Each had his or her story to tell. For Jane and the Boleyns, however, it was far from over. They hoped it was just a beginning.

So far, the whole family had profited. James was slotted in as Anne's chancellor, Mary was at court with her sister and Thomas's influence around his royal son-in-law remained strong. George's frequent absences on diplomatic missions to France meant that Jane saw less of him than usual but he, too, was an important player at court. By now, he was involved in Parliament and he had joined his father in the Privy Council so was busy even when he was in England. Chapuys, who often mentioned meeting the 'Lady's brother' when he went to court to see the king, remarked on how conversation sometimes stopped when the ever-watchful George came over to him. All were aware of his diligence in his sister's cause. And such devotion continued to bring rewards to him and to his wife. A prize had fallen into their laps a couple of months before Cranmer had placed St Edward's Crown on Anne's dark locks: they had been granted the wardship of Edmund Sheffield. Son of Sir Robert

Sheffield and his wife, Lord Strange's daughter, also a Jane, and a distant relation of the king, the little boy was heir to his father's lands, which were mainly in Nottinghamshire and Lincolnshire. Perhaps the Rochfords had a quiet chuckle at how fitting an acquisition the child was for them: his grandfather had once been in great trouble with Cardinal Wolsey, whose head, he had said, 'ought to be as red as his coat'. When given into the hands of George and Jane, the child was about twelve, a highly convenient age. As yet, they had no children of their own, but both were still young. Should Jane give birth to a daughter in the future, there would be a rich husband waiting in the wings. There was nothing wrong with being prepared. After all, if the lofty Duke of Suffolk had been willing to pay Henry more than £2,000 for the heiress Katherine Willoughby, clearly with an eye to marrying her off to his own son, there was no reason why they should not follow his utilitarian example. In the meantime, they could enjoy the fruits gleaned from administering Edmund's inheritance. The possession of a wardship was a matter of pride for Jane and George, confirmation of their place in the king's affections and of their status. Money was certainly plentiful. George had enough spare cash to send a servant to Calais with 20 marks simply to purchase hawks for the falconry he so much enjoyed, the first of several errands of this kind.

As for Anne, the gifts continued to flow. Francis gave her a 'fine rich litter with three mules', much to Chapuys' contempt. She needed more furniture for her privy chamber so Lord Windsor, keeper of Henry's Great Wardrobe, sent her several elaborate chairs, two of which had gilt and enamel pommels and were covered in cloth of gold. Her initials and arms were engraved upon the royal plate. She was bedecked in Katherine's jewels and flaunted them at every opportunity. And, although Anne was extremely wealthy by virtue of her investiture as Marquess of Pembroke, Henry quickly set about ensuring her a suitable jointure. To add insult to injury, the lands chosen were those allocated to Katherine when she had married Arthur, the transfer confirmed by Act of Parliament.

The jointure increased her fortune considerably. Assuming that she received everything once granted to her predecessor, she gained a huge boost from specified rents, as well as hundreds of acres of land in Essex, Surrey, Buckinghamshire, Berkshire, Wiltshire, Suffolk, Norfolk, Cambridgeshire, Hertfordshire, Herefordshire and Lincolnshire. She now owned castles scattered around the country, including Fotheringhay, destined to be the place where her daughter was to eventually execute Mary, Queen of Scots. She was given Baynard's Castle in London, with its fairytale towers and turrets and useful river-front position, as a further residence. She was even given the rights over the 'dragging of mussels' in Essex. Then, never one to hold back, Anne astounded Chapuys by cajoling Henry into asking Katherine to send her an exquisite cloth she had brought from Spain as a christening robe for the babies she had expected to have. Katherine's answer must have infuriated the Boleyns. 'God forbid that I should ever be so badly advised as to give help, assistance, or favour, directly or indirectly, in a case so horrible and abominable as this,' was the heartfelt response of the outraged former queen. For once, Anne did not get her way. However, as Jane saw, she certainly hardened her heart against both Katherine and Princess Mary.

Katherine's obstinate refusal to accept what appeared to be a fait accompli was exasperating. She would not be addressed as Princess Dowager rather than Queen. She would not agree that her marriage was over. She still believed that Henry, whom she professed to love, would come to his senses and save his immortal soul by returning to her. She had 'perfect confidence', she told Henry's messengers when they informed her she must acquiesce to his will, that God would effect a miracle in the king as he had done when turning St Paul 'from a persecutor into a preacher', and would so 'inspire the king's conscience' that he would not 'continue in error, to the slander of Christendom and ecclesiastical authority'. Such brave defiance worried Chapuys. 'The moment this accursed Anne sets her foot firmly in the stirrup, she will try to do the queen all the harm she possibly can,' he had informed Charles even before the coronation. Without the emperor's intervention, Chapuys believed that Anne would 'not relent in her persecution until she actually finishes with Queen Katherine, as she did once with Cardinal Wolsey, whom she did not hate half as much'. Katherine herself feared that Anne's vengeance would fall upon her daughter, a girl whose determination and courage matched that of her mother.

Grass-roots support for the former queen and princess disconcerted the Boleyns. An innate sense of self-preservation ensured at least outward conformity to the new regime from most courtiers, but winning over the general populace was proving an uphill struggle. Both Katherine and Mary were, according to Chapuys, greeted everywhere with outpourings of affection and allegiance. When the former queen was spotted as she was moved from one residence to another, the local people wished her well, 'filling the air with their acclamations' and hoping that 'mishap' would befall her enemies. As she made a similar journey, Mary, too, aroused such love from the ordinary people that Anne was reported to have complained to Henry that it was 'as if God Almighty had come down from heaven'. Neither she nor the king would countenance disobedience from Katherine and Mary for ever, although bringing them to heel would not be simple or straightforward.

It would be far easier to silence the seditious words of those who did not have such powerful friends. Jane may have heard of Mrs Amadas, who was married to the master of the king's jewels. She recklessly predicted that Anne, 'a harlot', would be burnt and the king lose his throne. Norris, she maintained, had acted as a 'bawd' for Henry, bringing Anne to him. Further, she accused Thomas Boleyn of prostituting both his own wife and Mary Carey, in addition to Anne herself. Since Mrs Amadas also alleged that the king 'had often sent her gifts' and had slept with her at 'Mr Compton's house in Thames Street', it is hardly surprising that she was considered mad. A little more worrying were the words of a priest in Lancashire who declared that he would 'take none for queen but Queen Katherine'. Anne, he said, was a nobody and an immoral nobody at that. 'Who the devil made Nan Bullen, that whore, queen?' he enquired. Fortunately, the Earl of Derby was equal to silencing him. More dangerous were the utterings of Elizabeth Barton, the Holy Maid of Kent, who also prophesied that only disaster would come to the king from his marriage to Anne. The entire court knew about her; some had even listened to her words. She could not be ignored for ever. She, and her followers, would soon be crushed with all the force that Cromwell could muster.

So, as Jane knew, the Boleyn sky was not entirely cloudless. But, as long as a pregnant Anne retained the king's affections, there was no need for too much concern. His love should see them through any repercussions that could result if Clement finally gave his verdict in Katherine's favour, a nagging anxiety which so frequently sent George post-haste to France to negotiate with Francis. Chapuys, optimistically, informed Charles that, the king's affection waning already, he had fallen in love with someone else. The ambassador reported a fierce quarrel between the royal couple when Anne, though 'not without cause', berated the king so soundly that he ordered her to behave as her betters had done before her. Furiously, Henry threatened that he could easily 'humble her again in a moment more than he had exalted her'. Overcoming his own wishful thinking, however, Chapuys was forced to concede that 'these things are lovers' quarrels, to which we must not attach too great importance'. And that was the rub. The relationship between Henry and Anne was, for the king at least, achingly intense, passionate and all-consuming. His devotion had not faded; he had no regrets. For her sake, he had risked religious discord, rebellion and war, dangers that were still far from overcome, but it was worth it. He had the woman he truly adored at his side. And the child she carried was, he was certain, the son and heir he craved. His physicians and astrologers promised him that this was true. Anne, they asserted, would give birth to a boy. He had already chosen Edward or Henry as the baby's name. Letters announcing the 'deliverance and bringing forth of a prince' were ready to be sealed and sent. So the king watched and waited impatiently, like everyone else, as the weeks passed.

In the meantime, Anne presided over her new household as queen, a vastly different role for her. She was determined to enjoy every minute, filling her apartments with the sounds of laughter and music. Or so it seemed to Sir Edward Baynton when he told George that there was so much 'dancing and pastime' in her chamber that any absent gentlemen who had ladies who 'they thought favoured' them, and 'would mourn at parting' from them, should think again. Not, of course, as Baynton pointed out, that every man was immediately flocking towards the girls. 'There is a hawk called a merlyon [merlin], that I think is not yet ready to fly at the larks in this country,' he added tantalisingly.

Jane, so often in her sister-in-law's society, was soon familiar with the many young gentlemen who joined Anne and her attendants. Some, like Henry Norris, Groom of the Stool and a particular favourite of the king, whose coat of arms, coincidentally, featured a merlin, were old acquaintances. An accomplished man, equally at home in the tiltyards and in the masques, he was always welcome in Anne's rooms. Sir Francis Weston, knighted with Jane's brother, was another who dropped by and was quick to join in the hum of merriment on which Baynton remarked. Skilful at dice and cards, Weston had sometimes partnered Anne when she was Marquess of Pembroke against the king in the fashionable Pope Julius's game, with Henry usually losing. Anne's former love, Thomas Wyatt, who had served her at her coronation, was also sometimes at court. It is tempting to conjecture that, in her panelled and candlelit quarters, he and Anne occasionally reminisced over those bygone years, but it is more likely that music and poetry formed the basis of any personal discourse they may have had.

For Jane, this was one of the best periods of her life. Her marriage was successful and there is no reason to believe it anything other than happy. Love matches were rare but they could happen and they could certainly develop. Then, too, Jane had every reason to feel proud of her husband's blossoming career. Trusted by his king, emerging as a politician in his own right, George was the epitome of the flourishing, prosperous courtier. Jane, as his wife, was a woman of importance. Very much the grand lady, she acquired a scholar, William Foster, who later spoke warmly of her as the 'most special patroness' of his studies. She either financed him completely or subsidised him at King's College, Cambridge, a college close to Boleyn hearts since their supporter Edward Foxe was Provost. Foster's name first appears as a scholar there when he ate his dinner in Hall on Saturday, 21 August 1535. Since King's scholars were drawn from Eton, she may have paid for his education there as well. He probably came from Aylesbury, one of the manors listed in her jointure. Jane's father, never happier than when surrounded by his books or absorbed in his writing, would have been proud of his daughter. So would her husband. When he was given a copy of a French work on chivalry by Suffolk, he commissioned the transcriber, Thomas Wall, to translate it into English for presentation to the king. Wall was fulsome in his praise of George whom he called his 'especial good lord'. This hitherto overlooked handwritten document has crossings-out, underlinings and corrections that may well have been made by George himself. His French was more up to date than Wall's and he would not have wanted his name to be associated with a shoddy piece of work that was meant to be a gift for Henry.

Jane, then, could feel satisfied that she was fulfilling her duties to her tenants and following family footsteps in promoting knowledge. And, on a personal level, she was at court – her home since adolescence – she was a member of the most powerful family in the land, she was on intimate terms with the queen. She dressed well and expensively. Her sleeves were of velvet, damask and satin. Her prayer book was edged with silver and gilt. The beads on her rosaries were of gold and pearls. There was so much to enjoy. If there were tournaments or banquets, there would be a place for her. She took part in the 'pastimes and dancing' in Anne's private rooms. When Henry came to dine with his wife, Jane may well have been privy to their conversation. And, accompanied by George if he was in England, Jane travelled with the royal couple in those months following the coronation. After the exertions of the festivities, Anne and Henry were rowed back to Greenwich where they would remain for the next three weeks before Henry indulged himself in a month or so's hunting. Rarely, however, did he stray far from Anne.

It was during August that Henry was given news he did not want to hear: Clement made a pronouncement on the Great Matter. He censured Henry for his actions. Henry should return to Katherine and send Anne away. If he did not obey, Henry faced personal excommunication and his realm being placed under an interdict. Nothing would happen quite yet, the way was still open for further negotiation, but it was simply a matter of time before the pope declared fully in Katherine's favour. The omens were there. The king was sufficiently concerned for Anne's well-being to try to keep this from her. He pretended to go hunting but, instead, went to Guildford, where he met his Council for crisis discussions, leaving her at Windsor.

The frantic negotiations which ensued did not concern Jane. She had other tasks ahead, for the time had come for Anne to get ready to give birth. There was a defined procedure for this, just as there was for everything associated with the royal family. Because it is all meticulously written down in the Royal Book, we know exactly what was required of Anne's lying-in chamber. Even Cromwell was involved in the preparations. Anne's rooms were luxurious, a scene of total opulence. The floor was carpeted. Splendid tapestries lined the walls and the ceiling, their bright colours and golden threads glowing in the candlelight. The room was kept warm but dark. As fresh air and daylight were thought to be dangerous for women in labour, the windows were covered, although one of them was 'hanged that she may have light when it pleaseth her'. Carpenters had made a 'false roof in the queen's bed chamber for to seal and hang it with cloth of arras'. They also made a special cupboard 'with three shelves for the queen's plate to stand upon'. There were two sumptuous beds, one a 'royal bed', the other a day-bed, each made up as the rules required. As Chapuys reported to Charles, 'The king has taken from his treasures one of the richest and most triumphant beds which was given for the ransom of a duke of Alençon.' He was convinced that it was delivered to 'the Lady' for her bedchamber. Doubtless he was right, and perhaps it really was the one chosen for her to lie upon as she brought the most important baby in the land into the world. After all, only the very best would do when Henry's son opened his eyes for the first time.

Nothing was left to chance, all was planned. At the end of August, the time came for Anne to occupy these apartments, even though she had not yet felt the slightest twinge of a labour pang, for Tudor queens were required to take to their lying-in chamber a few weeks before the birth was expected. Accompanied by the leading figures of the court, Anne walked in state into the chapel at Greenwich where she made her confession, before being escorted to the door of the carefully prepared rooms. Once inside, alone with Jane and her other gentlewomen – for this was a mysterious, secret world reserved for women not men – she could gather her strength for the ordeal ahead. Her women would support her, encourage her, talk about their own experiences of childbirth, perhaps play cards or sing to pass the time. Some would know the best herbs and potions to use to dull the pain, perhaps making them up from lilies, roses, cyclamen or columbine. Male servants could bring any necessary supplies only to the entrance, not beyond. Goods were taken in by her ladies whose jobs entailed acting as her cupbearer, her butler, her server, and, of course, as her midwife. Now all that was needed was for one of those ladies to bring the anxious king the news he was certain he would hear. Then, with the prince sleeping peacefully in his cradle, the Boleyns would reign for ever.

15

Birth of a Niece

As Henry waited for confirmation of the arrival of his son, Anne went into labour. We cannot be certain that Jane was with her sister-in-law, but it is entirely possible that she was there and was one of the first to see the face of the child who would one day become England's most famous queen. For the baby, of course, was a girl, not a boy. After years of anticipation, Henry still had no male heir. The documents proclaiming the arrival of a prince had to be speedily changed; there was only room to squeeze in one letter after 'prince' to turn the word into 'princes'. Chapuys announced the tidings baldly and with a note of satisfaction. 'On Sunday last, the eve of Our Lady, about 3 p.m., the king's mistress was delivered of a daughter,' he wrote to Charles, 'to the great regret both of him and the lady.'

A *Te Deum* was sung in the Chapel Royal and in the churches throughout the City of London, but there was no denying the first crack in Boleyn invincibility. For Jane's family, it was a blow; their fortunes were bound up with the sex of the child. Anne had failed in her most important task. Yet it was not all bad news. Anne was recovering well. She had conceived quickly, the pregnancy had gone smoothly, and the delivery was relatively swift and certainly uncomplicated. The infant seemed strong, healthy, and was likely to live. All of these things placed Anne in a different league from Katherine. With God's will, the next effort would produce the desired result. Fortunately, this appeared to be Henry's approach too. For now, the best policy was to prepare for a glittering baptism for the new princess, in accordance with the dictates of the Royal Book, and put on a confident front.

In the meantime, there was much for Anne's ladies to do. The queen could not leave her apartments until she was churched to remove the taint of childbirth. From the moment the baby was born, some of Anne's attendants began to care for her while the others devoted themselves to Anne. The little girl was washed gently in warm water and her navel soothed with powder of aloes and frankincense before she was wrapped in swaddling cloths and placed in her crib to sleep. Ladies offered Anne refreshment, perhaps some thin broth or a caudle, a warm and nourishing drink made from a mixture of gruel, wine and spices. She was not permitted to rise from the bed for some time; these things could not be rushed. Only when she was considered able to sit up, in itself a celebratory affair, did her ladies wash her, and change her clothes and bedding. There was no question of her attending the baptism. For the childless Jane, this was likely to have been her first direct contact with the rituals associated with childbirth. About a year previously, her brother's wife, Grace, had had a son, named Henry after his father and grandfather, but Jane probably did not travel home for the delivery. Her own court commitments would take precedence.

As Anne regained her strength, preparations began for her daughter's christening. The place selected for the grand event, and it certainly was going to be grand, was the Church of the Observant Friars, adjacent to the palace and linked to it via an enclosed gallery. Anne and her family could only approve. While Marquess of Pembroke, Anne had received a letter from Robert Lyst, a lay brother there who championed her cause, complaining that some of the friars were vociferous advocates for Katherine. Using the church for the baby's christening, then, was a sweet revenge. In other ways, too, it was a significant venue, since the church, with its superb window portraying the family of Henry VII, was very much a royal creation; in fact, it was where Henry himself had been baptised. Ironically, however, so had Princess Mary, for Greenwich had been her birthplace, as it was that of her half-sister. At first Chapuys was convinced that Anne's child was actually to be named Mary, both as a deliberate insult and to indicate that Henry's eldest daughter was about to be deprived of her title. He was partly right, for the Boleyns could not countenance any child except their own possessing that rank, so

Mary's status was indeed soon to plummet. But the baby was called Elizabeth after Henry's mother and, coincidentally, after Anne's.

Jane may well have been present as her niece was officially received into the Church. She may equally have remained with the queen in her closed apartments, although many ladies of the court were definitely at the christening on that early autumn afternoon, just three days after the baby's birth. If Anne wanted her sister-in-law at her side, they could both rely on George for a detailed description of everything that happened.

Sir Stephen Peacock was having a most exciting period as mayor. Hardly had his servants put away his best robes after the coronation than they were needed again, for he was a leading guest. After lunch, Peacock and his aldermen, dressed in crimson or scarlet velvet and with their golden chains gleaming once more upon their breasts, took to their barge as their oarsmen rowed them back to Greenwich. A second barge, with forty of the city's leading citizens on board, brought up the rear. Once they had arrived, a procession was assembled and the christening could commence.

Just as the streets had been decorated for Anne's days of triumph, so the way from the palace to the church was decked with golden tapestries and cloth of gold hangings. The ground was covered with green rushes – it would not do for anyone to slip. Inside, the church was ablaze with light and glittering with cloth of gold. The font, of solid silver, stood railed off in the middle, underneath a crimson satin canopy and on a covered dais three steps high, so that everyone could see the proceedings very clearly.

The citizens of London, walking in pairs, formed the vanguard of the cavalcade. Various gentlemen, squires and chaplains came next, followed by the aldermen, and Peacock, quite an old hand at parades by now, was allowed the honour of processing in alone. Henry's Council came in after the mayor, then the musicians of the Royal Chapel, the nobles and the bishops. All were magnificently attired in deference to the new arrival. Some of the nobility were entrusted with specific tasks: the Earl of Essex was responsible for the gilt basins, the Marquess of Dorset held the salt, Lady Mary Howard bore the christening cloth of pearls and precious stones. Then came little Elizabeth for her first public outing, carefully carried by the Dowager Duchess of Norfolk, on duty once more. The baby was wrapped up warmly in a purple velvet mantle, her ermine-trimmed train supported by the Countess of Essex, the Earl of Derby and, in pride of place, Thomas Boleyn. Family prominence did not end with Thomas. One of the four lords holding a canopy over Elizabeth was her uncle, George. Her great-uncle, the Duke of Norfolk, walked solemnly on one side of her, while the Duke of Suffolk was on the other.

The ceremonies, led by John Stokesley, Bishop of London, began at the church door as was customary. Cranmer acted as godfather, and the godmothers were the Dowager Marchioness of Dorset, the Marchioness of Exeter, and the ever useful Dowager Duchess of Norfolk. Once the baby had been christened in that magnificent silver font, Garter King of Arms cried out, 'God of his infinite goodness, send prosperous life and long, to the high and mighty Princess of England Elizabeth.' To a triumphant burst from the trumpeters, Elizabeth was carried to the altar where she was confirmed by Cranmer. The services and prayers took some time, these things always did, so the congregation were grateful for the sweetmeats and spiced wine which servants brought them before they left the confines of the church.

Then everyone returned to the palace to the joyous sound of trumpets, their way lit by five hundred torches. Some remembered taking part in the sombre procession escorting Prince Henry to his resting place more than two decades ago, but today's occasion was a happy one. If there were fleeting thoughts of Katherine or Mary, they were wisely kept private. Norfolk and Suffolk went straight into the king's rooms to reassure him that the proceedings had gone smoothly. It was they who came out to thank Peacock and his aldermen, on the king's behalf, for their attendance and to offer them refreshment before the journey back to London.

Once Elizabeth was sleeping in her cradle in Anne's rooms, she and her ladies could admire the fabulous christening gifts that her godparents had presented. Jane, who certainly saw them, could not fail to be impressed. Cranmer gave a gold cup, no silver for him. The Duchess of Norfolk gave a similar cup, also of gold but studded with pearls. The Marchioness of Dorset's offering was three beautifully worked gilt bowls, together with their covers. The Marchioness of Exeter gave three more, despite her devoted support for Katherine and Princess Mary and her constant communication with Chapuys. Together with further gifts, which were no doubt received from other guests, it was a most welcome haul. Proper respect had been paid to the latest Boleyn. Anne must have been satisfied. Chapuys might sniffily report to his master that 'the christening has been like her mother's coronation, very cold and disagreeable both to the court and to the city,' but in fact the whole occasion had been a notable success. Jane and the Boleyns knew it.

As they discussed the day, the name of Suffolk was bound to raise a smile. With his wife Mary, the French Queen, barely cold in her grave, the indomitable duke, who was almost fifty, had usurped his son's place and himself had married his ward, the fourteen-year-old heiress Katherine Willoughby, on the very day that Anne gave birth. For light entertainment it could hardly be bettered, although the worldly Boleyns would applaud his practical streak. He had not only lost the French Queen, he had lost her French pension, and now in debt to the king, Katherine Willoughby was too good a prize to let slip. The situation so amused Chapuys that he could not resist informing the emperor. 'In contracting such a marriage,' he wrote, 'the duke will no doubt please the ladies of this country, who, imitating his example, will no doubt take their revenge, when accused of marrying again immediately after the death of their husbands, as they are in the habit of doing.' The demise of the French Queen had little impact on the Boleyns, especially since she had never liked Anne and was not a frequent visitor to court. She would not be missed. Even Henry accepted his favourite sister's death with surprising equanimity. Jane's contact with her had been slight. Together they had performed in the masque for the French ambassadors, but that was a lifetime away. The innocent young Jane of those days was gone; in her stead was a poised, mature woman, whose niece was in line to inherit the throne, a prospect that she could never have envisaged when she had donned her mask and danced amidst the tapestries and flickering candles of Wolsey's York Place. The world had moved on. No, she would not grieve unduly for the dead wife of Louis XII.

Jane had very little time to become acquainted with Elizabeth. By the end of 1533, Henry had provided the three-month-old child with her own household. From now on, Anne's role as a mother was limited to visits rather than direct daily contact. All major decisions concerning the child would be taken by the king. He would even determine when Elizabeth should be weaned. Anne accepted her restricted role but, characteristically, she was deeply concerned that her daughter, a royal princess, should look the part. She bought her caps of purple and crimson, one of white satin 'laid with a rich caul of gold', and decorated her cradle with over two yards of crimson satin and crimson fringe. But purchasing pretty things and paying her brief visits were all she could do for her baby daughter. Breast-feeding, as Jane and every other woman of her time understood, was out of the question. At best a messy inconvenience, it was also a hindrance to conception. And that, as the Boleyns appreciated only too well, was the key to maintaining the position they had all fought so hard to attain and to which all of them, including Jane, had become accustomed. Anne simply had to become pregnant again.

16

The Boleyns Rampant

'The queen hath a goodly belly,' wrote George Taylor, Anne's receiver-general, to Lady Lisle, the wife of the Deputy of Calais, adding that he was 'praying our Lord to send us a prince'. Within three or four months after Jane's niece first opened her eyes to the land she would one day rule, Anne was pregnant again. Her entire family breathed a huge sigh of relief. This time, surely, she would produce the prince that George Taylor prayed for. Taylor was not the only supplicant. Jane was firmly settled at court, frequently at her sister-in-law's side, and very much in the heart of her country's affairs. She did not want to give that up. It simply had to be a boy, and Henry was confident that it would be. He would soon have a son, he told Chapuys. Gloomily, the ambassador confided in Charles that Anne was 'in a state of health and of an age to have many more children'. The Boleyns could only hope that his forebodings proved true.

As she watched Anne's stomach swell, Jane enjoyed her life behind the doors of the queen's privy chamber. It was almost as if Anne needed to prove the aptness of her chosen motto, 'the most happy'. There was gossip and fun and dancing and cards. There was music and song. There were the lilting notes of the queen's linnet, a gift from Lady Lisle, in the background. There were visitors to chat to, men like Norris and Weston and Richard Page, another of the king's gentlemen. There was lively discussion on the important topics of clothes and fashion, and what was chic and what was not, and who was paying court to whom. It was a whirlwind of fun and laughter, repartee and wit. Then there was the frolicking of Anne's little dog, Purquoy,* a creature of whom she was inordinately fond, and a further present from the solicitous Honor Lisle. Anne was so enchanted by Purquoy that when she heard that Honor had asked Sir Francis Bryan to deliver the animal, she 'took it from him before it had been an hour in his hands'. The dog ran around excitedly, following his devoted mistress, amongst the ladies and their beaux, until a terrible fall cut short his life. Knowing how upset Anne would be, no one dared tell her what had happened, so the king, very sympathetic in circumstances like this, took the task upon himself. Henry loved his own dogs dearly enough to pay generous rewards to those who found his favourites, Ball and the spaniel Cut, when they got lost, so he quite understood his wife's distress.

Jane, who had always delighted in masques and dancing, was very much at home with her current lifestyle. It was not all dalliance; many peaceful hours were given over to the serious business of embroidery and sewing, but to sit and work amidst the tapestries and luxurious furnishings of Anne's apartments was hardly taxing. She could not complain. By repute, Anne was a good needlewoman and expected high standards of craftsmanship from her ladies. Jane could take pride in helping to produce the 'shirts and smocks for the poor', which, according to Wyatt's grandson, Anne insisted her 'maids and those about her' turned out every day and which were 'rich and precious' in God's eyes.

And what was important in the eyes of God was, as Jane understood, fundamental to the Boleyns. Those early days, when Henry had felt so strongly about Luther's doctrines that he had once written a book against them, earning himself the title of 'Defender of the Faith' in the process, were long gone. So was his subservience to the pope. While still no Lutheran, the king was now Supreme Head of the Church, a title that Parliament would confirm. It was wise to accept it. Jane, brought up with a Latin Bible, no doubt felt at ease when Anne studied the exquisitely illustrated fifteenth-century Book of Hours she had owned before her fate became linked to that of the king. But she also grew used to seeing her mistress poring

---

* As it was customary to give an animal a name relevant to its character, I suspect that 'Purquoy' was really 'Perky'.

intently over the superbly bound edition of Lefèvre d'Etaples's French version of the sacred text, which she and Henry shared, and which had their initials engraved in gold upon the cover. Or at least, she did once the initial shock had worn off. To possess a copy of the Bible in the vernacular had often been a short cut to the stake when Jane was a girl. Now, it would be just a matter of time before the once-forbidden work was readily available, and with the king's permission. It was highly confusing, but Jane's world was changing, and the family into which she had married were busily promoting that change. She knew that.

She also knew that George and Anne, together with Thomas, were marching further along a dangerous road. Even the clerics they patronised, men like Hugh Latimer, Thomas Cranmer, John Skip, William Barlow and Matthew Parker, were all of avant-garde opinions. Around brother and sister particularly was a highly charged, exhilarating atmosphere as they debated and argued and deliberated on questions of faith, on what was wrong with the old ways and right with the new, and on how the gospel must be brought to everyone. Chapuys once said that George could never 'refrain' from entering into Lutheran discussions whenever he saw him. It was probably George who gave Anne *The Ecclesiaste*, bound in black velvet and sporting the royal emblems in brass and enamel roundels. He is also closely linked to a further book, based on a set of gospel readings and epistles gathered by Lefèvre d'Etaples, one for each week of the year. Every passage is accompanied by a meaningful essay, which George translated from French into English. He then gave the entire volume, complete with an affectionate and fulsome dedication, to his sister. George inscribed it for her too, sending greetings from her 'most loving and friendly brother'. That, however, was but one of several books and manuscripts that Jane saw in the queen's privy apartments, some of outstanding beauty, most with bindings that were themselves works of art, and many of a tone that risked censure with the more conservative members of the court. Whatever Jane's thoughts were about this aspect of the life she led, she kept her counsel.

Safer by far was to give serious consideration to the tricky business of New Year's Gifts, always a minor distraction for those in Henry's circle. Anne was lucky; Henry would pay for hers, and Cromwell was on hand to remind him 'of the expense' in case it slipped his mind. Jane was lucky, too, for amongst Anne's gifts for 1534 were 'palfreys and saddles for her ladies'. So another horse joined Jane's stable, this one with a finely worked saddle. Proximity to royalty remained profitable. It also brought responsibilities. Henry took a particular interest in what he was given, frequently accepting his presents personally and sometimes with a gracious comment, but sitting in the background would be Brian Tuke, treasurer of the chamber, calmly 'penning all things that were presented' and no doubt noting their value. Fully aware of the system, Jane's offering to Henry was a shirt with silver decoration on the collar. Then, as now, a shirt was always safe, but it could not, of course, compete in any way with Anne's gift to her husband. She gave him a gilt basin with a fountain inside it, water issuing from the nipples of the three naked women standing at the fountain's base. Since the entire item was studded with rubies, pearls and diamonds, Tuke had a good deal to write down. No one else could match that but, for any courtier short of ideas, Henry's love for his animals offered other possibilities: dog collars were always most welcome, particularly if they were of silver-gilt or gold damask, like those from the Earl of Huntingdon or Lady Bryan.

These few months of Anne's latest pregnancy were spent largely around London, often at Greenwich or at Westminster. Because she was a member of her sister-in-law's household, and George was in attendance upon the king so often, Jane and her husband usually accompanied Henry and Anne in their travels. When in London, they already had rooms at York Place and could always stay at Durham House if they wanted a change, but George also had his own quarters inside the palace at Greenwich. This was not out of the ordinary, he did need to be always on hand, but for Henry to pay for various alterations, such as the construction of a mullioned window, to make him more comfortable, was. Both royal residences had plenty of distractions, so there would have been no excuse to be bored. Hunting was a perennial interest, especially for Henry, and there were sometimes opportunities for George to fly his rather expensive hawks, a pastime his sister relished as well. Anne liked archery too, but although Henry had bought her bows in the past, it was hardly an advisable activity for the woman carrying his son. Jane, however, could have taken part. Then there was bowling, at which both George and his father were expert, although Anne's condition again made her a spectator, not a participant. Nevertheless, they could all enjoy the excitement of the cockfights held in the newly built cockpit at Greenwich, and bet on the result.

So, superficially at least, the days passed very easily. But, as Jane could see, life for Anne was not trouble free. The continued defiance of Katherine and Mary was a definite thorn in Boleyn flesh. No matter how much she was coerced and despite the pressure put upon her servants, the former queen still refused to acknowledge her redefined rank of Princess Dowager, which she saw as a wrongful and wicked demotion. Her scornful replies to such demands were faithfully conveyed to Charles by an admiring Chapuys. 'Knowing for certain that she is the true and legitimate wife of the king,' he reported, 'she will never as long as she lives, on any consideration, take any other title but that of queen, and, if addressed by any other will not answer to it.' She would not 'consent to damn her soul, or that of the king, her lord and husband' for 'a thousand deaths'. It was an impasse that might also prove perilous to the former queen. Chapuys was truly anxious about poison, as was Katherine herself. 'The little food she takes in this time of tribulation is prepared by her maids-in-waiting within her own bedroom,' he wrote.

Mary was just as intractable. Neither Henry nor Anne would allow her to remain a princess; only Elizabeth could retain that rank. And soon there would be a brother to join her in the royal nursery, his right to the throne confirmed by the recent Act of Succession hurriedly pushed through Parliament and requiring an oath of acceptance from every subject. Woe betide anyone who refused to take it. Indeed, amongst those in prison for such a refusal were More and Fisher. That, at least, was satisfying for the Boleyns, especially when Clement finally stirred himself to declare in favour of Katherine. Almost immediately after Elizabeth was born, Henry ordered that Mary should be notified that her household and allowance were to be reduced to correspond with her adjusted status. However, to persuade Mary to become 'Lady Mary' proved well nigh impossible;

Jane's sister-in-law was not the only determined female in the royal family.

Jane knew both Katherine and Mary well. She had grown up with Katherine as queen. She had seen her resplendent at Henry's side at the Field of Cloth of Gold and at so many court celebrations or state occasions, as she fulfilled her role as consort with the graciousness and majesty so natural in a daughter of Ferdinand and Isabella. Like everyone else, Jane was aware of the queen's raw anguish when she failed to give her husband the male heir he so craved. Herself a childless woman, Jane could empathise only too well. She had watched Mary develop from a little girl, who danced so prettily at court, worked at her studies and was the pride of both her parents, into the young woman whose world was suddenly destroyed and who was separated from the mother she loved. Yet, any sympathies that Jane had for Katherine or Mary had to be suppressed. Her first loyalty had to lie with her husband and the family into which she had married. She had cast her lot in with them and had been very willing to accept the prizes that had resulted. If she felt little pleasure at the harsh treatment meted out to the former queen and her daughter, she must keep it to herself.

Harsh treatment there certainly was. Katherine was moved from castle to castle, from country house to country house, anywhere but near the court or near Mary. It was upon Mary that Anne's attention particularly fell, and she was supported by George and Thomas, quick to realise how dangerous Mary was to Boleyn ambition. Henry, furious that anyone, let alone his own child, could even contemplate disobedience to his legitimate orders, was fierce in his support. 'She is my death and I am hers,' Anne was reputed to have said about Mary, 'so I will take care that she shall not laugh at me after my death.' As so often in the past, the Boleyns worked together. They began by securing the appointment of Lady Anne Shelton, Thomas's sister, to replace the decidedly partisan Margaret Pole, Countess of Salisbury, as Mary's governess. From now onwards, there would be a Boleyn in constant attendance upon the former princess. For Jane, Lady Shelton's was another familiar face: her sister, Margaret Parker, was married to Lady Shelton's son and would bear him five children, and Lady Shelton's husband, Sir John, was a friend of Jane's father.

Gossiping about ordinary domestic family matters, should she and Jane meet, would provide a welcome relief for the new and frequently harassed governess. Coping with the recalcitrant Mary was no easy task.

No one really knew how best to handle the ex-princess. Jane would have heard many a discussion between George, Thomas and Anne on the vexed subject. George and Anne were keen to press as hard as possible to force Mary to conform to the new Boleyn regime. Together with Norfolk, George castigated Lady Shelton, who was already doing her best to control Mary, for being too lenient. 'She ought to deal with her', they said, 'as a regular bastard that she was.' An exasperated Anne suggested similar methods. If Mary persisted in calling herself a princess, Lady Shelton should 'box her ears as a cursed bastard', she ordered. Fortunately for Mary, Lady Shelton, while quite willing to be a reliable spy, was not wantonly vindictive or cruel and was prepared to treat her only with 'respect and honour'.

Because of her own privileged position, Jane knew how Mary was being treated, but so did the rest of the court, not all of whom were enthusiastic Boleyn supporters. For anyone to take up Mary's cause openly was suicidal, especially since speaking publicly against Henry's current marital situation was by now against the law, but mutterings in dark corners were another matter. Even the eagle-eyed Cromwell could not be everywhere. Mary's humiliation intensified when she was required to join Elizabeth's household rather than have her own, which meant that Anne's child always took precedence as the only true, legitimate princess. Stories spread of Mary's evasions to avoid taking second place to her despised half-sister. Mary would not 'walk by the side of her when they are taken anywhere', Chapuys informed the emperor. Somehow, she managed to be 'in front of her or behind'. News of Mary's property being confiscated, or of the girl being bundled into a carriage with Lady Shelton and threatened, shocked many susceptibilities. Maybe even Jane's.

Whenever Anne visited Elizabeth, Jane may well have been one of the ladies accompanying her. A glimpse of Mary, then, could easily have occurred. In the early months, at least, Anne hoped that her stepdaughter would see sense. Kindness had once captured a king; it might be worth trying it on a princess. On one journey to

Elizabeth, she sent a message to Mary 'requesting her to visit and honour her as queen which she was'. If Mary would only do this, Anne promised to plead with Henry on her behalf so that she would regain 'the good favour and pleasure of the king, her father', and be 'treated as well or perhaps better than she had ever been'. Mary's tart answer bordered on recklessness. She knew of no other queen than her mother, she said, but 'should the king's mistress . . . do her the favour she spoke of, and intercede with the king, her father, she would certainly be most grateful to her'. Jane may not have been with Anne when Mary's reply was received, but doubtless she heard Anne's furious response. The queen would, she vowed, 'put down that proud Spanish blood' and do her 'worst'. It was war. The situation was fraught, but Jane's place had to be with the Boleyns.

In any case, Jane and George benefited considerably from Mary's disgrace. When the princess was bundled unceremoniously out of the royal palace of Beaulieu, the house was simply handed over to George. This was an amazing coup. While George had been granted keeper's rights to the palace previously, they were of a much more limited extent than this very special benefaction. It was not a gift, of course, but, in the fullness of time, anything was possible. The moment he got it, George began to move in his household and some of his furniture. Beaulieu was less than twenty miles from Jane's family seat at Great Hallingbury, so her new home was not only in an area with which she was very familiar, it was also ideally situated for occasional visits to her parents and brother. Since George had recently acquired a comfortable litter, she could do this in considerable style. George was even more delighted. To receive such a prize was a resounding signal of Henry's approval, but it was symbolic too: the old Ormond residence was in Boleyn hands again. However, it was the old Ormond residence with a significant difference, for Henry had spent about £17,000 in a massive building programme to upgrade it in accordance with his own exacting standards. The highly experienced William Bolton, prior of St Bartholomew's in Smithfield, who had already worked for Wolsey at Hampton Court and on Margaret Beaufort's tomb in Westminster Abbey, had been entrusted with the work there, so it was bound to be particularly fine. Jane and George really did have a palace to live in, and it was not one they would be required to share. It was solely for the two of them.

Although they were both likely to have visited Beaulieu as part of the court, they saw it with fresh eyes now. The lovely brick house was surrounded by acres of well-kept parkland. Through an arched doorway between the two sides of the gatehouse, above which were fixed the carved stone arms of the king, pronouncing his authority and majesty, they passed into the inner court around which the main wings of the palace were arranged. Beaulieu offered everything they could possibly want.

The chapel, with its hangings, glass windows and two organs, was on the left of the quadrangle. With the soul so well catered for, the body was not neglected, for behind the chapel was an indoor tennis court, which would have appealed to George, always such a keen sportsman.

The other side of the house was just as impressive. The great hall was huge and the kitchens, pantry and bakehouse were served by fresh water from a newly installed supply with lead cisterns for the waste. Jane and George could live in regal style, although daring to use the king's flower-decorated bathroom, complete with hot and cold running water, was probably a presumption too far, even for the Boleyns.

However, George and Jane could make use of some of the myriad soft furnishings, carpets, wooden tables, stools and cupboards that were stored there. They could sit upon the leather chair 'painted with the story of Venus', listening to musicians playing upon the lute and virginals, while the 'clock with a bell' marked the passage of time, or read some of the many books, such as Caesar's *Commentaries*. 'Great coffers bound with iron' would be useful to safeguard their ever-increasing stock of valuables.

But most of all, George and Jane could use their own furniture. Jane had grown up amongst the Parker plate but now she possessed her own. She and George could dine from silver platters and silver dishes, emblazoned with the Rochford arms coupled with those of the king, in a room lit by candles held in Rochford candlesticks. They could drink from silver and gilt goblets. They owned magnificent engraved gilt bowls, great gilt trenchers and gilt pots. They could use their own intricately worked tablecloth trimmed and fringed with gold thread and with the letters G and B proudly displayed at each end. Their wealth was on show everywhere.

And, on those nights when Jane and George slept together as man and wife, they could snuggle up behind red and white damask curtains in their superb bed, lying on a soft feather mattress, their heads resting on pillows of down. The painted and gilded wooden bedstead was draped in cloth of gold, its white satin canopy embroidered in tawny cloth of gold embellished with 'Rochford knots' and bordered with yellow and white silk fringe. Linen quilts filled with wool and a luxurious yellow counterpane lined with yellow buckram ensured that they would not be cold even in the depths of winter.

All that was needed for complete security until every Boleyn's dying day was for Anne to give birth to a prince. And, for a while, Anne's pregnancy seemed to be going well. Henry ordered an elaborate silver cradle from his goldsmith, Cornelius Hayes, together with swaddling clothes, and bedding of white satin and cloth of gold. George was told to ask for the postponement of a projected meeting with the Queen of Navarre, Francis's sister. Anne was 'so far gone with child', he was to say, that 'she could not cross the sea with the king'. Nor could Henry go without her for 'she would be deprived of his Highness's presence when it was most necessary'. Then, quite suddenly, we read no more in the documents about the baby. Anne had miscarried.

THE WINDS OF CHANGE

17

The King's Displeasure

One daughter, one miscarriage: no amount of spin or propaganda could convert such blatant failure into success. For Henry, it was achingly familiar; he had been here before. For the Boleyns, it could spell disaster. So far, the family had done remarkably well by backing Anne, but that in itself courted danger. Should she fall, they would fall with her, and the fall might be catastrophic. No one who risked the king's displeasure was safe, even those who seemed untouchable. Jane's memories of Buckingham's death may have faded as the years passed, but he could not be forgotten, and Wolsey's pathetic demise was yet more recent. Jane knew that she could have far more serious concerns than a mere reduction in her collection of extravagant clothes, jewelled sleeves and silk stockings for masques if the unthinkable happened. But it did not. Henry's love for Anne burnt as brightly as ever and, while it did, the Boleyns were still at her side.

Not only was the king committed to his wife, he was determined to make sure that everyone else was as well. As Jane watched, the bloodbath began. Opposition, real or suspected, was about to be rooted out across the land, from the teeming streets of London to the smallest hamlet in Cornwall or the tiniest village in Yorkshire. As far as Henry was concerned, his people should be grateful to him. He had saved himself from an adulterous marriage, them from the usurped power of the pope, a man who was nothing more than the Bishop of Rome, and would deliver the true gospel to all his subjects. He was a David, he was a Solomon; above all, he was right. The Boleyns agreed with him; or at least, Anne, George and Thomas definitely did, and the rest of the family simply acquiesced. As did most of the population. Cromwell made sure of that. With Acts on the statute book making it treason to deny that the succession rested in Henry's issue by Anne and, a little later, to deny that the king was Head of the Church, Cromwell was equipped with a full arsenal of ammunition. He used it.

Unaffected by respect for gender, he embarked on the first of a series of high-profile cases with a woman: Elizabeth Barton, the Holy Maid of Kent. Her fame had grown long before he chose to act. It had started when, as a young servant girl, she had suddenly succumbed to a mysterious sickness, in the course of which she had visions of 'heaven, hell, purgatory, and the state of souls departed'. Her recovery had been as dramatic as the onset of her illness. During one of her trances, voices had told her to go to the Church of Our Lady of Court at Street. Once there, she had lain in front of a statue of the Virgin. Then the miracle had begun. 'Her face was wonderfully disfigured,' the spectators had said, 'her tongue hanging out, and her eyes being in a manner plucked out, and laid upon her cheeks.' Eventually, she 'came to herself again, and was perfectly whole'. The bystanders had been convinced that God had cured her. The trouble was that once the Holy Maid had become a nun at the convent of St Sepulchre in Canterbury, not only had her visions and trances continued, but she had gained the additional power of prophesy. And her prophesies had been uncomfortably linked to the consequences of Henry's likely second marriage. He would die within six months 'in a plague of unheard-of severity', she had said, if he really did marry Anne; indeed, she had seen the place in hell that was already reserved for him.

Elizabeth Barton had become the talk of the court. There is no proof that Jane met her, but she certainly knew all about her, for her fame spread. The Holy Maid of Kent was fashionable and she seemed genuine. There was even a book written about her. Despite the fact of Henry's obvious survival beyond the six months that she had foretold, there were plenty of people prepared to listen to anything else she had to say, and she was voluble. She maintained that Wolsey had ascended into heaven through her penance, she knew when the king would die, she knew that she would 'receive the crown of martyrdom', she knew about angels, and popes, and abbots and she knew about 'a golden letter' written by Mary Magdalene. It was heady stuff, and it had to be stopped.

Stopped it was. Cranmer questioned her, Cromwell interrogated her. Between them, they managed to extract a confession that she had 'never had a vision in her life, but feigned them all'. It could not, of course, be allowed to end there. Cranmer might well tell Henry that people were delighted that Elizabeth Barton's calumnies had been exposed but the difficulty was that she had passed them on. Cromwell set about discovering who had listened. His detective work caused panic. Particularly satisfying to the Boleyns was the Marchioness of Exeter's grovelling letter to Henry. She was, she said abjectly, 'the most sorrowful and heavy creature alive' since she had 'been so unfortunate as to offend the king and his laws, or be in danger of his indignation or displeasure'. She was sufficiently desperate to point out that she was only a woman, 'whose fragility and brittleness is easily seduced and brought to abusion and light belief'. 'I will receive my Maker,' she wrote to Cromwell, 'that I never offended' the king, 'even in thought; but if I have offended through simplicity and lack of knowledge, I submit myself, accepting his gracious pardon'. The marchioness was lucky; she escaped with humiliation and a considerable fright, rather than a grim sojourn in the Tower as the headsman sharpened his axe.

Elizabeth Barton and her immediate circle were not so lucky. Jane knew precisely what had happened to them because George, Thomas and her father could give her a first-hand account. All three were summoned to the Parliament, which passed Acts of Attainder against the nun and her alleged accomplices, thereby condemning them to death. That death was public. Gawping crowds, accustomed to the carnage of such things, but curious to see a nun and five members of the clergy executed, watched them drawn to Tyburn from the Tower to die. There, they were granted the relatively merciful end of hanging and beheading. The government could have insisted that they suffer the infinitely slower and more painful death usually accorded to traitors.

The sheer terror of such an end proved an excellent deterrent to many as Cromwell beavered away to ensure conformity. Henry's subjects were ordered to take the oath accepting the legality of

Anne's marriage and the succession of her children. Most of those in the City of London did so on the very day that Elizabeth Barton was hanged. Henry issued Suffolk with full authority to imprison without bail any who preached or spread 'or otherwise set forth pernicious opinions and doctrines, to the exaltation of the power of the bishop of Rome'. That, too, was a crime. Every careless word could be reported, Cromwell's spies were everywhere. The minister himself was inundated with messages about miscreants of every type and every degree of seriousness. Sir Francis Bryan was pleased to report the capture of a certain George Taylor who had called Henry a heretic and said that he would play football with the king's crown if he had it. Despite Taylor pleading that he had been drunk at the time, Bryan felt that his execution would be 'a very great example and the safeguard of many'. He even suggested the most appropriate towns for the displaying of Taylor's four quarters, one of which, coincidentally, was Jane's manor of Aylesbury. In Suffolk, Margaret Chancellor was reported for calling Anne 'a goggle-eyed whore' and praying that she would never have another child by the king. Hugh Lathbury, a hermit, was another casualty for saying that Katherine would soon be queen again. He was obviously disturbed since he also said that he had seen her recently in Lincolnshire 'and she would make ten men against the king's one', but his mental state did not save him. Nor was royal mercy likely to be extended to Friars Hugh Payn and Thomas Hayfield who, 'in great pain and sickness', begged for forgiveness for praying for the pope 'by name after the old custom', until they heard such prayers were forbidden.

Those keen to prove their own loyalty to their king knew exactly what they had to do. They included Jane's relatives who lived in the more far-flung corners of the realm. Sir Piers (Peter) Edgecombe, a leading figure in the South-West and married to her mother's sister, Katherine, clearly knew his duty. He informed Cromwell that he had committed Friar Gawan, warden of the Grey Friars at Plymouth, to the castle at Launceston until 'the king's pleasure be known', and that he had also 'punished by pillory and stocks in the market places such persons as spoke opprobrious words of the queen'.

Whatever Jane thought about all of this, she could see its inevitable logic. Convinced in his own mind that what he was doing was morally correct, Henry would not countenance rebellion, disobedience, protest or even the mildest and most tentative disagreement. Everyone about him knew that. When Wolsey had warned Kingston all those years ago to beware 'what matter ye put in his head, for ye shall never put it out again', he had been devastatingly percipient. In the king's head now was his own assessment of his rights, duties and role in both Church and State. It was safest to go along with that assessment.

That was easier for some than for others. Anne, Thomas and George were genuinely exhilarated by the new religious ideas and sometimes they interested Henry in them. Jane's father Lord Morley perfected the art of bending with the wind. He accepted the loss of the pope's political powers readily enough and turned up punctiliously for every treason trial or parliamentary sitting. Kings, he knew, had to be obeyed without question. 'It often chanceth that tyrants do range and occupy the higher powers to afflict their subjects,' he wrote, 'and yet this notwithstanding the commandment of the king must be observed.' Fortunately he believed his own prince to be gentle and devout but, even had he not been blessed with such a ruler, Jane's father advocated a pragmatic approach. He counselled against the folly of resistance. Aiming to die in his own bed with his family about him, he saw no virtue in placing himself in needless danger. 'It is a great point of wisdom', he said, 'to dissemble some time and to give place.' Brought up in such a school, his daughter appreciated the value of silence.

Others did not, and the harsh policies continued. This time the victims were austere Carthusian monks, together with some from other orders, foolish enough or brave enough to deny their king his brand-new title, turning themselves into traitors in the process. Their treatment whilst in prison was barbaric. Yet, half starved, sick, and completely undeterred by the agonies they faced if found guilty of treason, some spoke out forcefully in support of their beliefs and the supremacy of the pope. Before an audience which included Cromwell, Audley and Thomas Boleyn, Richard Reynolds from Syon Abbey asserted that the majority of the population were behind him. 'I dare even say all this kingdom,' he said, 'although the smaller part holds with you, for I am sure the larger part is at heart of our opinion, although outwardly, partly from fear and partly from hope, they profess to be of yours.' This was not what Henry wanted to hear. Those who refused to conform were sentenced to the full horrors of a traitor's death. Again, Jane knew every last grisly detail of what that entailed, for Thomas and George had ringside seats as knives seared through flesh and the stench of burning organs permeated the air.

Tied to hurdles and dragged along the sharp and bumpy ground from the Tower to Tyburn, Reynolds and three Carthusian priors, John Houghton, Robert Lawrence and Augustine Webster, were hanged until almost dead and then cut down. For the spectators, and George and Thomas were not the only members of Henry's Council present to watch unmoved as the victims choked and gasped for breath, the best was yet to come. The hangman cut into the men's living bodies to remove their testicles, hearts and bowels, which were then ceremonially burnt. To increase the agony, each victim had to watch his companions die while awaiting his own turn to suffer the same fate. All died with great 'constancy', showed no fear and, during that inhuman period of dread anticipation, actually 'preached and exhorted the bystanders with the greatest boldness to do well and obey the king in everything that was not against the honour of God and the Church'. Finally, the bodies were beheaded and cut into quarters, which were then displayed prominently as a warning to anyone recklessly considering the idea of displeasing the king. As the executioner and his assistants removed the blood-drenched straw, George, Thomas, the Duke of Richmond, Norris and the rest could return to the court or to their own homes for supper. So perish all traitors. It had been a good day's work.

It was not the only one. Katherine's stalwart advocate, the elderly, frail Bishop John Fisher, was the next to pay the price. He was attainted for meeting the Holy Maid and not condemning her, his goods were seized and he was imprisoned. Barely had he been released than he was arrested again, this time for refusing the oath to the succession. As far as the Boleyns were concerned, the oath secured their descendants' inheritance. Fisher found the issue much more complicated. He made it plain that while he was prepared to accept the succession, and was ready 'to swear never more to meddle in the validity' of Henry's marriage to Katherine, he could not agree to the preamble of the Act, which amounted to a tacit denial of papal supremacy. To do so would be to deny the ideals which had governed his life. Cranmer's attempt to argue for the compromise by which the bishop was allowed to swear to the succession alone was completely rejected by the king. Henry was determined to have every last detail of what he wanted, right down to the tiniest of small print or, he said, 'it would give occasion to all men to refuse the whole' and thus deny both his supremacy and the validity of his marriage to his beloved Anne. In that, the Boleyns could only concur.

So the bishop, now in his mid-sixties, languished in the Tower, from where he wrote pitifully to Cromwell, asking for adequate clothes and food. He possessed 'neither shirt nor sheet nor yet other clothes' except ones that were 'ragged and rent too shamefully'. He was not complaining of their condition but they did not keep him warm. As for his diet, he said, 'God knows how slender it is at many times.' Because he was old and weak, there were certain foods he needed. Without them, he wrote, 'I decay forthwith, and fall into coughs and diseases of my body, and cannot keep myself in health.' For the first few months of his incarceration, his friend, the merchant Antonio Bonvisi, sent him meat, wine and jelly, and his brother, Robert, did his best to help, although this was 'to his great hindrance' as he was not wealthy. Fisher's pleas for better treatment, books and a priest, fell on deaf ears. As the court repaired to Greenwich for the festivities and frivolities of the Christmas season, and as Henry and Anne smilingly received their New Year's Gifts, the elderly cleric shivered in his cell. It was indeed unwise to court the king's displeasure. Jane could see that for herself.

Ultimately, it was also fatal. Once the Act of Supremacy was on the statute book, making it fully fledged treason to persist in refusing to acknowledge the king as Head of the Church, the screws were tightened. Fisher was questioned relentlessly, sometimes by Cromwell, sometimes by the Council. Henry – and doubtless Anne – was kept fully up to date on the minutest of developments. Her family, too, followed every single move, a process made easier by Thomas's position on the Council. Thomas definitely helped to interrogate Fisher's fellow prisoner, Sir Thomas More, who had also fallen foul of the draconian new laws.

Jane's acquaintance with Fisher was slight. She knew about him as Katherine's champion but he had never been a daily court attender, minister or courtier like Suffolk or Norfolk, Gardiner or Cranmer. She was unlikely to know much about him on a personal level. Sir Thomas More was different. Henry liked him. He was famous for his rapier wit, his humour, his learning, his writing, his integrity, his devotion to the Catholic cause. Like Thomas Boleyn, he was a friend of Erasmus, the Dutch humanist, but his religious views were vastly different from those of the Boleyns, whom he probably considered heretics. They had always known that More would never become an ally, particularly when he had swiftly resigned from the chancellorship and then pointedly declined the summons to Anne's coronation. But he had been at court, and quite often. George and Thomas knew him well. Jane almost certainly met him and talked to him at some point. And those who met him usually liked him.

Nothing would help him now, however, unless he changed his mind and took the oath. Just like Fisher, he might well have agreed to the succession if that had been the only issue, but for him it was not. He could not bring himself to accept that Henry actually had the right to bring about momentous changes within the Church without the consent of a General Council. No individual could, not even his king. 'A man', he avowed, 'is not so bound in conscience by a law of one realm as by a law of Christendom.' To take the oath would be to lose his soul. It was a point of principle which would cost him his life, but that was of no matter. 'I have lived, methinketh, a long life,' he wrote, 'and now neither I look nor I long to live much longer.' And should he go to the block, he did not want his family to grieve. Instead he would pray that they would all meet again in heaven 'where we shall make merry for ever, and never have trouble hereafter'.

Die he did, of course. So did Fisher. Thomas was named on the commission set up to try the bishop, and both he and George were named on the one established for Sir Thomas More. The two Boleyns, father and son, together with Cromwell, Suffolk, Audley and Norfolk, were amongst those who sat on the bench alongside the judges for the trial of the former chancellor, listening to every single word. The time would come when the Boleyn presence and involvement were remembered and would be avenged but, for the moment, they were firmly on the winning side. Neither prisoner really stood a chance, although More, ever the brilliant lawyer, argued his case admirably, despite only hearing the precise charges laid against him for the first time on that day. They were read out in Latin, a process which took almost an hour. Skilfully, he trod the tightrope of answering questions where he could without entrapping himself. Only when he was found guilty, after the hand-picked jury had deliberated for just fifteen minutes, did he speak out and proclaim his views. His words were devastating:

> Since I am condemned, and God knows how, I wish to speak freely of your statute, for the discharge of my conscience. For seven years I have studied this matter, but I have not yet read in any approved doctor of the Church that a temporal ruler could or ought to be head of the spirituality.

When Audley remonstrated on his presumption of superiority to 'all the bishops and nobles of the realm', More rounded on him:

> My lord, for every bishop of your opinion, I have more than a hundred saints of mine; and for one parliament of yours, and God knows of what kind, I have all the General Councils for a thousand years; and for one kingdom, I have France and all the other kingdoms of Christendom ... I say further, that your Statute is ill made, because you have taken an oath and sworn never to do anything against the Church, which through all Christendom is one and undivided, and you have no authority, without the common consent of all Christians, to make a law or Act of Parliament against the unity of Christendom.

More finished his address to the stunned room by praying that God would protect the king 'and give him good counsel'. Even Richard Reynolds had not dared go quite that far. The doomed man left Westminster Hall for his journey back to his prison cell in the Tower, the point of the ceremonial axe pointing symbolically towards him to indicate that he had been found guilty.

Waiting at the wharf where his boat landed was Margaret Roper, his most adored daughter. Knowing that it was the only chance she would have to embrace her father for the very last time before he was out of reach for ever, she pushed her way through the guards. She did so, her husband tells us, 'without consideration or care of herself'. The soldiers, of necessity usually unsentimental and unemotional, did not stop her. 'Margaret, have patience, and do not grieve,' said More. 'It is God's will ... For a long time you have known the secrets of my heart,' he told her gently. His composure slipped a little when, after 'having stepped back ten or twelve paces', she rushed to cling to him just once more. Fighting back the tears, he asked her to pray for his soul. More remained calm to the bitter end, but his last letter to Margaret, written with a charcoal stick on the night before his beheading, revealed his true feelings. 'I never liked your manner toward me better than when you kissed me last, for I love when daughterly love and dear charity hath no leisure to look to worldly courtesy.' Even the childless Jane, a Boleyn, was likely to be touched by that.

While the heads of More and Fisher, boiled in salt water and then tarred to prevent the gulls pecking at them too much, remained on their poles on London Bridge, a chilling warning to anyone else contemplating displeasing the king, court life seemed to go on much as before. Jane's father returned to the tranquillity of his library and his writings. Always keen to expand his property portfolio, Suffolk, true to form, let it be known that he would like some of More's lands in Chelsea, for, naturally, everything once owned by a traitor was forfeit to the crown and thus there for the taking. He did not get them. Cromwell concentrated on pleasing his master, keeping a wary eye on any potential troublemakers and carrying on with the normal matters of government. George, now appointed Warden of the Cinque Ports, a plum post, was as busy as ever. Thomas served on the Council with his son and kept an eye on their vast estates. Cocooned in her luxurious apartments, Anne supervised her ladies' sewing, listened to the melodies of her musicians, laughed with her companions. She visited little Elizabeth, bought her pretty things, fumed at the actions of the stubbornly recalcitrant Mary, and managed her husband in her own way. Every month, she watched anxiously until the first signs of menstruation dashed her hopes of pregnancy. But Jane was not always with her

For appearances could sometimes deceive. Over the year or so since Anne's miscarriage, subtle changes had been occurring. And they had been occurring very close to home: conflict within the Boleyn family coincided with disturbing hints of trouble between Anne and the king. To see his anger visited upon someone else was one thing; to be in the firing line personally was quite another. And, during that dramatic period when the Carthusian monks had rotted in prison, and Fisher and More had resorted to using charcoal as pens, Jane had become so involved in her sister-in-law's affairs as to draw Henry's wrath upon herself.

18

Happy Families

The horses stamped impatiently as the last of the baggage was loaded into carts. It was late autumn; the days were getting shorter, the nights darker and the weather colder. For Jane, this was reminiscent of a journey she had made so many years ago when, as a young girl, she had left the safety of her parents' home for the excitement and allure of the royal court. Now, it was the court that she was leaving, and in ignominy. At least she was not facing detention behind the stone walls of the Tower, where the Carthusians, Fisher and More still languished in an agony of suspense until the axe and the knife ended their lives. In view of the king's temper, that in itself was a considerable relief.

Over the next few months, while Henry's justice overwhelmed others, Jane had the leisure to reflect on her own situation. Ultimately, everything had stemmed from the vulnerability of the Boleyns' position. Anne had to give Henry the heir he needed. It was as straightforward as that. A slight edginess within the family had been inevitable after Anne's miscarriage but, for a while, life appeared to continue as normal. The king had accepted his loss and pushed on with crushing the merest hint of opposition, and, with her contacts, Jane already knew, or would know, every last gruesome detail about his methods. However, the fact remained that everything depended on Anne's reproductive abilities. Anne's relationship with Henry had always been one of intense passion. So far, she had proved to be the love of his life, his 'sweetheart', his 'darling', his soulmate. Sheer physical and mental attraction, as the Boleyns appreciated, was the secret of Anne's grip over Henry and the reason for their financial gains as part of the extended royal family. But such a hold could prove a chimera. The court was brimming with attractive women, many of them younger than Anne. The danger was crystal clear: a man who had strayed from one wife might get into the habit and make it a speciality. Until she gave birth to a prince, Anne's position would never be totally secure. Jane, like the rest of the family, was only too aware of that basic fact. And, like them, she would help her sister-in-law if she could.

Suddenly that help became necessary. Henry flirted with another woman at court a few months after the miscarriage. We do not know her identity, but she certainly gave Anne cause for concern. Chapuys, ever eager to pick up on any gossip that might mean that Anne's influence was waning, was soon on the scent. The ambassador wrote to Charles of 'a young lady whom this king has been accustomed to serve', expressing particular hopes that this girl might succeed in destroying Anne for she was, he reported, sympathetic to Mary. He reported that the lady in question had sent a message to the princess, 'telling her to take good heart', since 'her tribulations will come to an end much sooner than she expected', and that 'should the opportunity occur', she would, she assured Mary, 'show herself her true friend and devoted servant'. From Chapuys's point of view, it could not have been more promising.

Anne's response was to try the direct approach; it had always worked before. She went straight to Henry, demanding that her rival be sent away immediately for not treating her 'with due respect in words or deeds'. This time, however, she managed only to infuriate her husband. Not prepared to be taken to task by his wife, the king 'went away in a great passion, complaining loudly of her importunity and vexatiousness'. It was at this point that Jane came into the picture. She and Anne were close enough for the queen immediately to turn to her, of all her ladies, for help. Caution required such sensitive discussion be kept within the family. Jane could be trusted. Together they plotted how best to deal with the interloper and they hatched a plan: Jane would pick a quarrel 'or otherwise' with her so that Henry, finding the fracas too tiresome and preferring a quiet life, would dismiss the girl from court. As Chapuys mentions that Jane 'joined a conspiracy' to that effect, the family machine was obviously involved too. Since this crisis had happened at the moment when Henry, with Cromwell in the vanguard, was dealing with such high-profile antagonists as More and Fisher, it was a courageous action on Jane's part. But she knew that her own fortunes were so inextricably bound to those of the Boleyns that the risk had to be taken.

Unfortunately, the plan backfired. It was Jane who was exiled, not Anne's rival. Henry's rage must have terrified her. He had changed. The truly beautiful young king, with his slender body and chivalric values, who had so entranced all who saw him, had long since vanished. His waist had thickened, his muscles were less toned, his hair was thinner, his good humour less reliable. It was no longer advisable to count on his laughing, as he once had when his standard bearer, Sir Andrew Flamock, 'having his belly full' broke wind, excusing the loud noise as merely complementing the sound of the king's hunting horn. The old prophesy, that he would be 'mild as a lamb' at the beginning of his reign, but 'more fierce than a lion' towards the end of it, seemed to be coming true. Unexpectedly, it was Jane who felt the full force of that ferocity. The result was that on that October day, Jane left court under a cloud. We do not know where she was sent, although Beaulieu is a possible destination. At that time, Henry was not using the palace for himself or his family, as the former princess was living with Elizabeth, and the king had never considered it a suitable venue for Katherine's enforced rustication from court. Although inconvenient, to be removed to Beaulieu was not too terrible a fate. The Boleyns had other residences, however, and it is very likely that Jane divided her time between them. To be banned from the court did not mean that she could not reside anywhere else in the capital. In any case, Jane hoped that, with luck, it would not be too long before Henry relented and she was allowed to return to the court itself.

However, no doubt to Chapuys' disappointment, although not, perhaps, to his surprise, Anne's rival sank into oblivion, for the queen quickly regained her husband's affections. 'The young lady who was lately in the king's favour is so no longer,' Chapuys reported to the emperor regretfully. As the Boleyns perceived, the relationship between Henry and Anne was volatile, which was probably what gave it its spice, so their blazing rows simply burnt themselves out. They were but the 'lovers' quarrels' about which the shrewd ambassador had already informed his master. With her sister-in-law as beloved as always, it is likely that it was not long before Jane was back in the royal bedchamber again. Indeed, her exile must have been short if she was to gain the intimate knowledge of what went on there that she undoubtedly possessed.

In the interim, an enforced absence did at least allow a chance for contemplation, since hers was not the only problem to beset the Boleyns over those months. So far, they had all pulled together, but cracks had started to appear in the Boleyn façade. Sometimes in the past they had colluded on matters as mundane as New Year's Gifts to the king. Playing safe, like Jane, Mary Carey once gave Henry a shirt with a black collar. In the very same year, her mother, Elizabeth, presented him with six shirt collars, three of gold and three of silver. The Boleyns were a team. Jane understood that, but Mary had forgotten it. In the despatch in which he announced Jane's exile, Chapuys gleefully told Charles that Mary Carey had also been sent from court. She was, he said, 'guilty of misconduct' and was pregnant. Widowed when William Carey died of the sweat, Mary, like Jane, had been with Anne through those endless years of waiting as Henry wriggled out of his union with Katherine. She had been there to share in Anne's glorious coronation, albeit in a place lower than Jane's. Now she shared Jane's disgrace, but there was a fundamental difference: while Jane's removal was due to loyalty to the family cause, Mary's was for baser reasons. She had fallen in love and secretly married William Stafford, a scion of the minor gentry. This would not do. She had failed in her duty. Semi-royal now, she could have been married off advantageously for the Boleyns. Thomas was furious; George was furious; Anne was incensed. Sister or not, Mary was cut off at once. Although joined only through marriage, Jane had proved herself a more dependable Boleyn than Anne's own flesh and blood, especially when trouble had loomed. In the face of Boleyn anger, there was no way in which Jane could have helped her former masque partner, even supposing she had wanted to. This was not her dispute. Mary needed to make her peace herself. That, of course, was easier said than done. In comparative poverty and at her wits' end, Mary did the only thing possible: she wrote to Cromwell, as, one day, would Jane. The tone of entreaty so apparent in their letters is remarkably similar.

Calling herself 'a poor banished creature', she begged for the minister's aid 'for the love that well I know you do bear to all my blood'. Acknowledging that she and Stafford had been 'hasty' and 'bold' in marrying without the royal consent, she accepted that they deserved 'high displeasure ... both of the king's highness and the queen's grace'. She had, she said, been unable to stop herself. 'Love overcame reason,' she confessed, 'for my part I saw so much honesty in him, that I loved him as well as he did me.' In a sentence that proved she appreciated only too well that family ambition might have produced a more suitable husband, she wrote that she 'could never have had one that should have loved' her more deeply, even though she 'might have had a greater man of birth and a higher'. Their devotion was such, she wrote, that 'I had rather beg my bread with him than be the greatest queen in Christendom.' And his feelings were 'in the same case with me; for I believe verily he would not forsake me to be a king'. She begged Cromwell to intercede with her mother and her father for their blessing, and to ask Norfolk and George 'to be good to us'. She dared not write to either directly, as 'they are so cruel against us'.

Above all, Mary knew that her sister, the woman who had replaced her in the king's bed, was totally implacable. The only way to move her was for Cromwell to approach the king and persuade him to intervene, presumably for old times' sake.

> And, good master secretary [she begged], sue for us to the king's highness, which ever was wont to take pity, to have pity on us; and that it will please his grace of his goodness to speak to the queen's grace for us; for, so far as I can perceive, her grace is so highly displeased with us both that, without the king be so good lord to us as to withdraw his rigour and sue for us, we are never like to recover her grace's favour: which is too heavy to bear.

Yes, Mary knew her sister through and through. We will never be privy to Cromwell's reply, or to what the Boleyns said to one another behind closed doors as they fumed over Mary's conduct, but she was not forgiven and brought back into the fold until after Anne's death.

Then, all was different: her children represented the future. For the moment, however, as Jane walked in the gardens or sat sewing in her comfortable exile while she waited for news from George or from friends at court, she can only have looked on Mary's fate and learnt from it. To cross the family was unwise even for those who believed themselves at its heart, like Mary, or for those who thought themselves at its head.

That was Norfolk, and he was another niggling worry for the Boleyns, something else for Jane to ponder on as winter set in. Premier duke he might be, head of the Howard clan he certainly was, but his wings had been clipped by the rise of his niece who, if anything, took after her wily great-grandfather, Geoffrey, in values and courage. In the early days, Norfolk had been a vital ally, especially when the family had worked together to destroy Wolsey. The cardinal was gone now, his corpse rotting in his grave at Leicester Abbey. Norfolk could never again be quite as useful and, as the years had passed, that fact had become plain, both to the Boleyns and to the duke himself.

Chapuys, who usually rubbed along reasonably well with Norfolk, was quick to report a growing rift between uncle and niece. 'I am informed on good authority', he told Charles, 'that the said lady [Anne] does not cease night or day to procure the disgrace of the duke of Norfolk, whether it be because he has spoken too freely of her or because Cromwell, desiring to lower the great ones, wishes to commence with him.' Never one to mince words, the queen could be acidly sharp when talking to her uncle, indulging in altercations which Jane, while in the queen's apartments, was likely to have witnessed. When Anne used 'shameful words' to him, in a way in which 'one would not address a dog', a humiliated Norfolk 'was compelled to quit the chamber'. Once outside, he was sufficiently incandescent to complain 'to one to whom he did not generally show good-will'. Momentarily careless, he let his polite façade drop far enough to utter 'reproaches' against Anne, and call her a '*grande putain* [a great strumpet]'. Rumours of the confrontation spread throughout the court remarkably quickly, as any gossip concerning the queen always did. Anne's high-handedness endeared her to no one.

As the months went by without Anne becoming pregnant, one previous action returned to haunt her. Anne had persuaded Henry to allow Norfolk's daughter, Mary, to marry the king's illegitimate son, the Duke of Richmond. 'The king's grace had never a penny for my lord of Richmond,' wrote Norfolk's estranged duchess to Cromwell, 'for Queen Anne got the marriage clear for my lord my husband, when she did favour my lord my husband.' Since the betrothal was arranged long before she became queen, Anne had probably consulted her own family before suggesting a policy which had seemed so beneficial. It was a clever move to reward Norfolk, despite his initial uncertainty of the value of the union to his house, binding the king's illegitimate son to the Howards and preventing a foreign match that could turn the boy into a rival. The wedding took place in the same month as Anne's coronation, so Jane may well have been one of the guests. But with no son from Anne, the one Henry did have, whether born out of wedlock or not, was the apple of his father's eye. As he was fourteen when they married, Richmond and Mary Howard were considered too young to consummate their union, but they would soon grow up. The day might come when Norfolk's grandson would sit on St Edward's Chair; perhaps the clever move was not quite so clever after all.

To turn Norfolk into an outright enemy could be short-sighted but, so far, it had not come to that. Not quite. Anne and George recognised that their religious ideas were far more radical than Norfolk's; they knew too that he was bound to be jealous, and probably wary, of Cromwell's influence, as most sensible people were. Then, as the entire court could not fail to be aware, the great duke had his own personal problems in the shape of his formidable wife, who refused to countenance his adulterous affair with Bess Holland. Although forcibly kept from court, the duchess was adept at causing scenes and creating friction, writing vituperative accounts of her tribulations to Cromwell. It was hardly surprising that Norfolk was not enamoured of women as forthright as his niece. Yet, as even Jane knew, the ambitious duke would never put himself at risk by opposing Anne, unless the king tired of her and she became vulnerable. For as long as she was adored by her husband, there was no imminent peril, but Norfolk and his arrogant son, the Earl of Surrey, a close friend of Richmond's, could prove dangerous foes if Henry's eyes ever alighted on another pretty woman and the queen produced no son.

Jane's enforced exile from court, if anything, gave her even greater leisure to think about these tensions. The king's favour would be regained in the end, it was simply a matter of patience, but rifts within the family would not be healed easily, and enemies made could not be unmade. Whether she heard from, or even visited, her father and mother over these months is unknown. If she did go to Beaulieu, it is entirely possible that she took the opportunity to make the journey to Great Hallingbury, which was not many miles distant, and walked through the gardens and the orchard or sat by Lady Morley's pond. Her infant nephew, another Henry, was likely to have been brought up in Jane's childhood home, so on any visit he would have been present as Jane talked to her sister-in-law, Grace, in those familiar rooms, surrounded by the tangible mementoes of her grandmother. Since her marriage to Lady Shelton's son, Jane's sister, Margaret Parker, had left the Morley household but she, too, may well have come home for the occasional visit, or written to her family about her new life and her own children. Jane remained childless herself, something else that no doubt preyed upon her mind. Time was running out. To be a barren wife, while not uncommon, was undesirable and, although physicians were aware that either partner could be the root cause of childlessness, most men tended to blame the woman, who was supposed to be too moist to retain her husband's seed. Anne was not unique in watching for her monthly 'courses'.

Then, out of the blue, William Foster, Jane's scholar at King's College, Cambridge, asked for her aid. With all that was going on within the family, this would be an added burden. Foster had become involved in a scramble for jobs, in particular one concerning the priory of Swaffham Bulbeck in Cambridgeshire. The story was complicated and, had Jane not had more pressing matters to contemplate, amusing. The small priory owned the nearby parish church with the right to appoint the parish priest and, when the post fell vacant, the prioress, Joan Spylman, who was conducting an illicit and long-standing affair with a friar, Father Bassam, nominated her lover, who would then be conveniently close. The scandal was notorious for miles around; the nuns all knew that Bassam had been 'naughty' with Joan. Despite her strenuous efforts on his behalf, however, the friar was more inclined towards moving on to higher places, in fact to a King's College parish in the gift of the Provost, Edward Foxe. Bassam persuaded Foxe to give him the King's College parish in exchange for Swaffham, but this in turn meant an exchange with a Fellow of King's who had already been promised it. Fortunately for Bassam, the Fellow accepted the swap, which should then have gone ahead, but disaster struck in the person of Dr Leigh, Cromwell's commissioner, who visited Swaffham Bulbeck as part of the general visitation of all the monasteries ordered by the king. Dr Leigh said that no exchange could occur while the status of monastic property was under review. When, a few months later, Parliament enacted that all foundations with an annual income of less than £200 should be closed, Swaffham Priory fell into that category and so lost its right to appoint the new clergyman for the local church. The Fellow who had agreed to the swap, therefore, realised that his chance of obtaining the Swaffham living was so slim that he surrendered it to William Foster. All Foster had to do was to work out a way to get it.

With his connection to Lady Rochford, the 'special patroness' of his studies, Foster thought he would be home and dry. His sponsor was not simply a noblewoman but a member of the foremost family in the land, linked by marriage to the king. He was confident that, with her aid, his benefice was in the bag. Surely she would approach the king and queen for him and, as his surroundings at Cambridge made all too evident, the royal couple could do whatever they wished, including bypassing the implications of the recent Act. Evidence of the monarch's wealth and might was all-encompassing. Whenever he prayed in King's College Chapel, he knelt beneath the great vaulted ceiling amidst glowing shafts of light through its breathtaking stained-glass windows. These had been superbly fashioned by the artistry of Henry's glaziers into ethereal depictions of the saints and the Virgin and the holy figures of the Bible. Foster knew that Italian craftsmen had virtually finished carving an intricate screen, a screen on which the initials of Anne and Henry were prominently displayed, sometimes intertwined as signs of their love, and with Anne's falcon badge, together with the bulls of the Boleyns, clearly visible to every Fellow.

In the event, it was not his reasoning but his timing that was at fault. Naturally, when he contacted her, Jane did her best. Duty implied obligations. She passed the letter on to Cromwell. He gave some help which Foster appreciated, but unfortunately his hands were tied. By then, so were Jane's. She was too busy struggling to preserve her own position to be of any use to Foster, who left Cambridge shortly afterwards, certainly by October 1536. He never did get the benefice of Swaffham, although there is every chance that he was the William Foster who became vicar of Billingshurst in Suffolk. If so, he did owe something to his 'special patroness' who had, at least, started him on the road to a career. She could take pride in that.

In any event, there was certainly plenty to occupy Jane in those months away from court, but, if there were underlying anxieties, there was good news as well. Although Jane had paid a high personal price for her devotion to the Boleyn cause, at least the mysterious woman, who had temporarily distracted the king and for whom Jane was banished, was gone. She disappears into the archives as swiftly as she surfaced. Then, even if Mary Carey had let them all down by marrying Stafford, and they were a little uneasy about Norfolk, the rest of the family were still united. George and Thomas never faltered in their allegiance to Anne. James was acting responsibly as Anne's chancellor and William Boleyn continued to live his quiet, blameless, celibate life without causing a moment's concern. Anne reigned supreme again. The family's domination was far from over.

19

The Final Flourish

With Anne safely back in the king's arms, the entire family breathed a collective sigh of relief. More and Fisher knelt before the block, the Carthusians took their last agonised breaths, their broken bodies testament to their courage, and Henry's critics were learning the bloody results of opposition. It was business as usual. For Jane, an end to her banishment was entirely possible at any time after Anne's resurgence, perhaps in the early months of 1535. Even if she was forced to stay away from court for a while longer, she was likely to be very well informed on what was going on. Her loyalty meant that she could not be ignored.

Nor, from Anne's point of view, could Katherine and Mary. As far as the queen and the rest of the Boleyn family were concerned, the two women had to be brought into line. They were still refusing to accept their changed circumstances. Katherine would not relinquish her title of Queen and, while Mary was prepared to acknowledge Elizabeth as her father's daughter in the same way that Richmond was his son, she believed that the only true princess was herself. She was legitimate, they were not. For her, it was simple; for the Boleyns, it was exasperating. In fact, it was worse than that, for Elizabeth's position had to be protected: she was, after all, a Boleyn as well as the current heir to the throne. Thus, the poor treatment of Katherine and Mary continued unabated. Kept apart from each other, mother and daughter could only correspond and even that was difficult. The solicitous Chapuys did his best for them both, constantly negotiating with Cromwell on their behalf and bravely taking on the king himself to try to improve their living conditions. Their only reliable link with the outside world, he was a true and constant friend in what for them was a living nightmare.

The ambassador was convinced that somehow Anne would organise their deaths. Alarmed, he disclosed to Charles that Anne had said that if the king was out of the country at a meeting with Francis I, and she was left in charge, she would 'certainly cause the death of the said princess [Mary] by the sword or otherwise'. When George sensibly counselled that this might 'offend the king', Anne's response was of a type that a rueful Mary Stafford would have recognised. She 'cared not', she said, 'even if she were to be burnt or flayed alive in consequence'. Anne could be rash, as Jane had learnt over the years, but she was not that rash, nor, most definitely were the family.

To act against Katherine and Mary legally, though, was an altogether different proposition, and there were plenty of rumours circulating about that possibility. Whether at court or not, Jane would have heard them. Again, Chapuys feared for the two women's lives. According to him, Anne asserted that they should be 'punished as traitresses according to the statutes'. Others had paid the due price for their disobedience, she said; so should they. She was 'incessantly crying after the king' to act decisively because they 'deserved death more than those' already executed, for 'they were the cause of it all'. She tried another tack as well, he reported: she bribed an unnamed man to pretend to have a revelation that she would not be able to conceive while Mary and Katherine were alive. Chapuys was so desperately troubled that, via wonderfully far-fetched cloak-and-dagger schemes, he tried to plot an escape route for Mary, after which she would live happily ever afterwards in her cousin's dominions until it was time for her to become queen in her own right. That is, if Katherine did not become pregnant in the interim – despite the fact that she was post-menopausal, the ambassador had not quite given up the pipe-dream that Henry might take back Katherine who would then produce the longed-for son.

As it was, now that Anne was back in favour, mother and daughter were kept in relatively close confinement. At least the Boleyns could rely on Lady Shelton to keep a sharp eye on the former princess. With Mary stubbornly intransigent and so frequently ill, her task was far from easy. At the slightest whisper of indisposition,

Katherine always begged to care for her daughter. There would be 'no need of any other person but myself to nurse her', she entreated the faithful Chapuys, her 'especial friend', to tell the king; 'I will put her in my own bed where I sleep, and will watch her when needed.' That, of course, would never be allowed. Anne and Henry were convinced that Katherine would strengthen Mary's current obstinacy. 'Although sons and daughters were bound to some obedience towards their mothers,' an irate Henry told Chapuys, 'their chief duty was to their fathers.'

All health matters were, therefore, left to Lady Shelton, although the king's most trusted physician, Dr William Butts, was sent to check on the princess when her condition deteriorated. Illegitimate she might be in Henry's eyes, she was his daughter nonetheless. Deep down, every Boleyn was aware of that fact, inconvenient though it was. The king informed Chapuys that Mary could not be in better hands than those of Anne's aunt, as he said Lady Shelton was 'an expert lady even in such female complaints'. Mary was lucky to have her, he implied. So were the Boleyns. Anne Shelton could not bring herself to be as disrespectful or unkind to Mary as they had sometimes demanded, but she could be trusted to do her job efficiently. It required her to do more than pander to Mary's complaints. When a letter from Mary to Sir Nicholas Carew, a courtier who was very much her adherent, reached him unchecked despite her vigilance, Lady Shelton questioned her charge thoroughly on how it had been achieved and on who had acted as courier. She revealed all she had discovered, including the contents of the reply from Carew's wife, directly to Henry. The Boleyns were indeed fortunate to have the capable Lady Shelton in post. The family were pulling together again.

For Anne, George and Thomas, that was equally the case in religion. It seemed to Chapuys that they were set on destroying his Church and infecting the king with their wicked radicalism. They, of course, saw it differently: they were helping to bring the true message of the gospel and ending centuries of superstition. Anne's status and place in Henry's heart made this more possible. She continued to enjoy reformist literature, which George and others imported from France, and her influence spread out from the court as her bishops and clergymen were appointed to sees and parishes across the land. She took a keen personal interest in their preferments and in the welfare of her scholars. When a Dr Edward Crome proved tardy in taking up a benefice that she had obtained for him, she wrote to chide him for his delay and commanded him to leave immediately. She considered, she said, that 'the furtherance of virtue, truth and godly doctrine will be not a little increased, and right much the better advanced, by his better relief and residence there'. Education, too, was central to promoting the true gospel. She wrote imperiously to the Abbot of Whitby who had recalled one of her students, John Eldmer, from university in Cambridge, and had 'charged him with certain offices, to the great disturbance of his studies'. That she would not permit. Eldmer was to learn, not perform routine tasks in the monastery. 'We, therefore, desire you will allow him to return to the University, with sufficient maintenance to pursue his studies,' she instructed the chastened abbot. And Eldmer was only one of the queen's scholars. Whatever she really believed about her husband and sister-in-law's avant-garde religious views, Jane could empathise completely with the furtherance of education. Despite not obtaining the living at Swaffham, her own scholar, William Foster, had reason to be grateful to her, although she would never have been able to give him help on Anne's lavish scale.

Brought up to value good works as a holy duty, Jane also agreed with Anne's desire to help the poor. Many hours had already been spent sewing shirts for the destitute while Jane was in Anne's privy chamber. There were stories of huge sums being distributed to the needy on the queen's orders, individual cases of special hardship investigated and assistance given, and of Anne's personal intervention when she thought it necessary. Her final summer progress with the king gave her several opportunities for largesse. Of course, she could well afford it. In one year alone, George Taylor, her receiver-general, accounted for an income of over £6,000 and Anne was never personally short of assets. As late as February 1535, she was busily helping herself to some of Katherine's possessions left at Baynard's Castle. Amongst the items she appropriated then was 'a horn cup with a cover, garnished with antique works, with foot and knot of ivory', a coffer covered in crimson velvet, and a useful set of wooden trenchers. She saw no incongruity between maintaining the style expected of a queen and charitable works. Yet Anne wanted more than random charity, she wanted proper schemes for poor relief. This explains her delight when it was decided to look into the ways in which the monasteries were run: when some were closed, the money gained by the crown could be used for education and organised forms of aid. Such schemes would be in line with her own convictions. Henry and Cromwell, she felt sure, were bound to agree wholeheartedly.

What Jane knew from family tales or reminiscences was the extent to which this was part of the Boleyn inheritance. Although Anne's grandfather, Sir William, had left most of his wealth to his relatives, he was mindful of his obligations both to the Church and to the poor. Norwich Cathedral, where he wanted to be buried next to his mother, received £20 and each monk 20 marks, while the parish church at Blickling was the richer for four candlesticks and £20 pounds. It even gained an extra 20 marks that Sir William threw in because he had forgotten to pay his tithes. Whenever Jane prayed in that church, she saw those candlesticks. William's tithes might have slipped his mind, the people of his village did not. Every householder in Blickling was given the princely sum of £5 and his own household was to be kept in place, and therefore paid, for six months after his death. No one would be abandoned. It was a generous and unselfish gesture.

Sir William was merely following in the footsteps of his own father, Sir Geoffrey Boleyn, and it was his genes too which Anne and George had inherited. Everything that Anne intended to do conformed to the blueprint her great-grandfather had provided in his will. In many ways a conventional Catholic, Geoffrey wanted masses said for his own soul, for that of his wife and for those who were buried alongside him in the same church. He asked for burial in the chapel of St John in the Church of St Lawrence Jewry, ironically the church in which the young Thomas More had spent hours in prayer during his formative years. Geoffrey left money for that church as well as for the one at Blickling. But he went radically further. Like Anne, he believed in the value of preaching. He wanted

a 'convenable, honest, virtuous priest of good governance and conversation' to be employed for twenty years after his death to say the
necessary masses four times a year. In addition the priest could
engage in learning or teaching or – and Anne would have thoroughly
approved of this – he could 'labour in preaching the word of God'
on the highways and byways of the land. Even at the services he
gave for Geoffrey's soul, he was to preach a sermon. Like Anne,
Geoffrey was way ahead of his time.

Then, again just like her, he had cared about the disadvantaged
and those who really were at the bottom of the heap: he had left
sufficient money for food to be given to the prisoners in London
four times a year. On the anniversary of his death, every four prisoners were to share dishes of beef and mutton, or two types of fish,
should it be a fish day, with a pennyworth of bread, the whole meal
to be washed down with a pottle of ale. In addition, he bequeathed
money for five years to be spent on the general welfare of prisoners,
both in London and throughout the country. Leper houses received
financial help too, and so did the mendicant friars in London, the
'poor, sick and feeble' in hospitals in the city, and the women in the
almshouses within the hospital of St Katherine beside the Tower.
Jane was involved with the hospitals Geoffrey aided, as one of them,
the house of Our Lady of Bethlehem (or Bedlam), was in George's
keeping. Geoffrey did not stop there. He went on to leave funds for
poor householders in various named parishes, including Blickling,
and for those reduced to poverty through misfortunes of 'fire' or
'water'.

Education, too, mattered as passionately to Geoffrey as it did to
Anne. He had his own scholar, Master Thomas Randolf, to whom
he left 10 marks a year for ten years, providing he prayed for his
soul, worked at his studies in divinity in Oxford or Cambridge, or
preached. For Anne and Jane, supporting scholars was genuinely in
the family. Jane could feel a Boleyn in that also. Proving that he
appreciated how impoverished junior clergymen could be, Geoffrey
allowed 10 marks to the vicar of Fulbourn, Geoffrey Bishop. Anne's
great-grandfather understood how his world worked: he knew that
the best stipends and profits were reserved for those in the higher
echelons of the Church. Finally, if there was anything left of his vast

fortune after his debts had been settled and the personal bequests to members of his family had been given, Geoffrey Boleyn ordered that the residue of his estate should be used for the relief of the poor, setting up schools for children, arranging the marriages of poor maidens, and in 'other works and deeds of mercy and piety' according to the discretion of his executors.

As Jane watched Anne poring over plans to alleviate poverty and put her religious ideals into practice, she knew that the same ideals were in her blood too. Anne could carry on where Geoffrey had stopped. In her private apartments there was always music, song, dance and fun, all taking place in the most splendid surroundings that her royal husband could provide, but Jane appreciated that there was more to Anne than mere hedonism. And, now that the storm caused by Henry's dalliance had passed, life continued much as before. Jane was secure because Anne was secure.

Chapuys dutifully conveyed to Charles the bad news that Anne was back in favour. If anything, she seemed more powerful than ever. Even before the executions of More and Fisher, she laid on amusements and banquets to divert Henry, a task that 'she so well managed' that 'the King loves his concubine [Anne] now more than he ever did'. Mary's fears for her life may have become 'considerably increased' but there were fewer sleepless nights for the Boleyns. Anne felt sure enough of Henry's feelings to tell him how grateful he should be to her for rescuing him 'from a state of sin'. It was through her, she told him, that he had become 'the richest Prince that ever was in England' and that 'he would not have reformed the Church, to his own great profit and that of all the people' without her encouragement. Her affection was reciprocated. When Henry watched a play which portrayed him cutting off the heads of the clergy, he thought it so funny that he told Anne she should see it too.

Whenever she could, Anne went to see her daughter, Elizabeth, who was a toddler by now. There was talk of a marriage for the little girl with the Duke of Angoulême, one of Francis's sons, a matter for George to raise when at the French court. For the Francophile Anne, this was a delightful prospect. Keen for visiting French ambassadors to report back on little Elizabeth's perfections, she insisted they went to see her. The diplomats were kept well away from

Mary, of course, even though she was still housed in her half-sister's establishment.

Jane had lived amongst the Boleyns long enough to anticipate that, while the ultimate decisions were Henry's, whatever was being planned for Elizabeth would be of considerable interest to Anne. Her hands-on approach to policy was not new to her family. It was her way; it always had been. Years earlier, Wolsey had been surprised that Anne was present, and became involved, when he discussed matters of state with the king. Henry had accepted that she always wanted to be kept up to date on every development. In one of his own letters to her in those early, heady days of their romance, the king told her that George would give her all the latest information when he saw her. Thus, when George returned from a mission to France, therefore, it was natural for him to rush straight to his sister's side to let her know in minute detail exactly what had been said, even before reporting to Henry. While in the queen's privy chamber, Jane was used to seeing her husband and her sister-in-law totally engrossed in private conversation. This was quite usual; Anne had no reason to think it could ever be remembered and used against her.

So, as Anne set off with Henry on the summer progress, blissfully unaware that she would be in her grave by the time he embarked on such a journey again, she could feel satisfied that not only had she placated her husband, but she was doing all she could to uphold and, indeed, propagate her beliefs, living up to family traditions. If Jane was back at court by then, she would have joined Anne and the king. The trip, which lasted much of the summer and autumn, included parts of Oxfordshire, Hampshire, Gloucestershire and Wiltshire, the couple staying with selected courtiers who would take pride in receiving and entertaining their monarch. They spent four nights or so with Lord Sandys, in his luxuriously rebuilt and refurbished home, The Vyne, with its wonderful carved oak panels and sumptuously appointed royal apartments. Then there was Sir John Seymour, whose able son, Edward, served Henry while his daughter, Jane, was one of Anne's ladies. Sir John courteously welcomed his king and queen for several days at his seat of Wolf Hall near Marlborough. The weeks passed pleasantly enough. Henry and Anne spent their time hunting, hawking, meeting the great and the good, and being seen by the general population. Although a planned visit to Bristol was cancelled due to an outbreak of plague, all else went well. Anne shone. If she wanted to, she could be all graciousness and charm and, on this progress, she wanted to.

A sudden demonstration in Mary's support was the only cloud on the otherwise clear horizon. While Anne and Henry were on the progress, a group of women gathered at Greenwich, where Mary was staying, to catch a glimpse of her. As she left the palace, the women shouted out to her that 'she was Princess, notwithstanding all that had been done'. They were quickly dispersed, of course, and their leaders imprisoned in the Tower, conveniently a short river boat-ride away. Although the episode was a petty irritation to Anne and Henry, it was of little importance. The document recording the demonstration is intriguing, however, as there is a marginal handwritten note which reads 'Millor de Rochesfort et millord de Guillaume', which suggests that one of the women involved and ferociously punished was Jane. To break the habit of a lifetime and speak out, particularly against her husband's family, would be most uncharacteristic of her. Doubtless, she heard about the brouhaha but she knew her destiny lay with the Boleyns; to jump ship at this stage would have been folly. Only once in her life would Jane commit an act that was naive and foolish in the extreme. It was not this. She was much more likely to have been at court than protesting for what seemed a lost cause. In any case, if Henry and Anne were lovers again, the future most definitely lay with Anne and not with Mary.

By the end of the year, Anne's practised smile was genuine. She was proudly and very clearly pregnant. The family had endured a traumatic time. Jane had been unexpectedly exiled from the court which she had grown to regard as her home; Mary Stafford remained disgraced; Anne herself had come to realise that she could never take Henry's devotion for granted. Even after Chapuys' mysterious lady vanished into obscurity once more, Henry cast lovesick eyes on one of Lady Shelton's daughters, a pretty girl whom the court knew as Madge. Then there had been the odd scene, played out in public, when Anne burst out in hysterical laughter because she saw her husband become so wrapped up in talking to one young woman that he quite forgot that he had set off to talk to someone else altogether.

But, as the child grew in Anne's womb, so much that had happened paled into insignificance. It was of no consequence. The Boleyns were flourishing once more. Or were they?

20

The Wheel Turns

Jane could pinpoint the very day on which her world collapsed. It was Tuesday, 2 May 1536, the day after the May Day Jousts. When the end of the Boleyn ascendancy came, it came with terrifying speed and a bewildering inevitability. Yet the year had begun well enough. Anne's pregnancy continued to advance and the future was promising. The birth of a son would ensure that the family lifestyle continued unabated. Jane would wear her special stockings to masques, she would eat from the engraved silver bowls and eventually breathe her last in that wonderful Rochford bed with its embroidered knots and yellow counterpane. But it was not to be.

Had she thought back, Jane might have seen the demise of Katherine as the moment when it all started to fall apart. Katherine's illness and death, an event that Anne and George had always yearned for, actually gave the former queen her final victory over the woman who had supplanted her in her husband's affections and on her throne. Katherine had been ill, on and off, for some time. Chapuys constantly begged Cromwell to persuade Henry to treat her more kindly and respectfully, and to move her to what he thought would be a healthier environment. He was never happy with her living at Kimbolton in Cambridgeshire, a sprawling medieval castle that was bound to be damp and cold in winter. But Henry, encouraged by Anne, would only agree to improve Katherine's situation if she would acknowledge the invalidity of her marriage and the legality of his second one. Impasse.

It is not known whether Jane was aware of the full details of the former queen's last days, although her years at the centre of power meant that she heard of Katherine's frequent bouts of sickness. It is Chapuys who leaves us the best account of precisely what happened. On learning from her doctor on 29 December that Katherine was seriously unwell, Chapuys asked permission to visit her. Apparently, she had been unable to either eat or drink anything 'that would remain in her stomach' for two days, and could not sleep for more than an hour and a half as the pain in her stomach was so bad. She was also extremely weak. Chapuys mounted his horse the moment he received royal consent to see her, arriving at Kimbolton on Sunday, 2 January 1536. Much to the consternation of her custodian Sir Edmund Bedingfield, the ambassador spoke to Katherine comfortingly in her native language, although, as Bedingfield, was quick to point out in his report to Cromwell, 'Mr Vaughan, who was present, can declare to your Mastership the effect of their communication.' Katherine was delighted to see Chapuys, saying that should she die while he was there, it would be a 'consolation' to her to take her last breath in his arms 'and not all alone like a beast'.

The ambassador sat with Katherine on each day that he spent at the castle, talking with her about the emperor, about her own woes and those of her daughter, her fears for the country, and her will. Gradually, she seemed to improve. She kept a little food down and felt so much better that she advised Chapuys to leave. If he stayed too long, he might not be allowed to come again. Only after consulting her doctor, who 'gave full hope of her recovery' and promised to recall him should she suffer a relapse, did the devoted man set off for London.

The doctor's assessment of Katherine's condition was wrong. Within three days of Chapuys' departure, she was dead. It was true that at first she appeared stronger, once managing to comb and dress her hair herself. As night approached on Thursday, however, she rapidly grew weaker. Realising that the end could be near, she kept asking what time it was as she wanted to hear mass and receive the sacrament for the final time. Even *in extremis* and exhorted by her confessor, the Bishop of Llandaff, who was willing to conduct the mass straightaway, she would not allow the rules to be broken and waited until dawn, the earliest time that she believed scripture permitted, for her request to be granted. She 'took the Holy Sacrament with the greatest fervour and devotion that could be imagined', and prayed that the king would soon 'follow the right path' and gain 'good counsel'. Once she had been given extreme unction, Katherine asked her doctor to take down her last requests. She wanted to be buried in a convent of the Observant Friars, she wanted to leave little legacies for the staff who had so loyally tended her, and she wanted Mary to have her furs and a necklace with a cross on it, which she had brought with her from Spain when she had arrived on foreign shores as a young bride almost forty years ago. She died at about 2 p.m. on Friday, 7 January. It was Cromwell who sent the news to a distressed Chapuys.

Jane may not have known exactly what had happened at Kimbolton as Katherine slipped away, but she did know how the news of Katherine's death was greeted at court. Everyone knew that. 'Thank God, we are now free from any fear of war' was a relieved Henry's immediate reaction. While Katherine's relatives abroad donned sombre black as funeral obsequies were performed in the imperial dominions, he decked himself out in yellow, a jaunty white feather in his cap. Little Elizabeth joined her parents at church that Sunday, her way heralded by trumpets and 'great display'. Henry carried his daughter proudly in his arms, showing her off to all and sundry. There was dancing and jousting in the Greenwich tiltyards. Any outward semblance of grief was markedly absent. Those who lamented Katherine's demise did so in private. Jane had known the former queen for much of her own life but she, too, remained silent.

With Katherine gone, Mary was very much alone. Chapuys, stalwart as her protector, was convinced that Thomas and George, pleased to see the decease of one antagonist, were now calculating the further benefits that would accrue if Mary died too. Maybe they were. Anne tried a different tack. She proposed an olive branch to her stepdaughter, offering to become a replacement mother if Mary would only accede to Henry's demands. She even added the inducement that Mary would be excused the more subservient duties of court service, such as carrying her train, should she be sensible and give way. Unsurprisingly, the bereaved girl failed to respond to her overtures.

So, superficially, nothing had changed in that quarter, and court life in general continued much as usual. Anne should have felt more secure than ever. With Katherine dead, there was no one else who could claim to be queen, a comforting thought for the entire family. Yet Chapuys informed the emperor that while Anne was jubilant, she was also anxious 'lest she herself might be brought to the same end'. Anne understood only too well that the spectre of a forcible return to Katherine had been lifted from her husband. Should anything befall her, he would be free to dip his toe into the waters of matrimony for a third time, and enjoy a union unblighted by controversy or scandal. And Henry, who at one time would never have so much as glanced at another woman, had strayed twice in recent months, once with her own cousin. Still, providing she gave birth to the longed-for son, her position would be impregnable. No breath of criticism, no hint of disrespect, would be allowed to touch the mother of the next Prince of Wales, the prospective king. With a little prince slumbering in his cradle, any future affairs Henry might choose to wallow in would be conducted with the utmost discretion. It was not a situation that Anne would relish, but it might be tolerable.

So she listened to music in her chambers, some performed by the talented young Mark Smeaton, conversed with her ladies, exchanged pleasantries and, occasionally, her characteristically risqué brand of repartee with the gentlemen who drifted in and out of her apartments. In quieter periods, Anne sewed those shirts for the poor, she read, she planned what could be done with the proceeds of the monasteries Cromwell was so diligently closing. And she waited, as did every Boleyn, for her baby to be born.

Henry did the same. Or almost. His wife was quite right to be anxious: he had indeed spotted someone else, but she was proving as elusive as Anne had been. He was hopeful, however. After all, persistence had paid off with the reluctant Anne, and it might do so again. Time would tell. In the meantime, there was dancing, a spot of hunting and perhaps, while in the masculine world of his own privy chamber, playing chess with the ivory set he had purloined from Baynard's Castle a short while before. Most of all he must rest a little, for he had suffered a terrible accident: he had fallen from his horse, a huge one able to support his increasing weight, and had gone for two hours 'without speaking'. It was a miracle he was not killed, wrote Chapuys, half wistfully. And there was a funeral to arrange.

Bedingfield dared do nothing without the king's express command and there was one point upon which Henry was adamant: Katherine would not be interred as a queen. Even Anne, with her general misgivings about the current situation, but happy to see Henry cuddling Elizabeth, could not quarrel with that. Nevertheless, Henry was determined that Katherine would be given the reverence due to a princess of Spain and the widow of the Prince of Wales. Established protocol was to be followed to the letter. Katherine's embalmed body lay in state in her private apartments and in the chapel until her coffin was taken on the two-day journey to Peterborough Cathedral where her tomb was waiting. Since the king had closed down the houses of the Observant Friars, Katherine's request for burial amongst them could not be granted. The solemn cavalcade to the cathedral was impressive, however. The wagon on which her corpse lay was draped in black velvet with a frieze of cloth of gold, and was pulled by six horses covered in black. Priests, servants, gentlemen and mourners accompanied the late queen. Four heralds walked in the procession, each carrying a crimson banner, two with Katherine's arms emblazoned upon them, one with the arms of England and one that combined the arms of England and Spain.

Chapuys, invited to attend and even offered a gift of black cloth, politely refused. He did not wish to be present at what he saw as a shabby occasion which belittled the woman he had always regarded as the true queen. He remained convinced that she had been poisoned, presumably by Anne. When her body was opened for the embalming process, he said, the chandler who performed the operation found that Katherine's organs were all sound but with one exception: her heart was totally black and had 'something black and round' clinging inside it. Despite the ambassador's suspicions and his contemptuous dismissal of the whole affair, the funeral ceremonies were conducted as tradition demanded. Katherine's friend, the Dowager Lady Willoughby, who had managed to sneak in to see her just before she died, was one of the chief mourners, who also included the Countess of Worcester and the Countess of Surrey. Francis Brandon, the daughter of the Duke of Suffolk and the French queen, was there too, creating a royal link. Inside the Abbey Katherine's motto, 'Humble and Loyal', was picked out in gold letters near where her body lay, and four bishops stood ready to officiate at the requiem masses. Finally, she was laid to rest close to the high altar, where she remains to this day. Chapuys was correct: she was not buried as a queen, but she was treated with dignity and some pomp. In this area at least, Henry did not shirk his responsibilities to the woman he persistently regarded as Arthur's wife, but not his own.

It was Henry's current wife who was then to become the centre of a catastrophe. On the same day that her predecessor was buried in Peterborough, Anne miscarried. Worse, the child had the appearance of being a boy. Anne's desperate excuses, blaming Norfolk for telling her too abruptly of the king's fall, and her anguish at his infatuation with one of her own maids, made no impression on her angry husband. 'I see that God will not give me male children,' he spat. To make matters worse, instead of consoling her, he left a distraught Anne, exhausted from the physical as well as psychological effects of her ordeal, with devastating parting words. 'When you are up I will come and speak with you,' he said dismissively. They were parting words indeed, for she remained at Greenwich recovering while he returned to London to spend days in 'festival and rejoicing'. This was a man who, in happier times, could hardly bear to be in a different room from his beloved, let alone in a different palace. He had been more sympathetic to her when her favourite dog had died. Henry, hauntingly accustomed to stillbirths and miscarriages, was treading familiar ground and doing so in a familiar way. No wonder the Boleyns were distressed.

One of the most distressed was probably Jane, for she was privy to a secret. Anne's salvation, and that of the Boleyns, depended upon her enticing Henry back into her bed and away from his latest fancy.

As soon as she had regained her strength, she simply had to become pregnant once more. But, as the queen had once confided to Jane, that was not as straightforward as it might seem. All England assumed that the larger-than-life king was virility epitomised. His wife knew otherwise. In fact, there were times when he found it difficult to perform at all, his sexual prowess highly erratic. An incredulous Jane passed on the news to her own husband, little realising that the day would come when possessing such intimate knowledge would help to seal George's fate.

By now, Jane, like Thomas and George, was unhappily conscious that Henry's new favourite was more than a passing fling. It was serious. The woman was Jane Seymour, daughter of Sir John, who had welcomed Anne and Henry to Wolf Hall on the royal progress the previous summer. Her two brothers, Edward and Thomas, were ambitious and, in Edward's case at least, disturbingly able. That was an additional cause for anxiety. Mercifully, Jane Seymour lacked Anne's intelligence and perspicacity. However, with her brothers behind her and backed, as she was soon to be, by members of the court who had tired of Boleyn dominance, arrogance and advanced religious views, the whole situation quickly developed into a crisis for the Boleyns. They could even glimpse a replication of the family machine approach that had so assisted Anne. The shrewd Seymours and their supporters had a clear blueprint already mapped out for them of how to succeed in supplanting one wife for another, if they wanted to use it. And indeed they did.

Just like Anne before her, Jane Seymour refused to become the king's mistress but, unlike the vivacious Anne, she did so sweetly. Sweetness was her trademark. Probably even the Boleyns did not know exactly when Henry became besotted with the woman who was such a contrast to Anne, but, from the reports of the vigilant Chapuys, she was undoubtedly on the scene by February, just after the disappointment of the queen's latest miscarriage. And, as the weeks passed, Henry became more and more infatuated. Jane Seymour behaved perfectly, not putting a foot wrong. When Henry sent her a tempting present of a purse filled with sovereigns together with a letter, she would accept neither. She kissed Henry's missive and gave it back to the messenger, asking him to remind the king that she was 'a well-born damsel, the daughter of good and humble parents without blame or reproach of any kind'. Nothing, she protested, mattered as much to her as her honour and 'on no account would she lose it even if she were to die a thousand deaths'. Instead of giving her money at that time, she asked that Henry would save it until God sent her an 'advantageous marriage'. Such modesty was music to Henry's ears, so different, yet so similar, to Anne's approach almost a decade ago. To find out that the king was putting pen to paper again compounded the Boleyns' despair.

And for them, as the Marchioness of Exeter cheerfully informed Chapuys, matters were going from bad to worse. Henry was so touched by Mistress Seymour's response to his note and the gift that he comfortingly assured her that he would speak to her only in the presence of her relatives He would be scrupulous. To make such discourse easier, he proposed that their meeting place should be the room just requisitioned from Cromwell that he had assigned to Edward Seymour and his wife, and which happened to have private access. Naturally, the carefully tutored young lady regretfully declined this too. And, equally naturally, Henry admired her virtue still more.

Alarm bells were ringing for Anne and the Boleyn family, yet it was also very difficult for any of them to find consistency or coherence in Henry's behaviour. Chapuys jubilantly told Charles that the king had not spoken to Anne for weeks even before the miscarriage. He felt that he could see light at the end of the tunnel in the form of Anne's removal. But it did not occur. She was still in position in April. The family land portfolio was increased, too, when Anne was given grants of land, as were Thomas and George. Perhaps the storm was subsiding again; Henry always had been fickle. Plans were made for the queen to be at his side on a forthcoming trip to Calais and, most significantly, Chapuys was inveigled into publicly acknowledging her. Jane knew just how much that precious moment meant to her husband and his sister. On a visit to Greenwich to discuss foreign policy issues, now so much easier with Katherine out of the equation, Chapuys agreed to go into the chapel. Anne was there already. George escorted him and watched the ambassador's encounter with his sister. Anticipating an acrimonious confrontation, many courtiers flocked to the scene to see 'what sort of mien' queen and ambassador would adopt. If hoping for fireworks, they were disappointed. Carefully manoeuvred so that he was behind the door as Anne emerged, the two came face to face as she returned the 'reverence' Chapuys made to her. Sensibly, she was at her most gracious, 'affable and courteous' to the man who frequently called her 'the Concubine' in his many despatches to the emperor.

But just when Jane might begin to hope that Anne would weather the current uncertainty, George missed out on an honour that would once have been unquestionably his. When a vacancy arose for a new Knight of the Garter, George was a clear contender. He could have joined his father, a member of that august order for more than ten years. George's rival, Sir Nicholas Carew, was currently in the Seymour camp. The king allowed Carew to be elected, Anne's influence notwithstanding. She did not have 'sufficient credit to get her own brother knighted', reported Chapuys with obvious satisfaction.

It was a body blow, all the more damaging because it was so blatant. And it was with this snub to brazen out that the Boleyns took their places for the traditional May Day Jousts at Greenwich. As both Anne and the king watched the proceedings, George, still a keen sportsman, faced Henry Norris on the field. It was all good-humoured and ostensibly quite normal. What was not normal was the peculiar behaviour of the king. To everyone's surprise, including Anne's, he left the jousts abruptly to travel to Wolsey's old palace of York Place in London. Spurning his barge, he rode back, having ordered Norris and a mere handful of attendants to accompany him. Anne and George were left behind at Greenwich, unable to make sense of the king's conduct but, presumably after a hurried con-ference between them, George rushed to London in desperate pursuit of his brother-in-law to try to find out what was happening.

Blissful ignorance was not to last. On the following day, 2 May 1536, brother and sister were taken, separately, to the Tower. Accom-panied by Norfolk, Anne was rowed in full daylight, a stark parody of her triumphant entry into the city for her coronation. Then, the banks had been lined with spectators agog to catch a glimpse of their new queen; now, anyone by the side of the river would have seen a sight that was barely credible as she was moved from palace to prison. Anne and George's nightmare was about to begin. So was Jane's. And the origins of her own posthumous vilification started to take shape.

21

The Edge of the Precipice

News of Anne's disgrace spread like wildfire, as did the rumours. Chapuys, in his report to the no doubt astonished emperor, asserted that her imprisonment was 'by the judgment of God'. He managed to find out immediately who was taken although the details of individual offences were still hazy. The 'Concubine' was incarcerated for adultery 'with a player on the spinet of her chamber', he said. Norris was arrested too, 'for not having revealed the matter', and so was George Rochford, but even the sharp Chapuys could not work out what George was supposed to have done. Roland Bulkeley, rushing the news to his brother Richard, the Chamberlain of North Wales, threw in additional victims for good measure: Thomas Boleyn, 'one of the king's privy chamber, and sundry ladies' were also captured, he wrote, all with a treason charge hanging over them, but he assessed Norris's crime more correctly as having 'a do with the Queen'. The Bishop of Faenza was convinced that Anne's mother was another detainee.

In fact, these tendencies towards exaggeration were not that far from the truth. Thomas and his wife escaped detention but the existence of a complete list of the grants accumulated by Thomas and George, which was compiled after 3 March 1536, suggests that George's father had every reason to feel threatened. The sheer speed of the arrests was staggering. Mark Smeaton was actually the first behind the walls of the Tower, escorted there on May Day, followed by Henry Norris at dawn on the following day, then Anne, and then Jane's husband a few hours afterwards. But it did not stop there. Two days later, the bewildered prisoners were joined by Sir Francis Weston and Sir William Brereton and, on Monday, 8 May, by Sir

Richard Page and Anne's early love, Sir Thomas Wyatt. It appeared that no one was safe. The question on many a lip during those tumultuous days was surely who would be next?

The investigation into the queen's 'incontinent living' was entrusted to Thomas Cromwell who set about his task with assiduous thoroughness and his usual lack of sentiment. He painstakingly examined 'certain persons of the privy chamber and others of her side', which in fact meant anyone connected to Anne, to find out exactly what had been going on. One of those questioned was Jane. She was in a unique, if somewhat unfortunate, position for she was the individual most intimately linked to both brother and sister and with freedom of access into the queen's most private apartments. If anyone had known what went on between Anne and George, and between Anne and those gentlemen who flocked to her chamber, it would be Jane.

When she was ushered into Cromwell's presence, therefore, she had every reason to be frightened. Her previous experience of rustication from court, the only time so far that she had felt the effects of Henry's wrath personally, was nothing compared to this. As a noblewoman, she knew that she would not face torture. Although this was a reassuring thought, Henry had just proved that imprisoning his wife, a crowned queen and his 'own sweetheart', left him completely unmoved, and Elizabeth Barton's gender had provided no protection against the death penalty. If Cromwell discovered that she had any knowledge that she should have divulged, then she was in the worst trouble of her life. Jane's peril was very, very real. And then, should she evade an unwelcome sojourn in the Tower, there was her financial status to consider. If George was convicted of treason, all their possessions were subject to confiscation. George would be dead, she would be penniless, with only her jointure to rely upon, and the lands and estates so carefully accumulated would be a thing of the past. She could forget her special stockings for masques, her silver and gilt plates and that glorious bed; she could, literally, be in the street. Jane had before her the example of the plight of Alice More, widow of the executed Sir Thomas: while she had been allowed by Henry's gracious mercy to retain a tiny proportion of their former property, the king had kept the bulk.

There was no guarantee that he would let Jane keep anything. No woman wanted to be destitute. Jane would not beggar herself if she could avoid it.

However, every potential witness had the considerable handicap of not knowing what information Cromwell had amassed so far, or what the scope of his enquiry entailed. Even the prisoners themselves were not told the full extent of the charges. 'Do you know wherefore I am here?' Anne had asked the Constable of the Tower, Sir William Kingston, her gaoler, who feigned ignorance. Although there was a precious minute when she allowed herself to believe that she was somehow being tested by the king only 'to prove' her, laughing in the same way that she had in front of the French ambassadors on a happier occasion, she did not maintain that illusion for long. She could not work out why she was under suspicion but she understood that a number of men were somehow involved and, in her fear, kept on blurting out incriminating scraps of conversations and events, which the loyal Kingston dutifully reported.

One in particular stuck in her mind. On the day before the jousts, she had had an exchange with Norris in her privy chamber. This time the banter had got dramatically out of hand. In her usual fashion, she had teased him over his relationship with Madge Shelton whom court gossip maintained he would wed. Why had he not married her? she wanted to know. He was a widower, so there was no reason to hold back. When Norris had replied that he 'would tarry a time', she had foolishly retorted that he looked 'for dead men's shoes' for he would have her if any harm befell the king. Norris, stunned by the danger that he saw they were both in, quickly responded that if any such thoughts crossed his mind 'he would his head was off'. He had understood at once that even such ostensibly trivial badinage could be construed as a plot to murder Henry. It was terrifying. Realising that she had gone too far, Anne had rushed him off to her almoner to swear that she was a 'good woman'. But it was too late, the damage was done. The king's life was clearly threatened. This was treason.

In her incoherent babblings in the Tower, all carefully noted by Kingston and the unsympathetic ladies set to serve her, Anne unwittingly presented the king's chief minister with more and more circumstantial froth that he was only too happy to use against her, and against any man whose name tripped from her tongue. Indeed, within hours of her idly mentioning chiding Weston for flirting with Madge Shelton despite his being married, and his gallant response that the woman he loved more than both his own wife and the delectable Madge was the queen, he found himself behind bars, as did Brereton, Page and Wyatt, to whom she also made reference in her almost hysterical outpourings. In those early days, the formerly shrewd queen was a prosecutor's dream. She wondered about the Countess of Worcester, whose child, she said, 'did not stir in her body ... for sorrow she took of me'. She worried about her 'sweet brother', about her father and her mother who, she thought, would 'die with sorrow'. She managed to remember a potentially incriminating conversation with Smeaton as well. Finding him standing forlornly by the window in her presence chamber, she reminded him that he could not expect her to speak to him in the same way as she would a nobleman, as he was 'an inferior person'. His riposte that 'a look sufficed' him, coupled with a perfunctory 'fare you well', demonstrated her occasional over-familiarity wonderfully clearly. It was another gift to Cromwell, for no one would have addressed Katherine with such a lack of respect, and Mark had been his first prey.

For, although Jane was unaware of it, Cromwell had collected a plethora of evidence that he could use when the trials came. The pivotal confession of Mark Smeaton, the 'spinet player' of Chapuys' missive, made a comfortable start. Mark's downfall had begun even before the May Day Jousts. On Sunday, 30 April, Cromwell had ordered the young musician's arrest. Smeaton was taken to Cromwell's house in Stepney where he was questioned about just how familiar his relationship with his queen truly was. A statute of 1351 had pronounced it treason to 'violate' the king's companion even with her consent. The minister's agents were skilled interrogators, highly accomplished in prising secrets out of even the most reluctant or most courageous of prisoners. Few could resist for long. We will never know what pressure they applied to Mark, although there were suggestions that he was racked, or that a rope was tightened around his head with a cudgel until the pain was so intense that he had no choice but to say anything that might stop the agony. Perhaps he was promised his life if he co-operated. But, whether tortured or not, confess he did: he had, he said, slept with Anne. Once the king was told, there was no going back. Enquiries had to be undertaken, and Cromwell was the man to pursue them. No one doubted that he would approach his mission with diligence. After all, Henry's honour was at stake and, if Anne's foolish comments to Norris were taken seriously, so was his life.

Jane, and the rest of the Boleyns, were completely in the dark about these proceedings. Naturally they had agonised over the various difficulties that had beset them over the past few months. It was plain that Anne and Henry could be closer, or he would not be looking at any other woman. The lack of a son was the main stumbling block, but there was still a chance that Anne might conceive, and the royal marriage had always been a roller coaster of emotions. They could come through this. Even the inevitable fallout from Katherine's death was not insurmountable. Should Henry want to shift allegiances towards the emperor and away from Anne's beloved France, which was very much a current possibility, they could accept that. In those circumstances, the rehabilitation of Lady Mary would be a major problem, of course, but there might be room for accommodation there too. As for Anne's disappointment that the proceeds from the current round of monastic closures were going into Henry's pocket rather than into her cherished schemes of poor relief, she would have to get over it for the time being and work on Henry once she regained her influence. She ought also to patch up her recent quarrel with Cromwell, no longer a staunch ally.

But, for Henry, there was a hidden agenda. What the minister understood was the depth of his master's involvement with the gentle and demure Mistress Seymour, whom the king was no nearer to enticing into his bed. With Anne's shining example before her, she was holding out for marriage. If anything so dented the king's faith in Anne that he made up his mind to get rid of her, Jane Seymour would soon wear a crown. Then, anyone who helped him achieve his goal, and the happiness that he was sure he would find with a new bride, would gain his gratitude. Jane might have the fate of Alice More before her; Cromwell had that of Wolsey before him.

Henry was used to getting his own way. It was his minister's job to get it for him, or suffer the consequences of failure. The evidence we have on when or why the king decided that he no longer wanted Anne as his queen is inconclusive, but it was probably a sudden decision, perhaps taken shortly after Chapuys was forced to acknowledge her in the chapel at Greenwich. Jane, naturally, had even less forewarning than her sister-in-law. The first she knew was the dramatic arrest of her husband and her own subsequent interrogation.

The process, however, had started a little before that. By the time he got round to interviewing Jane, Cromwell's dossier was getting thicker. John Husee, writing to Honor Lisle, told her that three women had accused the queen of infidelity, 'the lady Worcester, Nan Cobham and one maid mo[re]'. Of the three, Husee offered no clues about what Nan or the maid might have said but he identified Elizabeth, Countess of Worcester, who had stood at Anne's side during the coronation banquet, as 'the first ground'. The story was that she had betrayed Anne's secret affairs with Mark and with George when reproved by her brother, Sir Anthony Browne, for her own immorality. Nothing that she had done, she was supposed to have said wildly, was as bad as the behaviour of the queen. As Jane was to find out for herself, anyone who concealed knowledge as spectacular as that was in peril. Browne, concerned for his own safety, therefore discussed the matter with Sir William Fitzwilliam, Elizabeth's half-brother, and the matter eventually reached the ears of Cromwell. This may well have been what did in fact happen. In view of Anne's friendship with the countess it seems far-fetched, but certainly something prompted the arrest of poor Smeaton.

What we do know is that Cromwell sent for the private correspondence of Bridget, Lady Wingfield, because one particular letter to her from Anne can be found amongst the Cotton manuscripts in the British Library among documents extracted in the seventeenth century from the State Papers. Had Cromwell not kept the note, it would not have ended up there. It would instead be in the private archive of the Wingfield family; as it is, it was seized at Cromwell's fall and is therefore a matter of public record. Anne had written this puzzling letter some time before becoming Marquess of

Pembroke. The note is conciliatory to the point of obsequiousness, for Anne apologises profusely for appearing to neglect Bridget, acknowledging that she had not 'at all times' showed 'the love that I bear you as much as it was indeed', but reassuring her that she did in fact love her 'a great deal more than I fair for'. Anne's love, was, she stated, 'unfeigned'; she loved Lady Wingfield 'so entirely'. Indeed, she said, she hoped that Bridget would accept that she would 'write nothing to comfort you in your trouble' but would 'abide by it as long as I live'. The nature of that trouble must have perplexed the minister as much as it does us. What he surely realised, however, was that Anne wanted to keep on the right side of Bridget, she did not want her as an enemy. And the only possible reason for that was that Lady Wingfield knew something that Anne preferred to keep hidden from her royal lover, which presumably originated either from Anne's early years in Kent or from when she had first come to court. When Bridget died, which was sometime in 1534, she is alleged to have made a deathbed confession. This was the golden nugget which Cromwell gathered up and which put him on the scent of Lady Wingfield in the first place.

Thus, Jane Rochford found herself dragged into a maelstrom of intrigue, innuendo and speculation. For when Cromwell sent for Jane, he already had much of what he needed, not only to bring down Anne and her circle, but to make possible the king's marriage to Jane Seymour, the woman Henry was positive was his soulmate. A few more details were all that was required. The questions to Jane would have come thick and fast. There is no word-for-word transcript of what they were, but the record of the trials of both Anne and George give us a plethora of clues. How often did George and Anne meet? Who was present on those occasions? Were they ever totally alone? Did he ever go into her bedchamber? Was she in bed at the time? Was he ever there alone with her? How did they behave when they were together? What did they talk about? Did either of them ever speak about the king? What did they say? How did they say it, respectfully or mockingly? Did they say it to each other or to someone else? If so, to whom? How often? When? Did Anne ever confide any intimate details about her sexual relationship with Henry to Jane? Had the queen conducted love affairs with anyone else? Did she ever mention Harry Percy, now Earl of North-umberland? How did she behave with Norris? With Weston? With Brereton? With Page? With Wyatt? What was her demeanour with the other gentlemen of the court? What did she say about the Princess Dowager? About the Lady Mary? About the Duke of Richmond?

Faced with such relentless, incessant questions, which she had no choice but to answer, Jane would have searched her memory for every tiny incident that occurred to her. This was not the moment for bravado and, in any case, the arrests had been so sudden and unexpected that there was no time to separate out what testimony might be damaging, what could be twisted to become so, or what could only be innocuous no matter what the interpretation. By the end of the various sessions, Cromwell had what he wanted. All he had to do was to put together all the 'facts' he had gleaned from all those whom he had interrogated and finalise the details on how the trials were to be conducted. Coincidentally, or some would say with considerable preliminary planning and foresight, commissions of Oyer and Terminer had been established on 24 April in Middlesex and Kent to look into serious criminal activity.* These, of course, would cover any cases of treason which might surface. On 27 April, Parliament had been summoned, less than two weeks after it had been dissolved, which would equally prove useful. By May Day, then, the necessary apparatus was already in place and much of the ground prepared.

There was still much work for the minister and the Council to do before all was ready for the trials of such high-profile prisoners. The minister wanted a watertight case. In the meantime, Henry consoled himself with the solicitous Jane Seymour, sure that he was lucky to be alive, free from the ensnarements of the evil Anne. His children were lucky too. Chapuys informed Charles that when Richmond went to his father to wish him goodnight on the evening of Anne's arrest, Henry 'began to weep, saying that he and his sister,

---

* Oyer and Terminer was the legal term for judicial commissions that could be set up in different counties to try serious crimes such as treason and felony within their area.

meaning the Princess Mary, were greatly bound to God for having escaped the hands of that accursed whore, who had determined to poison them'. As for the Boleyns, there was little they could do. Norfolk swiftly disassociated himself from his niece, as did the prudent Thomas from his son and daughter. Like Jane's father, both Thomas and Norfolk could be expected to serve on the panel of peers that would be constituted to try them.

Jane's main concern was for her husband. She had not deserted him through all their years of marriage, she did not do so now. Neither a visit nor a personal letter would have been permitted so she tried a more circuitous route: she sent a message to Kingston for George. In a letter to Cromwell, part of a cache of damaged documents saved from a fire at Ashburnham House, Westminster, in 1731, Kingston reported what she said. She asked how George was and promised that she would 'humbly [make] suit unto the king's highness' for him. The message was gratefully received by the otherwise abandoned George, who wanted to 'give her thanks'. The prospect of a petition to Henry, or perhaps the Council, from his wife, obviously gave him comfort. He asked Kingston at what time he would see the Council, and wept. In one of the tantalising fragments which survived the fire, he went on to say, 'for I think I [may not] come forth till I come to my judgment', presumably meaning that without Jane's aid he knew that no one would listen to his case before his trial.

Unfortunately, Jane's chances of pleading with the king were slim. Access to the royal presence was virtually impossible, and in any case, it was too late. The die was cast, and it was cast against the Boleyns. George was right. Only the formalities of the various trials stood between him and the block. Jane was about to become a widow.

22

Death of the Falcon

'M r Kingston, shall I die without justice?' asked Anne shortly
after her arrival at the Tower. His sanctimonious reply, that
'the poorest subject the King has, has justice', prompted merely her
laughter. Jane, anxiously waiting for the trials to take place, did not
hear this exchange. Had she done so, she could only have trusted
that Kingston was right and Anne wrong. The fate of every Boleyn
was at stake. Jane had once been sent from court but, other than
that, she had reaped nothing but benefits from her marriage. She
had attained a higher status than that of her own mother, she had
moved amongst the most influential people in the land, she had
lived in unbridled luxury. Now her world stood on a knife's edge.
The family to which she now belonged could be totally ruined, the
man whose bed she had shared for twelve years could be condemned
as a traitor and was likely to die with his sister, with whom Jane had
shared so many confidences and who was currently branded a whore.
And, from Cromwell's questions, she had an uncomfortable knowledge of the almost unspeakable charges that George and Anne
would face.

For the whole of her life, Jane had been accustomed to revere her
monarch. Whatever he decided had to be correct. He did not have to
reveal his reasons, but they were bound to be sound. The chronicler
Edward Hall understood this concept perfectly when he stated that
'the affairs of Princes be not ordained by the common people, nor
were it convenient that all things were opened to them'. Cranmer,
so very much one of Anne's bishops, grasped this too. Shocked by
the revelations about her, for he 'had never better opinion of woman',
he accepted that Henry 'would not have gone so far if she had not

been culpable'. Neither man was emotionally involved, unlike Jane, who had to balance allegiance to her king with her loyalty to her husband. Nothing remains extant about her feelings at this time. For contemporary reporters, if not for those writing soon afterwards, she was a minor figure, hidden in the chorus as she had been so frequently over the years, someone who was always present but who was not centre stage. In any case, Jane had been born into a family who appreciated the advantages of silence. Her father was never prone to speak out and invite retribution, nor was she. Jane had become practised in keeping her personal views private, like so many who surrounded the king, and the situation in which she found herself was not one in which it would be wise to break the habit of a lifetime. There was no queue to follow in the footsteps of Fisher and More. If Thomas dared not speak in his children's defence, then neither did she. She had already said more than she would have wished.

When the trials began, therefore, Jane could but watch and listen as the events unfolded and the revelations tumbled out. Prominent amongst the commissioners of Oyer and Terminer were Cromwell, who intended to keep a firm eye on all proceedings, Suffolk, who was getting older but was still ambitious and Norfolk, who had no intention of being pulled down by his sister's errant offspring. Norfolk, indeed, was officially put in overall charge of the whole process. Amongst the others were Sir John Spelman, who has left us his notes on the testimony given, and Sir John Baldwin, a man whose business dealings were linked to Jane's future security. They, with the remaining commissioners, could be counted on to do their duty. On Friday, 12 May 1536, with the preliminaries complete, the trial of the four commoners, Norris, Smeaton, Brereton and Weston, began in Westminster Hall, the site of Anne's triumphant coronation dinner just three years earlier. Page and Wyatt were not charged and were later released, thoroughly frightened but unscathed. Wyatt never forgot his experience, however, a vivid stanza in one of his poems expressing how deeply it had affected him:

> These bloody days have broken my heart;
> My lust, my youth did then depart,

And blind desire of estate;
Who hastes to climb seeks to revert:
Of truth, circa Regna tonat.*

This was a sentiment with which Jane, desperately watching from the sidelines, would agree.

Already greedy eyes were cast on the offices that would be there for the taking once the expected guilty verdicts were returned. The mysteriously compiled list of Boleyn grants would prove useful, but all of the prisoners had offices and lands worth fighting over. Richard Staverton rushed to put pen to paper, writing to Cromwell for his 'remembrance' when the 'various rooms in the parts' near him in Windsor became available. Staverton was keen to point out that he had fourteen children so was very interested in 'the Little Park, the Park of Holy John, Perlam Park, and the room of the Black Rod in Windsor Castle'. Although Thomas More's nephew, Staverton had fitted into the new regime fairly easily. He was not the only man with expectations. On the day before the first trial started, the Abbot of Cirencester wrote to Cromwell confirming that he had promised the stewardship of the monastery at Cirencester, currently held by Norris, to Sir William Kingston 'when it is void'. Kingston, of course, was the Constable of the Tower, where Norris was incarcerated.

Since the abbot referred to Cromwell's previous correspondence on the subject, it would seem that the minister was confident of conviction. Jane's chances of remaining a wife rather than a widow were few. To be certain that there were no slip-ups, Cromwell went further: some of the names on the juries are significant. Even in the early stages of these trials, Cromwell was remarkably thorough. Strictly speaking, although it was the role of the sheriffs to determine the composition of juries, they were likely to be responsive to a quiet word from the minister. The commissions of Oyer and Terminer had been established for Kent and Middlesex, the counties in which the offences were deemed to have been committed. In each county

---

* About the throne the thunder roars.

the grand juries,* which agreed that there was a case to answer, included those with a grievance against some or all of the defendants. A key figure on the jury register in Kent was Edmund Page, one of the two Members of Parliament for Rochester. The second Member had been Robert Fisher, the brother of the executed bishop. Robert† had died the year before Anne fell, but as he and Page were both elected for the 1529 Parliament, they were probably fairly close colleagues rather than mere acquaintances. The two of them had even been in some trouble, as they had opposed the Act ending appeals to Rome, the same Act that had driven a coach and horses through Katherine's right to have her case heard in the Eternal City. Page's sympathies would not lie with the Boleyns. In Middlesex, an even more significant name, that of Giles Heron leaps from the list. He was married to Thomas More's daughter, Cecily. Boleyn involvement in the condemnation of Henry's two most famous opponents would not be forgotten.

A glance through the trial jury itself for the four commoners is equally revealing since Giles Alington was one of them. He, too, was linked to More, for he was the second husband of More's stepdaughter, Alice, and she was particularly close to the former chancellor's favourite daughter, Margaret Roper. In fact, no one in that jury was in the Boleyn camp, each man wanted either to curry favour with the authorities or to seek revenge. Sir William Kingston and Richard Staverton would soon enjoy the fruits of Norris's offices. This boded ill for Anne and George. As Jane waited for news, she knew that the fate of her husband and sister-in-law was largely dependent on the verdicts on the four other accused men. If they were found guilty, then Anne and George were almost certainly doomed.

For the nature of the charges could mean nothing less. 'By sweet words, kisses, touches, and otherwise', the queen had enticed Norris

---

* Grand juries determined whether the case should proceed, so their role was similar to the current one of magistrates' courts in England and Wales, and grand juries in the United States.
† There is a Robert Fisher on the Kent jury list but this is a different man who, coincidentally, had the same name.

into her bed, it was alleged. They had had intercourse several times, with some dates and places known and others not. She used similar techniques with Brereton, with Weston and with Smeaton. Again, some specific times and venues were stated, with the phrase 'and divers other days' also included. Because the men grew jealous of each other, so it was said, she gave them presents and promised to marry one of them once the king, whom she would never love 'in her heart', was dead. She went, therefore, straight from 'frail and carnal lust' to planning murder. If true, this was undoubtedly treason, and the king was fortunate to have escaped unharmed. It was all astonishing. However, Mark alone would plead guilty. The others steadfastly maintained their innocence. It availed them nothing. Once the jury obligingly returned guilty verdicts on them all, the mandatory sentence of death was imposed. The four men were led to the waiting barge for the short voyage back along the Thames to the Tower. They would emerge only to meet the executioner, and they knew that they would have very little time to prepare themselves. For the fortress's chief officials – Constable Kingston, Sir Edmund Walsingham, the Lieutenant, and Anthony Anthony, surveyor of the ordnance – there would be arrangements to be made. They would not take long.

Once news of the judgment reached Jane, she knew that the odds against acquittal for the two principals were dramatically reduced. If the four men were judged to have committed adultery with Anne, the corollary was that *she* must have committed adultery with *them*. She had, therefore, betrayed her husband and would deserve her fate. Despite her inherent faith in the king, Jane surely did not believe in Anne's guilt. Even Chapuys, willing to disparage Anne when at all possible, thought that the four men had been 'sentenced on mere presumption or on very slight grounds, without legal proof or valid confession'. Jane had known Anne for years. She had lived in claustrophobically close proximity to her, as had all of her ladies. That was how the court functioned. These women were constantly on hand to attend to the queen's slightest whim. To elude their vigilance, and find suitable love-nests, would be no easy task. Jane, more than anyone, could see how impossible it was. Not, of course, that she would have the opportunity to say so. For the queen, the difficulty, as Anne said to Kingston, was how to prove herself innocent. All she could do was to deny any infidelity, unless there was a way to 'open' her body to show her purity. Unfortunately for Anne, she had only words at her disposal. And she used them. When asking for the sacrament to be brought to her so that she could pray for mercy, she explained that she was eligible to do so. 'For I am as clear from the Company of Man, as for Sin, as I am clear from you,' she affirmed to Kingston.

When the time for her trial came, there were no more ramblings. She was the old spirited Anne once more, ready to defend herself. By then, she knew the full extent of the charges. Not only was she accused of adultery with the four courtiers, and of conspiracy to murder the king, she was also alleged to have had intercourse with her own brother, George. For Henry, this was horrifyingly credible. He was overheard saying that he believed 'that upwards of 100 gentlemen have had criminal connection with her'. Later, he went further, reportedly telling the Bishop of Carlisle that he had had a premonition some while previously and had written a tragedy about it. A tragedy indeed it was. The allegations of incest were not merely astonishing, but very graphic. Anne had tempted her brother, according to the indictment, 'with her tongue in the said George's mouth, and the said George's tongue in hers, and also with kisses, presents, and jewels'. Then he, 'despising the commands of God, and all human laws ... violated and carnally knew the said Queen, his own sister'. If the trial of the four commoners had been sensational, this was spine-tingling. It was no wonder that a shocked John Husee wrote to Honor Lisle – whose presents to the queen had, naturally, suddenly ceased – that he felt that every evil thing ever written against women 'since Adam and Eve' was 'verily nothing in comparison of that which hath been done and committed by Anne the Queen'. He was almost too ashamed 'that any good woman should give ear' to her 'abominable and detestable' offences. Because of the line of Cromwell's intense questioning, little of this was entirely unexpected by Jane. She had been allowed no choice but to 'give ear', and she knew all too well what the wily minister had dragged out of her.

As was her right as Marquess of Pembroke, and a crowned queen,

Anne would not be tried by jury but by a panel of peers. The same was true of George. This time, Jane had access to insider knowledge of every word said in their cases, for her father, Lord Morley, was amongst those who were to sit in judgment in what was undoubtedly the trial of the century. Thomas was excused although, as Earl of Wiltshire, he should have been present. Only a couple of days previously, he had sat with his fellow commissioners in Westminster Hall while Norris, Brereton, Weston and Smeaton were tried, but he was spared the sight of his own children fighting for their lives. Norfolk presided, all his family feeling now rapidly dispelled. He had his own neck to protect. The Earl of Northumberland, Anne's love in happier days, had no option but to be present too.

The peers travelled to the Tower for the trial. On Monday, 15 May, Kingston escorted the queen from the royal apartments where she had been kept, into the King's Hall where her judges were waiting. She was given no legal counsel, as, at that time, was normal legal practice. She was on her own. As was traditional, she held up her hand as the charges were read out to her and then declared herself not guilty. In addition to adultery with the four courtiers, the allegation of incest, and the charge of plotting to murder the king, she was also accused of poisoning Katherine, of pondering doing the same to Mary and, last but far from least, laughing at her husband and ridiculing him. The most preposterous of accusations were treated as gravely as the most serious. With the eyes of Suffolk, Norfolk, Lord Morley and the rest of her peers upon her, she defended herself with considerable skill.

While Lord Morley may well have told his daughter all that occurred within that crowded room in the Tower on that day in May, we have no verbatim record. Much of what is extant comes from Chapuys, always so clever at finding those willing to brief him, but he was not present himself, although two men, both of whom have left us information, were. One was Anthony Anthony. A brewer, he owned an inn, The Ship, and was a churchwarden at St Botolph's in Aldgate. He also kept a journal covering the major events that he saw as 'an eye- and ear-witness' while working at the Tower. The journal has long since disappeared but Thomas Turner (or Tourneur), writing in the late seventeenth century, saw Anthony's 'old, original diary' and transcribed extracts from it. They make fascinating reading. It was Sir John Spelman, the second eye- and ear-witness, however, who recorded in his notebook that the 'matter was disclosed' by Lady Wingfield, reporting that she had made accusations against the queen in a deathbed confession. Perhaps she did, but quite what she said, and to whom, remains a mystery. Clearly whatever it was that she was supposed to have divulged must have been damaging to Anne, but it could have referred to anything that had happened before she was queen. It could equally have been a fairly minor indiscretion that was exaggerated out of all proportion.

Neither Anthony nor Spelman mentioned Lady Worcester, and they did not refer to Jane. She was not called upon to give evidence in person against her sister-in-law, nor was anyone else. In fact, no witnesses at all were called, much to Chapuys' surprise, As he wrote to Charles, it 'is customary in such cases, when the accused denies the charge brought against him'.

The lack of witnesses did not affect the outcome. At the close of the proceedings, the peers gave their decision. Beginning with the most junior, each of the twenty-six announced his verdict verbally. All said the same, single word: 'guilty'. It was up to the queen's uncle to pronounce sentence on his niece. She would be put to death, he said, 'and according to the old customs of the land she should be burned, but nevertheless it should stand in the king's commandment'. Her execution would take place on Tower Green, within the walls of the fortress. Calm and composed, Anne said that she was prepared to die but was sorry that others, who were innocent, were also condemned. Finally she asked for some time to 'prepare her soul for death'. For her, it was almost over.

Jane's husband was next. Since his sister, whom he was not allowed to see, had already been found guilty, his position was perilous. But, a Boleyn to the last, he held up his hand at the bar to plead 'not guilty' to all of the charges against him and proceeded to conduct his own case with commendable aplomb. His momentary weakness in the Tower, when he had wept in front of Kingston, was a thing of the past. He stood before the same judges who had just sentenced his sister to a terrible end.

They were all men he knew. Amongst them he could identify his uncle, Norfolk, in the seat of honour, Suffolk, with his instinct for self-preservation, and Lord Morley, his father-in-law, whose duty it might be to turn his own daughter into a widow. Although not trained as a lawyer, George defended himself so ably that many who were there 'had no difficulty in waging two to one that he would be acquitted'.

The evidence against him was weak, resting chiefly on his having remained for a while in Anne's bedchamber, probably when he had rushed to her side to give her the latest news from France, and enjoying her company. Again no witnesses were called, which continued to puzzle Chapuys. But then came the crunch, as Jane must have feared that it would. He was given a slip of paper, which he was told not to read aloud, but was asked to give a yes or no response to what it said. Defiant as always, George scornfully read it out, sealing his own fate in the process. Had Anne told Jane, he read, that Henry found it difficult to sustain an erection? It was most likely this that Cromwell had painstakingly extracted from a frightened Jane. The atmosphere in the King's Hall, already tense, was now electric. If the king truly was impotent, then Elizabeth was not his child and he could never have a son. But George refused to answer the question with the required yes or no, not wishing, he said, 'to engender or create suspicion in a matter likely to prejudice the issue the King might have from another marriage'. Nor would he respond to any suggestion that he had spread a rumour that Elizabeth was not Henry's. It was beyond contempt.

He knew his sister. She was as clever and sharp as he was; she had lived in royal courts for most of her life. She understood how they were organised. No matter what anyone might have insinuated to Cromwell, she would not have prejudiced the position that they had all worked so hard to help her attain by leaping into bed with an importunate courtier. Nor would she have tried to have a child by a man not her husband. It was too dangerous. The charge that George had fulfilled the role of surrogate himself was preposterous. The Boleyns were grasping and opportunistic, but to flout morality and religious law so wantonly was beyond even them. Like Anne,

George was sincere in his beliefs. Even if Henry was not virility epitomised, he was not impotent. What Anne told Jane, as she must have done, and what Jane repeated to George, as indeed she must have done, was surely not meant to suggest anything other than that Henry had intermittent sexual dysfunction. Getting pregnant by him was not easy, but it could be done. Anne's ill-considered remark proved to be George's undoing, as ripe for misinterpretation as his impetuous haste to keep her up to date with the delicate negotiations that he had been conducting in France. And Jane would remember until her dying day that the words Cromwell had gleaned from her during her interrogation had been turned so effectively against her husband. Perhaps there was some consolation in knowing that she did not volunteer the information, but it would be understandable if she wished that Anne had kept her own mouth firmly shut in the beginning. It was dangerous to be the queen's confidante.

The guilty verdict was inevitable, delivered by each of the peers in turn. Only Northumberland, 'suddenly taken ill', was not there to deliver the fatal word. Again, it was up to the stalwart Norfolk to pronounce the death sentence on a relative. Like Anne, George behaved with dignity. Acknowledging that he deserved to die, for everyone was a sinner, he asked the king to pay his debts. It always mattered to leave this earth owing nothing to anyone, and to die well was all that remained to him.

Henry's blatantly delighted reaction to the arrests and court cases astounded even the worldly Chapuys. On the day before the Boleyns were tried, he moved his beloved Jane Seymour to live within a mile of him, and ordered that she should receive only the very best of everything. There was even a report that he sent her a message on the day of his wife's trial to let her know that she would hear that Anne had been condemned by three o'clock that afternoon. His timing was impeccable, for so she was. He felt free of his 'own sweetheart', and he celebrated in style: he dined in company until the early hours of the morning. People living by the river heard music and song from musicians and minstrels as the royal barge glided by, taking the king to his untroubled sleep. His callous behaviour was compared to 'the joy and pleasure a man feels in getting rid of a thin, old, and vicious hack in the hope of getting soon a fine horse to ride', wrote the Spanish ambassador.

For Jane it was a different story. As the prisoners anticipated their end, their relatives' anguish began. While they were still alive, there was always a slim chance that the king might show mercy, although in this case it was a forlorn hope. The French ambassador, no less, tried to move Henry to spare Weston but failed. To attempt to plead for Anne or George would have been foolhardy and there is no suggestion that anyone sought to do so. Anne wondered at one point whether she might be allowed to retire to a nunnery but that was out of the question. Henry wanted her dead. And it would be preferable if her brother lost his head as well. Just to take care of any loose ends, and to distance the king completely from the woman for whom he had once yearned, a sick Northumberland was interrogated to ascertain whether he and Anne had agreed to marry in the distant days of their youth. However, that easy way of annulling her marriage to the king failed when the earl swore upon the holy sacrament that there had been no pre-contract. It was left to the faithful Cranmer to help his master by granting a decree of nullity, supposedly on the grounds that his affair with Mary Stafford had put him in a pro-hibited degree of relationship with Anne. It was the Katherine situation all over again.

Those incarcerated in the Tower could only await the inevitable. George was preoccupied by what he owed, in particular his respons-ibility to a monk whom he had helped to become an abbot, charging a total fee of £200 for his services, but whose new abbey was presumably closed by the king. George asked for Cromwell's help in settling the matter. Kingston does not tell us whether George was allowed to see Jane, or whether she communicated with him. Weston wrote a poignant letter listing his debts, asking his father and mother to pay them for him 'for the salvation' of his soul, and begging both his parents and his wife to pray for him. 'I believe', he said, that 'prayer will do me good'. Anne asked that Cranmer should hear her confession. She affirmed 'on the damnation of her soul' that she had always been faithful to Henry. One small consolation was that her sentence had been commuted to beheading rather than burning, Henry going to the trouble of sending for an expert swordsman from Calais to do the job. 'I heard say the executioner was very good, and I have a little neck,' she joked with Kingston as she laughingly put her hands around it.

The minutes ticked away. On Wednesday, 17 May, Kingston led the five condemned men – George, Norris Brereton, Weston and Smeaton – to a scaffold set up on Tower Hill just outside the fortress. The executions were, of course, in public. George was the first to die and by the axe. He did not face the terrible death which he had watched the Charterhouse monks suffer a few months earlier. There would be no hanging, no disembowelling and no quartering. For Norris, once so much liked by the king, for young Weston, for Brereton and for George, a magnanimous Henry allowed a swifter demise. Jane would have had little – probably no – advance warning of the time scheduled for her husband's execution, Kingston told him the night before, and he confirmed the hour with George and the other condemned men only in the early morning of the day itself. Contacting the wife of a convicted traitor was not a requirement of his post.

George stepped forward for the last time and gave his final speech. 'Christian men,' he said, 'I am born under the law, and judged under the law, and die under the law, and the law has condemned me.' He acknowledged that his many sins, which he would not enumerate but which were all known by God, meant that he deserved death. 'I am a wretched sinner,' he admitted, 'and I have sinned shamefully.' Everyone, particularly those at court, should learn from his great fall and 'trust not in the vanity of the world, and especially in the flattering of the court'. After asking forgiveness of anyone whom he had offended 'in thought, word or deed', he revealed his passionate involvement in religion. He did not, as Chapuys maintained, confess that he had been 'contaminated' with the 'new heresies'. On the contrary, he proclaimed himself 'a setter forth of the word of God', a man who 'favoured the Gospel of Christ'. If only he had practised in deed what he had read, he said, he would not have come to this. It was better to be a 'good doer' than a 'good reader'. Of the specific crimes of which he was accused, he said nothing.

The moment had come. He knelt down, laid his head on the

wooden block, the headsman's axe fell. As George's mangled remains were removed, it was Norris's turn, then Weston's, then Brereton's and, right at the end, having to endure the mental torment of yet more waiting, Mark Smeaton. He, however, was not beheaded, for, as Anne had explained as they stood by the window in her presence chamber, he was not a gentleman. Instead, he was hanged and his body cut into quarters. The corpses were carried back into the Tower to the churchyard of St Peter ad Vincula, where Norris and Weston were bundled into one grave, Brereton and Smeaton into another. George's head and body were taken inside the chapel and laid to rest there. Six years later, Jane would join him.

Anne did not die until Friday. She dressed with great care for this, her ultimate performance. Ever since her return from France as a girl, she had dressed well and today, of all days, was to be no exception. She chose a gable headdress, which was unusual for her, and a cloak trimmed with ermine. She would be attended by the four ladies set to guard and wait upon her, who included Lady Kingston, the Constable's wife, and her own aunt, Sir Edward Boleyn's wife, a woman who had once served Katherine of Aragon and whom she had never liked. At the appointed time, the queen walked out into the open air from the royal apartments and to the waiting scaffold, sited close to the chapel where her brother lay. There were plenty of people there to witness her death. Cromwell, a friend no longer, sat in the stands to watch, as did Suffolk, Audley and Henry's natural son, Richmond. Although the gates of the Tower were open, foreigners were excluded so that Chapuys was unable to see 'the Concubine', the woman he despised for her treatment of Katherine and Mary, receive her punishment.

Nor did he hear her short speech, so faithfully recorded by Anthony Anthony:

> You shall understand that I have submitted me unto the law, and so I am come hither to obey and fulfil the law. And so I can say no more, but I desire you all to be just and true unto the king, your sovereign, for he is a good virtuous king and a goodly king, a victorious king, a bountiful king, for I have found his grace always very good and loving

unto me, and [he] has done much for me. Wherefore I pray God reward his grace, praying you all to pray to God for his life, that his grace may reign long with you, and I pray you all for God's sake to pray for me.

Like George, she said nothing of the crimes which she was alleged to have committed. Taking off her cloak and her hood, she covered her still-beautiful dark hair with a thin linen hood and knelt down, modestly arranging her skirts. One of the ladies bandaged her eyes. There was no block. A sword does not descend vertically like an axe but slices off a head in one huge blow. This executioner was indeed an expert. Kingston had promised Anne that there would be no pain. It was certainly fast. When she fell, her ladies moved towards her. One covered her bloodied head with a white cloth and gently carried it into St Peter ad Vincula, the other women bearing her lifeless body.

Brother and sister were thus reunited in death, their ordeal finished. Jane's was not. In under three weeks, the once powerful Boleyn clan had been discredited and disgraced, their lives, and Jane's, shattered. Jane had been with Anne during the long years of Henry's courtship, she had ridden behind her through the bedecked streets of London on that great day of triumph, and she had watched as Cranmer had set St Edward's Crown on the new queen's head. She had shared in the disappointments of Anne's failed pregnancies; she had even tried to help her sister-in-law fight off a potential rival for the king's waning affections. She had been closer to the queen than she was to her own sister. She knew Anne through and through, and that knowledge would have led her to believe in her sister-in-law's innocence. Now she had lost her. Even more devastatingly, she had also lost her husband. George – the young gallant who had strode so proudly into the colourful little church at Great Hallingbury in the middle of the Essex countryside and whisked her off to a life of excitement and wealth – was buried under the cold floor of a very different church in a very different place. There would be no more cosy nights in that wonderful Rochford bed, perhaps trying for the child they had never had. Instead, Jane was a widow. But hers would be no ordinary widowhood. There could be no ornate funeral, no public grieving. No sympathy would be offered, any tears would be shed in private. It must be as though George had never been born. Jane was on her own.

CARVING A CAREER

23

Taking Stock

Henry's officers set about their task methodically. Every last item that George owned was recorded. It was the king's now, and he could not be cheated. The silver dishes, the candlesticks, the gilt trenchers, the gilt pots and the elaborately embroidered furnishings were all carefully packed to await the king's pleasure. Once they were securely stored with his other goods, the king might not even bother to glance at them. But when the executioner held George's bleeding head aloft to display to the watching crowds, Jane was not just made a widow: she became infinitely poorer.

Even her own personal possessions were rifled through by Henry's diligent scribes as they listed all that she had. She kept much of her 'stuff' in a chest 'in the chamber over the kitchen', probably the kitchen at Beaulieu, the palace that had so charmed George that he had moved his household in with remarkable speed. Now a note was made of her prayer book edged with silver and gilt, of a book covered in black velvet and with its silver clasp, and a book covered in crimson velvet. Her clothes were enumerated too. She had ten pairs of sleeves for her gowns, all of rich materials. Amongst them she had a pair of crimson velvet worked in gold, two pairs made of cloth of silver, a couple in tinsel or thin cloth of silver or gold, some in yellow or white satin, a pair in white damask, a pair in black velvet complete with eight sets of laces tipped with black enamel for fastening. She had intricate placards, the stiff panels that she liked to display beneath open skirts or gowns. These, too, were in satin, damask and velvet. She had two pairs of knives sheathed in black velvet. Henry's servants scrupulously wrote down that she had some broken beads, probably rosaries, of gold and white bone and gold and pearls. They did not forget the fabulous white silk stockings embossed in gold which she used for the masques she so loved. They were nothing if not thorough. It was humiliating in the extreme, emphasising that she was no longer the queen's sister-in-law, but the unimportant widow of a convicted traitor. Perhaps she was allowed to keep much of this. We do not know.

What she certainly could not keep was the proceeds of George's offices or any of the land that he had so painstakingly accumulated over the years. The vultures were soon out for those. Nothing was too small to be worth the asking. Robert Barnes, who was burnt as a heretic four years later, wrote a begging letter to Cromwell, asking him to procure for him the keepership of Bedlam, which he had heard, erroneously, was worth £40 per annum. The Earl of Sussex fared much better. He carried off the lion's share, gaining the stewardship of Beaulieu and some of George's manors in Essex. Andrew Flamock, who had made the king laugh when he broke wind, gained the constableship of Kenilworth in Warwickshire, and Sir Thomas Cheyney became the new Warden of the Cinque Ports and Constable of Dover. George's fall was a welcome bonanza for them. Jane's father, apparently not too squeamish to care about profiting from his daughter's distress, did quite well too. He received some minor offices in Beaulieu and the keepership of the park at King's Hatfield, but at least they stayed in the family. Also staying in the family were the manor of South Kent, the lordship of Rayleigh and lands around Penshurst, which had already been sold to Thomas. Yet, the one part of the family that they did not stay with was Jane herself. She saw every last vestige of George's estates snatched from her grasp.

Anyone who owed money to her late husband now owed it to the king and not to her. As George had faced death, concern about his debts and his obligations had preyed on his mind. He had hoped that the king would settle them for him, but could have been under no illusions about Henry's generosity. Perhaps the king did show compassion to the man with whom he had once played cards and bowls, but if he did, we have no record of it. What Jane knew, however, was that she would not see a penny that was due to her dead husband. Instead, Henry would ensure that everything went into the royal coffers. George Lovekyn, of East Greenwich, may have thought that in the circumstances he might escape the £100 he owed to George. He did not; he had to pay it to the king. The Archbishop of Dublin fared worse, enduring a long period of anxiety. Owing George £400, he repaid £250 and gave a further £50 'to redeem a gold cup of the said Lord Rochford's', leaving £100 outstanding. The archbishop had arranged for that sum to pay for a house of his which George wanted, but after the execution he could not even get the house back. Unfortunately, the king was now demanding the full £400. The issue dragged on for two years and was not resolved until after Jane's death, when the king magnanimously wrote off the debt. For Jane, whose finances had plummeted, recovering any of George's money would have been so very useful.

All she could count on was her jointure, the document signed at her marriage and designed to give her security should George die. On her wedding day at Great Hallingbury it had been perfectly natural for her to envisage herself as eventual mistress of the Boleyn estates when her husband took them over sometime in the future. That would include Blickling and Hever, the two jewels in the Boleyn crown. Her jointure was a form of insurance policy that she would have preferred not to cash in, certainly not at this stage of her life. It would, after all, mean living on much reduced means and Jane was not used to thinking about costs and living expenses. Over her years at court, she had come to take greatly for granted the considerable rewards of royal service. But her situation had changed beyond recognition now and she had to rely on Thomas to keep his part of the bargain.

And that was the problem. Thomas had just lost his only son and his daughter to the headsman. With his personal position at court so unenviable, he would have to practise his extensive diplomatic skills in minimising the damage that his children's fall had caused him. Perhaps had Jane produced a grandson for him as a living reminder of his dead heir, he would have felt, and behaved, differently, in which case the Ormond ancestral horn would have found a home. In Ormond's will, he had bequeathed a rather special item to his grandson, Thomas. The item was an ivory horn tipped with gold at both ends, together with a white silk ribbon decorated in gold to support it, both of which were to be handed through the family from father to son 'to the honour of the same blood'. Ormond had received the horn from his own father and, as he had only two daughters, Margaret Boleyn and Anne St Leger, he left it to Margaret's son, Thomas. It should have passed to George and then to George's son.

Since Jane and George had no son, Thomas was required by the terms of his grandfather's will to give the precious horn to Sir George St Leger, Anne St Leger's son, to descend through that branch of the family. It was yet another loss for Thomas. There was no relic of George left for him. A later suggestion – that George Boleyn, the colourful Dean of Lichfield who often took his badly behaved dog into church with him, was George's son – is unfounded. It is true that in his will the dean named Mary Carey's son, Lord Hunsdon, as one of his executors, perhaps hinting at a link with the Boleyns, but there is no record of Jane giving birth. Had the dean been George's illegitimate child, Thomas would surely have been involved in his upbringing, especially after George's death. If Sir Edward Howard could acknowledge his two bastards, there was no reason for George not to do the same for his. The child would not have been in line for the Ormond horn, as that was for legitimate issue only, but he might have been recognised as kin.

So, with no children as bargaining counters, Jane was entirely dependent on Thomas fulfilling his obligations to the letter. The precise terms of the jointure document, agreed between Thomas and Lord Morley all those years ago, were crucial. Even today, her story can only make sense in the context of these pivotal documents, hidden in the archives for almost five hundred years. Unfortunately, the original document itself has disappeared over the centuries, but as it is possible to reconstruct it from other references, we have the same information that Jane had as she considered her new position. For a woman like her, used to the very best that life could offer, the future looked bleak. And Thomas's typically shifty land dealings did not help.

Her jointure allocated her some lands in Norfolk, including the manor of West Laxham, together with the far more important manors of Aylesbury and Bierton as well as other lands in Buckinghamshire. Thomas had gained Aylesbury and Bierton through his mother's Ormond legacy and probably had no real intention of handing them over to Jane. His mother, Margaret, was still alive and retained an interest in them and they offered potential sources of profit if they came up for sale. Thomas, always happy to keep or preferably gain property, therefore opted for the clause in the jointure that allowed him to give Jane 100 marks a year during his lifetime in lieu of the lands. Jane had always known that this would be the case: it was why, even setting aside her emotional loss, it was so much better for her to be a wife than a widow. She also knew that widows were more commonly given ten per cent of the jointure price as a return, but she was getting only five per cent. Clearly, Thomas had managed to slip the 100-mark clause into the original agreement, conveniently forgetting that the king had doubled the jointure money from 1,000 marks to 2,000 marks.

Managing on 100 marks (£66) per annum would not be easy. George had happily paid £50 for a gold cup, he had willingly spent 20 marks on hawks, and had thought nothing of pocketing £58 as betting winnings from Henry in a single month. Jane was not used to budgeting. Even her wardrobe was expensive. Sufficient black satin for a cloak could cost almost £5, about the same as for a satin nightgown. Damask was a similar price, silk and velvet even dearer. At approximately £2 per yard, cloth of gold or cloth of silver would have to be things of the past. If she became ill and needed a good doctor, the costs could be astronomical. Henry had once paid £20 for Princess Mary's medical expenses. A mere 100 marks would not go far.

Until now, Jane had been very much under male protection and control, first her father's and then her husband's. With George dead, she could call on Lord Morley if necessary but his reluctance to become involved made him a weak ally. In fact, she knew precisely what she had to do if she was to find more funds: enlist Cromwell's help in persuading the king to take pity on her. As Brereton's widow, Elizabeth Savage, proved, sometimes the king could be sympathetic. Elizabeth Savage did remarkably well and remarkably quickly. Within weeks of her husband's execution, Henry returned much of his land to her. Later she knew whom to thank, sending a gelding to Cromwell when seeking yet more assistance from him. Uriah Brereton was helped too, for he gained some of his late brother's offices. No, pinning her faith on Lord Morley's efforts was not the answer for Jane. She must approach the minister.

That is what she did, virtually immediately There was no point in attempting to meet him: she had to write to him, phrasing her letter with considerable skill in accordance with set conventions. We know fairly accurately what her template would have been, for in the latter part of Elizabeth's reign, Angel Day, in *The English Secretorie*, produced what amounts to a 'Teach Yourself How to Write a Letter' manual based on the accepted Tudor norms concerning status, position, and chances of success. When Jane approached Cromwell, her language was that of an inferior to a superior. That might well have gone against the grain. Jane's aristocratic lineage and title were important to her and she was used to being closely associated with the woman to whom the king had once denied nothing. Cromwell was a commoner whose lowly origins were a matter for public derision. But this was not the moment for standing on her dignity, she was a supplicant, one of the many who turned to Cromwell in greed or despair every day and added to his mountainous correspondence. It was true that she had given him useful information about Anne and George, but the minister had dredged it out of her. She had done nothing to earn a reward, so she knew that she had to swallow her pride or he could choose to ignore her.

Therefore she appreciated that her tone must be one of humility. She must be self-deprecatory and she must not forget to flatter and praise the recipient. Her letter, which has survived, is a masterpiece. It had to be. She began by calling herself 'a poor desolate widow without comfort'. Her 'special trust' after God and the king lay in Cromwell. He was, she said, well known for displaying a 'gentle manner to all them that be in such lamentable case' as that in which she found herself. She really wanted two things: some of George's former possessions, and a better deal on her jointure payments.

She beseeched Cromwell to approach Henry for her. If only the king 'of his gracious and mere liberality' would return George's 'stuff and plate', which was 'nothing to be regarded' by him, it would be 'a most high help and succour' to her. She then moved on to her jointure, reminding Cromwell of Henry's lavish contribution, explaining that she found it very hard 'to shift [in] the world withal' on just 100 marks a year. She needed more, she said, entreating Cromwell to 'inform the King's Highness of these premises' and make the king think 'more tenderly' of her. The minister's assistance in this matter would, she felt certain, be 'a sure help'. He had it in his power to transform her current existence. If he did, he would be rewarded by God, who favoured those who 'doth help poor forsaken widows'. As for Jane herself, she offered Cromwell her 'prayers and service' for the rest of her life, as she was 'most bounden so to do'. She then signed the missive as 'Jane Rocheford', with her usual, rather old-fashioned flourish on the R.

She could do no more, now it was up to Cromwell. And he did help her. Clearly, he went to Henry on her behalf, and the king, perhaps mindful of his donation to her jointure, put pressure on Thomas, and so did the minister. The result was, for Jane, a great relief. She still did not get the promised lands, but she did get a rise in her living allowance. Grudgingly, Thomas bowed to the king's will on the very day he heard from his royal master. Despite his finances becoming 'much decayed', he agreed to pay Jane £100 rather than 100 marks, although he was quick to justify the original sum by referring to the jointure document itself to prove he had not cheated her. One hundred marks had been stipulated for while he was alive, she had been entitled to 200 marks only after his 'decease', and the latter he would now freely increase to 300 marks. Jane had, he thought, been treated generously. As a young man, he maintained, he had managed on an annual income of £50 despite his wife having a baby every year, thus implying that his daughter-in-law was simply avaricious.

Jane, however, felt she had achieved a fairer settlement, for the time being at least. In the long term, a new accommodation might well be possible. Cromwell had brokered the new deal, and he had done so because of her own prompting. Now in her early thirties, she was still reliant on the power of men, but that was to be expected in her society. The difference, however, was that this time the aid had come because she herself had been proactive. She had not quietly taken the 100 marks and settled into genteel obscurity, hoping that

Lord Morley might stir himself sufficiently to arrange a second marriage for her. As a widow with an assured income, she was not a bad catch, possibly for a younger son, but she was not a good one either. Unlike Brereton's widow, who had property from her first marriage, Jane had no lands of her own, her brother being first in line for the Morley estates. Only her jointure, hardly princely, stood between her and penury, or humiliating dependence on her family. So far she had produced no children, and that could also lower her worth in an age when the bloodline had to be perpetuated. Even Thomas must have handed on the Ormond horn with anguish, and not solely because he hated to see the back of anything valuable.

In addition, she had spent almost two decades at court. She had been at the heart of power. She had been present while the Boleyns had changed her world, and she had been there on those state occasions which flaunted those changes, and themselves, to the entire court. She had known the most powerful and influential figures of the country, including the king himself. Of course, the fallout from failure had been dramatic, the deaths of George and Anne were still raw, but to leave all of that excitement behind for ever was another matter altogether.

Perhaps there was an alternative. Jane's £100 brought her a measure of security. It was not a huge amount but it was far more than the majority of the population, toiling away in isolated villages, would dream of in their lifetimes. Yet it would not give her the standard of living that she had been used to, and it might mean that she would have to leave the environment where she had passed so much of her life. If there was a way to stay at court, to carve out a career for herself rather than as an appendage to a new husband, it would be worth consideration. Cromwell had helped her once, maybe he would do so again. But there would need to be something in it for him.

24

A New Beginning

We do not know how long Cromwell took to position Jane Rochford in Jane Seymour's privy chamber, but she was soon installed and it was more than a case of déjà vu. When she had last strolled through those intimate rooms, it had been to greet and serve her own sister-in-law, whose vivacious presence could not yet have been entirely eradicated or forgotten. Then Jane had been a woman of some importance, with George a rising star, and she herself with a scholar at Cambridge, enviable clothes and silver dishes with her initials etched on to them. Now Jane's world had moved on. Anne's name was anathema. The king considered himself fortunate to have escaped her wicked machinations, and George was equally smeared as an incestuous adulterer, the 'sweet brother' who was rather too sweet. Jane Rochford had to forge a new life for herself, and forget the ghosts of yesterday.

And being back in the royal privy chamber gave her the chance to do just that. She was at court again and she had a role. It was up to her whether she made a success of it, but perhaps a little of Anne's singular grit and determination – which even Cromwell ruefully acknowledged to Chapuys when he extolled 'beyond measure the wit and the courage' of both the dead queen and her dead brother – had rubbed off on Jane. She was on familiar territory, despite the changes in personnel.

The main change was that Henry had married Jane Seymour and with indecent haste. While Anne was taking her last few steps to the scaffold, delivering her short speech praising him for his gentleness and mercy and then fastidiously arranging her skirts, the king was waiting impatiently at Westminster for the news that the

French executioner had completed his task. The moment he heard that Anne really was dead and he was free, the bereaved monarch hurried to his barge and was rowed straight to Jane 'whom he had lodged a mile from him, in a house by the river'. They were betrothed the very next day and married at the end of the month, a mere eleven days after Anne's execution. The venue was the queen's closet at Whitehall, Wolsey's former palace of York Place that Anne had liked so much. Naturally, Henry did not want his people to believe that he had sacrificed Anne on the flimsiest of grounds to satisfy a personal whim. Instead, he wanted it known that he had only consented to a third marriage, and to Mistress Seymour, 'the most virtuous lady and veriest gentlewoman that liveth', because of the entreaties of 'all his nobles and council upon their knees'.

Jane was not the only courtier to see that Henry adored Queen Jane as he had formerly adored Anne, even if, perhaps, his love was softer and less intensely physical this time. Most of the court approved of the substitution. On the very day after Anne's death, Cromwell made a note to remind himself to write to Sir William Kingston and Anthony Anthony, presumably to thank them for all they had done to make her execution run smoothly, and to contact Sir John Gage. Clearly, Gage, a man who would play an important role at the end of Jane's life, and who had kept an extremely low profile during Anne's years as queen, was notified that his return to mainstream politics would be welcome. He was quickly ensconced in Queen Jane's council. Sir John Russell summed up the feelings of many when, in a letter to Honor Lisle's husband, he said that the king had 'come out of hell into heaven for the gentleness in this and the cursedness and the unhappiness in the other'. Russell went on to advise Lord Lisle to be sure to congratulate Henry on being 'so well matched with so gracious a woman as is reported', a comment which, Lisle was informed, would 'please the king'. No doubt Honor busied herself in deciding on the most appropriate presents to send to the current queen as she had done to the former. She would choose with care, for she was keen to place her two daughters at court.

Cromwell, too, knew that the royal couple seemed well suited. Once he had realised the extent of Henry's involvement with Mistress Seymour, he had been prepared to act against Anne. As a living reminder of Katherine's humiliation and with her advanced ideas on the proper use of monastic funds, she presented something of a problem in any case as royal policies had shifted. Cromwell took the sole credit for bringing about Anne's fall when he talked to Chapuys, whereas in fact he had laboured alongside Nicholas Carew and supporters of Princess Mary to engineer it. If the king wanted Jane Seymour, he must have her, and Cromwell had been willing to join forces with those who were working to the same end, particularly if it would cool their antagonism towards him personally. The trouble was – and this was where Jane Rochford might be useful to him – Mistress Seymour would not come alone. Cromwell would deal ruthlessly with Mary, Carew and their allies in due course, but he would not be able to take the same measures with the highly ambitious Seymour brothers, who were at court with their recently elevated sister. No sooner had Thomas and George Boleyn disappeared from the scene, along with the ever-present and influential Norris, than Edward and Thomas Seymour surfaced. Edward, the elder, had been at court for some years, first as a page of honour to Mary Tudor on her marriage to Louis XII, then as an esquire of the king's household, an esquire of the body and then a gentleman of the privy chamber. An able soldier, he had the makings of a particularly able courtier. And his brother came too. Although younger and less capable than Edward, Thomas was just as thrusting and ambitious and, within five months of his sister's wedding, he joined Edward in the king's privy chamber. They quickly gained offices, perquisites and, in Edward's case, titles. Five days after Henry lovingly looked into Jane Seymour's eyes at the wedding ceremony, he bestowed the title of Viscount Beauchamp on her brother. Chapuys found Edward Seymour conducting him to the king's chamber just as George Boleyn had done such a short while before.

Cromwell could keep a wary eye on the Seymours only up to a point, and he could not wander in and out of the queen's private rooms. Jane could. When she had begged him for help with her jointure payments, Jane had promised Cromwell her prayers and her 'service'. A source of information from behind closed doors might well be invaluable to the minister. To build up intelligence through personal contacts was sensible; after all, it was how Chapuys often operated. Whilst we have no concrete evidence that Jane was reinstated as a lady of the bedchamber through Cromwell's machinations, it is certainly a possibility. The bargain would have suited both of them. She would be back where she felt at home, despite the horrific events she had endured, and he would gain insider knowledge that could be invaluable.

So Jane returned to familiar territory. She was very well acquainted with her new mistress from their days of waiting on Anne. She has left us no clues about her own feelings as she performed her duties and made obeisance to Queen Jane, previously her equal, as she had done to Queen Anne. Maybe the differences between the two queens made the transition easier for her. Queen Jane was quieter, demure, of no 'great wit', according to an intrigued Chapuys. Her privy apartments would be calmer, more peaceful, but decidedly less vibrant and exciting, than those presided over by Anne. Nor was Queen Jane a beauty. Of middle height, she was 'so fair that one would call her rather pale than otherwise', Chapuys reported to Charles, and she was not in the first flush of youth. 'Over twenty-five', sneered the ambassador, before ruminating waspishly on the poor morals of English women, which, he felt, might be shared by Queen Jane. This would be useful should Henry ever want to divorce her, because he would soon find 'enough of witnesses' to testify to her premarital sexual romps. Whether the ambassador actually believed any of this is more doubtful. Certainly the new queen had behaved with conspicuous propriety during Henry's courtship, as Jane was fully aware. And Henry loved her. It would be as well to remember that, and not dwell on the past, if Jane was to stay at court.

In some ways, it was easy to think well of Queen Jane. She clearly portrayed contrasting character traits and sympathies to the volatile Anne, at least in public. To Chapuys' delight, she promised to do what she could for Mary, not an easy pledge to keep. The ever-hopeful ambassador saw light at the end of the tunnel for the former princess. If she would help Mary and persuade Henry to favour her, he affirmed, Queen Jane would realise Anne's motto of the 'Happiest of Women', a feat now beyond the dead queen, and earn herself the epithet of the 'Pacificator' in the process. As a Boleyn, Jane Rochford had never commented on Princess Mary's fate. With George and Anne rotting in their makeshift graves, she still stayed silent. The circumspection she had practised for so long would not be abandoned yet.

Mary's rehabilitation in royal affection, however, was a popular assumption. It was surely simply a matter of time before Mary took her rightful place at her father's side. Ostensibly the omens were good. Mary had viewed Anne as her chief enemy and now that she was out of the picture, Mary could see no reason for continued persecution. Mary wrote several letters both to her father and to Queen Jane, receiving 'kind words and encouraging hopes', although significantly not from the royal couple themselves, that tempted her to believe her troubles were over. She was even able to receive the odd visitor, although that was not to last. It was not long before Lady Shelton, in post as lady governess despite Anne's fall, was ordered to keep her incommunicado. Before Lady Shelton received that instruction, Lord Morley visited Mary at Hunsdon at Whitsun in early June, about three weeks after the executions.

As Hunsdon was only six miles away from Great Hallingbury, there was nothing remarkable about a courtesy call, although Jane's father had not visited the princess at Beaulieu or Hatfield, neither of which was too far for a day's journey. Plainly, Morley, ever careful where personal security was involved, felt that the fall of the Boleyns had changed the political landscape, as indeed it had, although not quite as much as he seemed to think. Mary and Morley hit it off. A friendship developed which was to last for many years and involve gifts on both sides. Mary even became godmother to Jane's nephew, and gave 15s to the baby's midwife and nurse. Lord Morley had the useful knack of being agreeable to all, of course. He had already sent Cromwell a greyhound 'for a gentleman to disport withal', hoping that the dog would be 'the best'. Cromwell so much deserved relaxation, an obsequious Morley wrote, after his 'great labours', which he 'hourly take for the wealth of many'. A little later, he sent the minister, somewhat appropriately, copies (in Italian) of Machiavelli's *History of Florence* and *The Prince*. For a man like Morley, approaching Mary was a rational move.

Jane's father did not go alone that Whit Sunday. His wife and daughter accompanied him. The daughter's name is not mentioned in the documents, which has led to speculation that she was Jane. However, since Jane was much too busy trying to sort out her jointure problems, the daughter referred to was far more likely to have been her sister, Margaret, married to John Shelton, Lady Shelton's son, a staunch Catholic who would later prove his devotion to Mary's cause. For Margaret to go with her parents and take the opportunity to talk to her parents-in-law was perfectly natural, and the princess came to like her. Mary gave £1 to the midwife and nurse at the christening of the Sheltons' baby and paid 8s for a frontlet* as a present to Margaret. For Jane, the wife of a convicted traitor, it would have been unwise to call on Mary before the princess's official reconciliation with the king. Once Mary was back in favour, it was to be a different story. Then, being on good terms with the king's elder daughter was a shrewd move.

Jane more than likely witnessed the reunion of father and daughter, although this took time. Henry did not welcome Mary back with open arms, as if all memories of her disobedience had been instantly erased. She would first be forced to recognise the invalidity of her mother's marriage and her own illegitimacy. Rumours of the pressure that was placed upon her would have reached Jane's ears. When Mary refused to accept her mother's divorce with all its implications, she was viciously abused and told that she was 'an unnatural daughter' who deserved to have her head beaten against the wall until it became 'as soft as a boiled apple'. Cromwell called her 'the most obstinate woman that ever was'. Faced with such merciless treatment, and with the danger to her supporters so great, she finally capitulated. Acknowledging her father as Supreme Head of the Church and the pope merely as the Bishop of Rome, she accepted that her mother's marriage to Henry was 'by God's law and man's law incestuous and unlawful'. She begged her father's pardon for not conceding more quickly: 'I do most humbly beseech the King's Highness, my father, whom I have obstinately and inobedi-

---

* A decorative band that could be worn around the forehead, perhaps as part of a headdress.

ently offended in the denial of the same heretofore, to forgive mine offences therein, and to take me to his great mercy.' As Henry demanded total surrender, complete humiliation, Mary had to go still further, making the promise, 'I will never vary from that confession and submission I made to your Highness in the presence of the Council.' In a state of inner turmoil, finding the stress almost unbearable, a broken Mary pleaded with Chapuys to ask the pope for a dispensation for what she had been compelled to say.

Now that he had his way, Henry could find it in his heart to forgive her. He and Queen Jane went to see Mary with a small group of attendants. The reconciliation was highly emotional. Henry was at his most loving and magnanimous. 'No father could have behaved better towards his daughter,' a relieved Chapuys told Charles. Queen Jane gave her a diamond ring, Henry gave her money, and immediately she was treated with more respect and reverence. It all boded well for the future, although Chapuys had to backtrack a few days later, when he informed the emperor that 'mixed with the sweet food of paternal kindness, there were a few drachmas of gall and bitterness', which he put down to the assertion of 'paternal authority'.

With Mary no longer judged as inferior to Elizabeth, who had also lost her title and her legitimate status, she was able to join the king and queen at court. Jane had no need to distance herself from Mary. An assessment of the current state of the succession suggested that it might indeed be politic to be on good terms with her. All of Henry's three acknowledged children had been bastardised. Because of his gender, the Duke of Richmond would probably have taken precedence but he died before his eighteenth birthday, possibly from a lung infection. When he had witnessed the swordsman strike Anne's head from her body, Richmond had little more than two months to live. That left Mary and Elizabeth, unless Queen Jane proved fruitful. Although the king allegedly told Mary that 'he was getting old, and feared he would have no children by his present wife', hope still sprang eternal in the royal breast. Just before Richmond's early death, Parliament passed a new Act of Succession by which the children of Henry and Queen Jane would inherit and, if there were none, the king could name his own successor.

Nonetheless, if the queen really did fail to produce an heir for him, there was always a possibility that Mary would succeed to the throne after all.

Perhaps it was with this in mind that Jane developed a relationship of a sort with her. The princess was on friendly terms with both the Morleys and the Sheltons, despite Lady Anne Shelton's tempestuous years as her lady governess. Sir John Shelton, Lady Anne's husband, remained in charge of Mary's household even after it was reorganised by the summer of 1536. Jane needed to make her own way; the Boleyn shield had disintegrated so building bridges was always prudent. Therefore she gave Mary a clock, probably as a New Year's Gift in 1537, although the princess had to pay 5s to have the item mended a few weeks later. A month later, Mary paid just over £4 for twelve yards of black satin as a present to Jane, and she gave money to Jane's servants and to one of her gentlewomen several times over the next few years. Mary and Jane met frequently at court during that time, and the payments and gifts show that some kind of bond certainly existed between them, although we do not know whether it was close or simply politeness. Nor, of course, do we really know what Jane had thought of Mary during her own years as a Boleyn wife. She may have felt more innate sympathy with the princess than she had ever dared reveal, although she had been aware that her own true interests depended on Anne's children ascending the throne one day. Since the chance that little Elizabeth would do so was now remote, maintaining a reasonable discourse with Mary was eminently pragmatic.

Thus Jane settled back into her usual life, albeit with an alternative mistress. In public, Queen Jane lived up to her chosen motto of 'Bound to Obey and Serve', an attitude which gratified her husband who wanted no more tantrums and interference from a wife. Subservience was a word that had never been in Anne's vocabulary. Queen Jane appeared to do all the right things: she seemed sweet and kind to everyone. She had even kept her word to Chapuys and had indeed pleaded for Mary, so much so that the king had told her she was being short-sighted and should save her care for the children she might have herself. If she pressed too much, she ran the risk of being 'rudely repulsed'. Few can have been more relieved than Queen

Jane when Mary's rustication ended. Relations between the two women were always respectful but affectionate, Mary writing to her as 'the Queen's Grace, my good mother'. The queen had not entirely learnt her lesson, however. Conservative in matters of religion, she sank to her knees to beg the king to restore the monasteries, only to be told sharply to get up and not 'meddle with his affairs'. Her predecessor had died, Henry warned, 'in consequence of meddling too much with state affairs', a threat that 'was enough to frighten a woman who is not very secure', reported Chapuys.

Perhaps that was why Queen Jane's sister, Elizabeth, Lady Ughtred, wrote to Cromwell when left in comparative poverty following the death of her husband. When William Carey had fallen victim to the sweat, Mary Carey had written first to her sister and Anne had gone straight to plead with Henry on her behalf. Elizabeth did not approach Queen Jane. Clearly she felt that her sister either would not help her, an interesting reflection on Queen Jane's studied kindness, or could not, which might illustrate the limited extent of her influence with Henry. Lady Ughtred wanted monastic land and specified which, so that at least she could secure a house for herself. She had been 'driven', she said, 'to be a sojourner' as her living was too poor for her to welcome her friends. Cromwell took the matter in hand, seizing the chance to marry off his own son, Gregory, to the grieving widow. Queen Jane's influence might be weak, he was determined to increase his own, and a union with the Seymours could be of benefit.

But there were areas in which Queen Jane maintained her authority with a quiet determination which belied her seeming diffidence, nowhere less so than on the vexed question of costume. Jane probably discovered that her wardrobe needed a few alterations to fit in with the queen's dictates, for the queen had her own style, essentially a contrast to that of the elegant, chic Anne. No more French hoods; the old-fashioned gable style was back in vogue, and eagle-eyed women spotted the odd difference in other areas of fashion too. Mr Skut, Anne's former dressmaker, found himself in demand, although Honor Lisle was 'disappointed' with the outfit he completed for her, which he had promised 'should be made like the Queen's gowns'. Her daughter, Anne Basset, fell foul of the queen's antipathy to the

French hood. After constant scheming, machinations and outright bribery, the indefatigable Honor had managed to get her daughter Anne into the privy chamber, only to find that yet more money had to be spent on equipping the girl for her tasks. The queen graciously allowed Anne to 'wear out her French apparel', but refused to countenance anything other than the correct headdress. Less than a month later, the queen changed her mind. The 'French apparel' would be tolerated no longer. Anne was to have 'a gown of black satin, and another of velvet'. She needed one or two bonnets, complete with a band of pearls.

Such restrictions affected Jane as well. Although of a higher rank than Anne Basset, now one of her junior companions in the privy apartments, Jane understood how crucial it was to accede to the queen's will on every issue. If Queen Jane wanted her ladies to sport the gable headdress, the favourite of Queen Katherine, then sport it they would. The queen had to be obeyed.

Jane's life, however, was quite a comfortable one. She was, after all, a viscountess; her rank had not been stripped from her, and that brought privileges. She was expected to have female servants, two above the number that her mother could have, but six below that of a duchess. If there was a court procession, she had a set place in the line, as did each of her women. The precise number that Jane employed eludes us, but she did not have to worry about fending for herself. The £100 that she had manoeuvred from a smarting Thomas would help. And as she served the queen, so was she served herself. Jane would receive two main meals a day: dinner, which was taken towards midday, and supper in the evening. She would not go hungry. The menus for each meal, or mess, were carefully selected. There were two main courses of several dishes. She could choose between beef, mutton, veal, a capon or coney (rabbit), possibly flavoured with a popular herb, aloe. The second course could involve lamb, plovers, teal (a small duck) or various tarts. Fruit was plentiful and so were eggs. She could nibble at two kinds of bread: circular roll-like manchets, made from the finest wheat, or chunks of a slightly coarser cheate loaf. She could quench her thirst on beer or wine. The pattern for dinner was replicated all over again at supper. Henry's chefs did not cook meat on Fridays, of course, but the sheer number of fish options was staggering: ling, pike, whiting, bream, chub, trout, conger eels, perch, crayfish, crabs, shrimps and lampreys. Should Jane still feel peckish, manchet and cheate loaf were always available in her room, which she could wash down with a gallon of ale three times a day or a pitcher of wine in the evening. Nor would she shiver. Between 31 October and 1 April, she was given two fires and plenty of fuel for her chamber. Wax candles ensured that she need not sit in the dark. This standard of living was what Jane had become used to as a Boleyn.

The only slight cloud on her horizon concerned the Parker family. Jane's brother, Henry, together with his relative, Sir John St John, had somehow managed to become involved in a hunting dispute. Such things could often involve serious repercussions, so Jane would have every right to feel concerned. Lord Morley, appreciating the young men's predicament, knew what action to take. There is no record of how much he had spent on Cromwell's greyhound, but it was a sound investment, for Morley contacted the minister to resolve the situation. And Cromwell complied. In one of his lists of 'Remembrances', he reminded himself to 'speak for' Henry and St John. Morley thanked him profusely for his 'favour' to the two men 'in their trouble' and expressed his gratitude 'for their deliverance'.

With that potentially unpleasant scrape dealt with, Jane could enjoy court life to the full. When Anne's confidante, she had always enjoyed taking part in court processions and, with her new mistress, she could now do so again. None would match Anne's coronation celebrations, when Jane had had such a prominent role but, while on nowhere near the same scale, the journey to Greenwich for the Christmas celebrations had nostalgic overtones for Jane. The winter was so very cold that the River Thames froze over. Barges could not negotiate the ice so the royal party had to ride from London to Greenwich. The citizens of London unpacked the cloth of gold and the arras to decorate the houses as the cavalcade rode through the gravelled streets where cheering crowds were just as eager to catch a glimpse of Henry's new queen as they had been to see Anne. The parade was led by Sir Ralph Warren, the Lord Mayor, and the aldermen, all beautifully dressed in their ceremonial robes. The members of the city guilds and crafts, in their livery and with their hoods on their shoulders, were represented too. Friars in their richly embroidered copes stood on one side of the narrow streets, holding candles, with crosses aloft and censers at the ready. The choir of St Paul's stood by the west door of the great church, while two priests from every parish church in the city lined the route for some way onwards, each proudly carrying the very best cross and candlesticks and censers that their individual churches possessed. As a demonstration of monarchical power, and as an assertion of the old faith to calm fears surfacing over monastic closures, it could not have been bettered. The king felt satisfied, Queen Jane no doubt felt at ease. The whole event was such a glittering spectacle and success that 'it rejoiced every man wondrously', Lord Lisle was informed.

It was definitely impressive. And, as Jane could see for herself, recent events notwithstanding, royal pomp was what it always had been. So was the court. Mary rode in the cavalcade, her years as a pariah blanked out. Blanked out too were Anne and George. As for Jane Rochford, she might be a lonely widow, her property and wealth considerably reduced, but she was back where she belonged.

25

A Prince at Last

How long Jane would last within the queen's privy chamber depended very much on how long the queen herself lasted. Henry seemed to love her, but his fickle, changeable nature made him a most unreliable husband. Indeed, just over a week after the announcement of his wedding, the king confided to Chapuys that, 'having twice met two beautiful young ladies', he was 'somewhat sorry that he had not seen them before his marriage'. And there was no coronation. The idea was mooted, a possible date earmarked, but nothing happened, plague being given as the excuse to postpone it for the time being. In his report to the emperor, the ambassador conveyed the rumour circulating to the effect that the queen would not be crowned at all unless she became pregnant. As Jane, and virtually the entire court knew by now, that would not be easy.

Miraculously, whether through Mary's prayers, for she was always telling her father that she prayed that he and Queen Jane would have issue, or through his own gargantuan efforts, Henry managed it. Queen Jane, within about eight months or so of her marriage, became pregnant. It was a commendable achievement. Having got this far, all that she needed to do was to give Henry the longed-for son. Whatever gender the child proved to be, Jane realised that any distant dreams of the throne for her niece, Elizabeth, were receding further into the distance as every week passed. With both Katherine and Anne safely dead, the legitimacy of Queen Jane's child would be beyond question.

The news of the royal pregnancy was greeted with delight in the City of London. It was officially announced on Trinity Sunday, 27

May 1537, almost a year to the day since Henry had ostentatiously acceded to the entreaties of his Council and married the woman for whom, in fact, he yearned. Audley and Cromwell, along with the mayor, the aldermen and guild officials, were amongst the congregation who celebrated the tidings in a *Te Deum* held in St Paul's. Bishop Hugh Latimer, ironically one of Anne's bishops, preached so effectively that his 'oration was marvellous fruitful to the hearers'. The poor could join in the jubilation too, drinking themselves silly from the free wine that was provided at the side of every spluttering bonfire. And, not to be left out, the people of Calais were treated to sounds of gunshot at 4 p.m. that afternoon.

Henry was overjoyed. Perhaps this time God would give him the heir he knew he deserved. The timing was particularly pleasing and opportune because the Pilgrimage of Grace, the rebellion that had greeted the monastic closures, and which had caused him tremendous concern and anger, was just being mopped up. London Bridge was decked with the boiled heads of some of those executed for questioning the royal will and, throughout the northern shires, a terrified populace could see the decaying bodies of those punished for similar presumption. Two of the leaders, Robert Aske and Sir Robert Constable, were hanged in chains until death mercifully claimed them. Since the list of the victims included Lord Darcy and Lord Hussey, the visible display of Henry's justice once again sent shivers down the spines of his courtiers. Neither noble blood nor years of service were any safeguard against the executioner. Everyone understood very clearly that the king must always be obeyed. No one, he had told the rebels, could 'rule' their prince.

Jane knew that from bitter experience. When Anne's influence had started to wane, Henry had had no qualms about asserting his authority with ruthless aggression. Even Queen Jane had experienced the force of his anger. With the Pilgrimage crushed and Mary forgiven, however, life within the queen's privy chamber settled back into a familiar routine. A more relaxed Henry was solicitous towards his pregnant wife, a thoughtful Mary sent her cucumbers several times to satisfy her cravings. And it was up to Queen Jane's ladies to care for her and keep up her strength for the ordeal ahead. Jane, of course, had been there before. She was an old hand in the birth room by now, she had been attendant on Anne and was now to be attendant on her successor. She was not the only person who had made the transition from one queen to another; Anne's former vice-chamberlain, Sir Edward Baynton, made a similar shift when he accepted the same office under Queen Jane. He had ensured that the correct protocol had been followed for Anne, he would do so for Queen Jane as well. Established procedure would be followed to the letter.

The venue was different, though. Anne had given birth to Elizabeth at Greenwich, but Queen Jane's confinement took place at Wolsey's former palace of Hampton Court. The court moved there from Esher and Stoke in the middle of September to give the queen time to rest and prepare herself. Henry wanted both his wife and his new child to have the very best accommodation, so he had already ordered alterations and improvements to be made in readiness. The bay windows in the queen's bedchamber were fitted with thick, no doubt richly embellished, curtains to protect her from any draughts and the dangers that lurked in fresh air. There was a wooden porch constructed over the door and a screen provided to shield her bed. Other arrangements for Queen Jane's comfort and security could be left to Baynton and her ladies, so she was given the same prescribed bedding and hangings that Anne had received not so long ago, with perhaps a card table to help while away the hours of waiting. For the child, there was a new nursery already prepared.

The queen retired to the female world of her chamber, away from public gaze, on Sunday, 16 September. Now it was just a case of waiting for the onset of labour. Jane, as one of the privy chamber, accompanied her mistress but, if she was able to take a little time off from her duties to rest and relax, her quarters at Hampton Court were particularly fine. She was entitled to double lodgings there, which meant that she was allocated two large rooms for her own use. There was a fireplace in each room, which was probably a great boon even in October, and she had the luxury of her own lavatory. It was all most satisfactory; she could start to put behind her the weeks of anxiety associated with the deaths of George and Anne. She had the chance to start again, but she was not starting at square one.

However, caring for the queen was her main role. The birth of the baby and Queen Jane's recovery were paramount. On Thursday, 11 October, the queen's labour began. With Jane amidst the ladies at her side, the midwife encouraging her and mopping her forehead, Queen Jane tossed on her lavishly furnished bed, her newly acquired royal status no defence against the intense pain. The moment news of her contractions was released, the Mayor of London, the aldermen and guild members, all wearing their liveries, joined in prayers for her safe delivery. Maybe their supplications were heard, for her child was born at about 2 a.m. on Friday morning. To the joy of her ladies, and the ecstatic relief of Henry, the baby was a boy. He was to be called Edward, because he was born on the eve of St Edward's Day. Even the day seemed special, a clear indication that Henry's heir was linked to England's royal saint, whose jewelled shrine was so close to the resting place of Henry's first-born son, the little Prince Henry who had died so tragically over twenty years previously.

Within the queen's bedchamber her ladies had no respite. Some cared for the exhausted but happy mother, while others gave their attention to their new prince. The procedure was standard: the infant's navel was gently dabbed with a cooling powder of aloes and frankincense, any blood washed away and the swaddled child lovingly placed in his cradle, the midwife making the sign of the cross upon him. It was never too soon to seek the sheltering power of the Church. Luckily, both mother and child were doing well. The baby was healthy and the queen had survived her travail. Now she needed rest and the ladies of her privy chamber were there to see that she got it.

Rest was the last thing on other minds, however. As Jane attended her mistress in that quiet darkened room, the court went into overdrive. Letters announcing the birth of the king's son, 'conceived in lawful matrimony', were sent out, courtiers not at Hampton Court hurriedly wrote to congratulate the king, and even the emperor was pleasant. He was 'as rejoiced as if it had been by his aunt', or so he said. London erupted with excitement. There was yet another *Te Deum*, this time sung in all of the parish churches throughout the city. Every bell in every church was rung for hours on end until the aching bellringers must have almost dropped from tiredness. The mayor and aldermen hastily donned their robes again, the best crosses and candlesticks were brought out by the various parish priests and, in the presence of the French ambassador, Cromwell, Audley, the Marquess of Dorset and all the judges, including Spelman no doubt, there was another service held at St Paul's. The noise was soon deafening, the pealing of the bells, the sounds of Henry's musicians and the gun salute from the Tower combining together in a cacophony of joy. The celebrations continued until late evening. There were bonfires, a further gun salute from the Tower, and free wine for the poor who probably wished that queens gave birth to sons more often.

None of this affected Jane, of course. She was preoccupied with the queen, who seemed to be recovering satisfactorily but would be remaining in her chamber for some while yet. The arrangements for Edward's christening, already being discussed, did not directly concern Queen Jane as by custom she did not attend. Also by custom, neither did Henry. Although we have a list of the most important gentlemen who were there, only a handful of women, those with set roles, are named. Jane is not mentioned. There was a defined place in the line for ladies of the privy chamber, however, and since Anne Basset, a very new and junior recruit, definitely was present, even needing a new dress for the occasion, it is highly probable that Jane was there too. It would certainly be an event worth attending. Elizabeth's christening had been splendid, and she had been but a princess. Edward was a prince.

On the following Monday, a bare three days after the birth, the ceremony that Henry had almost despaired of finally took place. Workmen laboured throughout much of the weekend to get the Chapel Royal and the processional route ready and to construct the traverses, or cubicles, that were needed. Knights, lords and barons travelled to Hampton Court in response to the king's summons, Jane's father and brother with them. They had their part to play as their prince was received into the Catholic Church. So too did the old guard like Norfolk and Suffolk and the Marchioness of Exeter (her indiscretions over the Holy Maid of Kent conveniently forgotten) and so too did the queen's officials Sir Edward Baynton and Sir John Gage. Of the younger figures, Queen Jane's brother Edward was in a particularly prominent position. Thomas Boleyn, eager to prove his loyalty despite his children's treachery, was in attendance, since he was, after all, one of England's leading peers. For Thomas, who had so hoped that it would be his grandson who was Henry's heir, the occasion cannot have been easy, but he could show no regret for what might have been, for he would be on full public view himself. So he fulfilled his allotted task, swallowing his grief and hiding his resentment at the continued rise and rise of Cromwell, to whom he had been forced to relinquish his post of Lord Privy Seal and who had joined the exclusive ranks of the Knights of the Garter in August.

The ladies of the privy chamber were not at the front of the procession. Gentlemen, squires and knights went first, two by two, each of them carrying an unlit torch. They were followed by the children, ministers and Dean of the Chapel, all of whom walked in silence. The Council and the Lords Spiritual and Temporal came next, with officials of the king's household and the queen's household after them, and then several foreign ambassadors. Cromwell and Audley walked behind, with Norfolk and Cranmer in the rear. The various items needed for the service, such as towels and basins, were solemnly carried by named members of the court. Sussex held two covered golden basins, Lord Montague at his side. Thomas held a taper of virgin wax, a towel around his neck, Essex bore the wonderful jewelled gold salt, which would be used when salt was sprinkled to save the baby from evil.

At last the key personages could be seen. Little Elizabeth, now four years old, carefully held the chrism. Because she was so young, Queen Jane's brother, Viscount Beauchamp, assisted by Jane's father, Lord Morley, carried her. And then came the most important baby in the land. Edward was in the Marchioness of Exeter's arms, with Suffolk and her husband, the Marquess of Exeter, beside her, the child's train borne by the Earl of Arundel and Lord William

Howard. Edward's nurse and the midwife entered at that point, walking proudly by Lord William. Gentlemen of the privy chamber held the beautifully embroidered canopy over Henry's precious heir, with an escort of four more gentlemen holding wax tapers. None was due to be lit until after the ceremonies were completed within the main body of the chapel. Mary, in visible recognition of her place within the royal family, was appointed her half-brother's godmother, so she had pride of place immediately after him, with Lady Kingston, Anne's erstwhile gaoler, supporting her train. Only after this long queue of people did the 'ladies of honour' take their place in the line. So, Jane would have been with them, in her required position, although it was a far cry from the period when she had been exalted beyond her rank in the days of Queen Anne.

The procession began at the prince's 'lodging', wound through the Council chamber to the king's 'great chamber', into the hall, then into the second court, then the gallery which led to the chapel itself. The floor was covered with rushes, and special barriers, draped with rich hangings, were erected along the route for the moment when the party moved into the open air.

At last everyone reached the chapel, passing through a specially erected porch which was covered in cloth of gold and had been thickly carpeted. Once inside, the congregation was greeted by a blaze of colour and the gleam of gold. Arras adorned the walls, carpets were on the floor, the high altar was 'richly garnished with stuff and plate'. The font was the focus of attention, no one could miss seeing it. Superbly crafted in silver and gilt, it stood upon a carpeted platform, underneath a canopy, and within barriers draped with silken fabric and cloth of gold. Special exits led from the enclosure towards the altar. Norfolk, Suffolk and Cranmer, the young prince's godfathers, waited beneath the canopy for his arrival. Standing with them were Sir John Russell, Sir Francis Bryan, Sir Nicholas Carew and Sir Anthony Browne, deputed to remain in charge of the font until the end of the service. In case the child wanted attention before the ceremony, there was another cubicle close by, also carpeted, draped in costly material and heated by a pan of coals.

The service was traditional, just as it had been for Jane's niece, Elizabeth, when she had been the king's favoured child. Those designated to hand out towels and basins, or uncover basins at the appropriate moment, did so as required. Edward was officially taken into the bosom of the Church and, like Elizabeth, was also confirmed. Once Garter King of Arms had proclaimed the baby's name and titles, it was almost at an end. Wine, wafers and spiced delicacies were served to Mary and Elizabeth, to Suffolk, Norfolk and Cranmer. Then it was the turn of the others, both those sufficiently favoured by the king to be allowed inside the main body of the chapel and those standing in the court near by. The former were offered spiced wine and sweetmeats, which were probably very welcome after the long ceremony, while those outside were simply handed sweet wine and bread.

Now, as the trumpets burst forth and the choristers raised their voices to the glory of God and their prince, candles and tapers were lit, their flickering flames reflected in the golden ornaments of the church and highlighting the glowing colours of the hangings. In their original order, the huge train processed out, returning to the palace. It was quite a marathon for the trumpeters, as they were expected to keep playing until Edward reached Queen Jane's bed-chamber. For the godparents, it had proved an expensive honour. None had dared be penny-pinching as their generous gifts reveal. Mary presented a cup of gold, carried for her by the Earl of Essex; Thomas Boleyn held Cranmer's offering of three bowls and two pots, all of silver and gilt; Sussex carried Norfolk's gifts, which were exactly the same as those of the archbishop; and Suffolk's silver and gilt flagons and pots were borne by Beauchamp.

Henry and Queen Jane were waiting to see their son and to formally receive the presents, which had been transported from the chapel. For the king, this was the triumphant conclusion of so many years of hope and despair. He had a son and heir. It had taken three marriages, but he had achieved his dream. Queen Jane had every right to feel secure: she had succeeded where the daughter of Ferdinand and Isabella had failed, as had her supplanter, Jane's sister-in-law, Henry's 'own sweetheart'. When her ladies gave her a minute account of every last detail that they had witnessed in the chapel that morning, Queen Jane felt confident that the king would never put her aside. She would remain Henry's wife and England's queen until the day she died. And Viscountess Rochford would be with her.

26

The Bitterness of Death

Clad in black, with a white cloth covering her head and shoulders, Jane knelt in prayer during the solemn mass. She was not alone, merely one of the ladies and gentlewomen of Queen Jane's privy chamber, all of whom were dressed alike and were undertaking the same sombre task. It was almost the last thing they could do for their mistress, for they were gathered around a huge hearse on which the body of the queen was lying. No one could quite believe it. The catastrophe had happened so swiftly.

There had been nothing to indicate that Queen Jane was within days of her death when she and Henry had received their infant son straight after the splendour of his christening. Henry was thrilled with the child, the visible sign that God had smiled on him after all those years of disappointment. The queen's relatives had benefited from her reflected glory as Cromwell himself read out the letters patent creating Beauchamp Earl of Hertford. That had been a very good day for the Seymours: the queen's second brother, Thomas, was knighted by the king a few hours after Edward had joined the ranks of the peerage. And, within the queen's apartments, all had seemed well. Queen Jane had progressed normally, young Anne Basset had anticipated the delivery of a new dress for the queen's churching. But the churching had never taken place.

Eight days after the christening, Queen Jane had become ill. Cromwell later blamed her women for neglecting her. They had, he said, 'suffered her to take cold, and eat such things as her fantasy in sickness called for'. With experienced ladies such as Jane about her, his accusation seems far-fetched. However, from whatever cause, she had passed what the doctors, hastily summoned to treat her, called a 'natural laxe', a massive loosening of the bowels probably, in her case, liberally laced with blood. Dr Butts, now the king's most trusted physician, assisted by Dr George Owen, had done what they could as her ladies gently tended the weakening queen. For a while she had rallied, but it was a short respite. The night proved sleepless and fraught in the queen's bedchamber as she rapidly deteriorated. In the early morning on Wednesday, 24 October, her attendants had called for her confessor; by 8 a.m. he had the priest ready to perform the last rites.

She had lingered throughout the day, gradually slipping away. We have no record of Henry visiting his dying wife, but we would not expect to find one. It was not the custom and, in any case, the king was always afraid of sickness, even in those he loved. Much though he had adored Anne, he had stayed miles away from her as she had burnt with the sweat. So, like everyone else, he had waited as the hours slowly passed and Queen Jane's strength ebbed, her chances of survival diminishing. Norfolk, worried about how Henry would react to the news that all were dreading, had scribbled a hurried note to Cromwell, begging him to return to Hampton Court instantly. The duke had written at 8 p.m. that evening, hoping that the minister could make it back to court by early morning on the following day. He was sure that Queen Jane would be dead by then, but Cromwell would be needed 'to comfort our good master'. There was 'no likelihood' that the queen could recover, Norfolk had said, signing the missive as from 'the hand of your sorrowful friend'.

And Norfolk had been right. The queen had not recovered. She had been beyond the desperate efforts of Butts and Owen, as well as the prayers offered up on her behalf. With her weeping ladies clustered at her side, one of them almost certainly Jane, the queen had died. She had enjoyed her new rank for less than eighteen months. When Henry had received the news, he had ordered Norfolk and Sir William Paulet, the treasurer of the household, to make the necessary arrangements for a state funeral and had then 'retired to a solitary place to pass his sorrows'. Her death hit him hard, in its immediate aftermath at least. To accept that 'the power of God ought to be esteemed all for the best', and that the queen was 'fortunate to live the day to bring forth such a prince', was easy only in theory. 'Divine Providence', he wrote to Francis, 'has mingled my joy with the bitterness of the death of her who brought me this happiness.'

For Jane, too, the death was bitter. She had worked hard to rehabilitate herself at court and carve out a career. A present of a gold tablet, probably a brooch, from Queen Jane as a New Year's Gift, proves how successful she had been in doing so but, as she knelt by the body of the dead queen, she knew that her own future was in doubt again. There would be no need for ladies of the privy chamber if there was no queen. However, such a problem had to be put from her mind for a while. At the moment all thoughts were focused on Queen Jane's burial, and that could not be rushed.

Katherine had been buried at Peterborough with considerable pomp, but Henry had been insistent that the ceremony should be commensurate only with her status as Dowager Princess of Wales. Jane Seymour was different. Although uncrowned, she had died a queen, and a queen moreover who had fulfilled her primary role of providing for the succession. In the king's eyes, she warranted the full obsequies that he had denied Katherine. Henry consulted Norfolk and Paulet, who looked into exactly what had happened at the interment of Elizabeth of York, Henry's own mother and the last reigning consort to die. He decided that Queen Jane would be buried at Windsor but there was much to do before she could be lowered into her tomb.

Thus it was that the queen's embalmed body lay in state underneath a canopy within her chamber of presence. At the foot of the hearse on which she rested stood an altar. It was here that the queen's chaplain said mass, and it was here that Jane as a lady of the bedchamber, robed in black and with the white cloth over her head, knelt amongst those praying beside the corpse day and night.

But the queen's body could not stay there for ever. A week after her death, the queen began the first stage of her final journey. Her bier, covered by a golden pall with a silver cross upon it, and with four noblemen holding the canopy to which were fixed four white banners portraying the Virgin Mary, was carried along the black-draped corridors and through the black-draped hall to the chapel, in a grim parody of the joyful procession for her baby's christening.

Jane was almost certainly amongst the black-gowned and hooded women who, walking two by two, followed the corpse into the chapel for the first of the many prayers that were intoned that morning.

The queen lay in the chapel for eleven full days of ritual, during which the grieving ladies of her privy chamber took their turn in watching over her. Jane was also at the centre of court protocol when the day came for the dead queen to be conveyed to Windsor.

At the crack of dawn on Monday, 12 November, Jane, robed in black, joined the other women and the most important figures of the land for a final requiem. It was, for Jane, almost a family reunion for Thomas Boleyn, Lord and Lady Morley and Jane's brother were all there. While the large congregation then went in to a welcome breakfast prepared for them by Henry's cooks within the palace – necessary because they faced a very long and tiring day – the queen's body was carried from the chapel on to the chariot that would take her through the countryside to Windsor. Drawn by horses with black trappings, it was draped in black velvet embellished with the royal arms. The canopy above it was also of black velvet, fringed with black silk and with a white satin cross upon it. But the black theme ended abruptly at the coffin itself. Jane Seymour went to her grave as the queen she had become, for a wax effigy lay upon her casket. The likeness was clothed in Queen Jane's robes of state, with cloth of gold shoes and embroidered stockings. Upon the head, which rested on a gold pillow, shone a golden crown; a sceptre glinted in the right hand, and rings of gold and precious stones adorned the fingers.

Once breakfast had ended, the solemn procession set out. The queen's chariot was preceded by a long line of guards, household officers, and officials, followed by two hundred paupers sporting her arms and clad in black robes with black hoods. Then came Cromwell, Audley, Cranmer in his full pontifical vestments, his cross carried before him by his chaplain, Norfolk, and the ambassadors, including Chapuys who, frustratingly, has not left us his own thoughts on the occasion. Just ahead of the chariot, heralds and gentlemen of the court, including Gregory Cromwell – the minister's only son, so recently married to Queen Jane's sister – held aloft banners of the saints, of the Virgin, of York, of Lancaster, and even one of Henry VII and Elizabeth of York. Thomas Boleyn, Suffolk and Sussex were three of the six lords riding, three each side, next to the chariot itself, closely followed by noblemen carrying six more banners.

Mary had been chosen by her father to be the chief mourner. Her horse, swathed in black velvet, accompanied her stepmother, with six ladies on horseback behind her. And then, clearly back in a place of honour, came Jane. Sitting with the Countess of Derby, Lady Carew and Lady Margaret Grey, she rode in a black-covered chariot drawn by six horses, each of which bore the royal escutcheons. Jane's mother, Lady Morley, rode behind her daughter in a second group of horsewomen. Three further chariots were filled with other court ladies, including Lady Kingston and Anne Basset. Although there were more riders, Jane's position in the first chariot was one of prominence. Widow of a convicted traitor she might still be, but she had successfully worked her way back into royal approval.

That approval was still more apparent when the procession arrived at Windsor. In fact, three Parkers were important in the ensuing rituals: Jane's brother, Henry, helped bear the queen's corpse from the chariot into the chapel, her father was one of the six peers who held the blue velvet canopy, fringed with blue and gold silk, over the body, and Jane was the second woman to enter after the queen. The first was Mary, the chief mourner, there in place of the king since, by tradition, he did not attend. Jane was immediately behind the princess, for she had been selected to hold Mary's long train. Seven noblewomen assisted her, but hers was the ultimate responsibility. When the *Dirige* drew to a close, the mourners returned to the castle where the king's cooks had 'prepared plenteously of all things necessary'. As they had not eaten since breakfast that morning, the repast was bound to be well received. The queen's interment, with all the appropriate ceremonies, took place the next day but, while we know that Thomas and Cromwell were there as Knights of the Garter, we do not know whether Jane or any of her female companions were present with them.

With Queen Jane buried with the fullest panoply the state could provide, life for those left behind had to continue. Jane's situation had changed yet again. While undoubtedly back in favour, she was also out of a job. Much would depend on whether the king decided to add a fourth wife to his growing tally and perhaps make another attempt at populating the nursery. Edward was a healthy baby, and there were high hopes of his survival through the pitfalls of infancy, but that could never be taken for granted. In those early years of Henry's reign, when he had still been married to Queen Katherine, Prince Henry had sickened and died without much warning. Now the king had Edward but only a second son would make the succession truly secure. And, for Jane, a new wife for the king might bring fresh opportunities.

Even before Queen Jane's funeral, Norfolk had written to Cromwell describing a conversation he had just had with the grieving king. He had, he said, spoken 'peradventure not wisely, but plainly'. Counselling Henry 'to accept God's pleasure in taking the Queen', he had exhorted him to take comfort in his newborn heir, the 'treasure sent to him and this realm'. But the duke had gone one stage further: he had 'advised him to provide for a new wife'. Cromwell was also working on the king to the same purpose. He found that while Henry had taken the queen's death 'reasonably', he was 'little disposed to marry again'. Nonetheless, the minister said, some councillors 'thought it meet . . . to urge him to it for the sake of his realm'. It might take a little while, but the chances were that the king would weaken. If he did, then Jane might well have a role in the bedchamber of the new queen. In the meantime, and totally unexpectedly, her fortunes took a slightly different turn.

27

A Woman of Property

Despite the efforts of his Council to cajole him into another marriage following Queen Jane's death, Henry was in no hurry to tread the matrimonial path once more. If he ventured on to it again, it would be at a time of his own choosing and only after exhaustive enquiries regarding the lucky bride had been undertaken by men he trusted. He had learnt his lesson: such things should not be rushed. In the interim, he delighted in his son. The child was strong and happy, cared for by a carefully selected team led by Lady Margaret Bryan, Edward's 'lady mistress'. The prince was 'in good health and merry', Lady Bryan wrote to the king in one of her many letters. It was a pity, she continued, that Henry could not have seen his son the previous evening when 'the minstrels played, and his Grace danced and played so wantonly that he could not stand still'. To have a healthy child, who had even inherited his own artistic interests, was music to the proud father's ears, but it did not bring Jane any nearer to another post within the royal household. Perhaps, however, she would not need one.

Suddenly, and out of the blue, Thomas Boleyn had made overtures concerning her jointure. After her own initiative in eliciting Cromwell's help, Jane had had to manage on the £100 per annum that her father-in-law had grudgingly allowed her. Combined with the perquisites of court service, this enabled her to live reasonably well, although not lavishly. She kept servants, she received and sent New Years' Gifts, she dressed according to prevailing diktats. Had George survived, of course, Jane's lifestyle would have been far grander, but at the very least she was managing to uphold the standards her birth and rank demanded.

It was probably confronting his own inescapable mortality that had made Thomas contemplate the future. In April 1538, Jane received the news that her mother-in-law, Elizabeth Boleyn, had died in London, very close to Anne's former property of Baynard's Castle. As a duke's daughter and an earl's wife, Elizabeth Boleyn was given a respectful and reverent funeral. Accompanied by the light from ceremonial torches, and with banners fixed to the black-draped barge on which her body lay, Thomas's dead wife was rowed along the Thames to Lambeth for interment. The couple had been married for almost forty years. Now in his sixties, Thomas was by no stretch of the imagination a young man. Although he was well enough to come to court the next January, the infirmities of old age could not have passed him by. He could rest more contentedly if he thought he had set his affairs in order.

That meant devising a property settlement, but Thomas's dilemma was to determine what it should be. Because he had no son, his brother, James, was next in line to inherit most of the Boleyn lands. But Thomas had a daughter, Mary Carey, now Mary Stafford. She lived in the manor house at Rochford in Essex with her father's blessing, his bitter response to her clandestine marriage to William Stafford quietly forgotten. After the executions of both George and Anne, she was his only remaining child, her son and daughter his only grandchildren. Other than via his siblings, which were not the same thing at all, his bloodline ran solely through Mary, and so it was to Mary and her descendants that Thomas wanted to bequeath whatever he could. What that really amounted to was the Ormond lands. They were his to bestow, providing Margaret Boleyn and his brother, William, agreed with his decisions. Neither should prove troublesome. Thomas had already gained control of his mother's inheritance years earlier and, even then, she had been declared a 'lunatic', interspersing periods of lucidity with bouts of insanity. There would be no problem in gaining her consent to anything. As for William, he was still content within the Church, having spent his whole life safely shielded from the excitement, and the corresponding dangers, of the court. Although no gullible innocent, for he was not a Boleyn for nothing, he was likely to be amenable to some form of deal. Edward Boleyn, apparently, was uninvolved.

However, as Thomas pondered his plans for posterity, he knew that there was one outstanding obstacle: his daughter-in-law, Jane.

For Jane's jointure provisions had included specified manors, Ormond manors. None had been handed over, as she knew only too well, and she had been given her £100 every year in recompense. Her manors of Aylesbury and Bierton in Buckinghamshire suddenly became crucial. Thomas wanted to sell them. There is no record of precisely why he wanted ready money at that moment: perhaps he did not want to saddle Mary Stafford with his debts. But what Jane was soon to discover was that her particular manors were valuable and that Thomas had a willing cash buyer waiting in the wings: Sir John Baldwin, chief justice of the Court of Common Pleas at Westminster. Baldwin – an existing acquaintance of Thomas from the trials of Fisher, More and, more painfully, from that of the courtiers accused of adultery with Anne – was a Buckinghamshire man born and bred. He had inherited lands around Aylesbury and had bought up others, including the manors of Danvers, Chearsley and Ludgershall, whenever they came on the market. The Ormond estates would considerably expand his existing property portfolio in the area, all of which he would be able to leave his son, William, in the fullness of time, and he was prepared to pay handsomely for the privilege.

With his customary business acumen, therefore, Thomas opened negotiations with Jane. While she did not have outright ownership of the coveted manors, she did have a life interest. Thomas could not sell the lands without her consent. Jane's father, a signatory of the original jointure, was also involved. Just as he had protected his daughter's interests so many years ago, it was his duty to perform the same task for her now. However, Lord Morley had a few distractions. His mind was very much on his purchase of Markhall, an estate he had leased since 1521, and he had recently been engaged in sorting out problems connected with the jointure of Lady Katherine Edgecombe, his wife's sister. Perhaps his attention was divided somewhat. There was also a major difference concerning the negotiations with the Boleyns this time: the very young, immature and inexperienced girl who had stood at the altar in St Giles with her bridegroom, her dreams intact, had grown up. And she had grown up in a merciless school. She had been widowed in the worst possible way, she had managed to recoup a proportion of her income through her own efforts and, by sheer determination, she had worked her way back into royal favour, gaining powerful support in the process. Jane, therefore, would not be an easy target. The deal would have to be worth taking.

The haggling took place over the spring and summer, the major indenture drawn up in October. The final price for the Buckinghamshire manors was fixed at the astronomical sum of £1,200, which was to be handed over in four months' time. However, while no doubt the dream purchaser as far as Thomas was concerned, Baldwin had a lawyer's eye for detail. He was insistent that when he paid the money there should be no potential entanglements or disputes outstanding on his new acquisitions. He had no intention of facing debts or lawsuits in the future. One impediment could be removed only by the king. While the manors were held freehold, Henry retained certain feudal rights over them so his permission was vital for Thomas to sell them. Thomas did not envisage the king's refusal, and he was right: Henry acquiesced. It was with Jane, the key figure, that there was a hitch.

For the deal to go ahead, she had to sign the deed as well as her father, who was administering the transaction on her behalf. If she was to give up Aylesbury and Bierton, she wanted something in exchange. Thomas offered her the manor of Swavesey in Cambridgeshire, in theory not a bad swap. In order to give up Aylesbury and Bierton and obtain Swavesey, Jane would have to agree to a series of legal conveyances known as recoveries in the Court of Common Pleas. Jane's father and brother, together with Robert Cranwell, Thomas's steward and surveyor, and Richard Sackville, who was married to Thomas's sister, Margaret, were to recover her new manor for her, while James Boleyn would recover Aylesbury and Bierton, which could then be handed over to Thomas to sell to Baldwin. The canny Thomas even managed to inveigle Baldwin into paying Jane's legal expenses on Swavesey in a one-off payment of £8.

Unfortunately, as far as Jane was concerned, there were catches in what at first sight seemed a very neat arrangement. Should

Baldwin find that Aylesbury and Bierton did not in fact come to him unencumbered on the set date, or should Thomas, his mother or Jane die before then, he would be able to stake a claim on Swavesey until everything was sorted out. As long as the preliminary paperwork had been meticulously completed, that should not happen, but it was a potential cloud on Jane's horizon since she was the youngest and least likely to die. As the survivor, she would then be left to pick up the pieces. And there was actually more than one cloud. Thomas did not really want Jane to have full possession of Swavesey. Maybe he hoped to pass it on to Mary and William Stafford sooner rather than later. It would come to them in the end, but only on Jane's death and she could live for years. So, Thomas suggested that Jane should allow him to keep Swavesey for himself, to do with as he pleased, in exchange for 100 marks (£66) a year, payable in two equal instalments at the font of St Paul's in London. Since she was already receiving almost twice that sum from Thomas, what had at first seemed an equable settlement was becoming thorny.

And so she did not sign. She knew that this was her one opportunity to secure her future, she would not waste it. Cranwell agreed with Baldwin, who was ready to part with his £1,200 only if he felt the sale was secure, that Jane would have a further five days to consent or Thomas would come to a new agreement with Baldwin concerning Swavesey. Frantic discussions must have taken place behind the scenes before Jane considered a satisfactory compromise had been reached, but eventually she did sign the original document.

The situation was complicated further because Jane schemed to obtain a private Act of Parliament as a form of insurance policy. She was no fool, she knew just how sharp Thomas could be if money was at stake, and she also knew that he was ageing. Should he die before the entire deal came to fruition, there was no way of knowing whether it would be honoured. An Act of Parliament, however, would be sacrosanct; to procure one was merely another form of the back-watching that was endemic in her family. Such Acts were not easy to get, and yet hers was special: the king signed it personally, a tremendous coup for Jane. She was no longer a pariah, contaminated by association with George and Anne; she had worked her way back into a position of trust. She even managed to obtain a grant of two

Warwickshire manors from the king in her own right, but she would never have dared approach Henry herself. Such a delicate matter required time and the intercession of an intermediary. In her case, that was likely to be Cromwell. He had helped her once and might do so again. Perhaps she had been of some use to him, or perhaps he was simply being generous to a woman who had lost so much. Sometimes the minister did put himself out to be of assistance to the wives and children of traitors, as he did for several dependants of those executed after the Pilgrimage of Grace.

And when news of Thomas's increasing ill-health filtered through, there was all the more reason for Jane to make sure that her hard-won concessions were not lost. Thomas survived his wife by less than a year. In March 1539, Jane's father-in-law died peacefully in his own chamber at Hever, 'the end of a good Christian man', as Cranwell informed Cromwell. On hearing the news, the king paid just over £16 for masses for the 'soul's health' of the man whose children he had executed. Thomas was buried in the church at Hever. His last resting place can be seen to this day, a monumental life-size brass over his tomb showing him resplendent in his robes as a Knight of the Garter. Typically, he had made a sound choice of executor in Cranmer. The archbishop spent years of labour in clearing up remnants of the late earl's affairs, tracking down any uncollected debts becoming his speciality. Thomas would have been proud of him.

There is no record of Jane inheriting anything from her father-in-law, but she did not expect to do so. Because she had opted for a jointure settlement confirmed by Act of Parliament and introduced in the House of Lords, her fortunes were very much improved. All three readings were completed in one day, Friday, 23 May 1539. With the king's firm signature already upon the document, the whole thing went through on the nod, and in the presence of men she had known at court for many years. Her father was there, keeping a watchful eye on his daughter's finances, in the same company as Norfolk, Suffolk, Cranmer, the Earl of Hertford and, most importantly, Cromwell himself.

Jane was entitled to feel delighted with the final bill. She was to receive a life interest in 'the manor of Swavesey within the county of Cambridge of the clear yearly value of a hundred marks above all charges and reprises, and 20 messuages, 1,000 acres of land, 300 acres of meadow, 1,000 acres of pasture, 200 acres of wood, 500 acres of firs and heath, and £10 rent with the appurtenances in Swavesey alias Swasey, Fen Drayton, Conington, Bixworth, and Great Stanton'.* That was not all. She also gained the 'manors of Blickling, Calthorpe, Filby, Stiffkey and Postwick with their appurtenances and 20 messuages, forty acres of land, 200 acres of wood, 500 acres of heath and firs, 300 acres of moor and alder, and £20 rent'. Her chief prize was the Boleyn stronghold of Blickling. Naturally the house would revert to James upon her death, but it was an excellent base in the meantime and, perhaps remembering how George had reacted when Henry had entrusted him with Beaulieu, she quickly moved in some of her goods. They are listed in the copious inventory of her possessions taken three years later.

Crucially, because of the Act, her right and title to all of these lands was assured. Even had they wanted to, the remaining Boleyns could not touch any of them. Jane had them for her lifetime. The Staffords and James Boleyn had already recognised this. When applying to Henry for his consent to their inheriting various other properties from Thomas, they had complied with the law and listed everything that they had gained immediately upon his death, together with respective values – the king was always keen to know about values and would penalise heavily anyone who foolishly attempted to cheat him – and they had also declared what they would inherit in the future. That meant lands that Jane currently held that would revert to the Boleyn family upon her death.

For Jane, the whole messy jointure episode was now closed. She now had a decent income, over £200 a year, and her own manor house at Blickling. Should she choose to do so, and it was something that she would have to decide, she could live very comfortably in the Norfolk countryside. She had achieved much more than the 100 marks of Thomas's first offer, so clearly hard bargaining had paid

---

* Messuages and appurtenances are legal terms. A messuage was usually a dwelling house, with land and outbuildings, while an appurtenance referred to additional, more minor property linked to larger assets.

off. But she also knew that what she now had was a drop in the ocean compared to what she would have enjoyed had George out-lived Thomas. On his father's death, George would have netted both his title and his estates. James affirmed that the total value of the lands that he inherited from Thomas, excluding what he would eventually get on the reversion of Jane's manors, was just over £116; the Staffords got more, declaring a little over £488. Both sums would have boosted George's income, rather than theirs, had he not been caught up in the maelstrom that destroyed his sister. Then, too, his property would not have been forfeit to the king and, with Henry's continued favour instead of his displeasure, George would probably have grown richer still. There would even have been the chance that, just like Suffolk, he might have been presented with a dukedom by his royal brother-in-law. So Jane's jointure settlement, while very welcome, and a great relief, served only to remind her of what she had lost. She was a widowed viscountess in comfortable cir-cumstances but, had events panned out differently, she could have been Countess of Wiltshire at the very least, living on more than four times what she would now get. She might also have had a family of her own; she had still been young enough to conceive a child when George was taken from her.

But the past could not be recaptured. She had put it behind her once, she had to do so again. She had rebuilt her life after what was perhaps the worst type of disaster to befall a woman of her age and class. To regret what might have been was a waste of energy; it was far better to concentrate on what was to come. A second marriage was always a possibility. With an income of £200, she was a reas-onable catch. The money would die with her, however, and she had nothing else to bequeath to a new husband's family. Perhaps that explains why, although so many widows remarried, sometimes with almost indecent haste, Jane never did. Or maybe her own first-hand experience had revealed the risks, pitfalls and grief that a second sortie to the altar might bring and she could not face that emotional trauma again.

So, with her marital status unchanged, Jane had to think about her next step. She had a definite choice: calm tranquillity at Blickling, or the excitement of the court. The house that Jane inherited at

Blickling is no longer there. All that remains is one chimney, which has been incorporated into the grand Jacobean mansion that replaced it shortly after James died, but the site, nestling in the gentle Norfolk countryside, is of course the same. It is pretty, but remote, a far cry from the noise and bustle of Henry's palaces. And it was to Henry's world that Jane was addicted. But, unless the king married again, there was no real place for her there. Without a husband in whose wake she could follow like a dutiful wife, the only chance for a lucrative return to court was if the king gave way to his Council and there was a new queen for her to serve. That is precisely what happened.

28

A Question of Trust

With Blickling now hers, Jane put behind her the anxious years following George's death. By dint of hard-nosed bargaining, she had money and property in her own right for the first time in her life. She had come of age. But for Jane, a creature of the court, the rumour that Henry was seeking a new wife was welcome. Blickling was all very well, but she needed more than the peaceful existence it offered. Henry wanted a change too. His mourning for Queen Jane was not prolonged; a dutiful son of the Church, he accepted that to wallow in grief was tantamount to challenging the will of God. There was still a world to enjoy, and in that world was a potential fourth wife. The French ambassador, Marillac, noticed Henry's demeanour. 'The king, who in some former years has been solitary and pensive,' he wrote, 'now gives himself up to amusement, going to play every night upon the Thames, with harps, chanters, and all kinds of music and pastime . . . all his people think this a sign of his desire to marry if he should find an agreeable match.'

And an agreeable match was found. With her mind set on a return to the privy chamber, Jane was agog for news of the identity of her new mistress. It took a while to narrow down the field, since Henry had no pretty English girl waiting patiently this time, Queen Jane's death having caught him unawares. Gossip about potential candidates intensified. Many bets were on the fetching young widow Christina of Milan, especially once Holbein's portrait of her was seen. Even in her black mourning clothes, with a tight-fitting cap covering her hair and her hands demurely linked across her stomach, there was a hint of promise in her eyes, a suspicion of a smile about her lips. She would make a worthy wife for any man. Henry certainly thought so but, disappointingly, nothing resulted from diplomatic overtures. Nothing came of any other candidate either.

Then, the pope's punishment of excommunication, threatened for ages, finally came into effect and at the same time Charles and Francis became closer and closer, meeting for discussions and parting 'with much love and affection'. The more complex international situation made everyone at court increasingly jittery. No one liked the idea of standing alone against the combined might of Spain, the Empire and France, especially with Henry's nephew, James V of Scotland, never trustworthy, prowling on the northern border. In this tense period Henry's choice of the Duke of Cleves's sister, Anne, came as a relief. Alliance with the German duchy made perfect sense. Jane was in familiar territory: some years earlier, George had been involved in negotiations with the Schmalkaldic League, the union of German Protestant princes. Any plans that Henry may have had then had failed to materialise; the current political landscape necessitated drastic measures.

Henry wanted this marriage and he wanted it fast, as soon as all the preliminaries could be sorted out. Allies were always valuable, particularly since he felt vulnerable at home too. There seemed to be almost constant plotting. No one knew whether the person with whom they were talking and laughing in the tapestried corridors and panelled rooms of the royal palaces was really a traitor, planning a foreign invasion or the murder of the king.

One particularly involved plot had recently been uncovered. The king's once-favoured choice for the archbishopric of York, Reginald Pole, who now lived in exile, had betrayed him by encouraging a foreign-led invasion to restore traditional Catholicism. It had been Pole's relatives and their friends who paid the price. Lord Montague, one of the cardinal's brothers, together with the Marquess of Exeter and Sir Edward Neville, had been arrested, put in the Tower and brought to trial for treason. Their servants and acquaintances had been thoroughly interrogated, but the most damning evidence had come from the other accused, Pole's second brother, Sir Geoffrey Pole. He had almost fallen over himself in his eagerness to dredge up every communication his fellow prisoners had ever had with Reginald, together with any apparently incriminating remarks or ambiguous conversational nuances that he could possibly remember. What was particularly staggering was the involvement of Mary's much-respected former governess, the elderly Countess of Salisbury, Richard III's niece and mother of the Poles.

Jane knew everyone implicated, from those on the fringes like the Marchioness of Exeter, never a Boleyn friend, who was questioned yet again, to the countess herself. Jane was also in a position to have insider knowledge of the various trials because her father, gaining further unwelcome experience in such matters, had been on the panel of peers who heard the cases against Montague and Exeter and, unsurprisingly, had found them guilty. Both, together with Neville, had been executed. The bewildered and bereaved countess was still in her prison cell, a death sentence hovering over her, while the king magnanimously pardoned Geoffrey for providing such useful information. For those with a sound instinct for self-preservation, coming clean sometimes worked. The whole episode was terrifying but at least the king had escaped unharmed, so his loyal subjects could sleep more easily in their beds. Yet, with traitors lurking behind every door, it was so difficult to be confident of the loyalty of anyone.

The death or capture of the conspirators, however, meant that such unpleasantness could be put aside. The focus of attention could now pass to the new queen and what she might be like. The bare facts were that she was twenty-four years old, and she was certainly a Catholic, for Cleves was not a Protestant state despite its links with those who were. The bonus was that she was supposed to be beautiful. Henry had ordered stringent checks on her appearance, such things mattered to him very much. After all, he was the one most affected, he was the one who would have to put his neck into a 'great yoke'. And all reports were favourable. Those who saw her, including Henry's envoys and some of his own councillors, praised her good looks. One went so far as to assert that she excelled the beauteous Christina 'as the golden sun did the silver moon'. Keen to see for himself, Henry sent Holbein to the court of Cleves just to make certain. The artist's finished portrait pleased him. Looking intently at the canvas, the king saw a young woman rather than a young girl, with soft eyes, a slightly wide nose and a delicate mouth.

Carefully nurtured by her mother, she was said to be virtuous, a good needlewoman, moderate in diet and gentle of temper. So far, so good. It was true that she spoke only German and was no musician, but no doubt both drawbacks could be remedied. He could not wait to see her. Neither could the ladies designated to attend her.

The sooner the arrangements were made, therefore, the better. Cromwell and the Council played their part: a marriage treaty was agreed, the dowry largely waived as the duke was hardly wealthy, a niggling concern that Anne had been betrothed to the son of the Duke of Lorraine removed. At last she set out for England, travelling via Calais, where she was fulsomely greeted. Jane was not there but could well have received the latest information from Anne Basset, who was to join her in the royal household, and whose mother, Honor Lisle, was the wife of the Lord Deputy of Calais. The queen would be 'good and gentle to serve and please', Anne Basset heard. If that was correct, life within the private apartments would be enjoyable. We do not know the precise date of Jane's appointment as a lady of the privy chamber, but once installed she was likely to come across several old friends and acquaintances, amongst them her mother's sister, Katherine, recently widowed by the death of Sir Piers Edgecombe, and young Katherine Carey, Mary Stafford's daughter. Baynton was once more in his usual role of vice-chamberlain and his wife, Isabel, was also in the privy chamber. There were to be new people too, including Norfolk's young niece, Catherine Howard, who coincidentally was Isabel Baynton's half-sister. Perhaps the missing faces would not be noticed.

Delayed for a while in Calais by bad weather, Anne of Cleves arrived in Dover at the very end of December 1539. Elaborate plans had been drawn up for her official reception, Cromwell working overtime to make sure nothing could go wrong. He covered everything from providing 'ready money for provisions' at Dover to appointing 'an honest man that can speak the languages to attend' with him. Jane's father was not the only one to appreciate the importance of back-watching. Suffolk and his duchess were the leading nobles designated by the king to meet Anne but Jane's name is not on the Dover list, so it is unlikely that she was amongst those ladies deputed for the first major round of introductions. However, since formal welcomes had been set up at various stages along Anne's route to Greenwich, and there was naturally the ubiquitous river display, Jane may well have been included in one of those ceremonies.

But what Jane could not be sure of was the king's reaction to his affianced bride. Indeed, even those who were there on what was to be a crucial encounter gave different versions. Officially, Henry was scheduled to see Anne for the first time at Blackheath but, mindful of the etiquette due to foreign brides, and with his curiosity getting the better of him with each minute that passed, he decided to visit her, incognito, at Rochester in Kent, long before she reached the outskirts of the capital. His intention was to give her a New Year's Gift on 1 January. He was confident that she would recognise him despite his disguise, and that the happy couple would be so entranced with each other that, after their wedding, they would live in connubial bliss ever after.

The fairytale plan backfired. Henry turned up in the late afternoon to find Anne engrossed in watching bull-baiting through the window. She took little notice when a group of six gentlemen, wearing cloaks and hoods, came into the room. She took still less notice when one of them, a tall, profoundly corpulent stranger, approached her, kissed her and offered her a present. Polite thanks, rather than instant recognition and protestations of love, were all the recompense he got. Anne was more interested in the bullbaiting. There was nothing for it but for the incredulous king, totally unused to being 'regarded ... little', to go outside, throw off his disguise, and re-enter as himself. It was not a good start.

Whilst Jane was not there to witness this initial disappointment, she would come to learn the depth of Henry's disillusionment. Although few at the Rochester meeting realised the full extent of the king's dismay, with some accounts stressing how amicable had been the whole occasion, he had been horrified by his first sight of his intended wife. Later his closest aides noted their master's reaction. Russell, the Lord Admiral, described how Henry was 'marvellously astonished and abashed' by Anne's lack of physical charms, an interpretation shared by Sir Anthony Browne, who observed that when Henry went to kiss Anne there was 'on his countenance, a discontentment and misliking of her person'. And, while all was sweetness and smiles in public – for the king was only too aware of the rapprochement between Charles and Francis, and was fearful of 'making a ruffle in the world and driving her brother into the Emperor and the French king's hands' – in private Henry was not slow to speak of his woes. 'I see nothing in this woman as men report of her, and I marvel that wise men would make such report as they have done,' said the reluctant bridegroom. 'Alas, whom should men trust?' he complained. 'I promise you I see no such thing in her as hath been showed unto me of her, and am ashamed that men hath praised her as they have done, and I like her not.' He could hardly have been more plain. 'What remedy?' he pleaded with Cromwell. In desperation, Cromwell suggested that she had 'a queenly manner'. That was not enough. It was not a 'queenly manner' that Henry wanted.

The situation rapidly deteriorated. Instead of the king's feelings abating as he found deeper qualities to admire in Anne, all he could see was that he would have to marry, and bed, a woman he was finding increasingly repulsive. While Jane and the other ladies tried to break through the language barrier and get to know Anne, Henry began clutching at straws to find a way out. Anne's alleged pre-contract with the Duke of Lorraine's son was the obvious exit route. He could say that he dared not marry a woman who was already betrothed. He had offended God with his first marriage, his conscience would not now permit him to repeat his offence. It was worth a try. Anne's brother could hardly object if a genuine impediment existed. Unfortunately, the king had to relinquish his grasp of that particular straw. Whilst the Cleves envoys could not produce the original documents concerning the alleged engagement, they assured Henry that no obstacle existed to their union and Anne herself affirmed this on oath. There was no instant escape. Marriage it had to be.

The wedding was a quiet one at Greenwich, the king pensive and resigned. 'If it were not to satisfy the world and my realm, I would not do that I must do this day for none earthly thing,' he told Cromwell plaintively. Anne's ladies, probably including the 'strange maidens' she had brought from her native duchy, helped her to dress that day with special care. The usual jokes and laughter were probably understood, whatever languages were spoken. With her long hair flowing loosely around her shoulders, a coronet of precious stones and pearls on her head and wearing a dazzling gown of cloth of silver embroidered with glittering jewels, Anne of Cleves became Henry's wife. The ceremony over, the newly married couple paraded through the court, Anne's ladies walking sedately behind her. Unfortunately, we have no record of whether Jane was one of them.

Whether she was or was not present on Anne's wedding day, she was certainly present within the bedchamber in the weeks that followed, and it was to be there that the next stage in the king's marital saga was played out. With the nuptial service completed, the celebratory meal eaten, and the festivities ended, Anne was undressed to await her husband. There could be no witnesses to what ensued next. In fact, if Henry is to be believed, there was nothing to witness. He was quite incapable. To an anxious Cromwell, who dared to ask him the next day how he 'liked the queen', the king's response was stark: 'Surely, my Lord, as ye know, I liked her before not well, but now I like her much worse.' Henry convinced himself that Anne's 'belly and breasts' indicated that 'she was no maid'. Once he had touched them, he 'had neither will nor courage to prove the rest'. The king therefore 'left her as good a maid as he found her'. His aversion continued although, nothing if not heroic, he admitted to having a couple of futile attempts at consummation.

Only those very intimately connected with Anne and Henry knew of the lack of activity in the bedchamber. In public, a contented and united front was maintained. Jane, no stranger to river processions, would have had the opportunity to enjoy yet another a month or so after the royal wedding, as she is likely to have been one of the attendants who accompanied Anne when the king and queen moved from Greenwich to Westminster. Just as they had with Anne Boleyn, the city merchants prepared to welcome their queen into the city. The barges were decorated, their pennants flying in the breeze, the mayor and his officials donned their very best robes, their polished golden chains gleaming upon their breasts, and the Tower gunners, still with Anthony Anthony in charge of the ordnance, fired off a thousand shots in salute, making a 'noise like thunder'. Anne and Henry travelled in separate barges, hers no doubt the one that had once been owned by both Katherine of Aragon and Anne Boleyn, while Jane was one of the ladies in the barge immediately behind that of their mistress.

When spring arrived, Jane had another sense of déjà vu during the May Day Jousts. Like her former namesake, Queen Anne was there in a place of honour. Although for her there was to be no imminent arrest or execution, the event was destined to be her farewell appearance as queen. It was the traditional extravaganza, with challengers in white velvet facing defenders who were equally richly dressed. The young bucks of the court acquitted themselves with customary bravado; Queen Jane's brother, Thomas Seymour, took part, as did Cromwell's son, Gregory, Norfolk's son, the Earl of Surrey, and Thomas Culpepper, a rising star in the king's privy chamber. Gregory Cromwell had every reason to feel especially satisfied since his father had just been created Earl of Essex, and he was his sole heir. The days of the jousts passed happily enough, with Anne and her ladies being entertained one evening to a wonderful banquet overflowing with 'all delicious meats and drinks', each course introduced by a drum roll, and consumed to the sounds of music and minstrels. Since the venue was Durham Place, with its lingering echoes of Anne and George, there was an acute sense of nostalgia for Jane Rochford.

It was also Anne's swansong. Within the queen's privy apartments, those ladies most au fait with current developments had started to realise that their king had found a new love, and it was not his queen. One of their own number, Catherine Howard, petite, pretty and appealing, had ensnared the besotted monarch and stirred his slumbering libido. There was no chance now of his consummating his union with Anne. Indeed, he had given up on that long ago, although, for appearance's sake, he still sometimes slept by her side, for part of the night at least. It was simply, as Jane was to discover, that nothing else happened.

Everything came to a head in June, 1540, a mere six months or so after Anne of Cleves had become Henry's wife, and once Henry had become more confident that the fragile reconciliation between

Charles and Francis had indeed reached its inevitable end. Jane, who had watched the fall of two queens, was about to see, and to contribute to, that of a third. But first there was another fall, one that must have taken Jane by as much surprise as it did so many others. On 10 June, Cromwell was arrested as he walked into a meeting of the Privy Council at Westminster. In a surreal scene, Norfolk tore the St George emblem from his neck as Southampton rushed to unbuckle the garter from his leg, between them stripping the minister of the most visible symbols of his meteoric rise from commoner to membership of the exclusive ranks of the Garter Knights. Then, the man who had seemed more powerful than all of the Council put together was bundled out of a side door into a waiting boat and incarcerated in the Tower, the fortress to which he had sent so many others in his heyday. He was charged with treason and heresy. It must have been his worst nightmare.

Three hundred years after the event, historians still debate the causes of Cromwell's spectacular end. Perhaps his enemies combined to destroy him, perhaps the king blamed him for the failure of the Cleves marriage, perhaps Henry was simply tired of him or wanted to move on to alternative policies. Stories abounded at the time as they continue to do today. Jane could only comprehend that the man who had helped her now needed help himself. He would not get it. No one ever wanted to be associated with those in Cromwell's plight, treason could be catching. Even Cranmer, who sometimes signed his letters to Cromwell as from 'Your own ever assured', dared not defend him. 'I loved him as my friend, for so I took him to be,' he wrote to the king, 'but I chiefly loved him for the love which I thought I saw him bear ever towards your grace.' The archbishop acknowledged that he had been wrong. 'But now, if he be a traitor, I am sorry that ever I loved him or trusted him, and I am very glad that his treason is discovered in time,' he continued, 'but ... who shall your grace trust hereafter, if you might not trust him?' Cranmer could only 'pray God continually night and day, to send such a counsellor in his place whom your grace may trust, and who for all his qualities can and will serve your grace like to him, and that will have so much solicitude and care to preserve your grace from all dangers as I ever thought he had'.

Cromwell would leave his prison only to walk to the block on Tower Hill, found guilty by Act of Attainder, but not before his useful testimony on Henry's attitude towards the Cleves marriage was demanded and willingly given. Perhaps he thought frankness and co-operation might save his life, as it had for Geoffrey Pole, but he should have known his master better than that. He was not Geoffrey Pole, he had too many enemies and too many rivals. Despite his pitiful pleas for mercy, 'prostrate at your majesty's feet', as he wrote to the king, Henry did not lift a finger to save him.

While the distraught minister lay in the Tower awaiting his fate, Anne's marriage was drawing to its close. Jane's response to the minister's end is undocumented, but she was Morley's daughter, and she appreciated the value of silence. Four years earlier, she had been dragged into the repercussions of a fall equally as dramatic and sudden as Cromwell's, and one which had touched her more closely. She had survived that, she would definitely survive this. But she would also look to the future, her future, and it did not lie with Anne of Cleves. It lay at Blickling, if she wanted it to, or it lay at court, if the king so decided. That decision was to end his union with Anne and marry the delectable Catherine Howard. Jane could not help Cromwell, but she could, and did, help her king during the ensuing annulment proceedings he instituted.

Together with two other senior ladies of the bedchamber, her aunt, Lady Katherine Edgecombe, and the Countess of Rutland, Jane related during the legal process an odd conversation that they had all had with the queen that summer. When they had joked about the possibility of a new prince, Anne's response had kindled Jane's retort that she thought the queen was 'still maid indeed'. Not so, said the queen, who had proceeded to tell them innocently that since the king kissed her night and morning she could be no virgin. She had seemed astonished to hear from the countess that more was needed before there would be a Duke of York. Perhaps the basic facts of life had passed her by; perhaps they had not. Even her ladies were bewildered that Anne could be so ignorant. And at least one, the countess, must have been aware before this June banter that all was not well, for Cromwell had suggested that her husband, Anne's chamberlain, should advise the queen to try to make herself more attractive to Henry and seduce him into a little more exertion within the privacy of the marital bed.

Whatever the real extent of Anne's understanding of her conjugal duties, the ladies' testimony was gold dust for Henry's case. The women confirmed his own assertion of non-consummation, one that was also supported by the evidence of the frantically squirming Cromwell, a series of Henry's councillors and Drs Butts and Chambers. Dr Butts was quick to assert that while the king was physically unable to copulate with Anne, he was perfectly capable of doing so with any other woman. Henry had, after all, recently had two 'wet dreams'.

Convocation's assent was needed for Henry to be granted his freedom. In early July the bench of bishops met at St Peter's, Westminster, to consider the matter. Sitting in the octagonal Chapter House, surrounded by medieval wall paintings still glowing with colour and life, and with their feet firmly planted on the tiled floor, the churchmen listened to every last salacious detail of the royal couple's embarrassing sexual relationship. They moved on to debate the knotty problem of Anne's pre-contract with the Duke of Lorraine's son, an issue which the king persisted in believing unresolved. If he was right, it was a further nail in the coffin of his marriage. Convocation decided that he was. So, with Henry's original unwillingness to wed Anne also laid in the balance, Convocation was quite ready to declare in his favour. The marriage was null and void, and both parties were free to marry elsewhere. Covos, the emperor's principal secretary, could not resist a smile. 'A very good joke of the king of England again divorcing his queen,' he wrote. 'Not in vain does he pretend and assume spiritual superiority that he may at will decide upon matrimonial cases whenever he himself is concerned.'

Jane's testimony had been useful. She was useful again, for Henry was only one of the two parties involved in the case. Anne's consent was required too. The queen had been stunned when she had been asked to move away from her husband to Richmond Palace ostensibly as a safeguard against disease. Once there – and with Jane and her other ladies at her side since their responsibilities were not yet over – she had been visited by members of the Council, who explained Henry's misgivings about the marriage and the need for

Convocation to look into it. They took an interpreter with them to ensure that there would be no misunderstandings. Anne soon realised that she had little choice but to accept. Similarly, when informed by Sir Richard Rich, Suffolk and other councillors that the marriage was annulled, she had to agree to that also. Her initial reluctance was partly overcome by the king's offer of two palaces – Richmond and Bletchingley – jewels, and his promise to treat her as his sister with all the privileges that that status conferred. Her verbal acquiescence deemed insufficient, Anne 'freely signed certain letters of consent to the said divorce'. One of the witnesses to her signature was Jane; there were some people left upon whom the king could rely. All that remained for Anne was to settle into her new role. Choosing to stay in England, where she was to spend the rest of her life, the former queen returned to Henry 'the ring delivered unto her at their pretended marriage, desiring that it might be broken into pieces as a thing which she knew of no force or value'.

That ring was indeed worthless, representing a wedding that the king preferred to forget. Now all he wanted was to lavish rings, necklaces, furs, and his precious person upon his beloved Catherine Howard. For Jane, this was very good news. With her erstwhile companion as her queen, and that queen needing her own ladies of the bedchamber, there should be a place for her. And that place would be back within the court that was, despite everything, her true home.

THE PATH TO THE BLOCK

29

The King's Jewel

The final chapter in Jane's life began on 28 July 1540. On that day, the bungling executioner clumsily hacked Thomas Cromwell's head from his body and the king, 'being solicited by his Council', married Catherine Howard, his 'jewel for womanhood'. Thankful to have won her, the ageing Henry was convinced that he had found true happiness at long last. He was not to know just how brief that happiness was to be. For little Catherine, the former maid of honour, who now dined under a cloth of estate and was prayed for as queen, a glittering future beckoned. It was very exciting and wholly unexpected. Although she was a Howard, and therefore of good marriage potential, her father, Lord Edmund, was a younger son and frequently so financially stretched that he did not dare leave his house for fear of being accosted by his creditors. At best, young Catherine might have found herself the wife of a minor noble; she could never have dreamt of a husband such as the one she had netted. It was almost too good to be true. Her uncle Norfolk, regarded by the French ambassador as 'the author' of the union, was bound to be pleased that another Howard was in Henry's bed, especially one who was presumed to be committed to the old faith.

Catherine's unexpected elevation was also a bonus for Jane. With the death of Cromwell, she had lost her protector and was now alone again, just as she had been at George's death. But this time her situation was different: she owned Blickling, she had an annual income of rents, she possessed status at court, she was a respectable lady of the bedchamber. She had been useful to her king in helping him extricate himself from the embraces of Anne of Cleves, so any debt Jane owed him for consenting to the settlement of her jointure had been paid. She had proved her worth and had fought her way back to prominence. There was no reason for her to believe that she would have further use for a defender. As she had already served at court alongside Catherine, this queen was not an unknown foreign princess. She was even a sort of relation, since her father and George's mother, Elizabeth Boleyn, had been siblings. The future looked promising for Viscountess Rochford.

It was true that Catherine could be difficult. Mrs Dorothy Josselyn, writing to her brother, John Gates, certainly found her so. 'The Queen's work troubles me so much and yet I fear I shall scant content her Grace,' she complained. She was not the only one to feel the full force of Catherine's displeasure. Mary had a similar experience when the queen decided to exert her authority by interfering in her stepdaughter's household. According to Chapuys, 'The Princess did not treat her with the same respect as her two predecessors,' so Catherine punished her by taking away two of her maids. Only when Mary 'found means to conciliate her' was the issue resolved and Catherine appeased. After that initial contretemps, in which the queen could claim victory, the two women rubbed along fairly amicably. Wisely, Mary sent Catherine a present for the New Year, 'at which her father was pleased', and, with the queen's gracious consent, Mary was soon allowed to reside at court. She and Jane would have met on state occasions, or perhaps within the privy apartments, so their old acquaintance could be renewed.

Should Jane ever need to understand how best to please Catherine, she could follow Mary's method, or she could emulate Anne of Cleves's superlative behavioural exemplar. When Henry allowed Anne to visit the court, as he had promised he would, her first encounter with her supplanter might well have been sticky. That it was not was because Anne's technique was faultless. When admitted to Catherine's presence, Anne fell on to her knees before her ex-attendant and treated her with all the respect and deference that the diminutive queen now regarded as her due. Catherine, satisfied by Anne's calculated display of self-abasement, 'showed her the utmost kindness'. Anne was invited to supper with Henry and Catherine

One of Henry's love letters to Anne Boleyn. After giving her his recent news, the king writes, 'No more to you at thys present, myne owne darlyng, for lak off tyme, but that I wolde you were in myne armes or I in yours, for I thynk it long syns I kyst you'.

Anne Boleyn.

Hever Castle, the Boleyn scat in Kent, where Dr Butts once fought for Anne's life against the sweating sickness. The castle was bought and restored by William Waldorf Astor in the early years of the twentieth century.

Cardinal Wolsey travelling by barge from his palace of York Place to Greenwich for a meeting with Henry VIII.

(*Above left*) Sir Thomas Wyatt, Anne Boleyn's poet suitor.

(*Above right*) The brass tomb effigy of Thomas Boleyn, Earl of Wiltshire, Jane's father-in-law, wearing the robes and insignia of a Knight of the Garter, and with the family falcon emblem above his right shoulder.

Thomas Cromwell.

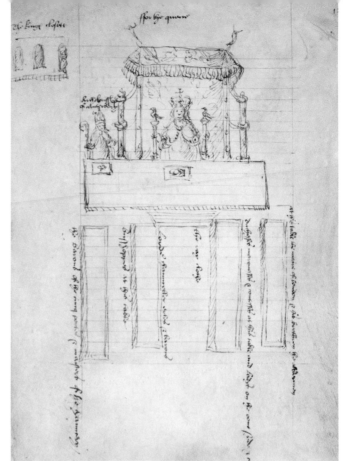

The seating plan for Anne Boleyn's coronation banquet. Jane sat at the second table from the right.

Hans Holbein the Younger's design for Mount Parnassus, the tableau provided by the merchants of the Steelyard to honour Anne Boleyn during her coronation procession.

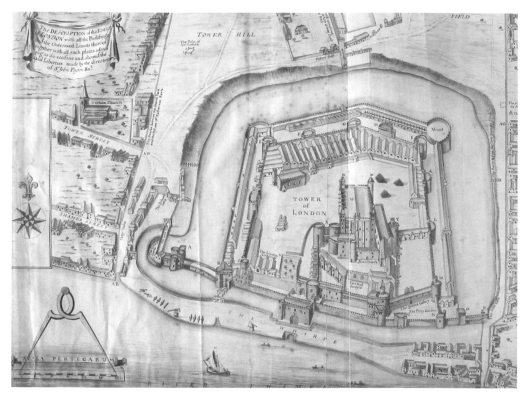

The Tower of London, 1597. The Chapel of St Peter ad Vincula, where Jane lies with George Boleyn, Anne Boleyn and Catherine Howard can be seen to the north-west of the White Tower.

Thomas Howard, 3rd Duke of Norfolk, the uncle of Anne and George Boleyn.

Jane Seymour.

Anne of Cleves.

Catherine Howard.

Charles Brandon, Duke of Suffolk,
with his wife Mary, the French Queen,
Henry VIII's sister.

Henry Fitzroy, Duke of Richmond, Henry VIII's illegitimate son by Elizabeth Blount.

(*Right*) Mary Tudor, the daughter of Henry VIII and Katherine of Aragon.

Edward VI, the son of Henry VIII and Jane Seymour, as a baby.

Elizabeth I, Jane's niece, as a young girl.

Sir John Russell.

Pendant designs by Hans Holbein the Younger.

A costume design by Hans Holbein the Younger.

and, once the king had retired, his two wives 'danced together, and next day all three dined together'. Rounding off the highly successful visit, Catherine then presented to Anne the two dogs and the ring which Henry had just given her. As her ladies probably knew, however, Catherine was to remain wary of her husband's relationship with the German princess.

Jane was lucky. She and Catherine hit it off, so much so that it was to Jane that the queen turned when she wanted a confidante, and it was to be upon Jane that she most relied. Since Henry was so besotted with Catherine, Jane might be excused for considering that she had acquired a post for life. In a way, she had. The king found Catherine enchanting. He could scarcely keep his hands off her even in public, much to the French ambassador's amusement. 'The King is so amorous of her that he cannot treat her well enough and caresses her more than he did the others,' Marillac wrote. For Jane this was reminiscent of those heady days when nothing had been too good or too costly for Anne Boleyn. Seeing the myriad flashing stones purchased to adorn the king's own jewel brought back the past. There were countless brooches set with diamonds, rubies and pearls, there were gold chains, gold girdles, decorated rosaries, there was a little gold purse 'enamelled red, containing eight diamonds, set in goldsmith's work'. When Catherine had chosen her motto of 'No Other Wish than His', she could not have envisaged that Henry's wish was to give her so much. If Jane was used to this splendour, she was also used to the French fashions that Catherine reintroduced. Queen Jane's severe, unflattering gable hoods were decidedly banished, probably to the relief of Anne Basset, who had held on to her post in the privy chamber, and who had never looked her best in them.

For Jane, then, life seemed to have turned full circle. She had managed to build up an array of possessions once more, perhaps not quite so many as she would have owned by now had Anne remained on the throne, but an impressive collection nonetheless. She tended to wear black, the accepted colour for the ladies of the bedchamber, and had gowns in damask and satin. Her nightgown was black taffeta, her kirtles velvet or satin. She had jewellery too, nothing like Catherine's, of course, but of considerable value in its own right.

She had a 'fair brooch black enamelled with six small diamonds', another with an agate, and one of gold on which there was an 'antique' (classical) head. She had a diamond cross from which three pearls were suspended, she had pearls, she had rubies and a 'flower with a ruby and a great emerald with a pearl pendant', she had red cornelian bracelets. She had a steel casket in which she kept a purse. There was £40 in it when she died, more than half the annual allowance with which Thomas had intended to palm her off on George's death. She had silver flagons, a silver and gilt salt, a silver-gilt ewer. And somehow, she had inveigled Henry into returning her wonderful wooden bed, with its Rochford knots and yellow and white silk furnishings, for which she now had red and white damask curtains, as well as yellow and white sarsenet ones. There were pillows filled with down for her head, and woollen quilts to keep her warm in the long winters. If she still shivered, there was also a counterpane of yellow sarscnet, which was quilted and lined.

She was still a widow, of course, but her jointure gains had made her more eligible and, as she was only in her thirties, there was always the chance that her marital status might change. Anything was possible. If it did not, or if the consequences of her first marriage had made her value her independence too much to relinquish it for the uncertainties of matrimony, she had a good career in her own right. Blickling was a peaceful retreat if she needed to escape the pressures of the court for a respite, and it would offer a permanent bolt-hole for whenever she wanted to retire. Jane, however, was not yet ready to do that. Despite its dangers, its backbiting and its intrigue, the court retained its allure, especially with Henry so devoted to his pretty little bride, and she increasingly devoted to her trustworthy lady of the bedchamber. Proximity to power was addictive.

All that was missing to complete the king's domestic happiness, and to ensure a permanent residence at court for Jane, was the news that Catherine was pregnant. The impotence that he had endured with Anne of Cleves now a distant memory, Henry entertained hopes that Catherine would produce a Duke of York to make the succession completely secure. Rumours of her pregnancy abounded, with Marillac reporting in the spring of 1541 that Henry intended to have her crowned as a reward and that preparations for a coronation were already in hand. 'The young lords and gentlemen of this Court are practising daily for the jousts and tournaments to be then made,' he said. It was not to be, or not on that occasion anyway, but Catherine and her ladies grasped that Henry would never discard her if she could give him the spare heir he craved. In time, perhaps, with stamina on his part and courage on hers, his wish might be granted.

They may have made a slightly incongruous couple, however: he, tall, stout and almost fifty, she, less than half his age and size. Catherine was brimming with vitality and exuberance; Henry was starting to feel his years. He had grown much fatter with the passage of time, so dragging his vast frame around was becoming a chore. The handsome young king that Jane remembered from the Field of Cloth of Gold had a waist measurement of 87 centimetres (35 inches). When she saw him now, his waist was fast approaching the 135 centimetres (54 inches) that we have recorded for 1545 and he was in almost constant pain from horribly ulcerated legs. Sometimes the sores oozed pus, in which case he usually felt a little better, but sometimes they closed up and the pain almost drove him mad. 'For ten or twelve days the humours which had no outlet were like to have stifled him, so that he was sometime without speaking, black in the face, and in great danger,' a French envoy had written in 1538. Then, Henry had recovered, but he was constantly terrified that the wounds would close again and that he would be in the same perilous condition as before; this had happened once and he had had to undergo the agony of having them reopened. This was not the image that he wanted to portray to the youthful Catherine. He wanted her to view him simply as a man in his prime. Already, however, stairs were becoming awkward for him. When Sir John Russell, with whom the king and queen stayed, undertook building works in preparation for their visit to his Buckinghamshire mansion of Chenies, he arranged for a special state bed, complete with cloth of gold and silver hangings and with Henry's arms upon it, to be placed in the 'lower chamber' allocated to the king. Fortunately Henry was usually able to ride and hunt, but sometimes he resorted to enclosing deer and watching greyhounds tear them to pieces rather than expending his precious energy in chasing them. He had discovered more pleasurable ways of utilising that energy, especially if he was to impregnate his jewel of womanhood.

Until that happy announcement could be proclaimed, there were court events and festivities for Henry and Catherine to attend, escorted, naturally, by their favourite attendants. Jane was probably one of the party who accompanied Catherine as she savoured the triumphant river procession which the mayor and officials in London laid on as their customary welcome for a new queen. The decorated barges came out again, the pennants flew, Anthony Anthony supervised the Tower gunners who fired their weapons in salute as Henry showed off his fifth wife to his subjects. It was a repeat experience for Jane, but a novelty to Catherine. She probably loved it and, mindful that it was a queen's responsibility to beg for mercy, she knelt sweetly before her husband to plead for the release from the Tower of Anne's old flame, Sir Thomas Wyatt, no stranger to trouble, and for that of Sir John Wallop, who had also displeased his king. Unable to refuse her, Henry pardoned both in a display of genial magnanimity.

Shortly afterwards, Jane joined her queen in a summer progress; Henry was determined to visit the northern parts of his kingdom, territories which he had never seen before. When she mounted her horse at the end of June 1541, Jane understood that the journey would be important for the king. He could quell any murmurs of dissent in areas that were still reeling from the effects of the Pilgrimage of Grace, and he was also due to meet his Scottish nephew, James V, for discussions. Henry would be at his most majestic, magnificent and awesome. The rationale for his chosen itinerary was commonly known at court. Of the ultimate significance of the progress for herself and the queen, Jane had no conception.

The trip was dogged by troubles from the outset. The weather was foul, so bad in fact that they had barely left London before the bitter cold and driving rain held them back. Soon the roads became so flooded and waterlogged that 'the carts and baggage could not proceed without great difficulty'. Then Jane and the other ladies were called upon to care for Catherine who had become ill. With the queen recovered, and Norfolk and Suffolk, braving the ferocious storms, sent ahead to prepare the route as much as practicable, the whole train eventually got going once more.

As far as the king was concerned, the corner had been turned and all was going well. He particularly relished his ceremonial entry into the city of Lincoln. The citizens had never witnessed anything like it as the king's procession rode into their town, every bell in every church pealing to proclaim his arrival. He was dressed in cloth of gold and mounted on his 'horse of estate'. Catherine, shimmering in cloth of silver, was a perfect counterpart to her husband. Behind her came her ladies, doubtless Jane amongst them. Slowly the long lines of gentlemen, guards and officials made its way through the streets to the great abbey church to pray. The king and queen knelt upon cushions of cloth of gold as the Bishop of Lincoln gave them the crucifix to kiss, after which they both walked solemnly into the body of the church, the choir bursting forth in a glorious *Te Deum* as they did so.

Many towns, including Pontefract, Stamford, Scrooby and York, were honoured by a visit from their king that fateful summer. The populace decorated their streets and watched agog as the cavalcade passed by. For the royal party, it was tiring but satisfying. The king was greeted everywhere with outpourings of loyalty and thanks. Despite James's failure to keep his appointment, Henry enjoyed himself. And so did Catherine. There were new places to see and different people to meet, and being the focus of attention and the recipient of admiring and sometimes envious glances was deliciously gratifying. At most places, she and Jane liked to seek out all the nooks, crannies and secret places of the queen's lodgings. Catherine loved to explore.

There were undercurrents, however. Even before the journey had started, Jane had been aware of a few unsettling occurrences. The immediate threat of foreign invasion seemed to have receded, but disturbances at home had continued. A sudden rebellion in the North had flared up out of the blue a few months before the progress had begun. Easily quashed, it had led the king to order the execution of the aged Countess of Salisbury, although as she was almost seventy years of age it was hard to see quite why she was so dangerous. Those towns involved with the rebellion had proved pleasingly contrite when the king had arrived on his progress but it was impossible to pretend that it had not happened. Nor could anyone forget that James V was just as untrustworthy as ever, or that Ireland was far from content under Tudor rule. Fear of rebellion there was a constant dread in English hearts. With so many cares of state to wrestle with, it was fortunate that Henry was so much in love with his wife, although there had been a couple of tense moments even there.

Catherine's first scare had come within a few months of her wedding. 'Feigning indisposition', Chapuys had informed the Queen of Hungary, the king 'was ten or twelve days without seeing his queen or allowing her to come into his room', fuelling gossip that he was considering divorce. Nothing had come of this, and she and Henry had been reconciled swiftly, but the incident had rankled. Then, concerned by his bonhomie towards her predecessor, Catherine had begun to wonder whether the king intended to rekindle his fourth marriage and end hers. Anxiety about Anne of Cleves had made the queen 'rather sad and thoughtful'. When Henry had noticed, Catherine had poured out her worries. Dispelling them, Henry had said that 'she was wrong to believe such things of him'. Even if he had to marry again, he had comforted her, he 'would never retake' Anne. That had been good for Catherine to hear, although she might have wondered why Henry might think he would ever need a sixth wife when he was married to her. The possible resurgence of Anne had been upsetting for Jane too: Anne would not have welcomed her back as a lady of the bedchamber after she had testified against her. However, the stormclouds passed.

But these episodes had illustrated the root of Catherine's own dilemma. As long as the king worshipped her she was safe and secure but, as Jane was in a position to know, Henry was fickle. Just a few years earlier, he had recklessly risked the vengeance of the greatest power in Europe, together with the wrath of the pope, for the sake of one woman, only to destroy her without a qualm, on the flimsiest of grounds, when his ardour had cooled.

Queen Jane, of course, would never have been discarded: she had produced his precious heir, Edward. Even had Henry become bored with her simpering goodness and amused himself elsewhere, the mother of his son would have been secure until her dying day, which, of course, she was. At least Catherine aroused her husband sexually, as Anne of Cleves had not, but she could never rest entirely easy unless she could give him that Duke of York to grace the nursery.

There was still time, however. Catherine was young, healthy and active, and Henry optimistic. With the misgivings of the previous year that Chapuys had sensed now a thing of the past, in the weeks after his return from what he had considered a highly successful progress, Henry settled down to his blessed domestic life with his jewel. He was so happy that he ordered the Bishop of Lincoln to thank God for the 'good life' he had with his wife 'and hoped to have with her'.

Henry's nightmare began the following day, on Wednesday, 2 November, All Souls' Day. As the king went to the chapel to pray, Cranmer handed him a letter. The archbishop had received information so heinous about Catherine's morals that he felt that the king had to be told, but since 'he had not the heart to tell it by word of mouth', he had written it down instead. Unable to conceive that his jewel could be flawed, Henry ordered a discreet investigation in order to root out those who had dared to slander her. Assuming the issue was under control, he simply followed his usual routine while he waited for the results of the enquiry, which would, he was certain, exonerate his queen. He would then punish the perpetrators of such wicked lies.

For the time being, life continued as normal. The court was at Hampton Court, perhaps relaxing after the long progress. Catherine and her ladies sewed, danced, listened to her musicians, chatted, walked in her gardens, all blissfully unaware that soon, for some, life would never be normal again. And all the while, Henry's most trusted councillors were rounding up witnesses, listening to their stories, writing out statements, uncovering more and more scurrilous details as the days slipped by. The first inkling anyone had that something was wrong was when Henry attended a special Council meeting on Saturday morning and remained closeted away until noon. That in itself was not unheard of, although Henry was not usually prone to spend quite so long on state business. At midnight, he instructed messengers to fetch Audley and Norfolk. Even then, Jane and Catherine knew nothing. Both could sleep soundly in their beds.

Matters came to a head the next day. Henry pretended to be going hunting so that he was well away from the main body of the palace. There in the fields, unobserved by his courtiers, he could talk over the shocking facts with his councillors. Action would have to be taken. There was proof positive that Catherine had been no virgin on her wedding day: she was damaged goods; she had betrayed her gentle prince. So, after supper that evening, and without bidding farewell to the queen, the king suddenly ordered his small barge to be made ready. He left immediately, his oarsmen taking him to Westminster. If he wished, he could spend the night at York Place, although the place where he would pass the night was not uppermost in his mind. That, of course, was his disappointment in his queen, whom he would never lay eyes upon again. Once back in London, he went straight into another Council meeting, which went on through much of the night. Unaware, Catherine slept peacefully.

On Monday it was a different story, however. The king's abrupt departure had become common knowledge, but the cause was a mystery. Catherine could only sit within her luxurious apartments, waiting for news. No one told her anything as the hours dragged by but, unlike the French ambassador who repeated to Francis the initial rumours that such feverish activity was caused by trouble with Scotland or Ireland, she was in a position to know that the meetings might well be about other issues entirely. For Catherine had secrets, one of which concerned events that were very recent, and which Jane shared. She knew that the architectural explorations that she had undertaken with the queen whilst on the progress were designed for a specific purpose, one that was far from innocent. If Catherine's escapades in the North and the Midlands ever came to light, Jane's world would be shattered even more devastatingly, and fatally, than it had been when George had been arrested.

Then, as the two women sat in anxious silence, with time almost suspended, there came a knock on the door of Catherine's chambers. Archbishop Cranmer had arrived with serious questions to put to her.

30

In the Maidens' Chamber

When Cranmer, accompanied by a handful of other councillors, entered Catherine's apartments, she and Jane were in mortal danger. The outcome hinged on exactly what Henry had discovered. But, although the peril remained grave, both the queen and Jane could feel only overwhelming relief that the archbishop's focus was solely on Catherine's life before she had met the king, rather than afterwards. What Catherine realised, and what Jane did not, was how much dirt could surface concerning her teenage years.

Jane, like everyone else at court, knew about the queen's upbringing. It was common knowledge, arousing minimal interest. Because her mother, Joyce, had died when she was little and her father, Edmund, at one point Comptroller of Calais, had found it impossible or inconvenient to look after her, Catherine had been despatched to Agnes Tylney, the widow of the second Duke of Norfolk, and her step-grandmother, to be brought up in the dowager duchess's houses at Horsham in Sussex and at Lambeth in London. Since children were frequently sent away from home to the households of rich patrons or relatives, few at court had felt much sympathy for Catherine's plight, although it was true that she had probably been younger than was usual when she first went to Horsham. The dowager duchess had kept a fairly open house. She had other youngsters in her care including, sometimes, Catherine's siblings and cousins, as well as the daughters of various neighbours, so Catherine's childhood had not been lonely or unhappy. At night, there would have been chatter and laughter in the maidens' chamber, where they all slept together, often sharing beds. By day, there were lessons. The busy duchess had arranged for the girls to be taught to read and write and, with a pragmatic eye on acceptable feminine accomplishments, she had even paid for one Henry Manox to give them music lessons. Manox, however, had been interested in giving the bubbly and precocious Catherine something more than music lessons.

It was the extraordinary details of Catherine's romps with Manox, and with Francis Dereham, another of the bucks at Horsham, that had been relayed to the archbishop, and which he had in turn passed on to the king by letter a few days earlier. There is no reason to assume that Jane had known anything of the queen's youthful adventures. She knew quite enough about what Catherine had been up to over the past few months to disturb her sleep, but the queen had hoped to keep her earlier genie safely locked in its bottle as well. Unfortunately, too much was known by too many.

And one of them, Mary Hall, born Lascelles, had let the genie out. When Mary's brother, John, had come to visit her in Sussex, he had suggested that she should ask Catherine for employment since Mary had known the queen at Horsham. His sister's response had put John in a terrible position: Mary vowed not to approach Catherine because she was 'light, both in living and conditions'. When pressed, Mary had gone further. Manox, she had maintained, knew a 'privy mark' on Catherine's body, and Francis Dereham 'had lain in bed' with Catherine 'in his doublet and hose'.

John's dilemma had been acute, and it was one that Jane could appreciate. If he buried the information, only for it to come out later, he would be in dire trouble for concealing it. Then, he could be deemed guilty of misprision of treason, an offence carrying a maximum penalty of life imprisonment and confiscation of all property. On the other hand, if he passed on Mary's remarks, and they were shown to be false or unproven, he would have slandered the queen and incurred Henry's displeasure. Either way, his position was grim. On balance, he had felt it better to tell someone, although quite whom to tell had been another difficulty. In the end, he had confessed all to Cranmer, who, 'being much perplexed', and wary of bearing Hall's burden alone, had consulted Audley and Hertford, Queen Jane's brother. Thus it was that the archbishop had written to the king and the investigation had been initiated. Everyone remotely connected with what might have occurred in the maidens' chamber had been rounded up and interrogated with the utmost rigour. So devastating were the results that the wounded king had left Hampton Court and sent Cranmer to question his jewel.

By the time Cranmer walked into Catherine's apartments, the material already amassed by Henry's councillors was staggering. This information was at the king's fingertips while he waited to hear of Catherine's responses to Cranmer's gentle probing when she faced the archbishop on that winter's day at Hampton Court.

The queen began by denying everything, but was confronted by a mountain of evidence. For a start there was Mary Hall's testimony, collected by the Earl of Southampton, Cromwell's successor as Lord Privy Seal, who had rushed down to Sussex to interview her. Mary had been very forthcoming. After working as a nurse to the children of Lord William Howard, the Duchess of Norfolk's son, she had become a chamberer to the duchess herself, which meant that she had met the nubile Catherine. Henry Manox, Mary Hall maintained, fell 'so far in love' with Catherine that Mary 'did abhor it'. Tokens were carried back and forth between them by Mrs Isabel and Dorothy Barwick, and Mary had become worried enough to take Manox to task. If the duchess ever found out what was going on, she warned him, she would 'undo' him, for Catherine came 'of a noble house'. She was so far out of Manox's league that should he marry Catherine, Mary prophesied, 'some of her blood will kill thee'. Manox had shrugged off her remarks. 'Hold thy peace, woman,' he had retorted, 'I know her well enough for I have had her by the cunt and know it amongst a hundred.' Catherine, he said, had even promised him 'her maidenhead'. According to Mary, when Catherine later berated Manox, he had responded that 'he was so far in love with her that he wist not what he said'. For a fleeting moment, Mary had thought that Catherine had dealt firmly with the bragging Manox, but then she saw her walking with him behind the orchard 'and no creature with them but they two alone'.

To compound her foolishness, when bored by Manox, 'Catherine had quickly moved on to the charms of Francis Dereham. Mary confessed to seeing 'them kiss after a wonderful manner, for they would kiss' and hang together as though they were 'two sparrows'.

It was not long before Catherine ordered Mary to steal the key to the maidens' chamber so that she could let Dereham in. Catherine 'would go to naked bed', said Mary, and Dereham 'would lay down upon the bed in his doublet and his hose'. Mary discussed the situation with another colleague, Alice Wilkes, who told her that Dereham would lie on Catherine's bed 'till it was almost day', and that many times there was 'a puffing and blowing betwixt them'. When she could think of no more to report to Southampton, the obliging Mary provided the minister with a list of several other people whom she thought might know something. The diligent councillors set to work to trace them all. Trace them they did.

Manox was easy to find. He had in fact done rather well for himself after leaving the duchess's employment. He had married Margaret, the widow of Nicholas Jennings, a wealthy London alderman, and now lived very comfortably with her in the late alderman's residence in Streatham. He, too, proved most forthcoming. He agreed that he had asked to touch 'her secrets', a favour that he demanded as a special sign of her love. Clearly dismissing his request as unimportant, Catherine had consented on the condition 'that he would desire no more' for, she had asserted, 'I will never be naught [wicked or sinful] with you and able to marry me you be not.' Although he had touched her private parts quite often, he maintained that that was all he ever had done, but he, too, confirmed that Dereham had replaced him in the fickle Mistress Howard's affections. Dereham, he said, and his friend Edward Waldegrave, who was infatuated with another maiden, 'haunted nightly' Catherine's chamber 'and would commonly banket [banquet] and be merry there till two or three of the clock in the morning'. Indeed, Manox had felt so jealous of his successor that he had written an anonymous letter to the duchess to advise a random check on her maidens' bedchamber to see whether it contained more than maidens.

Catherine would surely be able to remember the incident. She could hardly have forgotten her intimacies with Dereham, now so meticulously documented from the statements of Mary Hall and so many other deponents. Dereham, who was 'seriously examined', a code for torture, confessed 'that he hath had carnal knowledge with the Queen afore marriage, being in bed with her in his doublet and hose divers times and six or seven times in naked bed'. When Dereham's close friend, Robert Davenport, was also interrogated 'seriously', he corroborated Dereham's statement. He had, he affirmed, 'seen the said Dereham and Catherine Howard kiss oft and lie together upon the bed'. He had even heard Katherine Tylney, who at that time had to share Catherine's bed, plead, 'I pray you, Mr Dereham, lie still.' Since Davenport went on to say that he could 'hear Dereham blow and strive to have had his will', poor Katherine Tylney's entreaties for a peaceful night were clearly ignored. Davenport also mentioned other times when Dereham had visited Catherine's chamber and 'no woman was with her'.

The councillors were thoroughness epitomised. All evidence was carefully substantiated, cross-checked and cross-referenced, no possible witness ignored. They took particular care to track down any servants who had left the duchess's employ but might possess valuable information. One such was Andrew Maunsay. He swore that 'he thrice saw the Queen, then Mrs Catherine Howard, lie in her bed and one Durnand [Dereham], a gentleman then in the house, lie suspiciously on the bed in his doublet and hose'. Unaware that she had already been interrogated, he suggested that the councillors should contact Katherine Tylney who 'lay in the bed at the time and can tell more'.

Still Catherine continued to lie. When, finally, she decided to co-operate and start to tell the truth, up to a point at least, Cranmer felt sorry for her. He 'found her in such lamentation and heaviness, as I never saw no creature', he wrote to Henry. 'It would have pitied any man's heart in the world to have looked upon her.' She wept, she raged, she worked herself up into a 'frenzy' of fear. She did admit her relationship with Dereham but swore that all that he 'did unto her was of his importune forcement, and, in a manner, violence, rather than of her free consent and will'. Yet she hoped for a miracle: that Henry might pardon her. Calling herself his 'most sorrowful subject and most vile wretch in the world', she begged him to take into account her 'youth', her 'ignorance', her 'frailness'. Although she acknowledged herself 'worthy of most extreme punishment', she trusted to his 'infinite goodness, pity, compassion and mercy'. Her confession was so perfectly pitched to tug at Henry's heartstrings as to suggest that she was given help to compose it.

The atmosphere in the queen's apartments during the next few days was tense. Their routine interrupted, her ladies tried to calm and comfort Catherine as more and more revelations emerged. The agony of suspense was so much worse for Jane. Whilst every new disclosure was horrifying enough, she knew it was but the tip of the iceberg. Even the once fun-loving Catherine was far too apprehensive for amusement. 'Whereas, before, she did nothing but dance and rejoice,' Marillac informed Francis, 'now, when the musicians come they are told that it is no more the time to dance.' Soon, Hampton Court was strictly guarded. For as long as the interrogations focused only on Catherine's life before her wedding, both she and Jane felt that they might survive. It could be a matter of holding their nerve. The king would be furious, he would be disillusioned, he would be hurt, but he would not be branded a cuckold for the second time. He might, therefore, be compassionate. The Duchess of Norfolk, oblivious to her own impending imprisonment, was optimistic. Davenport told his interrogators, Sir John Gage, Sir Richard Rich and Henry Bradshaw, that he had heard the duchess say that she believed Dereham and Catherine were in trouble 'for some matter done when they were here', in which case they 'should not die for it'. She may have been right, for Cranmer himself had at one point reassured Catherine that the king was inclined to mercy.

There could even be a way out. If Catherine and Dereham had agreed to marry and had then copulated, that could amount to a pre-contract. Since Anne of Cleves's presumed pre-contract with the son of the Duke of Lorraine had provided a major cause for the annulment of her union with Henry, a comparable situation could now arise. But Catherine refused to grasp the lifeline. Whilst she admitted that Dereham had left the huge sum of £100 with her for safe-keeping when he had gone away, and that marriage talk had been bandied about between them, she would not concede that it amounted to a pre-contract. The archbishop reported back to the king that what she had said was 'not so much as I thought', but he still believed it 'sufficient to prove a contract'. Unfortunately, further revelations would make the pre-contract escape route irrelevant.

Until that happened, it was a waiting game. The queen hoped that her confession would stop the questions. It did not. The questions went on, moving in ever widening circles. Sooner or later, the councillors would latch on to Catherine's more recent conduct, and that would entrap Jane too. A distraught Catherine almost lost her mind with worry. She 'refuses to drink or eat and weeps and cries like a madwoman, so that they must take away things by which she might hasten her death', wrote a well-informed Marillac to the French king. Although less serious than the damning facts that so far lay undiscovered, an additional complication was that Catherine had had fresh contact with Dereham. Her relationship with Manox had indeed petered out once he had carved himself a new life with his rich widow and, for a while, she had lost touch with Dereham too. Much to the suspicion of the investigating councillors, he had gone to Ireland when his frolics with Catherine had come to an end. It would have been better for both had he stayed there. But the break was only temporary. In a gesture that could be misinterpreted as acquiescence to blackmail, which perhaps it was, the queen had employed Joan Bulmer, an acquaintance from her Horsham days, after Joan had written to her seeking a position for old times' sake. Stupidly the queen had also welcomed Dereham into her household upon his return from Ireland. Now there were questions about whether they had resumed their affair. Since she had met her former lover within the confines of her privy chamber 'divers times' and had once advised him to 'take heed what words you speak', a belated nod towards discretion, there was yet more scope for Henry's unremitting investigators.

And discretion was not Dereham's watchword. Recklessly, he had boasted of his connection with the queen. Davenport, under pressure again, described a particularly telling incident. When Dereham had come back to court, Davenport related, he 'fell out' with Catherine's gentleman usher, Mr Johns, because the queen 'favoured him [Dereham]' and because Dereham obstinately sat with the queen's councillors for meals, a place to which he was not entitled. A furious Mr Johns had sent over a messenger to ask sarcastically whether Dereham was one of the queen's council. 'Go to, Mr Johns,' spat back Dereham, 'and tell him I was of the Queen's Council before he knew her and should be when she hath forgotten him.' The councillors solemnly wrote down all of Davenport's recollections but it was still not quite enough to nail Dereham for anything more than bedding a flirtatious Catherine before her marriage. However, Davenport suddenly delivered the *coup de grâce*. He asked his gaolers to fetch someone from the king's Council because he had something to tell them. Wriothesley, Sir John Gage and Sir Richard Rich hurried to the Tower before he changed his mind. What they heard was worth its weight in gold: according to Davenport, Dereham had said that, should the king die, 'I am sure I might marry her.' It was a capital crime to imagine the king's death. Davenport had condemned his friend.

He had not condemned Catherine, however. She had already managed that for herself, for she had embarked upon an entirely new relationship within months of becoming queen. Manox and Dereham were her past; Thomas Culpepper was her present. 'The Queen 3 or 4 times every day since she was in this trouble', Jane confessed later, would ask her 'what she heard of Culpepper'. Since Jane had become entangled in Catherine's illicit passion from its early stages, the queen's disquiet was no surprise. What was surprising was that Catherine had indulged in such folly to begin with. Revelling in the pleasures of the flesh as a girl was one thing; giving way to similar temptation when queen was quite another, particularly with her own cousin's death at the hands of the Calais swordsman proving a pertinent reminder of the consequences.

It is true that Culpepper had many obvious attractions and that Catherine had met him, and appears to have liked him, when she was serving Anne of Cleves. A very distant relation of Catherine's, he came from a respectable and fairly wealthy gentry family, and was well established within the king's privy chamber. He was also unmarried, probably charming, courteous and solicitous, and close to Catherine's age. The contrast between this appealing young man and Henry, with his thinning hair, bloated body and suppurating ulcers, could not have been more marked. Perhaps, for Catherine, it was as simple as that. Certainly, she was not deterred by an unsavoury story associated with the young man, which linked him to the rape of a park-keeper's wife whom his attendants 'held down for him in a thicket', and then to a 'murder committed when some villagers tried to apprehend him for the crime'. She told Jane that she 'trusted Culpepper more than her own brother'. In fact, she more than trusted him, she loved him. She said as much in her one surviving, incriminating letter to him. 'I heard you were sick,' she wrote, 'and never longed so much for anything as to see you. It makes my heart die to think I cannot be always in your company. Come when my Lady Rochford is here, for then I shall be best at leisure to be at your commandment.' She signed it, 'Yours as long as life endures, Catherine.' It was scarcely the tone to be expected of a queen to a subject, not least since at the time the word 'company' had a well-known sexual resonance.

Catherine's desire for Culpepper led her to abandon caution. It was to cost the queen her life, but it was also to cost Jane hers. We shall never know whether Jane realised what she was getting into when the Culpepper fiasco commenced. The most viable explanation for her otherwise incomprehensible behaviour is that what started innocently enough developed, with terrifying speed, into a deadly vortex of deceit and intrigue. When the queen first ordered her to take a note, a token or a verbal message to Culpepper, Jane had to make a split-second decision. She had no real reason to think that the queen's request was connected to a passionate affair. Attendants were expected to run errands, that was part of their function. Indeed, when Culpepper received gifts from Catherine, the queen told a male servant, Henry Webb, to escort him to her apartments. Jane had clawed her way back into a senior post within the royal household, she wanted to stay there. That meant she must obey her mistress. Although not born to rule, Catherine could be as imperious and demanding as her royal husband. Blatantly to refuse her instructions was unthinkable.

If she had done so, Jane's career would have been over. It would have meant permanent withdrawal from court to the tranquillity, or boredom, of Blickling. When her jointure had been agreed, Jane had rejected that lifestyle. Alternatively, she could have gone to the king and told him that his wife was communicating with one of the gentlemen in his privy chamber. But should it have come to the queen's word against hers, there would have been no contest. Henry could easily have dismissed the missives as innocuous and blamed Jane for tale-bearing. Even had she decided to risk it, the sheer practicality of gaining access to the king posed almost insuperable obstacles. As a woman, especially one about whom a whiff of treason might still linger, she could not approach Henry directly. She would have needed a male go-between. Cromwell would have been the ideal choice, but the minister had perished.

As for her father, Jane knew his interests were intellectual rather than political. Lord Morley was not unworldly: he came to court when required, he fulfilled his duty by sitting on the various panels of peers, he was not averse to accumulating ex-monastic property despite his religious convictions. In particular, he was contentedly settling into his new estate of Markhall in Essex, the childhood home of Alice Middleton, Sir Thomas More's widow, which he had purchased in 1538 from Thomas Shaa, in the very year that Jane's jointure was agreed. However, he was at his happiest when engrossed in his books and his translations. He had never been one to raise his head above the parapet, he was hardly likely to break the habit of a lifetime now. Clearly, Jane did not approach her father, nor is there any hint that she consulted her brother, Sir Henry Parker. She was on her own, as she had been during other key episodes in her life, and she chose the path of silence. For her, it was much trodden.

And, once she had decided to take that first message, and that message became part of a series, Jane had passed the point of no return. 'Come when my lady Rochford is here,' the queen had written to Culpepper. What may have started harmlessly had taken on a momentum of its own and Jane could not extricate herself. It was now too late to crave country air or to attempt to see the king. Her situation was actually worse than that of John Hall when he listened, probably with mounting horror, to his sister's unsolicited confidences. Mary Hall had heard Catherine's love-making, she had helped her procure the key to the maidens' chamber, but Catherine then had been as free as a wild bird, she had not been the king's wife. When Jane became immersed in Catherine's intrigues, the bird was caged and the king kept the key. Because she had not acted immediately, Jane had drastically reduced her options. If she opened her mouth now, charges of misprision of treason would loom and all of the property she had so painstakingly regained since George's death would be forfeit yet again.

All she could do, even though her danger intensified when Catherine's romance went beyond the letter stage to nocturnal trysts, was to go along with it, do her best to minimise the dangers and hope that, somehow, it would not be discovered. Paradoxically, as Jane may have realised, should Catherine become pregnant, the baby could be their saviour. Henry was still sharing his wife's bed, his optimism undiminished; if Catherine did have a child, it could as easily be Henry's as Culpepper's. And, should it be a boy, Henry would be so overjoyed that Catherine would be his precious jewel for ever. If that were so, the loyal Viscountess Rochford's place within the bedchamber would be secure too.

But this scenario had depended on secrecy. The exposure of Catherine's youthful adventures had jeopardised everything. For the few days that the archbishop and the councillors questioned the queen about her years at Horsham and Lambeth, and about Manox and Dereham, Jane was in limbo. Catherine told her that if the Culpepper 'matter came not out, she feared not for nothing'. Unfortunately, too many of those already in custody knew enough about it to make sure that come out it would. It was just a question of time.

31

'That bawd, the lady Jane Rochford'

A week after Henry had sat back in his small barge while his bargemen rowed him upriver from Hampton Court to Westminster and his waiting councillors, the Culpepper affair was out in the open. It could hardly have been otherwise. Catherine, Jane and Culpepper must each have known that their chances of escaping detection were slim once the councillors really set to work. According to Marillac, it was Dereham who first blew the whistle. Desperate that his forceful interrogators should believe his protestations that he had not slept with Catherine after her marriage to the king, he said that 'Culpepper had succeeded him in the Queen's affections'.

That was enough. For Catherine to say to Jane, as she had, that if the 'matter' of Culpepper 'came out ... she would never confess it' and to demand that Jane should 'deny it utterly', was pointless. Catherine had already cracked under pressure from Cranmer about Manox and Dereham, her transparent lies quickly exposed. She would fare no better now; neither would Jane. By the time that Henry's diligent councillors had tracked down every potential witness, they were able to compile a formidable dossier. They had times, places, the names and statements of those whose suspicions had been aroused, and they were soon ready to take depositions from the three most fatally implicated: Culpepper, Catherine, and Jane. Henry was determined to 'find out the bottom of the pot'.

With her normal household dispersed, their ears buzzing with lurid details of their mistress's immorality, Catherine was taken from a desolate Hampton Court along the Thames to the former nunnery at Syon where she was to live in much reduced circumstances. Three chambers were prepared for her, hung with 'mean stuff, without any cloth of estate'. She was cared for by four gentlewomen, one of whom was to be Lady Isabel Baynton, and two chamberers. Jane, of course, was separated from her. Sir Edward Baynton was deputed by the king to be in overall charge of the queen's establishment, in addition to Nicholas Heath, Bishop of Rochester, Henry's almoner. Catherine had had to leave behind the more ostentatious trappings of royalty, such as her fabulous jewels. The king even specified the clothes that she was allowed to take with her. She could have six French hoods, six pairs of sleeves, six gowns and six kirtles. She could wear satin, damask or velvet. Her hoods could be edged with gold, but she was to have no precious stones or pearls on any of her garments. It was quite a comedown for this jewel of womanhood. It could have been worse. Culpepper was conveyed to the Tower. So was Jane, and she would have barely enough time to collect her thoughts before the questioning would start.

At least she knew that she had not engineered Catherine's first major encounter with Culpepper. When the queen had initially sent for Culpepper back in April, he was escorted to her apartments by a male servant, Henry Webb. As Culpepper stood in the 'entry between her privy chamber and the chamber of presence', Catherine gave him 'by her own hands' a velvet cap 'garnished with a brooch', a chain and three dozen pairs of aiglettes.* The gifts were a secret between them. 'Put this under your cloak so nobody see it,' the queen advised.

Jane's role as intermediary began shortly after that. Noticing a cramp ring† on her finger, which she had been given by Catherine, Culpepper daringly stole it. When Jane told the queen of his playful theft, Catherine took another one from her own finger, asking Jane to take it to him. He needed two, Catherine said, as 'it was an ill sign to see him wear but one'. Other than saying that it was 'in the progress time', Culpepper does not date this incident in his

---

* Aiglettes were cord-like fasteners made of silk or cotton threads woven together. Sometimes they were metal-tipped and could have gold or silver bands at their ends, below which the threads were left loose to billow out rather like tassels. Aiglettes could be both elaborate and expensive.

† Cramp rings were intended to ward off pains and other ailments.

confession, and Jane does not mention it at all, but there is no reason to doubt its veracity.

With the progress under way, Jane proved very useful indeed to the queen. Margaret Morton, one of Catherine's attendants, testified that when the royal party were at Liddington in late July, the queen felt unwell and ordered Margaret to take a 'privy letter' to Jane. The note was sealed but not addressed. Margaret was to tell Jane that the queen 'was sorry that she could write no better'. Jane then 'had her desire the Queen to respite her [give her more time and wait] till the next morning for an answer'. When Margaret returned as ordered on the following day, Jane handed her a sealed letter for Catherine, instructing her to warn 'her grace to keep it secret and not to lay it abroad'. About a week later, when the royal train arrived at the Duke of Suffolk's Lincolnshire mansion of Grimsthorpe, there was a similar event when Katherine Tylney, one of Catherine's Horsham friends and now her chamberer, was also sent off with a message for Jane. 'When should she have the thing she promised her?' Tylney was to ask Jane, whose response was that she would sit up for it and 'would next day bring her [Catherine] word herself'. By now, Jane had indeed reached that point of no return.

But it was at Lincoln, the scene of the wonderful mass in the abbey at which the dutiful queen knelt beside her husband, that events moved into another gear. This time Jane did not just deliver an epistle, she helped arrange a tryst. Everywhere that the royal party stopped, Culpepper said, Catherine searched for quiet nooks and crannies 'that would have served' as meeting places. She 'would in every house seek for the back doors and back stairs', he continued, and at Lincoln she was particularly lucky. In a visit that lasted only three days, the pair were able to meet on two nights, although their assignations did not go unnoticed.

Tylney reported that Catherine was 'out of her chamber when it was late'. The queen was with Jane in Jane's room, which was 'up a little pair of stairs' conveniently close to hers. When Tylney went there with Margaret (presumably Margaret Morton), the queen sent both women off to bed. Tylney obeyed, but the curious Margaret crept up again to see what was going on. She did not return until 2 a.m. 'Jesus, is not the Queen abed yet?' asked Tylney. 'Yes, even now,' was the enigmatic response.

In fact, as Jane knew only too well, Catherine had spent most of that night with Culpepper, who later said, much to the fastidious disgust of the councillors, that he thought the assignation was in Catherine's stool-chamber.* He had arrived at 11 p.m. and stayed until three in the morning, simply talking, he maintained, 'of themselves and of their loves before time'. Jane listened but heard little of what they said as they talked softly and 'secretly', although she did pick up that they spoke of Bessie Harvey, another of Culpepper's loves, a woman to whom Catherine had contemptuously donated a damask gown. He had actually been fortunate to get into the room at all. Catherine and Jane had been watching out for him in the darkness at the back door, when the watch suddenly appeared. 'Having a light', the watchman, who clearly took his duties seriously, realised that the outer door was unlocked and, much to the ladies' consternation, proceeded to lock it. When Culpepper appeared a short while afterwards, they 'marvelled how he came in'; it seems that his resourceful servant had picked the lock.

The careless use of attendants was, as Jane came to appreciate, foolhardy, as many of them could, and did, give evidence against her. On the second night at Lincoln, Catherine went into Jane's room again, having sent all her ladies, except Katherine Tylney, to bed. Tylney sat with Jane's female servant some distance from the queen 'in a little place by'. They stayed there while the queen 'tarried also in a manner as long as she did the other night', Tylney informed Wriothesley helpfully, but she had neither seen nor heard what went on. Staying up half the night might suit Catherine and Culpepper, but Jane, their supposed chaperone, had fallen asleep. She had not woken up, she said, 'until the Queen did call her to answer Lovekyn', another of Catherine's ladies, who had come to knock on the door. Catherine, clearly furious that Lovekyn had appeared at all, ordered that no one should come to her bedchamber unless specifically summoned. She later vowed to dismiss Lovekyn, together with Margaret Morton. This would have been 'without reason', said an

---

* A stool-chamber was a lavatory.

aggrieved Morton, going on to suggest that Catherine's intention was to bring some of Jane's cronies into the privy chamber. It was Margaret Morton, now watching out for anything untoward, who reported that she 'first suspected the Queen at Hatfield when the Queen looked out at her privy chamber window at Mr Culpepper'. Catherine stared at him 'after such sort that she thought there was love between them', said Morton, perhaps wise after the event.

Morton proved a valuable source for the queen's activities at Pontefract too. There, she said, Catherine, alone with Jane every night, 'locked and bolted her chamber door on the inside'. The queen was too occupied with Culpepper to countenance any interruptions, even from her own husband. Indeed, when Anthony Denny of the king's privy chamber went to Catherine's room one evening, presumably to escort her to an amorous Henry, he found the door locked. As Morton alone reported the occurrence, the queen's explanation is tantalisingly lost to us. Catherine's mind was focused on Culpepper, not on Henry. Jane, acting as intermediary, told Culpepper where to be and at what time. By now Catherine was becoming a little jumpy, unnerved by the watchman locking the door on the outside at Lincoln. Convinced that the king had 'set a watch' near her apartment, she consulted Jane. Jane then persuaded her own maidservant to stay up as a lookout. Since the coast was clear, Culpepper came the next night, remaining with her until the king went to bed. According to Culpepper, they were just talking. They seemed to do rather a lot of that. Jane maintained that she never knew what they actually said because she was always stationed too far away to hear. She knew that Catherine's fears of discovery had not entirely abated, however. Culpepper stood upon the stairs, she said, 'ready always to slip down if noise came', with petite Catherine standing on the step above the much taller young man.

Catherine's trepidation was not enough to make her call a halt to the affair. They met again at York, where Catherine teased Culpepper about the other lovers she could take if she chose. She accepted a ring from him, sending him two bracelets in return 'to keep his arms warm'. And they were still enamoured at the end of the progress, for Katherine Tylney, worth her weight in gold to the busy councillors, declared that yet again the queen had sent her to

Jane with one of those cryptic requests about when she should 'have the thing she promised her'.

If Catherine, Culpepper and Jane ever imagined that all of this could stay hidden for ever, they were roughly disabused of their fancies once the arrests began and Dereham, thinking about his own neck, passed on what he suspected of Culpepper. Tylney, present both at Horsham and on the progress, was a star witness against Catherine with regard to her conduct both before and after marriage. Morton, so frequently in the right place at the right time, was another who was quick to tell her story, which was sometimes so close to that of Tylney as to indicate that they had spent many a cosy hour discussing what they had observed. There is no record of Culpepper's servant, that expert lock-picker, being questioned but he may well have been, and the same is true of Jane's servant, Richard, who was probably the woman with whom Tylney had sat at Lincoln.

By the time Catherine had been sent to Syon, and Jane and Culpepper arrested, the councillors had pieced together virtually the whole story. Culpepper was taken straight to the Tower, to be questioned in that bleak atmosphere so conducive to confession. Although not tortured, he seemed to be co-operative, purporting to give a full account of all he could remember about the progress, Catherine's gifts and what they had talked about. He admitted that she had told him that if she 'had tarried still in the maidens' chamber, I would have tried [made love to] you'. At Lincoln, when she pleaded that 'she must never love him', he responded that he was so 'bound' to her that he loved her 'above all creatures'. At York, he said, the queen 'desired communication with him how well she loved him'. Always, though, he said, they had simply talked. Their romance was rooted in the language of love, not in its practical application. He did not seem to think that the concept of this very experienced couple spending hour after hour in the middle of the night engrossed merely in conversation stretched credulity as, frankly, it does. When pressed, however, he uttered the one sentence that could condemn him whether or not the rest of his evidence was truthful. 'He intended and meant to do ill [go to bed] with the Queen,' he said, 'and that in like wise the Queen so minded to do with him.' In any case, he stated, the real culprit was Jane. Not only was she 'the carrier of all messages and tokens' between himself and Catherine, but she 'provoked him much to love the Queen'. The offence was not his and certainly not Catherine's. It was all Jane's fault.

In that, at least, he was joined by the garrulous Margaret Morton. Growing envious of Jane's pre-eminence within the privy chamber, Morton pointed the finger at her as 'the principal occasion of the folly'. Catherine, too, also shifted the blame squarely on to her lady of the bedchamber. In a confession extracted just before she was sent to Syon, Catherine denied any sexual intimacy with Culpepper, stating that the only 'bare of her' that he had ever touched was her arm. Everything that took place between them was perfectly innocent, she maintained. They had done no more than talk. In that, her story meshed with Culpepper's, although, unlike him, she was careful not to divulge that they had talked of love or that she was prepared to 'do ill' with him, if she had not already done so. And the only reason they had talked in the first place, she said desperately, was because Jane had pushed her into it. It had never been her own idea. It had been Jane, she claimed, who had begged her to speak to Culpepper, telling her that he 'desired nothing else' and meant the queen 'nothing but honesty'. It had been Jane who had calmed her fears that 'this will be spied one day' and that then they would 'be all undone'. It had been Jane who had chosen and bought the bracelets for Culpepper, after entreating the queen to let her do so. It had been Jane who had warned her to tell no one what was happening, promising, that she (Jane) would be 'torn with wild horses' before she would confess it herself.

Catherine in her distress and confusion had forgotten her own highly incriminating invitation to Culpepper: 'It makes my heart die to think I cannot be always in your company. Come when my Lady Rochford is here, for then I shall be best at leisure to be at your commandment.' This devastating note hardly supported her attempt to assert that, all along, it had been Jane who had talked her into the affair. Two days later, the councillors would raid Culpepper's lodgings at court and seize his possessions, including this explosive document.

Nor could Catherine consult Culpepper to make sure that their stories tallied. While Culpepper said that it was he who had pulled the cramp ring from Jane's finger, and that when she had heard of it, Catherine had taken another from her own finger and had sent Jane to give it to him with a message, Catherine gave a conflicting version of this incident. She insisted that Jane had deliberately taken one from her to give him and had then taken another to 'match it'. And while Culpepper alleged that it was the queen herself who 'would in every house seek for the back doors and back stairs', Catherine claimed that it had been Jane. 'At every lodging', the cornered queen said, Jane would 'search the back doors and tell her of them if there were any, unasked'. Jane, she continued, had even found 'an old kitchen' at Greenwich where Catherine and Culpepper could 'speak'. And during these nocturnal liaisons, said the queen, it was she herself who had to make Jane sit 'near' rather than wander off or turn a blind eye, which, she said, Jane had tended to do.

The more she talked, the more Catherine tied herself up in knots in her frantic attempt to extricate herself. At one point, she tried to throw the blame on Culpepper, protesting that when she had wanted to end the friendship, he would not listen. 'Sweet little fool,' she said she had called him. But mostly she blamed Jane. She had started the whole thing, insisting it would be safe, reassuring her that men at court would be bound to look at her. Jane, she added, had even said that another man, Thomas Paston, Culpepper's colleague in Henry's privy chamber, 'bore her favour'.

Perhaps Catherine really thought that she might escape Henry's vengeance and leave Jane to pay the price. After all, Jane was a Boleyn, a woman whose own husband, according to Henry and the judgment of the courts, had thought nothing of having an incestuous relationship with his whore of a sister; anything, therefore, could be believed of her. It was worth a try. Yet for Catherine to think that Henry's hardened councillors would be taken in by her story – that she was little more than putty in the hands of her lady-in-waiting – was a forlorn hope. For was it not Catherine who had already confronted, and defeated, Princess Mary in the matter of her two maids? A woman who could stand up to Henry's daughter could certainly stand up to Jane.

Jane saw herself as the victim, not the instigator, of the whole sorry mess, but Catherine's evidence, so useful as the basis for an indictment against everyone involved, ensured that her sojourn in the Tower would be terrifying. Because Jane was a viscountess, she had the consolation of knowing that Henry's skilful torturers would not touch her body, but the incessant questioning, so horribly reminiscent of her interviews following the arrests of Anne and George, was enough to petrify her. Her sworn deposition, taken at her interrogation, is quite short and to the point. She catalogued meetings between her mistress and Culpepper. She mentioned Bessie Harvey, she remembered Culpepper's servant picking the lock, she talked of Catherine standing above Culpepper on the stairs, she accepted that she had helped the queen look out for him. She denied nothing, but she did go one step further than Culpepper: she did not think his affair with Catherine was platonic. 'What they might speak and do together', she said, she was 'never the privier'. As she was also asleep on at least one occasion, they had had every opportunity to express their love. 'She thinketh', she finally said outright in her sworn statement, 'that Culpepper hath known the Queen carnally considering all things that this deponent hath heard and seen.'

She stuck to the truth as she saw it. That was what she had done in 1536 and she had survived. No lady-in-waiting had followed Anne to the block, so perhaps she hoped that none would this time either. Even if she was brought to trial, found guilty and condemned, the king had the power to pardon her. He could grant a reprieve up until the very last minute. Only recently he had done just that to Sir Edmond Knyvett, who had been sentenced to lose his hand for a violent blow he had struck Thomas Clere, ironically a Boleyn relation, 'in the tennis play within the court'. All had been made ready for the amputation: the king's cook had his knife, the sergeant of the scullery had his mallet, irons to cauterise the stump were heating in the fire. Then, just as the cook was about to perform his gruesome task, Henry had called a halt to the proceedings and the errant Knyvett had been freed. So, from Jane's point of view, telling the truth might be worth while.

What Jane did not know was the depth of Henry's despair or his anger. The situations concerning Anne and Catherine were entirely different. He had wanted to end his marriage to Anne in order to marry Jane Seymour, so he had been eager to believe the worst of her. Not so with Catherine. She had been his 'jewel'. He had adored her and believed his love was reciprocated. But, it transpired, she had not only misled him into assuming her 'of pure and honest living before her marriage', she had gone on to betray him with one of his own servants. He would never forgive her. He even demanded a sword 'to slay her he had loved so much'. The 'wicked' Catherine, he vowed, 'had never such delight in her incontinency as she should have torture in her death'. Any hope of clemency from the king was indeed forlorn. And with the whole torrid story out in the open, there really was no hope at all.

On 1 December, Sir John Gage, in his capacity as Constable of the Tower, brought Dereham and Culpepper to the Guildhall in London where they were tried for treason. With Norfolk, Suffolk and most of the Council at his side, Audley read out the various indictments, to which the two men pleaded 'not guilty'. Then, 'after sufficient and probable evidence had been given on the King's part', but before the jury retired to consider their verdict, the prisoners changed their plea to 'guilty'. There was only one sentence for treason, the full agony of hanging, drawing and quartering. When the Council were certain that they had 'gotten as much of Dereham as would be had', the king ordered that the executions should take place, providing that the two men had been given 'convenient respite and warning of the time, that they may prepare themselves to God for the salvation of their souls'. The king refused Dereham's request that he be beheaded rather than disembowelled, considering that he 'deserved no such mercy'. Because of his lineage, Culpepper suffered the swifter death of decapitation, although the Council instructed that since his offence had been 'very heinous', his execution should be 'notable'. That translated into being drawn on a hurdle across the sharp, cobbled streets to Tyburn where the headsman would be waiting.

Next it was the turn of those who had kept silent about Catherine's 'abominable' life. The elderly Dowager Duchess of Norfolk found herself in the Tower along with her daughter, her son, her son's wife, Robert Davenport, and the queen's various attendants.

Only Mary Lascelles escaped detention, on the direct intervention of the king, as a reward for bringing the whole issue to light, even if somewhat tardily. The duchess was in special trouble for breaking open coffers belonging to Dereham and Davenport. The Council spent many hours trying to force the scared and confused woman to tell them precisely what she had read and what she had destroyed. There could have been love letters in the coffers or worse: maybe the jittery councillors were anxious about Dereham's trip to the often rebellious Ireland. The grim fortress became so full that the harassed Lieutenant, Sir Edmund Walsingham, ran out of rooms in which to house his prisoners and was forced to ask the king whether he could use the royal apartments. The king consented but there was a delay when Walsingham checked to see whether Henry had the keys to the locks on the doors. When Henry could not remember, Walsingham had to change them all. Eventually the captives were freed, but not before they were found guilty of misprision and frightened so much that they appeared physically changed by the rigours of their ordeal.

While this was going on around them, neither Jane nor Catherine was brought to trial. Catherine was left at Syon, officially a pariah. Norfolk, terrified that he might be blamed for this second Howard niece's immorality, wrote an abject letter to his sovereign to distance himself from her and to beg the king's favour, without which he did not 'desire to live'. To Marillac's wry amusement at what he saw as an odd English custom, Catherine's brothers rode ostentatiously through London 'to show that they did not share the crimes of their relatives'. We do not know whether Jane's brother did the same, but any despair that he may have felt on his sister's behalf did not hinder a property transaction that he undertook with Lord Morley at the end of January. James Boleyn, aware that Jane's interest in Blickling was only valid during her lifetime, could anticipate its reversion to himself with some satisfaction. Indeed, he actually profited from her death, even managing to buy some of her property at a knock-down price.

Meanwhile Jane was hysterical and overwhelmed. Conscious that the king's officials were busily listing and valuing all her possessions, and that her own life hung by a thread, 'she went mad' on the third day of her incarceration, Chapuys tells us. In view of the trauma that she had suffered when the king had struck at Anne and George, finding herself in the firing line again – and this time at the epicentre, not the periphery – her breakdown is understandable. It did not suit Henry, however. While, grudgingly, he was to pardon the other women dragged into the affair, Jane was different. She alone had taken messages, she alone had stood guard, she alone had known the full extent of what had been going on. She might even have been laughing at him behind his back, just as her husband had done with Anne. None of that could be allowed to go unpunished, and that punishment should be public. His rightful justice must be properly witnessed. Therefore, she must be nursed back to health. He sent his own doctors to treat her, allowed her out of the Tower, and placed her in the care, and custody, of the Admiral Lord Russell's wife, Anne. Jane knew the Russell family both from court and from the progress visit to their seat at Chenies in Buckinghamshire. Their London residence, Russell House, was on the Strand, so Jane could easily have been taken there by river at dead of night without anyone knowing. Then, once out of the bleak stone stronghold with its haunting memories of Anne and George, and back into a familiar world of warm fires, wood panelling, tapestry hangings, rich food and wine, Jane could recover her wits. Henry's vengeance could wait until after Christmas, which he spent, as usual, at Greenwich.

There was no trial for his queen or her attendant. Henry decided to proceed via Act of Attainder, such a neat and clinical method. He opened Parliament himself in January 1542. Audley outlined the case against the queen and 'that bawd, the lady Jane Rochford'. In a speech which Chapuys considered 'aggravated the Queen's misdeeds to the utmost', Audley was punctilious in omitting none of the more salacious and sordid facts. Jane's father, Lord Morley, sitting in the Lords, listened impassively as his daughter's life hung in the balance. The guilty verdicts, however, were a foregone conclusion. The king did not have a last-minute change of heart: Jane and Catherine were to die.

All that remained was to have them taken back to the Tower. Gage went to Syon to break up Catherine's household. She had lived through the past couple of months as though in a dream.

Chapuys informed the emperor that she took care of her appearance, she was cheerful, she was demanding. She was, he wrote, 'more imperious and commanding, and more difficult to please' than she had ever been. But, on Friday, 10 February, when she was brought down to the waiting barge for her journey to the Tower, reality hit her. It was only after overcoming 'some difficulty and resistance' that the councillors persuaded her to board the small covered vessel. There were three barges in total at the river's edge. Southampton climbed aboard the first one, with other councillors and servants. Catherine, dressed in black velvet, sat in the second, together with four ladies and the four sailors whose job it was to row their queen to her prison. Suffolk brought up the rear, 'in a big and well-manned barge, with plenty of armed men inside'. When the sombre group arrived, Catherine was received 'with the same honours and ceremonies as if she were still reigning'. And, although forced on to the boat, she soon regained her composure. When told on Sunday evening that she was to die early on the following morning, she asked that the block be brought to her chamber so that she could practise what she would have to do on Monday. She would die as befitted her birth and her rank.

Jane was rowed back to the Tower on Thursday, the day before her mistress, each stroke of the oars bringing her closer to her destiny. For her, there was no formal reception committee but she, too, would have been treated with courtesy and consideration. She had almost three days in which to consider the enormity of what was about to happen before Gage, or possibly Walsingham, brought her the news that her execution had been fixed for early the following morning. Now only hours remained.

32

Royal Justice

As the long night slowly turned to day, the anguished waiting was almost over for Jane and for Catherine, the last of the queens she had served. It was time for them to make their final preparations. As the two women began to don the clothes they had carefully chosen, the executions of Anne and George, less than six years before, must have crossed their minds. Jane and Catherine knew exactly what to expect; they came from families only too familiar with the horror of decapitation. They also knew that they would die well. They would hide their terror and accept their fate. Their birth and their honour demanded it. They would play their part in the ritual to come, a ritual that required compliance, not resistance, from the victims.

So mistress and servant, each in their separate chambers in the royal lodgings, rooms that were comfortable without being comforting, gradually made ready to face the world for the last time. Catherine had her four ladies to assist her into a plain velvet dress, one of those that had been allowed her by the king. Her nightdress was removed and she put on her silk chemise. Then there were the underskirts to give her gown the fashionable shape she liked, a velvet kirtle, separate embroidered sleeves, a hood with gold edging, silk stockings, soft leather shoes and leather gloves. Finally, for Tower Green was in the open air, a mantle was slipped around her shoulders to protect her against the cold and frost of that early February morning. She would be the queen just once more.

Jane, too, was helped to dress. As Lord Morley's daughter, she expected this. Servants had been around her since her childhood, women who would see to her every need. Now, although a convicted traitor, she remained a viscountess. She could not be treated as an ordinary prisoner. The formalities had to be preserved. So she took off her black damask nightdress and, over her chemise and kirtle, put on a velvet gown, again in the black which she usually wore as a lady of the bedchamber. Her black shoes and gloves were leather, but her stockings were probably plain. She was not going to a masque.

Sir John Gage* had much to do. The execution of a queen was hardly an everyday occurrence and there could be no mistakes. This was too important a task to be left solely to Sir Edmund Walsingham. Gage was very conscious that the king was waiting to hear that Catherine and Jane had paid the ultimate price for their wicked betrayal. At least Gage and Walsingham had the precedent of Anne's death to follow, and Anthony Anthony was still in post. That made it easier; there was no need for constant consultation with the Council. Walsingham had been Lieutenant then too, so he knew exactly what to do. The scaffold was ready; draped in black, some three or four feet high and covered with straw to soak up the blood, it stood starkly on the grass. Upon it rested the block on which Catherine had practised the night before in her bizarre dress rehearsal. When she laid her neck upon it this time, it would be for real. The headsman had arrived – no swordsman was coming from Calais for this queen. The guards were prepared. All that was lacking now was the king's councillors and the small group of Londoners who were also to watch royal justice being administered. Gage waited for them to arrive for this was, after all, a ceremony, a performance. It would not be complete without an audience.

The councillors had spent the night at Westminster, close to Westminster Hall where Jane had banqueted with Anne on the day of her sister-in-law's coronation, and near St Peter's Church, where the king's son, Prince Henry, slept peacefully. Had he lived, perhaps the tragedy that was about to unfold would never have happened.

* Gage's office of Constable was more an honorary position than one carrying with it everyday responsibilities, which were in the remit of the Lieutenant, Sir Edmund Walsingham. At Anne's execution, however, Kingston, the then Constable, was very much involved, so I suspect the same is true of Catherine's.

When it began to get light, the councillors boarded the barges which were bobbing up and down on the dark waters of the Thames, waiting to take them to the Tower, about two and a half miles downriver. Norfolk was not with them. We do not know why. Perhaps watching Catherine die was too much even for him, maybe he had been excused or chose to be unwell. The Duke of Suffolk was not present either. He was ill, Chapuys tells us. Whatever had laid him low, it was not serious enough to prevent his attending the Council meeting the next day, along with Norfolk. The other councillors all knew that they had no choice but to attend. For some, like Sir Richard Rich – that key witness against More and Fisher who had risen to be Chancellor of the Court of Augmentations, overseeing the administration of ex-monastic lands – it was simply a job to be done. For Russell, perhaps, whose house-guest Jane had so recently been, the coming hours would be more taxing.

The councillors were accompanied by Catherine's cousin, Norfolk's proud son and heir, the Earl of Surrey, himself destined to die in a similar fashion within five years. In his despatch to Charles describing the event, Chapuys referred to 'various lords and gentlemen' being present amongst the official party but their identities are unknown. All of them, however, would have been acquainted with the queen and with Jane. They were there to see what befell those, no matter what their rank, who displeased the king and to learn from their experience. As Jane was only too aware, the luxury, the wealth, the power, and the exhilaration of Henry's court carried their own price tag. This was about to be made crystal clear to every member of the court party on that chill February morning. And, as the grim walls of the Tower, gradually appearing through the lingering mist, came ever closer with each rhythmic stroke of the oars, they hoped that their duty would be accomplished quickly so that they could try to put the terror of what they were about to see out of their minds.

A select group of Londoners also set off for the Tower that day. They went on foot. Some walked along Tower Street, passing the houses of wealthy merchants in which servants were beginning to stir for a day which to them would be like any other. Along their route lay the Clothworkers' Hall in Mincing Lane, the Bakers' Hall, hidden in the maze of buildings between Harp Lane and Water Lane, and, on the corner of Seething Lane, the Church of All Hallows, where it was believed that the heart of Richard I was buried. Clearly visible was the public scaffold erected on Tower Hill, just outside the walls of the stronghold, a permanent fixture now, always waiting to receive and despatch the king's less important enemies, like George Boleyn. Some walked along Thames Street, through the parish of St Dunstan, where rich importers, salters and ironmongers had their warehouses or lived comfortably in their large timber-framed dwellings, a stone's throw from the river with its wharfs and customs house.

Eventually, they would have reached Petty Wales and the western entrance of the Tower, the place at which the wide, deep moat could be crossed. The Bulwark Gate, the main land gate, was used by visitors and tradesmen alike. Usually it was guarded, but that morning it was open for witnesses to the executions of Jane and Catherine. Henry had decided that the woman he had once loved should have the privilege of a private end, which meant that it would be carried out inside the walls, just as Anne's had been, but nevertheless it still needed spectators. Amongst them was a cloth-dealer and victualler, Ottwell Johnson, whose customers had included the officials of the queen's household. In his letter to his brother, scribbled almost immediately after the event, we have the only genuine eyewitness account of the deaths of Jane and the queen.

As streaks of dawn appeared in the sky, the small crowd crossed the drawbridge over the first section of the moat towards the Lion Tower, where the slumbering lions, lionesses and leopards of the king's menagerie were housed, cared for by James Worseley, their keeper. Once they reached the Middle Tower, protected by a port-cullis at each end, they were halfway across the moat, but there was another section of the bridge to cross before they were allowed through the iron portcullis of the Byward Tower and inside the precincts of the walls. Getting this far was a major undertaking. The Tower, combining the functions of citadel, palace, prison, armoury and jewel house, had been designed to withstand long sieges and ferocious attacks. It could not be entered easily. Ottwell Johnson and his companions had to pass through three security gates and had yet to make their way past the Bloody Tower before they could gain admittance to the Inner Ward. Eventually, they came to the huge square walls of William the Conqueror's White Tower, recently repaired, on their right and the Beauchamp Tower on their left. Walking along the west side of the White Tower, as they turned the corner they could see the scaffold that Walsingham had made ready, standing between the north side of the White Tower and the royal armoury opposite.* To the left of the Londoners, some fifty yards away, stood the chapel of St Peter ad Vincula, to which the bodies of both women would shortly be taken. The decaying corpses of Anne, George, and the Countess of Salisbury, interred there already, would soon become their neighbours.

As the Londoners gazed curiously around, the barges from Westminster drew up at the water gate of the Tower. Sir John Gage received his fellow councillors and the other members of the court as they disembarked, then led them through the security cordon. He escorted them to their places in the wooden stands beside the scaffold, probably the specially constructed stands left over from Anne's execution, where they sat huddled in their fur-trimmed robes. One thousand people had attended then; this was to be a paltry spectacle by comparison.

With everyone in place, Gage could at last fetch the prisoners. Catherine, as befitted her rank, would be the first to die. The agony would be prolonged for Jane. Gage walked the few hundred yards to the queen's lodgings, which stood to the south-east of the White Tower. The only access was through the Cole Harbour gate leading to the courtyard of the palace area. He climbed the stairs and knocked politely on the door of Catherine's chamber. She deserved that courtesy. Catherine was ready for him. Wrapped up warmly and followed by her small group of ladies, she left her rooms. There was no point in looking back. Passing through the apartments rebuilt by a devoted Henry to please her once-beloved cousin Anne, she descended the stairs to the ground floor and, walking through the gateway and around the White Tower in the footsteps of the spectators, reached the foot of the scaffold.

* The present-day scaffold monument is regrettably in the wrong place.

It was over very quickly. Catherine glanced at the assembled councillors and courtiers, recently so respectful of her and eager to do her bidding, but separated from her now by a vast gulf. She mounted the scaffold with Gage and her ladies still beside her. Ottwell Johnson watched transfixed as the process took its established course, one of many onlookers who would live to tell their children and their grandchildren what they had seen that day. In Marillac's report to Francis, he said that Catherine 'was so weak that she could hardly speak'. Marillac, however, was not there; Johnson was. And, in his letter to his brother, he gave unstinting praise to Catherine for her bravery. He particularly noted her 'steadfast countenance' and 'constancy'. There was no suggestion of fear or trembling. She was a Howard, and a queen, she would die as such.

The masked executioner stood there silently, his axe resting on the block. As was customary, he knelt to ask his victim's pardon for what he was about to do. Catherine forgave him and handed him a few coins, as tradition demanded. She was playing her part in the charade, and she was playing it well. She knelt in prayer and then turned to those watching. In a clear voice, she spoke the words that she had rehearsed. She acknowledged her faults, stated her belief in Christ and asked everyone to pray for the king. There were no recriminations, no protestations of innocence, no last references to Culpepper, merely a regal acceptance of her fate.

Her ladies stepped forward. They removed her mantle, put a linen cap over her hair and bandaged her eyes so that she would not see the axe fall. They gently positioned her head on the block – she already knew what that would feel like – and arranged her skirts modestly around her feet. Then the headsman struck. Mercifully, Catherine's head came off in one blow; the executioner raised it by the hair for all to see. It was done.

But it was yet to be done again. Once the queen was dead, Gage instructed the guards to throw water over the scaffold, which was then covered in fresh straw, lest the new victim slip in the blood of the last. Gage made the return journey to the royal lodgings. Jane was probably kept either in the king's or the queen's apartments, since Walsingham had run out of suitable accommodation for his horde of illustrious prisoners, most of whom, including the Duchess of Norfolk, were still incarcerated.

It was now Jane's turn to die. Gage knocked on her door and escorted her down the stairs, past the White Tower – that symbol of royal power, dominating the skyline and meant to overawe London as much as to protect it – and thence to the scaffold. Those watching had a second death to witness and the executioner another task to perform.

Jane was not a queen, but for this last walk she was treated royally. Gage conducted the affair with civility and with deference. She had seen nothing of Catherine's death and, by this time, there was little to see. The queen's ladies had already wrapped her head in a white linen cloth and laid her small body in a black cloak, before carrying her remains, dripping with blood, into St Peter's and to her grave.

From her room in the royal lodgings, Jane had almost certainly heard the cries and gasps of the spectators as Catherine's head was held up by the executioner. Those last few minutes, while she waited for Gage's polite tap on the door, were the longest she had ever experienced. But the waiting was finally over and she faced her end with the bravery and composure faithfully recorded by Ottwell Johnson. Like Catherine before her, Jane was met by a sea of familiar faces, people with whom she had once laughed and danced but who now stared impassively, not meeting her eyes. With calm dignity, she ascended the scaffold as Catherine had done before her. The executioner moved forward to seek her pardon, which she gave graciously.

And then she faced her audience. It was her last chance to speak. Marillac maintained that she gave a 'long discourse' but, although Jane did not know it, Ottwell Johnson would tell a different tale. There is no word-for-word transcript of her final speech – she was not important enough for that – but Johnson has left us enough to reconstruct it. She began by declaring her complete faith and trust in God. 'I have', she said, 'committed many sins against God from my youth upwards and have offended the king's royal Majesty very dangerously, so my punishment is just and deserved. I am justly condemned by the laws of this realm and by Parliament. All of you who watch me die should learn from my example and change your own lives. You must gladly obey the king in all things, for he is a just and godly prince. I pray for his preservation and beseech you all to do the same. I now entrust my soul to God and pray for his mercy.' Not once did she refer to the specific offences that had brought her to the block. Neither did she have anything but praise for Henry, the man who had ordered her death. There were conventions governing final speeches. Anne and George had both adhered to them and so did Jane.

It was then her turn to have her cloak removed and her hair bound so that nothing would impede the axe. With a final prayer, she knelt down. Her eyes were bandaged and the executioner severed her head. Blood stained the straw yet again as he held the head aloft.

The spectators were free to go home. Justice had been done, and had been seen to have been done. Every man knew the fate of traitors. The Londoners returned the way they had come, through the portcullises and over the drawbridge across the moat, back into the narrow, rambling streets of the city, now teeming with glorious life. They had much to tell their families. Ottwell Johnson wrote his note to his brother, convinced that the souls of both Jane and Catherine were 'with God, for they made the most godly and Christian's end that ever was heard tell of (I think) since the world's creation'.

The courtiers and the councillors returned to their barges to be rowed back to Westminster. It was already past ten o'clock, so there was no need for the torches that had been so necessary on their outward journey. The business of the day awaited them. Henry was expected back in the capital within a matter of hours. Never one to be close to any death that he had ordered, he had spent the night at Waltham Abbey in Essex, a monastery which he had just confiscated but which had always kept special apartments for him in case he happened to be hunting in the area. He had been less than twenty miles from Great Hallingbury. Still stung by his ungrateful wife's treachery, he would expect to hear a full account of the morning's events. Chapuys was to say that the king was 'in better spirits' after Catherine's execution and to remark on the court's 'much feasting' in the build-up to Lent but the strain of the whole affair had aged

Henry. Two months later, Marillac noted, on seeing the king, how old and grey he had suddenly become. Chapuys, too, often found him 'sad, pensive, and sighing', despite his initial resurgence.

For Gage and Walsingham, there was the clearing up to supervise. The scaffold was washed down again, then dismantled, the executioner sent on his way with his fee and the victims' clothes as a perquisite, and the guards dismissed to their quarters. Catherine and Jane were buried together, close to Anne, in the chancel beside the altar. With George near by, Jane was finally reunited with the husband she had lost. It was a fitting resting place.

His tasks completed, Gage was free to return to court and resume his duties as a trusted councillor and the comptroller of Henry's household. Walsingham walked back to his newly constructed lodgings, which were located just inside the walls and to the south of St Peter's. Both men had fulfilled their duties honourably. Ordinary life could now resume. There would once again be processions, banquets, music and dancing. Yielding to the entreaties of his grateful Council, Henry would take a sixth and final wife in Katherine Parr. No tears would be shed for the king's jewel of womanhood or for her confidante. They had to be banished from conversation and thought.

Like so many other families in Henry's England, the Morleys had no choice but to accept their loss. With his daughter's mangled body putrefying in its makeshift grave, Lord Morley settled down to what he did best: he shut himself away in his library and worked. The result was a translation of Boccaccio's *De claris mulieribus*. Written between 1361 and 1375, Boccaccio's Latin volume tells the story of 104 exceptional women, ranging from Eve to Queen Joanna of Naples. While praising some for their high moral standards or filial piety, Boccaccio castigates the majority for their immorality. Morley translated his accounts of forty-six of them, all classical figures.

Morley worked hard in the months following Jane's death and his completed and exquisitely decorated manuscript was his New Year's Gift to Henry in 1543. Ostensibly, it was his way of distancing himself from his daughter's crimes and recognising the justice of her execution, his unique equivalent of riding through the streets in the wake of Catherine's brothers. If her own father was so horrified by Jane's flagrant depravity as to feel compelled to write on the immorality of women and the need to keep them firmly under control, he must obviously have agreed that she was indeed 'that bawd' and her death well deserved.

But a close comparison of Boccaccio's Latin with Morley's English rendition suggests that he did not completely disown her after all; it is possible to discover a veiled valediction skilfully camouflaged within his work. Although his translation is usually precise, there are instances where he changes a word, a phrase, or adds an interpolation of his own, and it is in his passage on Polyxena that we can glean a hint of his true feelings. When Troy fell, Polyxena, the daughter of Hecuba and Priam, was sacrificed by Achilles' son, Pyrrhus, so that the gods would send the victorious Greeks the winds they needed to return home. She was the counterpart to Iphigenia, who had been killed for a similar purpose when the wars first began.

Morley inserts a complete phrase of his own when describing Polyxena's death: 'O, that it was against all good order ... that so sweet a maiden should be devoured by the hands of Pyrrhus for to satisfy for another woman's offence.' Clearly, the 'sweet maiden' was Jane. The other woman here could be Hecuba because of her involvement in the death of Achilles; it could equally be Helen, the cause of the Trojan Wars, or Morley could perhaps mean Catherine Howard, in whose service Jane had died. Morley went further yet. Boccaccio talks of Polyxena as a willing victim, an important concept in both Greek and Roman literature, as a sacrifice was deemed useless if the sufferer struggled and fought. He speaks of the girl offering her 'throat' to Pyrrhus 'with a deeply constant heart', to the admiration of everyone around. Morley, however, translates the word '*iugulum*' as 'neck', not as 'throat'. The two words have the same root, but the subtle difference between them surely relates to how the two women died: Polyxena's throat was cut, Jane's head was severed. And Ottwell Johnson had remarked on Jane's considerable 'constancy' when facing the axe.

Morley did not callously dismiss his daughter from his mind. The Catherine Howard inference is impossible to miss in his insertion; so is his respect for Jane's bravery in adversity. Perhaps, too, he hoped that just as Polyxena's death marked the end of the turmoil of war, Jane's would presage peace, a return to normality after the storms of religious change and factional jockeying for power. In that, he was to be disappointed.

In his own way, however, he had paid what tribute he could to his daughter. He was not the only person to remember her. In the very year in which her daughter mounted the scaffold steps, Lady Morley made an unprecedented gift towards the cost of the bells at St Giles, Great Hallingbury. John Tonne, who originally came from Sussex but worked extensively in Essex, cast a new bell for the little church. To imagine that Alice Morley thought of Jane every time the bell was rung may be fanciful. Equally, it may be true. And John Tonne's bell, the sole survivor of those early ones, is still there. It rings to this day.

History Finds a Scapegoat

When Jane placed her head on the block, she did so as 'that bawd, the lady Jane Rochford', a convicted traitor. She died because she had helped Catherine Howard pursue her wicked, lascivious life, or so it was said. What she did not die for was her Boleyn links, or for anything that she might have said or done in connection with the fall of Anne or George, and there is no suggestion of that in the Act of Attainder against her. As the years passed, her posthumous reputation, already tarnished by her relationship with Catherine, deteriorated further: a myth evolved, seeing her execution as a much deserved, if belated, retribution for giving false testimony against her own husband and sister-in-law. Eighteenth-century histories and biographies are littered with slurs. She was a 'wicked woman', a 'scandalous woman', a woman of 'infamous character'. She became 'the infamous lady Rochford, who justly deserved her fate for the concern which she had in bringing Anne Boleyn as well as her own husband to the block'. Her death was 'the judgement of Heaven'.

This myth, which makes Jane's name synonymous with deceit and betrayal, did not develop overnight. It can be traced back to its source: John Foxe, the doyen of the Protestant historians of Elizabeth I's reign. Within forty years of Jane's death, he named and shamed her in his *Actes and Monuments*, the work which charts the origins and progress of the Reformation and immortalises those martyred for their Protestant beliefs. Jane does not figure in the 1563 edition of Foxe's work, but she does become a marginal note in that of 1576. Foxe does not bring her into his discussion of the fall of Anne, and when he talks of the execution of Catherine Howard in the main body of the text, he merely mentions Jane as dying with her. It is the marginal comment which castigates Jane: 'It is reported of some that this Lady Rochford forged a false letter against her husband and Queen Anne her sister, by the which they were both cast away. Which if it be so, the judgement of God is here to be marked.' The same note appears in the 1583 edition, again in the margin and not in the text itself.

Foxe – if, indeed, the note was his rather than the printer's (as is often the case with marginal additions) – must have latched on to the false letter idea from some other source. Had Jane given direct evidence at the trials of Anne and George, his source would be clear. However, Jane did not appear in person at either trial. Chapuys actually said that the absence of witnesses was unusual. All he did say, and it is significant, is that the weight of opinion was in favour of George's acquittal until he read aloud from the paper that he was handed, referring to Henry's lack of potency. This was the only time, that we know about, when Jane's name cropped up at the Boleyn trials. When we examine who else was in a position to know what testimony was given or produced in the Tower hearings – information that Foxe could have used – we continue to draw a blank. Sir John Spelman, who sat on the bench throughout, did not touch on Jane at all. Instead, he wrote in his notebook that the incriminating evidence against Anne came from Lady Wingfield. He could hardly have confused 'Rochford' with 'Wingfield'. According to John Husee, the chief informant was the Countess of Worcester; he did not say that it was Jane. And Cromwell – who, we can be sure, prepared the case – simply made general remarks on the disgust at Anne's conduct felt by the ladies of the bedchamber. Had Jane been his star witness for the prosecution, there was no reason for him to withhold her name. In fact, he had everything to gain by proclaiming it to the rafters.

So if Foxe did not alight on Jane from what he could discover about the trials, he did so in another way. Several possibilities spring to mind. We know that he referred to documents and oral recollections, so one informant might have been the young George Wyatt, grandson of Anne's love, the poet Sir Thomas Wyatt. Writing towards the end of Elizabeth's reign, George Wyatt penned an account of the life of Anne Boleyn, which was eventually published in 1817. In this highly partisan story, Wyatt clearly wished to vindicate the queen who, he gushes, was not only of 'rare and admirable beauty', but had a 'heavenly flame burning in her'. Although he does not allude to any letters, he includes a damning reference to Jane, saying that she was the witness to the alleged incest between George Boleyn and Anne. Wyatt calls her George's 'wicked wife, accuser of her own husband, even to the seeking of his own blood'. Conveniently ignoring the comparative penury to which Jane would instantly be reduced by 'seeking his own blood' in such a dramatic way, Wyatt goes on to suggest that she was a hostile witness 'more to be rid of him than of true ground against him'. Jane's later execution after the Catherine Howard debacle – 'the judgment that fell out upon her' – was a 'just punishment by law after her naughtiness'. By dying as she had, Jane had provided every man and his dog with the chance to impugn her. Yet, after resoundingly maligning Jane, Wyatt proceeds to contradict himself by reporting that he had heard that George was 'condemned only upon some point of a statute of words then in force', which somehow contrived to 'entangle' or 'bridle' the truthful. His idea of exactly what had actually happened in the trials is patently hazy.

Another potential source for Foxe was George Constantine, a former servant of Henry Norris, who fell foul of Cromwell for remarks he was purported to have made to John Barlow, Dean of Westbury. In 1830, Thomas Amyot, Treasurer of the Society of Antiquaries, was handed an alleged transcript of Constantine's 'Memorial' to Cromwell with details on Anne's fall and, crucially, George's trial. 'I heard say', writes Constantine, 'he had escaped had it not been for a letter.' If authentic, this suggests that talk of a letter had surfaced, although Constantine gives no information on its contents, sender or recipient, and he emphatically does not say that Jane was involved.

Furthermore, Constantine's 'Memorial' may be a forgery. The original document has never been seen; all that was ever produced was the transcript, which Amyot received from the infamous John Payne Collier. A journalist, theatre critic, literary reviewer, essayist and subeditor at the *Morning Chronicle*, Payne Collier wrote a *History of English Dramatic Poetry and Annals of the Stage* in three volumes. Unfortunately, he regularly tacked on inventions of his own to the sources that he claimed to have rediscovered. So, although his transcript may be genuine, we should perhaps reserve judgement. Even if true, however, the document does not implicate Jane; it merely gives a hint of the origin of a possible letter known to Foxe.

Where letters do figure significantly is in a document sent by Alexander Ales, a Scottish Protestant, to Elizabeth at the beginning of her reign. In what was in reality a plea for money, he tells Anne's daughter that he wants to write 'the history or tragedy of the death' of her 'most holy mother'. Blaming Anne's death primarily on the failed embassy to the German princes, Ales also refers to Stephen Gardiner, 'a most violent persecutor of all the godly' and then ambassador to Francis, passing on to Cromwell the news that 'certain reports were being circulated in the Court of the King of France, and certain letters had been discovered, according to which the Queen was accused of adultery'. An additional letter, it transpires, supposedly written by Anne to her brother, tells him that she is pregnant. In spite of this, Jane's name never surfaces. Ales, keen to impress Elizabeth, explains away all of this circumstantial froth, but the idea that there were letters, some of which were possibly forged, has materialised.

We do not know whether Ales's own epistle ever reached the hands of Elizabeth, but it would certainly have been read by Sir William Cecil, her secretary of state and chief councillor, amongst whose official papers it is now preserved. A zealous Protestant, Cecil was Foxe's patron in publishing the *Actes and Monuments*. And Foxe's printer, John Day, who may himself be the author of the marginal note about Jane first appearing in 1576, had run a secret underground press for the Protestants not far from Cecil's country house at Stamford in Lincolnshire during the Catholic Mary Tudor's reign. Once Elizabeth was queen, Day continued to work closely with Cecil, to the point where one historian has called him Cecil's 'tame printer'. It is now that Jane's story becomes intertwined with politics. After the brief reigns of Edward VI and the unhappy Mary, Elizabeth ushered in a Protestant religious settlement. A Boleyn sat upon the throne. Although Elizabeth wisely preferred not to rake up the past,

Ales scored a palpable hit when he said that it could hardly be imagined that her 'most saintly mother', a Protestant heroine in her own right, was an adulteress. Since it was unthinkable that her 'serene father', the great king who had freed his country from the papal yoke, could act unjustly, he must have been misled into believing his wife false. Someone must have lied to him; Jane fitted the bill. Named a 'bawd' by Parliament, she had already lost her good name, so was the ideal scapegoat. To make her situation worse, she had been born a Parker. In 1570, Jane's nephew – her brother's son, Henry Parker – fled abroad as a recusant and became a leading Catholic exile. These were dangerous times. By then, the Catholic Mary, Queen of Scots, was a prisoner on English soil, memories of the Catholic revolt in the North of 1569 were still fresh and the potential repercussions of Elizabeth's excommunication by the pope were uncertain. In such circumstances, no stigma on the queen's parents could possibly be countenanced and anything, or anyone, remotely connected with Catholicism was bound to be suspect. Jane was doomed all over again.

It took no major stretch of the imagination for Foxe (or Day) to blame 'that bawd', who even had a recusant nephew, for forging a key letter to destroy Anne and George. The myth was taking shape. Foxe's book was made required reading by a proclamation issued by Cecil. It was a best-seller, readily available to those who wished to use it or to cite it, as perhaps one author may have done. Edward, Lord Herbert of Cherbury, published *The Life and Raigne of King Henry the Eighth* in 1649. Echoing the marginal addition to Foxe, he denounces Jane as 'wife to the late Lord Rochford, and noted to be a particular instrument in the death of Queen Anne'. Like Foxe, however, he does not bring Jane into his description of the events during Anne's own arrest or trial, but makes his damning condemnation only much later, and in parenthesis, when talking of the attainder and execution of Catherine Howard.

After Charles II's restoration, Peter Heylin takes the myth a stage further. In *Affairs of Church and State in England during the life and Reign of Queen Mary*, published in 1660, Heylin states that the evidence against Anne comprised only Mark Smeaton's confession and 'the calumnies of Lady Rochford'. Jane, he contends, had 'aggravated' the story that George had been 'found whispering' to Anne when she was in bed. Without concrete motives for Jane behaving so falsely, Heylin suggests that the cause could be 'jealousy' towards her husband or 'inveterate hatred' of Anne 'according to the peccant humour of most sisters-in-law'. Like Foxe before him, Heylin smugly points to the events of 1542: Jane 'most deservedly lost her head within a few years after, for being accessory to the adulteries of Queen Catherine Howard'. This was the best Heylin could manage to justify his exposition of Jane's life.

Bishop Gilbert Burnet delivers the *coup de grâce* in his *History of the Reformation of the Church of England*, beginning with the first and second volumes in 1679. Jane, he writes, was 'spiteful' and, blatantly picking up Heylin's jibe, 'jealous' of George. She 'carried many stories to the King, or some about him, to persuade, that there was a familiarity between the Queen and her brother'. As her conduct in the Catherine Howard affair proves, or so Burnet maintains, Jane was 'a woman of no sort of virtue'. Her execution, therefore, is 'God's justice' because she 'had the chief hand' in the deaths of Anne and George, her 'spite and other artifices' having 'so great a hand' in their fall.

Jane is damned indeed. And because Burnet's books have been used so frequently from his own time until the present day, his judgments have largely been followed. However, in the third and final volume of his work, published in 1714, there is a brief sentence which usually slips by unnoticed, but which actually contradicts what he had previously said about Jane: the 'confession of Smeaton', Burnet at last concedes, 'was all that could be brought against her [Anne]'. He cannot have it both ways.

Burnet's sources were vast. He could certainly refer to Foxe. He had access to the original documents stored in the Tower of London, the State Paper Office, and the Cottonian Library before the fire at Ashburnham House in 1731 that destroyed or damaged a quarter of those manuscripts. He could use the various chronicles, he could use Heylin and Herbert – the words with which he chooses to malign Jane are strikingly similar to Herbert's – but he also acknowledges an 'eye- and ear-witness' to the trial proceedings: Anthony Anthony, who wrote a journal of what he saw and heard whilst working at the

Tower. Sadly, the journal is now lost to us, but it was still in existence until the late seventeenth century. Burnet cites it as one of his sources for Anne's trial and execution, but does not say which parts of his narrative are based upon it. Anthony's work is also listed amongst the authorities used by John Stow in the *Annales of England*. This is fortuitous, since Stow – who was writing in Elizabeth's reign and would surely have taken the opportunity to provide corroboration of her mother's innocence had it been readily available, and to condemn Jane as her traducer – does not blame Jane at all. Nor do the chroniclers Edward Hall (first published in 1548) or Raphael Holinshed (in 1577). Even William Camden, a more independent-minded historian and antiquary writing partly in Elizabeth's reign and partly under James I, says nothing detrimental to Jane when describing Anne's fall. It is not known whether these authors apart from Stow were able to refer to Anthony Anthony's journal, but specific references made to it in another source have caused major confusion as late as 2004.

Thomas Turner, or Tourneur as he liked to call himself, was elected president of Corpus Christi College, Oxford, in 1688. A keen scholar, he had easy access to a wealth of material including a version of Anthony Anthony's journal and the first edition of Herbert's *Life and Raigne of King Henry the Eighth*. Still sitting in Oxford's Bodleian Library is the very same copy of Herbert that Turner read and annotated,* together with some crabbily written notes, usually on separate sheets and bound awkwardly into the volume, transcribed 'out of an old original diary or journal wrot with ye proper hand of one Mr Anthony Anthony, surveyor of the Ordinance in the Tower in the said K.H. the 8th's reign, the said Anthony being a contemporary to ye Action, and (as he saith himself) an eye- and ear-witness'. Other sources consulted by Turner for his remarks include Hall, Holinshed, Heylin, Richard Baker's *Chronicle of the Kings of England* (1670), and John Strype's *Ecclesiastical Memorials* (1721).

---

* An examination of the volume shows that it is the first edition of Herbert published in 1649, but its pagination is disordered. After p. 404, the numbering begins afresh at p. 369, even though the material is different and an earlier set of pages is numbered 369–404.

Turner, fortunately, was a meticulous note-taker with his own, unique system. When recording his comments, he begins with 'Memorandum that' or ends with 'A.A.' if drawing from Anthony Anthony, as he does, for instance, when commenting on the executions of Fisher and More. When citing his other sources, Turner is equally explicit: 'For better light in this dark business of the Queen's crimes, see Dr Heylin's Church History,' he writes on one occasion, carefully citing the specific folio he had been reading. Should he choose to express opinions of his own, however, Turner prefaces his remarks with 'Note that'.

His volume makes fascinating and, from Jane's point of view, essential reading.* The critical passage is where Turner comments: 'Note that the wife of Lord Rochford was a particular instrument in the death of Q. Anne (probably out of malice, because her husband had laid with the Q.) and yet this very woman was a conspirator in the adultery of Q. Katherine Howard afterward, and executed with her, see *postea* 474.' This is not, as has recently been claimed, an extract from the lost journal of Anthony Anthony. It does not begin with 'Memorandum that' or end with 'A.A.' but begins with 'Note that'. So the passage is Turner's own inference, most probably based on his reading of Herbert's remark that Jane was 'wife to the late Lord Rochford, and noted to be a particular instrument in the death of Queen Anne'. Furthermore, this probability can be clinched as fact, because Turner refers his readers to '*postea* 474', the exact page of Herbert on which (in Turner's own mispaginated copy) the reference to Jane as a 'particular instrument' is printed. On this same page 474, Turner interpolates an extract that genuinely was from Anthony Anthony's journal, but all it says is: 'and both of them [Catherine Howard and Lady Rochford] beheaded on the green within the Tower on Monday 13 Feb. 33 H. 8 with the Axe. Jesu pardon their souls for their misdeeds. A.A.' The damaging words here about Jane come from Herbert, not Anthony Anthony. What Turner adds to the debate is no more than a cross-reference coupled

---

* The interpolated sheets containing Turner's notes have been bound in the wrong order and therefore require sorting out and refoliating if they are to follow on and make sense.

with his own parenthetical, tentative suggestion as to why Jane might have acted as Herbert had described.

The remaining extracts that we have from Anthony Anthony, some quite lengthy, which Turner faithfully transcribes into the Bodleian volume, are very useful – including, for example, Anne's scaffold speech and Cromwell's too – but nowhere do they say that Jane Rochford caused the deaths of Anne and George. When Anthony describes Anne's trial, Jane's name is entirely absent. And, like Spelman, Anthony Anthony was an 'eye- and ear-witness' to what happened within the Tower walls in 1536 and, probably, in 1542. If he did not accuse Jane, then she had done nothing to warrant it, nor could he have been the vital, mysteriously elusive source for Foxe's devastating comment.

When the young Jane set out from her parents' home at Great Hallingbury for Henry's court, she believed that she had the world before her. And for a while, she had. She married a man of her own age, from an up-and-coming family, and whom her father considered a good match. She should have become the traditional Tudor matron, running her household and coming to court when required, rather like a carbon copy of her own mother. She was destined to be the mistress of Hever and Blickling, dividing her time between those two great houses and the court presided over by Henry and Katherine of Aragon. Her sister-in-law, Anne, could be expected to have married well, but should have been no more than a footnote in history, if that. Her husband, George, might well have become a royal councillor, following in the footsteps of his father, Sir Thomas, but under normal circumstances the Boleyns would not have been catapulted into positions of such supreme prominence.

But, for normality to have existed, Prince Henry needed to have survived. He had not and the king's doubts about the legality of his marriage had festered. That her sister-in-law, Anne, should not only catch the eye of the king but become his wife, with George constantly at her side, had not been foreseeable when Jane had taken her marriage vows. We cannot know what Jane really thought about the Boleyns' changed fortunes, but she had played her part in the ceremonies connected with Anne's new rank, settled into her part as a lady of the bedchamber, and accepted the rewards of royal favour with gratitude. The lure of the court had swiftly cast its spell.

However, disaster had struck. Just as her husband's world had crumbled, so had Jane's. Jane took with her to her grave the intimate secrets of her relationship with George, but to lie just to 'be rid of him', as Wyatt suggests, is absurd. A Tudor marriage was not predicated upon romantic love. Had she and George seriously quarrelled, and there is not a scrap of sound evidence to show that they had, they needed only to behave with dignity and decorum in public while leading virtually separate lives. George's duties often took him away from home, so he and Jane would scarecely have been closeted away together day after day. She had no need to slander her husband, especially when the financial implications of such a move would be ruinous. To slide from a luxurious court lifestyle to managing on 100 marks a year was not a prospect to be relished and, had she caused the death of his only son, she could hardly have envisaged Sir Thomas rushing to increase her allowance. He was reluctant to part with money at the best of times. Her letter to Cromwell had paid dividends, it is true, but the minister might equally have refused to help her. Even with his assistance, she had only obtained £100, which was less than ten per cent of the amount paid towards her jointure, the most usual proportion allocated to widows.

Jane had not been quick to tell tales, but she had buckled under the pressure of relentless questioning, once the investigation was in progress. Confronting the first major test of her courage, she had given way. She had repeated to Cromwell Anne's indiscretion about Henry's sexual inadequacies, the specific remark that was passed to George on a slip of paper at his trial and which he had been ordered not to read out but only to give a yes or no answer. And it was her weakness under interrogation that gave her future detractors – happy to find a scapegoat to exonerate the king from the heinous charge of callously killing his innocent wife – the ammunition to maintain that it was her evidence that had fooled Henry and destroyed Anne and George. She had repeated Anne's secret to her own husband, which in itself implies a relaxed rather than a failed union, and she had confessed the same to Cromwell. However, she had done no more than that.

It was, of course, enough. The piece of paper read out by George could so easily be twisted, or misunderstood, and become not a slip of paper but a letter, perhaps the very letter that Constantine mentions. That in turn could have become confused with the letters that may (or may not) have been in circulation in France, about which Ales wrote to Elizabeth. The stories of letters grew and grew. 'She hinted to the king that his wife carried on a criminal correspondence with her own brother,' wrote Smollett in 1759. The fictional letters ballooned into accounts of everything from rumours of adultery and whispers of incest to the supreme crime of treason.

What matters is that Jane's own actions made credible the accusations later levelled against her. She opened the floodgates herself. With considerable effort, she had carved a career for herself after George's death. She had showed just how far a woman alone could progress, despite the handicaps she had faced, but then she had thrown it all away. When faced with Catherine's demands, she succumbed once more. She could not break her addiction to the court. It was a fatal mistake. Supporting Catherine's silliness, for whatever reason, cost Jane not only her head but her reputation. Anything, even deliberately betraying her own family, could then be believed of such a woman. Jane had turned herself into the perfect target. She has been ever since. She is 'that bawd', 'the infamous Lady Rochford', a 'woman of vice insaciatt [insatiate]'. She is so 'vile and vicious' that Anne, 'a virtuous and truly spiritual Christian', could 'not but hate' her 'unworthy behaviour'. Small wonder then that she died 'unlamented' and 'unpitied'. Not only was she Catherine's 'associate', but her lies 'had plunged her husband and sister-in-law into an untimely grave'. Or so generation after generation has been educated to believe.

In fact, it is Jane who has been betrayed. She had told George what Anne had confided to her about Henry's sexual inadequacies, but a private conversation between husband and wife – even if she had confessed to it when interrogated – is not the same as inventing malicious falsehoods to bring down the Boleyns. She was not a tale-teller; she certainly did not inform against Catherine when she had good reason to do so. Indeed, it might have been better for her if she had. But, although she is innocent of the charge of bringing down the Boleyns, she is guilty of helping Catherine to conduct an illicit affair. She did not deny it. It was for this that Jane died, for this and for nothing else. And she died courageously. The woman who walked out on to Tower Green that morning walked calmly towards the scaffold, any former weakness overcome. She confessed that she had sinned, she asked those about her to learn from her faults, she prayed for her prince, she made a 'godly end'. Whatever she had done wrong, and it was in fact very little, she paid the price. Her life was stolen from her. So was her story.

APPENDIX

The Likeness of Jane Boleyn

Amongst Holbein's chalk drawings in the Royal Collection is a study of a young woman, just under half-length. She looks straight towards the viewer. Her features are delicate, her soft eyes wide apart, her nose perhaps slightly retroussé and her full lips form a perfect cupid's bow. There is a suggestion of high cheekbones. Her hair is fastened beneath a flattering French hood, her dress modestly high-necked but with a V-shaped, collar-like opening. Her fashionable full sleeves billow out from just above her elbow. She is a very pretty girl, anything from about seventeen to twenty-six or so years old. It is difficult to be precise. The drawing is inscribed 'The Lady Parker'. There is no corresponding oil portrait extant.

The sitter's identity has been disputed. Most experts suggest that she is Grace Newport, Jane's brother's first wife, although she could be Elizabeth Calthorpe, whom Sir Henry Parker married after Grace's early death. However, one authority, G. S. Davies, has stated categorically that she is Jane.

It is tempting to believe him, as that would provide the only likeness we have of her. The name is not necessarily an insuperable obstacle. Holbein did not inscribe them upon the drawings himself. We do not know who did, but many of the identifications were provided by John Cheke, who became tutor to the future Edward VI in 1544. Because he knew some, but not all, of the figures, some remain blank. Cheke was not always reliable, however, and a few drawings are labelled incorrectly. It is tantalising to speculate that Cheke was wrong in this instance and that 'Lady Parker' is in fact Jane. Lord Morley was drawn by Albrecht Dürer while in Germany on his sovereign's business, so he was not averse to portraiture, and Jane's marriage meant that she was closely connected to the royal circle. In such circumstances a sketch – perhaps followed by a lost portrait or, as is the case with several of the chalk drawings, not followed up at all – is credible.

Unfortunately, the girl in the picture is far more likely to be one of Sir Henry Parker's wives, with Grace the favoured candidate. Holbein's first visit to England was between 1526 and 1528, the period in which he made the chalk drawings of the More family and produced the family group portrait. Those who employed him at this time, notably Archbishop Warham and Sir Henry Guildford, were very much art connoisseurs, since most of the wealthy still preferred tapestries and wall hangings. His second visit to England was not until 1531 or 1532 and, some foreign excursions apart, he remained there from then until his death in 1543. For Jane Rochford to be the girl in the drawing, it would make much more sense if she had been sketched on his first visit or early in the second, because only then was she about the right age. By the time Holbein was undertaking more regular court commissions, she was a more mature woman. Conversely, Grace, who was ten years younger than Jane, would have been too young during Holbein's first visit to England to be the subject, but would fit neatly more or less anywhere after his return. And the colour of the paper points to the second visit rather than the first: Holbein's early drawings are on white paper, whereas he used pink-primed paper from the 1530s onwards. As 'Lady Parker' is on pink-primed paper, she was, therefore, probably sketched on the second visit.

This still does not entirely rule out Jane as the sitter. The exact chronology of Holbein's relationship with the royal court is uncertain. There are no confirmed Holbein likenesses of Anne Boleyn. He worked on the court festivities of 1527, and in 1533 produced the designs for one of the pageants that greeted Anne on her coronation. He was involved in planning an elaborate cradle intended for Henry and Anne's first son, and he designed a table fountain that she presented to the king as a New Year's Gift in 1534. In spite of this, Holbein's record as an established court artist, producing royal portraits, cannot definitely be traced back before the time of Jane Seymour. Then, of course, his work became the height of fashion; suddenly everyone who was anyone scrambled to commission him. Yet he had undertaken private work before then, so perhaps Jane was drawn between 1533 and 1536, although the costume that 'Lady Parker' is wearing hints at a later date. The main problem is that Jane had slipped out of favour once the Boleyns fell. She was also a widow, so it is difficult to see who would have wanted a portrait of her after her husband's death, especially a drawing that shows her as a young girl.

Also, while the names on the chalk drawings can be entirely wrong, Jane was never Lady Parker. When Holbein first arrived, she had already been married to George Boleyn for over two years; she was Lady Rochford by the time the artist returned.

So, while there is always a very remote chance that the girl who stares out at us is Jane, it is very remote indeed. We are almost certainly looking at Grace. Perhaps a picture of Jane will eventually surface, or she might be identified from one of the handful of anonymous faces who still beguile us. Time will tell.

Meanwhile, the best impression that we can have of Jane Rochford is Holbein's drawings of an unknown woman in Tudor dress, which perhaps he wanted as costume illustrations. The woman is wearing the gable headdress, she has full slashed sleeves with a little lace cuff, a pendant at her neck and golden chains across her bodice. In one pose, she faces us, almost as though she has paused specially to do so; the back view shows her raising her hand as if to emphasise a point in an engrossing conversation. She is elegant, poised and animated. It is not Jane, but it is how she really was.

Notes and References

The Harvard system is used in citing references to sources. Abbreviated citations of printed primary and secondary materials identify the works listed in the Bibliography, where full references are given. For example, Carley (2000) refers to J. P. Carley, *The Libraries of King Henry VIII*, (London, 2000); Carley (1989) refers to J. P. Carley, 'John Leland and the Foundations of the Royal Library: the Westminster Inventory of 1542', *Bulletin of the Society for Renaissance Studies*, 7 (1989), pp. 13–22. Manuscripts are cited by the reference numbers used to request the documents in the archives and libraries.

In citations, the following abbreviations are used:

BL	British Library, London
Bodleian	Bodleian Library, Oxford
CRO	Cornwall Record Office
CSPF, Elizabeth	*Calendar of State Papers, Foreign: Elizabeth*, 23 vols. (London, 1863–1950)
CSP Sp	*Calendar of Letters, Despatches, and State Papers Relating to the Negotiations between England and Spain, Preserved in the Archives at Vienna, Brussels, Simancas and Elsewhere*, 13 vols. in 19 parts (London, 1862–1954)
CSP Sp Supp	*Further Supplement to Letters, Despatches and State Papers Relating to the Negotiations between England and Spain*, ed. G. Mattingly (London, 1940)
CSP Venice	*Calendar of State Papers and Manuscripts Relating to English Affairs, Existing in the Archives and Collections of Venice and in Other Libraries of Northern Italy*, 38 vols. (London, 1864–1947)

CUL	Cambridge University Library
CWE	*Collected Works of Erasmus*, 76 vols. (Toronto, 1974–)
ERO	Essex County Record Office
HEH	Henry E. Huntington Library, San Marino, California
HLRO	House of Lords, Record Office
HMC	Historical Manuscripts Commission
KCAR	King's College Archives Centre, King's College, Cambridge
Lambeth	Lambeth Palace Library, London
Longleat	Longleat House, Warminster, Wiltshire (microfilm at Cambridge University Library)
LP	*Letters and Papers, Foreign and Domestic, of the Reign of Henry VIII*, ed. J. S. Brewer, J. Gairdner, and R. H. Brodie, 21 vols. in 32 parts, and *Addenda*, with revised edition of vol. 1 in 3 parts (London, 1862–1932)
MS	Manuscript
NA	The National Archives, Kew
NPG	The National Portrait Gallery, London
ODNB	*The New Oxford Dictionary of National Biography*, ed. Colin Matthew and Brian Harrison, 60 vols. (Oxford, 2004)
STC	*A Short-Title Catalogue of Books Printed in England, Scotland and Ireland, and of English Books Printed Abroad*, ed. W. A. Jackson, F. S. Ferguson and K. F. Pantzer, 2nd edn, 3 vols. (London, 1976–91)
WAM	Westminster Abbey Muniments
WRO	Worcester Record Office

Manuscripts preserved at the National Archives are quoted by the call number there in use. The descriptions of the classes referred to are as follows:

C 1	Chancery, Early Chancery Proceedings
C 54	Chancery, Close Rolls
C 65	Chancery, Parliament Rolls
C 66	Chancery, Patent Rolls
C 82	Chancery, Warrants for the Great Seal, Series II

C 142	Chancery, Inquisitions Post Mortem, Series II
C 193	Chancery, Miscellaneous Books
CP 25	Court of Common Pleas, Feet of Fines
CP 40	Court of Common Pleas, Plea Rolls
DL 25	Duchy of Lancaster, Deeds, Series L
E 36	Exchequer, Treasury of the Receipt, Miscellaneous Books
E 40	Exchequer, Treasury of the Receipt, Ancient Deeds, Series A
E 41	Exchequer, Treasury of the Receipt, Ancient Deeds, Series AA
E 101	Exchequer, King's Remembrancer, Various Accounts
E 150	Exchequer, King's Remembrancer, Escheators' Files, Inquisitions Post Mortem, Series II
E 163	Exchequer, King's Remembrancer, Miscellanea
E 179	Exchequer, King's Remembrancer, Subsidy Rolls
E 315	Exchequer, Augmentation Office, Miscellaneous Books
E 404	Exchequer of Receipt, Warrants and Issues
IND 1	Public Record Office, Indexes to Various Series
KB 8	Court of King's Bench, Crown Side, Bag of Secrets
KB 9	Court of King's Bench, Ancient Indictments
KB 27	Court of King's Bench, Coram Rege Rolls
KB 29	Court of King's Bench, Controlment Rolls
KB 145	Court of King's Bench, Files, Recorda
LC 2	Lord Chamberlain's Department, Special Events
OBS	Obsolete Lists and Indexes
PRO 31/3	Public Record Office, Transcripts from French Archives
PROB 2	Prerogative Court of Canterbury, Inventories
PROB 11	Prerogative Court of Canterbury, Registered Copy Wills
PSO 2	Warrants for the Privy Seal, Series 2
SC 2	Special Collections, Court Rolls
SC 6	Special Collections, Ministers' Accounts
SC 12	Special Collections, Rentals and Surveys
SP 1	State Papers, Henry VIII, General Series
SP 2	State Papers, Henry VIII, Folio Volumes
SP 6	State Papers, Henry VIII, Theological Tracts

SP 9   State Papers, Williamson Collection
SP 46   State Papers, Supplementary
WARD 7   Court of Wards and Liveries, Inquisitions Post Mortem

NOTES

PROLOGUE: pp. 1–4

The printed sources from *LP*, I, i, nos. 670, 671, 678 and 707, give details on the young prince and his funeral. NA, LC 2/1, fos. 159–74ᵛ is the fullest original document providing significant information omitted by the printed abstracts. Hall (1904), I, pp. 2-27, gives a vivid account of the young prince's life and death. For royal funeral protocol, Royal Book (1790) is an excellent starting point. Starkey (2004), pp. 120–3, provides the political background. For the life of Robert Fayrfax, see *ODNB*.

 For what Westminster Abbey was like in 1511, Perkins (1938–40) is invaluable. Annenberg School (1972) provides a useful context. *Monumenta Westmonasteriensia* (1683) is crucial to an understanding of the Abbey's historical topography, describing where the tombs are located, including Prince Henry's.

1, Childhood: pp. 7–13

In the absence of church records, my suggestion for Jane's date of birth as *c*.1505 is based on the fact that it is likely she was about sixteen or seventeen when she took part in a court pageant in 1522. This would also fit with Bell (1877), p. 27, which suggests that she was around forty when executed, an estimate based upon an examination of the bones discovered in the chancel and believed to be hers when the chapel of St Peter ad Vincula was repaired in 1876–7. I have also sited her at Great Hallingbury, the principal Morley residence, especially as Sir Edward Howard's will says that Alice Lovel used Morley Hall in Norfolk. The precise date of construction for Morley's new mansion at Great Hallingbury is unknown; although it is more likely that she grew up in the new building, Jane could have been brought up in the much smaller house or even on a building site. Since Jane's early life is undocumented, the details of her education are, inevitably, generic. Harris (2002), chapter 2 (especially pp.

32–42), is invaluable. The details of the baptism come from Cressy (1997), pp. 100, 125, 135, 139 and 141, from the *Sarum Missal* (1913), I, p. 13, and from the *Manuale* (1875), p. 11. Cavendish (1825), II, p. 71, asserts in *Metrical Visions* that Jane went to court early and, since he knew her and was concerned with her as a penitent, there is no reason to disbelieve what is, for him, a circumstantial detail.

For Lord Morley's life, see *ODNB*; Axton and Carley (2000), pp. 1–27, where D. R. Starkey shrewdly writes of him as an 'attendant lord'; see also Wright (1943), pp. ix–xlvii. Further family details come from the wills of Alice Lovel, Sir John St John, and Sir Edward Howard: NA, PROB 11/17, PROB 11/19, PROB 11/21. The Morley mansion at Great Hallingbury is described in Cocks (1997), pp. 5–8, 14–15, 28, and in Cocks and Hardie (1994), pp. 1, 7–10. The possible furnishings come from Alice Lovel's will.

2, All that Glisters: pp. 14–24

Until now, no one has identified Jane as the Mistress Parker mentioned in *Calais Chronicle* (1846), p. 25, and the *Rutland Papers* (1842), p. 38 but I believe that it was indeed her. There has been confusion with Margery Parker, one of Katherine of Aragon's women and later rocker to Princess Mary, a fairly menial position. However, in both the *Chronicle* and the *Rutland Papers*, Mistress Parker's name is juxtaposed with those who, like Mistress Carey, are not servants: Mistress Parker is the name under which Jane is listed at the 1522 pageant, and her fellow performers on that occasion, such as Mistress Dannet, are also listed with her at the Field of Cloth of Gold. If Cavendish is to be believed when he states that Jane spent her early years at court, she would have accompanied her parents to the great spectacle at Calais and Guisnes – everyone who was anyone was present. Hall (1904), I, pp. 188-218, contains a very full account; *LP*, III, i, nos. 632, 704, 826, 852 and 870, provide less emotive documentation; Anglo (1969), pp. 139–58, gives the best, fullest and most meticulous account. The *Musical Times* for 1 June 1920, pp. 410–11, has details on the music played. Campbell (2007), chapter 8, identifies the King David hanging as one of Henry's tapestries lining the walls of his palace at Guisnes. Details of food and victualling are taken from *LP*, IV, I, no. 2159. References to Wolsey are from Cavendish (1825), I, pp. 18–20, 43, 44, 50 and 131. Henry's description is from Hall (1904), I, p. 5, and *LP*, III, i, no. 402; his musical abilities are discussed by Starkey (1991b),

p. 104. Francis is described by Knecht (1994), pp. 105–7 and 170–5. Starkey (2004), pp. 160–3, gives an excellent account of Katherine's deteriorating physique. Ives (2004), p. 31, suggests that George Boleyn was likely to have accompanied his father and also, p. 32, makes the persuasive suggestion that Anne Boleyn was probably present in Queen Claude's suite. *ODNB* entries for Katherine of Aragon, Elizabeth Blount, Henry Norris and Cardinal Wolsey give good basic background.

3, Château Vert: pp. 25–31

Detail on Tudor costume is from Norris (1997), pp. 199–200, 203, 208 and 220–2. For documents concerning the execution of the Duke of Buckingham, see *LP*, III, i, nos. 1 and 1284, *LP*, IV, i, no. 2159. *CSP Sp Supp*, Preface, pp. xii, xiii, and xvii, provides information on the imperial ambassadors. My account of the Shrove Tuesday pageant relies on the information from *LP*, III, ii, no. 1522, Hall (1904), I, pp. 238–40, Ives (2004), pp. 36–9, 70, and Anglo (1969), pp. 120–1. The most authoritative and comprehensive account of the way in which tapestries were used for court festivals and as decorative objects is in Campbell (2007), chapters 6 and 9. For the five players in the masque who had been part of Katherine's entourage at the Field of Cloth of Gold, see *Rutland Papers* (1842), p. 38, and *Calais Chronicle* (1846), p. 25.

4, A Suitable Match: pp. 32–8

Details on Buckingham's income and lands are taken from *LP*, III, i, nos. 1286 and 1287. The sale of New Hall to Henry VIII, is in *LP*, II, ii, p. 1470, while the references to the grants to the Boleyns are in *LP*, III, ii, no. 2214 (29) and *LP*, IV, i, no. 5469 (2). There are many references to the Ormond lands: for example, NA, SP 46/183, fo. 124. See SP 46/183, fo. 140, for references to Aylesbury, SP 46/183, fo. 164 and SP 46/183, fo. 189, for references to Rochford; and SP 46/183, fo. 186, and SP 46/183, fo. 194, for references to New Hall. For Morley's diplomatic mission and ensuing letters, see *LP*, III, ii, nos. 3373, 3390, 3391, 3546 and 3619. *ODNB* references to Sir Thomas Boleyn and George Boleyn are useful, as is the *Complete Peerage* (1987), especially IV, p. 138, for details on George. His part in the Christmas revels is taken from *LP*, II, ii, p. 1501. The wills of Sir Geoffrey Boleyn and the Earl of Ormond are from NA, PROB 11/5, PROB 11/18. General background material on Lord Morley comes from

Starkey's Introduction to Axton and Carley (2000). See also Carley's *ODNB* entry on Morley.

The respective dates and order of birth of the Boleyn children have exercised historians for over a hundred years as the evidence conflicts or is inconclusive. J. H. Round debated the subject in Round (1886) while Gairdner (1893) is an excellent critique and summary. See also Friedmann (1884), II, Appendix Note A, pp. 315–22. A birth date of 1507 for Anne was given by Camden. However, contradictory evidence comes from the family of Mary Boleyn: her son, Lord Hunsdon, said that his mother was the elder sister, while the funeral monument to Lady Berkely, Hunsdon's daughter, gives Mary as the second daughter. To further muddy the waters, Weever (1630), p. 799, has a reference to William Boleyn in which he states that Anne was sixteen years older than Henry VIII, which supports a later birth date of about 1507; on the other hand, Brooke (1619) names Anne as the second daughter on one page and the eldest on another, p. 250. E. W. Ives follows in the footsteps of Paget (1981), pp. 162–70; he suggests about 1499 for Mary, 1500–1 for Anne, and 1504 for George: see Ives (2004), p. 17. Starkey (2004), p. 258, supports this order, although he places the dates a year or so later. Warnicke disagrees, arguing that Anne was the elder daughter, born in 1507: see Warnicke (1985a), pp. 939–52. Fortunately, there seems to be unanimity in accepting George as the youngest Boleyn sibling.

References to the king's contribution to Jane s jointure are from *LP*, X, no. 1010, and Ellis (1824–46), 1st series, II, p. 67. The fullest details, however, including newly discovered evidence not in the printed sources, can be found in WRO, microfilm 705:349/12946/498729; this should be read in conjunction with HLRO, MS PO/1/1539 (Original Acts, 31 Henry VIII, c.20). Lord Morley's payment to Thomas Boleyn is from *LP*, IV, Appendix 99, p. 3116. Elizabeth Edgecombe's jointure is taken from CRO, MS ME/824. Boleyn's indenture with his mother, Margaret, is enrolled on NA, C 54/379. Mary Tudor's bargain with Henry VIII is taken from *LP*, II, ii, no. 227. An excellent starting point for anyone wanting to understand the jointure system can be found in Harris (2002), pp. 44–50.

5, For Better, for Worse: pp. 39–44

The wording and proceedings of the marriage ceremony are taken from *Sarum Missal* (1913), II, pp. 143–61, which was the form of liturgy in use throughout southern England. General details on Tudor marriage customs can be found in Stone (1961) and Peters (2000). The most comprehensive survey is by Cressy (1997), pp. 285-375. Information on the costumes of Katherine of Aragon, Mary Tudor and Eleanor of Austria is from Norris (1997), pp. 209, 273 and 650. Wolsey's Eltham Ordinances are taken from *LP*, IV, i, no. 1939 (4), interpreted in the light of his crucial preparatory material in his own hand from NA, SP 1/37, fo. 102. There is no record of an application for a marriage licence listed in the allegations for marriage licences issued by the Vicar-General of the Bishop of London.

6, Kindness Captures a King: pp. 47–53

Good summaries of Mary Carey's early life are in Starkey (2004), p. 274–5 and Ives (2004), pp. 15–17. She is likely to be the 'Mademoiselle Boleyn' listed amongst the French Queen's attendants in *LP*, I, ii, no. 3357. The reference to her morals comes from *LP*, X, no. 450. Basic details on the life of William Carey can be found in *ODNB*. His wedding to Mary is from *LP*, III, ii, p. 1539; the Eltham Ordinances are from *LP*, IV, i, no. 1939 (4); and his rewards are pieced together from *LP*, III, i, no. 317, *LP*, III, ii, no. 2074 (5), *LP*, III, ii, no. 2297 (12), p. 973, and *LP*, IV, ii, no. 2972, p. 1331. Murphy (2003), pp. 38–9, has a useful account of Richmond's investiture. See also *LP*, IV, I, no. 1431, and *CSP Venice*, III, nos. 1037 and 1053. Ives (2004), p. 83, discusses the rumour that Richmond would inherit the throne. The reference to Katherine's commissioning a treatise on marriage is from *CWE*, XI, p. 308.

Rumours about the parentage of Henry Carey are from *LP*, VIII, no. 567. Interestingly, the precise date of his birth is contested. See Starkey (2004), p. 274, Ives (2004), p. 369, and *ODNB* entries for Mary Boleyn and Henry Carey. The inscription on his tomb, which can still be seen in Westminster Abbey, states that Carey was in his seventy-second year (*anno aetatis*) when he died on 23 July 1596 (*Monumenta Westmonasteriensia* (1683), p. 328), which means that he must have been born in 1525 as there appears to be little doubt that the month of his birth was March.

George Boleyn's post as cupbearer is from *LP*, IV, i, no. 1939, section 14 (p. 871), his entitlement to living at court with Jane is from *LP*, IV, i, section 4 (p. 865). The reference to the silver dishes comes from Starkey,

Ward and Hawkyard (1998), no. 1865, p. 60. George's ownership of the satire on marriage and his gift of the manuscript to Smeaton is taken from Carley (2004), p. 133, who has also noticed that the musician was so enamoured of the book that he wrote his name inside it. Carley suggests that the manuscript was a humorous wedding present, which seems very likely.

Stone (1961) gives details on Tudor marital customs. Information about the duties of the keeper of royal residences and dates of acquisitions is from Thurley (1993), pp. 49–50 and 83.

7, The Falcon's Rise: pp. 54–61

The accounts of the 'still' Christmas and Shrove Tuesday joust rely on Hall (1904), II, pp. 56–7. The description of Anne is from *CSP Venice*, IV, no. 824. Interestingly, this tallies very well with the description of Anne suggested by the discovery made during repairs to St Peter ad Vincula of what were reputed to be her bones. See Bell (1877), pp. 26–8, for a first-hand account of the nineteenth-century excavations. Cavendish's account of the Percy affair is from Cavendish (1825), I, pp. 58 and 66. For Anne's other suitors, see Ives (2004), pp. 72–80, Starkey (2004), pp. 268–71, and *LP*, III, no. 1762.

The complexities of the chronology of Henry's relationship with Anne are tackled by Ives (2004), pp. 81–92, and Starkey (2004), pp. 271–85. By establishing the date of the Percy marriage, Starkey redates the beginning of the affair. Trying to establish the sequence of the love letters is equally problematical as they are undated and, for the earlier ones at least, contain no clue to allow us to fix even upon a definite year. The order I have chosen for the six mentioned here is, therefore, speculative but does, I think, make sense of the overall chronology: see Halliwell (1848) I, p. 310 *(LP,* IV, ii, no. 3220); Halliwell (1848), I, p. 302 *(LP,* IV, ii, no. 3321); Halliwell (1848), I, p. 309 *(LP,* IV, ii, no. 3219), Halliwell (1848), I, p. 303 *(LP,* IV, ii, no. 3326); Halliwell (1848), I, p. 305 *(LP,* IV, ii, no. 3218); Halliwell (1848), I, p. 306 *(LP,* IV, ii, no. 3325). D. R. Starkey's decoding of letter 3 is explained in Starkey (2004), p. 281, and an analysis of the ship image can be found in Ives (2004), pp. 86–7; Starkey (2004), pp. 282–3, and Arnold (1988), p. 76. For Thomas Boleyn's accounts, see *LP*, IV, iii, Appendix 99, p. 3116, and, for his possible involvement in the developing relationship between Henry and Anne, see Ives (2004), p. 217.

8, Lady-in-Waiting: pp. 62–9

Henry's letters to Anne are taken from Halliwell (1848), I, pp. 311 *(LP,* IV, ii, no. 4537), and Halliwell (1848), I, p. 317 *(LP,* IV, ii, no. 3990). The entertainment for the French ambassadors is from Hall (1904), II, pp. 84–8, Anglo (1969), pp. 212–24, *CSP Venice,* IV, no. 105, and Starkey (2004), pp. 284–5. The significance of the King David tapestries is discussed by MacCulloch (1995), p. 180, Herman (1994), pp. 193–218, and Campbell (2007), chapter 10. T. P. Campbell explains that Henry ordered a new set of King David tapestries at the heart of the divorce controversy, but they did not arrive in England until 1528. Henry's comments on his relationship with Katherine are taken from Hall (1904), II, p. 146. Wolsey's early involvement is from Cavendish (1825), I, p. 139. Katherine's intention to remain Henry's wife is from *LP,* IV, ii, no. 4875; Charles V's support is mentioned in *LP,* IV, ii, no. 3312. The sack of Rome is from *LP,* IV, ii, nos. 3114 and 3200. Information on James Boleyn's interest in religion is mentioned in Susan Wabuda's entry on Nicholas Shaxton in the *ODNB.* Robert Wakefield is described in Lloyd Jones (1989), p. 186; see also *ODNB.* His lecture and writings are to be found in: Wakefield (1528), Wakefield [n.d.], and *STC,* nos. 24943 and 24944. See also Lloyd Jones (1989), p. 64, and *LP,* IV, ii, nos. 3233 and 3224. For Fisher's views, see *LP,* IV, ii, no. 3148, and no. 3232 for his comments on Henry's right to consult the pope. More's recollections of his meeting with Henry at Hampton Court are taken from Rogers (1961), pp. 206–8.

9, The Sweat: pp. 70–5

A comprehensive and fascinating account of the sweat is to be found in Caius (1552) (himself a doctor), and in *STC,* no. 4343. For a modern analysis, see Flood (2003), Thwaites, Taviner and Gant (1997) and (1998), and Dyer (1997). My description of the disease's symptoms is taken from Caius (1552), pp. 12–13, and *CSP Venice,* II, no. 945. The general fear it engendered is from *LP,* IV, ii, nos. 4332, 4510 and 4542, and the remedies come from Caius (1552), pp. 32 and 35, *LP,* IV, ii, no. 4409, *CSP Venice,* II, no. 945 and Wood (1846), II, p. 29. For Henry's reaction to the news of Anne's illness, see *LP,* IV, ii, nos. 4383, 4391, 4403, 4409, 4422, 4440 and 4542. His rather brazen building works at Tittenhanger are mentioned in *LP,* IV, ii, no. 4438. The news of Carey's death is from *LP,* IV, ii, no. 4408; the effect on the Boleyn family is taken from *LP,* IV, ii, no. 4410, and *LP,* V, no. 11. Carey's offices appear in *LP,* IV, ii, no. 4413; Russell's wardship requests are from *LP*, IV, ii, nos. 4436 and 4437. The Wilton Abbey case is explained by Knowles (1959), p. 161, Ives (2004), p. 102, and Starkey (2004), pp. 333–6. Relevant documents include *LP*, IV, ii, nos. 4477, 4507 and 4509. Anne's letter to Wolsey is *LP*, IV, ii, no. 4480, and the joint letter from Anne and Henry is *LP*, IV, ii, no. 4360. References to the divorce are from *LP*, IV, ii, nos. 3686 and 4742. Details of Anne's emerald ring are from *LP*, V, no. 276, and Ives (2004), p. 91.

10, Fortune's Wheel: pp. 76–84

For a comprehensive account of the divorce, see Scarisbrick (1968) or Starkey (2004). I have concentrated only on those events that particularly touched Jane as a member of the Boleyn family.

My account of the distrust of Wolsey is taken from *LP*, IV, iii, nos. 5255, 5635 and 5803, and *CSP Venice*, IV, no. 461. Cromwell's sudden prominence is evident in, for example, *LP*, IV, iii, nos. 5437, 5446, 5457, 5459 and 5460. Clement VII's desire to please Henry is from *LP*, IV, iii, no. 5516. The Duchess of Suffolk's hostility to Anne is from *CSP Venice*, IV, no. 761. Campeggio complains of the weather in *LP*, IV, iii, no. 5636. Henry's return to London is from *LP*, IV, iii, no. 5016, and Anne's farm is mentioned in the Privy Purse Expenses, *LP*, V, p. 753.

The proceedings of the trial are from *CSP Venice*, IV, no. 482, *LP*, IV, iii, no. 5702, Hall (1904), II, pp. 150–2, and Cavendish (1825), I, pp. 147–58. The testimony relating to Arthur is from *LP*, IV, iii, nos. 5774 and 5778. Clement VII's letter to Wolsey is from LP, IV, iii, no. 5759. Starkey (2004), pp. 237–40, gives a very full description of the Parliament Chamber at Blackfriars.

Wolsey's fall is described in Cavendish (1825), I, pp. 166–70 and 181–2, and also in *LP*, IV, iii, nos. 6017, 6019, 6025, 6026 and 6075. His loss of property is from *LP*, IV, iii, nos. 6026, 6184 and 6186. His reliance on Cromwell can be seen in *LP*, IV, iii, no. 6076.

The rewards and house for Jane and George are taken from *LP*, IV, ii, nos. 4779, 4993 (15), *LP*, IV, iii, no. 6115, *LP*, V, no. 686 (p. 314), and pp. 306, 312 and 754. Details of the New Year's Gifts are from *LP*, IV, ii, no. 3748, and *LP*, V, pp. 307 and 317. The grant to William Boleyn is from *LP*, IV, iii, no. 5815. The wardship awarded to Edward Boleyn is mentioned in *LP*, V, no. 80 (29). For the gift of Durham House, see Starkey (2004), pp. 356–8, and Colvin (1982), p. 76. Thomas Boleyn's investiture comes from *LP*, IV, iii, nos. 6083 and 6085, and *LP*, V, p. 316.

George's gambling is from the Privy Purse Expenses, *LP*, V, pp. 755, 757, 758 and 760. Gifts to Anne are taken from *LP*, IV, iii, Appendix 256, and *LP*, V, no. 276. The redemption of Mary Boleyn's jewel and the details of the satin are mentioned in *LP*, V, p. 752.

11, Almost There: pp. 85–95

The New Year's Gift list is printed in *LP*, V, no. 686 (p. 327) There are extensive accounts of York Place and the building works there in Thurley (1993), pp. 50–5 and 137, Thurley (1999), pp. 37–64, and Colvin (1982), pp. 300–15. Additional information is from *CSP Sp*, IV, ii, no. 720 and *LP*, V, no. 952. Anne's handwritten letter to Lady Wingfield is from BL, Cotton MS, Vespasian F.XIII, fo. 198 (formerly fo. 109), printed in Wood (1846), II, pp. 74–5. For its significance, see chapter 21. My quotations describing Wolsey's death are from Cavendish (1825), I, pp. 310 and 320. Cavendish reports Wolsey's advice to Kingston on p. 321. The loss of Katherine's jewels is from *CSP Sp*, II, no. 1003 (pp. 524–5).

Henry's infatuation for Anne is from *CSP Sp*, II, no. 995 (p. 512). Katherine's letter to Charles V is from *LP*, V, no. 513. An account of Anne's investiture as Marquess of Pembroke is printed in *LP*, V, no. 1274; the significance of Anne's sons' ability to inherit even if illegitimate is explored in Friedmann (1884), I, pp. 162–3. Rumours that Katherine was to be confined in the Tower are from *CSP Sp*, II, no. 993, (p. 509). The tantalising snippet of Henry's habit of beginning sentences with 'Well' is mentioned in *Lisle Letters* (1981), III, p. 412. For a very readable analysis of Henry's belief that the pope had no authority in the matter of the divorce and for his claim for supremacy in the Church, see Ives (2004), pp. 129–39. George's presentation to Convocation is from NA, SP 6/2, fos. 81–3 (formerly pp. 187–92), discussed by Lehmberg (1970), p. 114.

There is a brief account of the Calais visit in Anglo (1969), pp. 245–6. Hall (1904), II, pp. 218–21, gives a fuller account. Both should be read in conjunction with *CSP Venice*, IV, no. 824, *LP*, V, nos. 1484, 1485 and 1492, Anon. (1532a), Anon. (1532b), and *STC*, nos. 4350 and 4351. Ives (2004), p. 159, confirms that Henry lodged at the Exchequer and has a very full description of the building and its gardens on p. 161. The present from Montmorency to Anne is mentioned in *Calais Chronicle* (1846), p. 118, and her loss at cards on p. 121. Elyot's letter is from *LP*, V, no. 1554. Suffolk's opposition to the Boleyn marriage is described by Ives (2004), p. 164.

The rumour that Anne and Henry intended to marry in Calais is from *CSP Sp*, IV, ii, no. 1003 (p. 527). The date, place, and the officials involved in the secret marriage of Henry and Anne have been much debated: Friedmann (1884), I, pp. 182–4, and Ives (2004), p. 161, should be read in conjunction with Starkey (2004), pp. 461, 463, 474–7, and the Appendix in MacCulloch's *Cranmer* (1996), pp. 637–8. Starkey and MacCulloch's argument, that there were in fact two ceremonies, is compelling. Chapuys' comment about witnesses is from *LP*, VI, no. 180. Henry's remark to the Dowager Duchess of Norfolk is from *CSP Sp*, IV, ii, no. 1055. Anne's ceremonial entry to mass at Easter 1533 is from *LP*, V, no. 351; Friedmann (1884), I, p. 200, refers to public opposition. The letter concerning the Dunstable Judgment is from *LP*, VI, no. 528. For a discussion of the proceedings at Dunstable, see MacCulloch (1996), pp. 92–4.

12, Soaring with the Falcon: pp. 99–108

For my account of the river pageant, I used *LP*, VI, nos. 556, 562 563, 584, 585 and 601, in conjunction with Wriothesley (1875–7), I, p. 18, and Hall (1904), II, pp. 229–31. Very readable descriptions of the event are in Ives (2004), pp. 172–4, and Starkey (2004) pp. 493–4. Jane's letter to George is referred to in Sir Edward Baynton's letter, NA, SP 1/76, fo. 195 (stamped fo. 168), and *LP*, VI, no. 613. Katherine's defiant gesture is from *CSP Venice*, IV, ii, no. 923. The ceremonies associated with the investiture of Knights of the Bath is sketched out by Bayne (1910), but I relied on the fuller and more contemporary information from BL, Additional MS 38174, and HEH, MS HM 41955, fos. 129ᵛ–33. My focus was on Henry Parker, but Ives (2004), pp. 175–6, discusses the Boleyn links of others chosen for knighthood on that occasion.

Anne's procession from the Tower to Westminster is taken from *LP*, VI, nos. 561, 563, 564, 583, 584, 585, 601 and 602, although no. 585 is from a manuscript described as 'unfavourable to Anne'. The fact that she had a female fool is taken from *LP*, X, no. 913, in which the queen pays for a gown and a cap for her. See also Royal Book (1790), p. 123, for traditional regulations for the coronation of a queen. Anne's appearance was not a result of a whim or personal choice; every last detail conformed to the protocol prescribed. For a description of the various pageants performed for Anne, see Hall (1904), II, pp. 232–6, and for an analysis, see Ives (2004), pp. 219–30, and Starkey (2004), pp. 496–9. BL, Additional MS 71009, fos. 57ᵛ–60 (formerly fos. 48ᵛ–59), provides the exciting new information that I have included on the order of the procession and Jane's place in it. Courtenay's pleading letter to Cromwell is from *LP*, VI, no. 521.

13, The Falcon Crowned: pp. 109–14

All the standard accounts of Anne's coronation derive from Anon. (1533), *STC* no. 656, Hall (1904) II, pp. 237–9, Wriothesley (1875–7), I, pp. 19–20, and *LP*, VI, nos. 584, 601 and 661. In addition, I have used BL, Additional MS 71009, fos. 57ᵛ–60, for vivid details that are not in any of the above abstracts or references. For the traditional protocol, I followed Royal Book (1790), pp. 123–4, Bayne (1907), pp. 650–73, and Loach (1994). Modern descriptions covering the event, but lacking the benefit of the information in the BL Additional MS, are by Ives (2004), pp. 178–9, and Starkey (2004), pp. 500–1.

What is particularly intriguing is that Anne appears to have used St Edward's Chair as well as St Edward's Crown. Katherine, her predecessor, had been crowned only with Queen Edith's Crown as the major diadem was, naturally, reserved for Henry. Both Ives and Starkey point out the significant use of the crown and Ives agrees that Anne also used the chair. If she was given the king's crown, rather than that of the consort, it is only one step further to allow it to be conveyed on the correct chair. BL, Additional MS 71009, describes how the chair was decorated and places it upon the platform. It is this document that also describes the chair that I think she used as a throne. It was customary for more than one chair to be used by the monarch at coronations and it seems likely to place that upon a platform also. For comparison with the placing of the chair for Elizabeth I's coronation, see Knighton and Mortimer (2003), p. 124.

For Henry's personal revision of the coronation oath, see Ellis (1824–46), 2nd series, I, p. 176. The coronation banquet is meticulously described in Hall (1904), II, pp. 239–42, Wriothesley (1875–7), I, pp. 21–2, and *LP*, VI, nos. 561, 562, 584, 601 and 661. Sir Edward Baynton's reference to the Duke of Suffolk is from NA, SP 1/76, fo. 195 (stamped fo. 168), and *LP*, VI, no. 613. For Suffolk's rivalry with Norfolk, see Gunn (1988), pp. 121–7.

14, Long May We Reign: pp. 115–23

George's membership of Parliament is from *LP*, VI, no. 123. Chapuys lists him as being in the Privy Council in *CSP Sp* IV, ii, no. 1072. Ibid., no. 1127, shows how his presence could be a dampener to conversation. The wardship of Edmund Sheffield is listed in the king's grants of April 1533, taken from *LP*, VI, no. 419 (8), with background information on the boy from Bindoff (1982), III, p. 305. Suffolk's wardship of Katherine Willoughby is from *LP*, IV, no. 5336 (12). Details of George's hawks are taken from *LP*, VI, no. 1515, and *LP*, VII, no. 1273. Information on Anne's litter is from *LP*, VI, no. 720; items from the Great Wardrobe are from *LP*, VI, no. 602; the royal plate is from *LP*, VI, no. 1364: and Anne's jointure is from *LP*, VII, no. 419 (25).

The huge list of lands and rents originally given to Katherine, from which my highly abridged details come, is *LP*, I, i, no. 94 (35). Thurley (1993), p. 36, has a tantalising description of Baynard's Castle. Of the many references to Katherine's christening cloth, I have used *CSP Sp*, IV, ii, no. 1107. The references to Katherine's response to Henry's messengers derive from *LP*, VI, no. 805. Chapuys' antagonism to Anne comes from *CSP Sp* IV, ii, nos. 1058 and 1061. His accounts of the reception accorded to Katherine and Mary by the people are from ibid., nos. 1100 and 1107. Of the many references to English antagonism towards Anne, I have chosen *LP*, VI, nos. 923 and 964. Chapuys' hopeful reference to Henry falling in love with someone else is from *LP*, VI, no. 1054; his shrewd comment about lovers' quarrels is from ibid., no. 1069. Henry's choice of name for his son is from ibid., no. 1070. Sir Edward Baynton's highly informative letter is from NA, SP 1/76, fo. 195 (stamped fo. 168), and *LP*, VI, no. 613.

The Privy Purse Expenses yield further fascinating details: *LP*, V, p. 761, for instance, has Weston partnering Anne at Pope Julius's game. References to Jane's possessions are from NA, SP 1/104, fo. 82 *(LP*, X, no. 1011). Henry's desire to spare Anne worry over Clement VII's judgment on the divorce is from *LP*, VI, no. 918.

Clearly, a love of learning and study was inculcated in the Morleys. Books associated with the family are discussed in Axton and Carley (2000), pp. 70–2. The first reference to Jane's scholar is from *LP*, X, no. 1251, but sight of the original letter, now NA, SP 1/104, fo. 282 (stamped fo. 253), rather than the printed abstract, is illuminating, because William Foster needed help at the very time that the Boleyns were fighting for their lives. Fosters abounded in Aylesbury as the local records show: WRO, microfilm 705:349/12946/498724, 705:349/12946/498704, 705:349/12946/498700, 705:349/12946/498353.

Members of Eton College were tracked in Sterry (1943), who confuses and conflates two different William Fosters who later overlapped at King's College, and therefore presumably also overlapped at Eton. The career of Jane's William Foster at King's College is from KCAR/4/1/6, MS vol. 14 (unfoliated; entries dated between August 1535 and October 1536), not to be confused with a King's Fellow of the same name who had already graduated as an MA and went on to be Bursar. The newly discovered manuscript of Wall's translation of the French treatise is from NA, SP 9/31/2. The underlinings and corrections may well be George's. According to Carley (2004), p. 133, Suffolk gave George the copy-text, but this was still in French. The new document shows that George took it one step further.

My account of Anne's birthing suite follows Royal Book (1790), pp. 125–6, *LP*, VI, nos. 890 and 1069, and Cressy (1997), p. 21. See also Thurley (1993), pp. 140–1, for further detail on Anne's lying-in chamber. Despite fears about the dangers of childbirth, mortality figures for mothers, as Schofield (1986) convincingly argues, were far lower than was popularly believed.

15, Birth of a Niece: pp. 124–9

The birth of Elizabeth crops up in many documents. I have chosen Chapuys' fairly stark account in *LP*, VI, no. 1112. The officially pre-prepared document announcing the birth of a 'prince', which had to be hastily altered to 'princes,' is from *State Papers* (1830–52) I, p. 407; there was room only for one 's' in princess. The rituals of childbirth are from Cressy (1997), pp. 80–6, and Harris (2002), pp. 99–107. Information on Jane's nephew is from Bindoff (1982), III, pp. 58–9. Robert Lyst's letter to Anne concerning the Observant Friars is printed in Ellis (1824–46), 3rd series, II, pp. 245–9. Full accounts of the christening are from Hall (1904), II, pp. 242–4, and *LP*, VI no. 1111. The official protocol for royal baptisms is from BL, Additional MS 71009, fos. 27–8ᵛ. The partisanship of the Marchioness of Exeter is from *LP*, VI, no. 1125; see also Ives (2004), p. 185. Chapuys, ever vigilant of anything that might harm Mary, informed Charles V of his fears about the baby's name: *LP*, VI, no. 1112. He also could not resist informing him of Suffolk's sudden marriage to Katherine Willoughby: *CSP Sp*, IV, ii, no. 1123. Anne's determination that her daughter must be dressed as a princess comes from the list of some of the items she purchased for her: see *LP*, X, no. 913.

16, The Boleyns Rampant: pp. 130–9

Anne's second pregnancy is from *LP*, VII, nos. 232, 566 and 958, and *CSP Sp*, V, i, no. 7. The significance of Henry's purchase of a silver cradle, documented in *LP*, VII, no. 1688, is discussed by Ives (2004), p. 191. Lady Honor Lisle, the wife of the Deputy of Calais, wrote to Anne several times, fully aware of the benefits to be gained from a highly placed patron. She also sent many gifts to the queen, amongst which were the dog and the linnet: see *LP*, VII, nos. 92 and 654. The account of the dog's death and Henry's solicitude is from *Lisle Letters* (1981), II, no. 299a (p. 331). Henry's dogs, both buckhounds and pets, often got lost, usually when he was hunting in forests. The rewards to the finders of Ball and Cut are listed in *LP*, V, pp. 749 and 750.

The Boleyns' interest in the new religious ideas is well known. Chapuys often remarks upon it: see *LP*, X, no. 699. The reference to shirts for the poor is part of an account of Anne's charitable works described in the life written by George Wyatt, the grandson of Sir Thomas, printed in Cavendish (1825), II, p. 207. Whilst George Wyatt never met his grandfather, the suggestion is that there were family stories upon which he could draw. This is possible. The most outstanding work on the books Anne possessed is by James Carley, who found the inscription in the epistles and gospels and identified it as from George: see Carley (2004), p. 128. Other references to Anne's books are from Carley (2004), pp. 125–31, and Ives (2004), pp. 239–40 and 269–73.

There are many lists of New Year's Gifts and recipients. I have used *LP*, VI, nos. 1382 and 1589 for Anne; see also Ives (2004), p. 216, for Jane's presentation of a shirt. Anne's gift to Henry is from *LP*, VII, no. 9. Unfortunately, Henry's present to Anne is unrecorded. The dog collars are mentioned in *LP*, V, no. 686. For a vivid account of Henry receiving his presents while Tuke notes them all down, see *Lisle Letters* (1981), IV, no. 1086. For relations with Katherine, I have drawn on *CSP Sp*, IV, ii, no. 1100, and *CSP Sp*, V, i, no. 4. For relations with Mary, see *CSP Sp*, IV, ii, no. 1132, *CSP Sp*, V, i, nos. 1, 17 and 22, and *LP*, IX, no. 873. References to Greenwich are from Thurley (1993), pp. 130 and 190, and *LP*, V, pp. 750 and 758.

Chapuys informs us of George's acquisition of Beaulieu: *CSP Sp* IV, ii, no. 1137. Details on the rooms and construction are from Thurley (1993), pp. 44, 73, 103, 164, 170–1, 186 and 196, and Colvin (1982), p. 172. I have drawn on the detailed inventory of the house's furnishings and appointments in NA, E 101/622/31. See also Starkey, Ward and Hawkyard

(1998), nos. 789, 967, 1164 1307, 1701, 1888, 1889, 13147, 13685, 13686, 13706, 13708, 13741 and 17221, for lists of some of the items found at Beaulieu as well as confiscated goods from George and Jane, which became part of the royal property. Intriguingly, Jane appears to have persuaded the king to return to her the great Rochford bed, as it is listed in the inventory as her property rather than George's.

17, The King's Displeasure: pp. 143–53

A full and readable account of the main opposition to Henry's religious policies is given by George Bernard. He also provides an analysis of recent research on each opponent. For Elizabeth Barton see Bernard (2005), pp. 87–101; for the Carthusians, ibid., pp. 160–7; for Syon Abbey, ibid., pp. 167–72; for Fisher, ibid., pp. 101–25; for More ibid., pp. 125–51. For Elizabeth Barton, I followed *LP*, VI, nos. 1419, 1464, 1465, 1466, 1519 and 1546, and *LP*, VII, no. 522. Of the many references to those more ordinary folk who spoke against Anne, the divorce or the royal supremacy I chose *LP*, VII, nos. 498, 522 and 1652, *LP*, VIII, nos. 196, 278 and 809, and *LP*, VI, no. 1503. For Cavendish's remark on Wolsey's warning to Kingston, see Cavendish (1825), I, p. 321. The quotations from the writings of Lord Morley are printed, and discussed, in Wright (1943), pp. lxxi, lxxxviii, xciv and xcv. Morley's religious views are discussed by Richard Rex in Axton and Carley (2000), pp. 87–107. Reynold's speech is from *LP*, VIII, no. 661. Information concerning the trials and deaths of the Carthusians and the spectators' reactions is from NA, KB 8/7/1, *LP*, VIII, nos. 661 and 666, *CSP Sp*, V, i, no. 156.

My account of Fisher's conduct, incarceration and trial is from NA, KB 8/7/2, *LP*, VII, nos. 498, 499, 500 and 1563, and *LP*, VIII, no. 856. The case of More is discussed by Guy (2000a), pp. 186–205. He assesses More's reasons for refusing to take the oath and describes his trial. While both Fisher and More chose to die rather than betray their consciences, they do so for quite different reasons. Fisher was an outright papalist; More was not. He believed in the superiority of Church Councils and the received wisdom of the Church. A consensus was needed if change was to happen; one individual kingdom or country could not go against the universality of the Catholic Church, i.e. the common body of Christendom. For the list of high-profile judges in More's case, see NA, KB 8/7/3. For other details, I mainly used *LP*, VIII, nos. 815, 988 and 996, and *LP*, VII, nos. 1114 and 1116. More's speeches at his trial are translated from the Paris Newsletter, printed in Harpsfield (1932), pp. 263–4. Accounts of Margaret's last meeting with her father are from Roper (1935), pp. 97–9, and from the Paris Newsletter in Harpsfield (1932), p. 265. More's last letter is from Rogers (1961), pp. 256–7. Suffolk's bid for More's Chelsea lands is from *LP*, VIII, no. 1101.

18, Happy Families: pp. 154–63

Henry's latest infatuation, and its consequences for Jane and others, are pieced together from *LP*, VII, nos. 1257 and 1554, and *CSP Sp*, V, i, nos. 97 and 118. The fall from favour of the unidentified lady briefly in Henry's affections is described by Chapuys: see *LP*, VIII, no. 263. For a fuller analysis of this episode, see Ives (2004), pp. 194–5.

There is no record of Jane's return to court, but we would not necessarily expect to find one. Chapuys, the source of so much that was going on at the time, was alert for signs of Henry tiring of Anne, or flirting with other women, and was fearful for the lives and prospects of Katherine and Mary. After he reported the incident involving Jane, her fate was low on his agenda. When individuals were sent from court, however, many did come back after a short period, possibly after the next court move or 'remove' (as it was known), so it is reasonable to assume that Jane returned some time in the early months of 1535, before the executions of Fisher and More.

Chapuys' report of the prophecy is from *CSP Sp*, V, i, no. 230. Flamock's story is taken from Puttenham (1589), p. 324. The New Year's Gift list is from *LP*, V, no. 686. Mary Carey's exile from court is from *LP*, VII, no. 1554, and her letter to Cromwell is from Wood (1846), II, pp. 193–7. Anne's quarrels with Norfolk are taken from *LP*, VIII, nos. 1 and 826. For possible causes of their estrangement, see Ives (2004), p. 202. Boorde (1547) contains fascinating details on medical conditions and suggested remedies; see *STC*, no. 3373.5.

Information on William Foster, a scholar at King's College, Cambridge, is from NA, SP 1/104, fo. 282 (stamped as 253); KCAR 4/1/6, MS vol. 14 (unfoliated; entries dated between August 1535 and October 1536); NA, C 1/983/2; *LP*, IX, no. 708; *LP*, X, nos.1238 and 1251. He is not to be confused with a King's Fellow of the same name also appearing in KCAR 4/1/6, MS vols. 13–14 (unfoliated), who had already graduated as an MA and went on to be Bursar. For information on King's College Chapel, see Harrison (1953). The screen is still in situ today; the visitor can see the carved initials and symbols commissioned when Henry viewed Anne as his true and last wife. Ives (2004), pp. 243 and 249–50, provides a fuller description and analysis of the screen.

19, The Final Flourish: pp. 164–73

Anne's turbulent relationship with Mary and Katherine is chronicled in *CSP Sp*, V, i, no. 68, and *LP*, VIII, nos. 666 and 1105. Her assertion that she would not become pregnant while they were alive is from *CSP Sp*, V, i, no. 144. Chapuys' plot for Mary's escape is taken from *LP*, VIII, nos. 263 and 501. Katherine's heart-rending letter begging to nurse her daughter is from *LP*, VIII, no. 200. She refers to Chapuys as her 'especial friend' in *CSP Sp*, V, i, no. 134. Henry's attitude towards his former wife and daughter is taken from *CSP Sp*, V, i, no. 263, and *LP*, VIII, no. 263. Lady Shelton's letter is from *LP*, VII, no. 1172.

Anne's religious zeal is taken from *LP*, VII, nos. 693 and 710. See also Ives (2004), p. 286, and Ives (1996), pp. 83–102. For Anne's charitable works, see Ives (2004), p. 284. Her wealth can be estimated on the basis of an account of income and expenses for the year 1534–5 compiled by her receiver-general: *LP*, IX, no. 477. A list of items taken from Baynard's Castle is from *LP*, VIII, no. 209. For my theory that her interest in poor relief and education came from family tradition as well as her own religious beliefs, see the wills of Sir Geoffrey Boleyn and Sir William Boleyn: NA, PROB 11/5, and PROB 11/14.

Chapuys' report on Anne's comeback is in *CSP Sp*, V, i, no. 174. Her remark to Henry that he should be grateful to her is from *LP*, VIII, no. 666, and his reaction to the play is from *LP*, VIII, no. 949. The proposed marriage for Elizabeth is mentioned by Chapuys: *CSP Sp*, V, i, no. 213. George's interview with his sister is from *LP*, VIII, no. 826. Henry's letter from the heyday of their romance referring to George is from Halliwell (1848), I, pp. 317–18 (*LP*, IV, no. 4539). The royal progress is taken from *LP*, IX nos. 639 and 571; for a fuller analysis, see Ives (2004), pp. 291–2, and Starkey (2004), pp. 524–32.

The demonstration in support of Mary is from *LP*, IX, no. 566. Ives (2004), p. 293, believes that Jane was one of the women involved, while Starkey in Axton and Carley (2000), p. 14, disagrees. The evidence for her involvement rests entirely on the handwritten marginal note, but that is too vague and inconclusive to be relied upon. I feel that Jane's colours were still firmly nailed to the Boleyn mast at this point, when Anne's downfall was not yet in sight. Even had Jane suddenly developed feelings of sympathy for Mary, she was sensible enough to realise that taking part in such a demonstration was exceptionally dangerous. She had already felt the force of Henry's anger when she was sent from court; to invite that again would have been foolhardy. Henry's flirtation with Madge Shelton is from *LP,* VIII, no. 263; Anne's sudden outburst is from *LP,* VIII, no. 48. Ives views this laughter as genuine, but I suspect there was a little more to it than that. When Anne was imprisoned, she would often break out in uncontrollable laughter, which was presumably her reaction to stress. She had behaved in exactly the same way when she had met the ambassadors and had remarked on Henry forgetting a message because he was talking to another woman.

20, The Wheel Turns: pp. 174–83

Katherine's last days and death are pieced together from *LP,* IX, no. 1037, *LP,* X, no. 28, and *CSP Sp,* V, ii, nos. 3, 4, and 9. Starkey (2004), pp. 541–9, gives an excellent account of her illness and death. Court reaction is taken from *CSP Sp,* V, ii, nos. 9 and 13. Anne's offer to befriend Mary is reported by Chapuys, ibid., no. 9. The banter in Anne's chamber, which becomes crucial in the condemnation of Anne, Norris and Weston, is referred to in *LP,* X, no. 793. Henry's ivory chess set is listed amongst the goods seized from Baynard's Castle: see *LP,* VIII, no. 209. His riding accident is from *LP,* X, nos. 200 and 427. Katherine's funeral has many references. I have used *LP,* X, no. 284, as a basis combined with *CSP Sp,* V, ii, nos. 9, 13 and 21. For the fate of the monastery of the Observant Friars, see Bernard (2005), pp. 151–6.

Anne's miscarriage is from *CSP Sp,* V, ii, nos. 21 and 29. Jane's knowledge of Henry's lack of sexual prowess is repeated at George's trial, ibid., no. 55. Jane Seymour is first mentioned at court by Chapuys, ibid., no. 21. The gold purse incident, and Henry's offer to meet her on neutral ground, are from ibid., no. 43. Further grants to the Boleyns, even at this late stage, are listed in *LP,* X, nos. 243 and 597. The meeting between Chapuys and Anne is from *CSP Sp,* V, ii, no. 43a. Henry's revealing decision to elect Carew as a Knight of the Garter instead of George is from ibid., no. 47. For an account of the May Day Joust, see Ives (2004), p. 320.

21, The Edge of the Precipice: pp. 184–92

The causes of Anne's fall have long been debated by historians, who give a myriad reasons ranging from her failure to produce a son, the possibility that she miscarried a deformed foetus, Henry's infatuation with Jane Seymour, the potential for a foreign-policy switch towards the Holy Roman Empire now that Katherine of Aragon was dead, the chance that Anne may have been guilty, the disagreement over the use of monastic funds, right the way through to Cromwell taking over a plot to topple the queen and then toppling the conspirators. The most important literature is by Bernard (1991) and (1992); Ives (1992) and (2004), pp. 319–37; Starkey (2004), pp. 554–73; Walker (2002); Warnicke (1985b), (1987), (1989) and (1993).

There is something to be said for many of these theories or, indeed, for a fusion of several. My own view inclines towards Henry's growing dissatisfaction with a marriage that had not given him the son he craved, combined with Anne's failure to give up the role of mistress that had so enchanted him and become the more staid wife that was the Tudor ideal, coinciding with his falling for the quiet, submissive Jane Seymour. And Henry always was fickle, enjoying the chase but tiring of the kill. Of course it mattered that there might be a foreign-policy shift and that the mere existence of Anne was a thorn in Charles V's flesh, but even a cursory reading of Chapuys' correspondence shows that she was not an insuperable obstacle.

The use of monastic funds was again important, but Anne was a consort, not a ruling monarch; she could not have influenced policy for the rest of Henry's reign. I very much doubt that she was foolish enough to risk having affairs, even if she saw them as offering the opportunity to conceive with a more potent man. Norris, though, does have the intriguing heraldic link with the merlin, which, in the context of the Baynton letter, suggests that he might have been a more flirtatious character than previously thought.

My suspicion is that Anne's letter to Lady Wingfield is extremely significant, simply because it ends up in Cromwell's papers, a point unnoticed until now, and because it is couched in such unusually subservient tones for someone of Anne's social status. If Bridget Wingfield possessed information that could be dangerous to the queen, it is likely to refer to Anne's behaviour with Wyatt or Percy. In considering the letter important, I concur (if for different reasons) with Retha Warnicke (who also believes no concrete evidence exists against Lady Rochford).

I still, however, remain unconvinced by Warnicke's major thesis that Anne's last miscarriage was anything other than normal.

All this said, no one can deny that Cromwell's role in Anne's fall was vital. He was a superb tactician, utterly ruthless if he believed his own survival was at stake. It is entirely within character for him to act as E. W. Ives believes, masterminding the entire plot once he had quarrelled with Anne, and in any case the conservatives at court were already trying to depose her. G. W. Bernard's point that Henry was not someone to be easily manipulated also holds water. I cannot attempt to do justice to all the prevailing theories here, but would refer anyone interested in delving more deeply into the entire mystery to the literature cited. Since this book seeks to reassess the life and role of Jane Rochford, what is really important is not so much why Anne fell, but whether Jane was involved, and, if so, in what ways.

The intriguing document listing grants to the Boleyns is calendared in *LP*, X, no. 109, in which form it is sadly incomplete. An examination of the handwritten original, NA, SP 1/102, fos. 155–6 (stamped numbers fos. 139–40), opens the possibility that the arrest of Thomas, and also the fall of the Boleyns as a family, might have been considered earlier than is currently thought. Since the document is undated and ends with the final grants of March 1536, it could have formed part of the assessment of George's property, so that its significance must remain speculative. For the news of the arrests, see *LP*, X, nos. 782, 785, 798 and 838. For the 1351 statute, see Baker (2003), p. 588. Cromwell names those he interviewed in *LP*, X, no. 873. Anne's babblings in the Tower are from ibid., nos. 793 and 797. Husee's denunciation in a letter to Lady Lisle of the Countess of Worcester as the informant against Anne is from ibid., no. 953. Anne's letter to Lady Wingfield is from BL, Cotton MS, Vespasian, F.XIII, fo. 198 (formerly fo. 109), and *LP*, V, no. 12. Bridget Wingfield's date of death is confirmed by NA, C 1/1003/10–12.

Anne's uncharacteristic obsequiousness suggests that Lady Wingfield knew something to her detriment and could be a threat to her, making clear that there were many possible informants. George is alleged to have protested that he was condemned 'on the evidence of one woman only', but nowhere states that it was his own wife. In reality, Lady Worcester and Lady Wingfield are both far more likely contenders. Both are denounced in the sources as informants, Worcester by Husee (see above), and Wingfield by Judge Spelman in his notebook: Spelman (1976–7), I, p. 71 (see chapter 22). George's purported protest, which comes from a

French poem by Lancelot de Carles, chronicling the main events of Anne's fall, is discussed in Ives (2004), p. 331. Ives assumes that the informant is Jane, but goes on to prove with spectacular success that the major source given by de Carles for betraying Anne's alleged behaviour is probably Lady Worcester, ibid., p. 333. The foreign visitor mentioned (ibid., p. 331), who talks of an envious and jealous person divulging Anne's lasciviousness, could be entirely mistaken or, since no name is included, the visitor could be making allegations against anyone at all, either male or female. It sounds suspiciously like an example of the many fanciful and exaggerated rumours prevalent at the time.

Henry's reaction to Anne's arrest is from *LP*, X, no. 908. Kingston's report of Jane's message to George and his response is from BL, Cotton MS, Otho C.X, fo. 225 (formerly fo. 222), and *LP*, X, no. 798. I take this at face value, as there seems little point in Kingston's taunting George with a fictional missive, but see Ives (2004), p. 332, for a different interpretation.

22, Death of the Falcon: pp. 193–207

Kingston's letters to Cromwell detailing his conversations with Anne, her ramblings, and his dealings with the other prisoners are calendared in *LP*, X, nos. 793, 797, 798, 890, 902 and 910; they are also printed in Ellis (1824–46), 1st series, II, pp. 52–6, 56–9, 59–60, 62–3, 64–6, and in Cavendish (1825), II, pp. 217, 220–3, 223–5, 227–8 and 228–9. Unfortunately there are often words or even whole passages missing as, with two exceptions, they were part of BL, Cotton MS, Otho C.X, which fell victim to a disastrous fire at Ashburnham House in 1731. I also referred to Strype (1721), I, pp. 279–84, and quoted from p. 280, as he saw the letters before the fire. Hall's trusting comment on the nature of kingship is from Hall (1904), II, p. 197. Cranmer's letter to Henry is from *LP*, X, no. 792. Wyatt's poem is from Wyatt (1969), p. 187. The records for the trials of Norris, Brereton, Weston and Smeaton are filed in the so-called 'Bag of Secrets': NA, KB 8/8. See also *LP*, X. nos. 848 and 876, for relevant information.

I used the KB records for the Middlesex and Kent juries of presentment. For the trial jury, I followed Ives's masterly analysis, see Ives (2004), p. 339, except that, where Ives implies that the foreman, Edward Willoughby, was biased because he owed Brereton money, I suggest that such a debt makes no difference. The debt would not die with Brereton, since all debts owed to convicted traitors were still payable in full to the king by way of forfeiture (see chapter 23). For the correct identification of Edmund Page, see Bindoff (1982), III, pp. 40–1. He is sometimes wrongly transcribed as Edward. Of the several examples of the indecent scramble for the offices of those arrested, I have used *LP*, X, nos. 791 and 842.

The records of the trials of Anne and George are also in the 'Bag of Secrets': NA, KB 8/9; see also *LP*, X, no. 876. These are relatively uninformative as to what evidence was given on the day, as (like all such official documents) they concentrate on the charges, verdict and procedural matters. The fullest account of what really happened is from Chapuys: *CSP Sp*, V, ii, nos. 54 and 55. Some further details are taken from Thomas Turner or Tourneur's handwritten notes on the (now lost) 'Chronicle' by Anthony Anthony, an 'eye- and ear-witness' to the trial, bound into Turner's copy of Herbert of Cherbury's *Life and Raigne of King Henry the Eighth*, now Bodleian Folio Delta 624 [*sic*], pp. 381–5 (pages out of sequence; new numbering beginning after p. 404). Anthony Anthony's will is from NA, PROB 11/46. St Botolph's is described by Atkinson (1896), pp. 522–7. Spelman's exposure in his notebook of Lady Wingfield as the informant against Anne is from Spelman (1976–7), I, p. 71. John Husee's comment on Anne is from *LP*, X, no. 866. Northumberland's oath is from ibid., no. 864. Anne's affirmation of her innocence is from ibid., no. 908. For the executions, see ibid., no. 911, *CSP Sp*, V, ii, no. 55, and Wriothesley (1875–7), I, p. 38. There are many versions of the final speeches of both Anne and her brother, most with slight variations. I have taken George's speech from *Calais Chronicle* (1846), p. 46; Anne's speech is extracted from the journal of Anthony Anthony as transcribed by Turner: Bodleian Folio Delta 624, pp. 384–5.

23, Taking Stock: pp. 211–18

Jane's possessions are listed in *LP*, X, no. 1011, but I obtained the full details from the manuscript: NA, SP 1/104, fo. 82. The details on George's possessions, offices and debts are from *LP*, X, nos. 870, 878, 880, 890, 902, 1015 (16), 1256 (2 and 31), *LP*, XI, no. 1277, *LP*, XIII, ii, no. 1192, *LP*, XIV, i, no. 1006, and *LP*, XVII, no. 460 (9). Henry's help to Elizabeth Savage is from *LP*, X, no. 1256 (52), and her letter to Cromwell is *LP*, XI, no. 1024. Uriah Brereton's grants are mentioned in *LP*, X, no. 1256 (29) and *LP*, XI, no. 1217 (7). Information on the eccentric George

Boleyn, Dean of Lichfield, comes from *Complete Peerage* (1987), IV, p. 142, and from his will: NA, PROB 11/101. Details of Ormond's ancestral horn are from his will: NA, PROB 11/18. The will also gives information on his two daughters, Margaret Boleyn and Anne St Leger. His lordship of Aylesbury is referred to in NA, SP 46/183, fo. 140. The Chancery enrolment of Thomas Boleyn's indenture with his mother, which gave him control of most of her property, is from NA, C 54/379. Examples to illustrate the limitations facing Jane if she relied on an income of 100 marks per annum are taken from *LP*, V, pp. 755 and 758, *LP*, VI, no. 1515, and Madden (1831), p. 223. Henry's relative generosity to the Brereton family is from *LP*, X, no. 1256 (29 and 52), and *LP*, XI, nos. 1024 and 1217 (7). Details on Jane's jointure are pieced together from her letter, BL, Cotton MS, Vespasian, F.XIII, fo. 199 (formerly fo. 109ᵛ), which is printed in *LP*, X, no. 1010, and in Ellis (1824–46), 1st series, II, pp. 67–8. Thomas Boleyn's letter is in *LP*, XI, no. 17, and Ellis (1824–46), 3rd series, III, pp. 21–3. However, these references must now be reconsidered in the light of the newly discovered information about Jane's jointure and marriage settlement from WRO, microfilm 705:349/12946/498729, and HLRO, MS PO/1/1539 (Original Acts, 31 Henry VIII, c.20). For Angel Day's template on writing a letter of supplication in circumstances not dissimilar to Jane's, see Day (1586), pp. 169–82, and *STC*, no. 6401.

24, A New Beginning: pp. 219–30

For readers interested in the life of Jane Seymour, the best and most eminently readable account can be found in Starkey (2004), pp. 584–608. Starkey's assessment of her character and his analysis of the ways in which Queen Jane was such a contrast to Anne is masterly. Cromwell's comment about admiring Anne's courage and his assertion that he brought about her fall is from *CSP Sp*, V, ii, no. 61. Henry's dash to Jane Seymour's side is taken from *LP*, X, no. 926. Early reactions to Jane Seymour are from *LP*, X, no. 1047, and *LP*, XI, no. 29. The references to Sir John Gage are from Cromwell's 'Remembrances': *LP*, X, no. 929, and *LP*, XI, no. 580. Chapuys remembers Edward Seymour as escorting him to Henry's chamber: see *LP*, XI, no. 479. His description of Queen Jane is taken from *LP*, X, no. 901, and his allusion to her as the 'Pacificator' is from *CSP Sp*, V, ii, no. 61.

Mary's hopes of immediate reconciliation with Henry are from *CSP Sp*, V, ii, no. 70. My account of the realities of her situation is pieced together from ibid., nos. 70, 71 and 72, and *LP*, X, nos. 1110, 1134, 1137 and 1203. See also Starkey (2004), pp. 597–601, who provides a clear and succinct analysis of Mary's plight and the broader question of the succession. Lord Morley's visit to Mary is from *LP*, VII, no. 1036, which is wrongly dated, *LP*, XI, no. 222, and BL, Cotton MS, Otho C.X, fo. 262. For a full analysis of the burgeoning relationship between Morley and Mary, see Starkey in Axton and Carley (2000), pp. 14–17 and 44. Mary's payments or gifts to the Parkers and Sheltons are from Madden (1831), pp. 11, 42 and 57. The reference to Jane's clock is from ibid., p. 13. Mary's payments to Jane are from ibid., pp. 17, 25, 51, 64, 65 and 82. Information on Mary's new household is from Loades (1989), p. 106. Morley's gifts to Cromwell are from NA, SP 1/93, fo. 207 (stamped fo. 168), *LP*, VIII, no. 957, and *LP*, XIV, i, no. 285. Queen Jane's efforts on Mary's behalf are from *CSP Sp*, V, ii, no. 184. Mary's affectionate greeting is from *LP*, X, no. 1204.

Henry's rebuffs to Queen Jane are from *LP*, XI, nos. 860, 880 and 1250. Letters to Cromwell from Lady Ughtred are printed by Wood (1846), II, pp. 353–8. Honor Lisle's attempt to buy a gown in Queen Jane's style is from *LP*, X, no. 1193. Anne Basset's costume problems are from the *Lisle Letters* (1981), IV, nos. 895 and 896. Richmond's death is from Murphy (2003), pp. 164–5 and 176–8. Jane's entitlements at court as a viscountess are from HEH, HM 41955, fos. 32^v–33; see also BL, Additional MSS 45716A–B, 45717.

The predicament of Henry Parker and Sir John St John is taken from *LP*, XII, i, no. 128, and *LP*, XII, ii, no. 1151. As we do not know exactly when Jane returned to court, I have chosen to omit Queen Jane's river pageant and various other court functions, which occurred very early after her marriage. My account of the ride to Greenwich for Christmas is from *LP*, XI, no. 1358, and Wriothesley (1875–7) I, pp. 59–60.

25, A Prince at Last: pp. 231–9

Henry's aside to Chapuys on the two ladies he had seen is taken from *LP*, XI, no. 8. The ambassador's belief that Queen Jane would not be crowned unless she became pregnant is from *CSP Sp*, V, ii, no. 103. Mary's letters to her father, in which she expresses her prayers that he should have issue, are from *LP*, X, nos. 1083, 1109, 1133 and 1203. The Trinity Sunday *Te Deum* and celebrations are described by Wriothesley (1875–7), I, p. 64; the gun salute at Calais is from *LP*, XII, ii, no. 11.

Mary's gifts of cucumbers to the queen are listed in Madden (1831), p. 34. Henry's comment on the obedience due to princes is from *LP*, XI, no. 780. The information on Hampton Court is taken from Thurley (1993), pp. 89, 131 and 141, and Loach (1999), p. 4. The joy and thanksgiving with which the news of Edward's birth was greeted is from *LP*, XII, ii, nos. 889, 905 and 1053, and Wriothesley (1875–7), I, pp. 66–7. My account of Edward's christening relies heavily on the handwritten recollection of Robert Boys, a young man at the time who later went on to be in charge of providing provender for Elizabeth I's horses. His version is from HEH, MS HM 41955, fos. 127–9. I also used *LP*, XII, ii, nos. 905, 911, 922 and 923, Loach (1999), pp. 5–6, and Wriothesley (1875–7), I, pp. 66–7. Cromwell's new posts are from *LP*, XI, no. 202 (3), and *LP*, XII, ii, no. 445.

26, The Bitterness of Death: pp. 240–5

Edward Seymour's elevation to the peerage and the knighting of Thomas Seymour are taken from *LP*, XII, ii, no. 939. Anne Basset's new dress is from ibid., no. 923. For the death of Queen Jane and the various reactions to it, I have relied on *LP*, XII, ii, nos. 968, 970, 971, 972, 1020 and 1084. Cromwell's suggestion that the queen's death was caused by the negligence of her ladies is from ibid., no. 1004, but the most commonly held view is that she died from puerperal fever. However, J. Loach suggests retention of sections of the placenta as the possible cause of death: see Loach (1999), p. 7. The reference to Queen Jane's gift to Jane Rochford is taken from *LP*, XII, ii, no. 973. The preliminary enquiries made by Norfolk and Paulet into the funeral ceremonies for Elizabeth of York are from ibid., no. 1012. A basic calendared description of Queen Jane's funeral may be obtained from *LP*, XII, ii, no. 1060; see also Wriothesley (1875–7), I, pp. 71–2. I based my description upon the fuller handwritten version in BL, Additional MS 71009, fos. 37–44v. The attempts by Norfolk and Cromwell to persuade the king to consider remarriage are from *LP*, XII, ii, nos. 1004 and 1030.

27, A Woman of Property: pp. 246–54

Lady Bryan's letter to Henry is taken from *LP*, XIV, ii, Appendix, no. 9; see also Loach (1999), pp. 8–9. Descriptions of Elizabeth Boleyn's death and funeral are from *LP*, XIII, i, nos. 696 and 717, and *Lisle Letters* (1981), V, nos. 1137 and 1139. Information on Sir John Baldwin's background relies on Bindoff (1982), I, pp. 372–3. Details relating to Thomas Boleyn's death are from NA, C 1/1110/65–9, *LP*, XIV, i, no. 511, and *LP*, XIV, ii, no. 781 (p. 309 at fo. 71) As an example of Cromwell's willingness to help the widows and orphans of those executed, I chose *LP*, XIII, i, no. 1. Lord Morley's purchase of Markhall from Thomas Shaa is from NA, C 54/420. His distraction over Lady Edgecombe's jointure is from CRO, MS ME/829 (dated 31 July 1538). The reference to Margaret Boleyn's precarious state of mind comes from her inquisition post mortem in Cambridgeshire: NA, E 150/87/6 (31 Henry VIII).

The piecing together of the intricacies of Jane's jointure and marriage settlement requires patience and considerable detective work as the full details, unfortunately, are not neatly contained in one document. The licence to alienate Aylesbury and Bierton is from NA C 66/680, and also *LP*, XIII, ii, no. 734 (24). The information concerning the series of legal recoveries by way of conveyances for the cluster of manors in Norfolk and Cambridgeshire, and the manors of Aylesbury and Bierton in Buckinghamshire, is from NA, IND 1/17181, fos. 117–17v, CP 40/1099, mm. 317, 411 (Norfolk and Cambridgeshire); NA, IND 1/17218 (index to feet of fines for Buckinghamshire, Hilary term, 30 Henry VIII), CP 25/2/3/16/Henry VIII Hil [*sic*] (manors of Aylesbury and Bierton, document annotated 'Buk' 55); WRO, microfilm 705:349/12946/498360, 705:349/12946/498361, 705:349/12946/499489, 705:349/12946/498729, 705:349/12946/499490, 705:349/12946/498711, 705:349/12946/499476, 705:349/12946/499484 and 705:349/12946/498713. Other information is from Cranwell's letter to Cromwell: *LP*, XIV, i, no. 854. Jane's final jointure settlement is worked out from WRO, microfilm 705: 349/12946/498729; HLRO, MS PO/1/1539 (Original Acts, 31 Henry VIII, c.20); NA, C 65/147; *LP*, XIV, i, nos. 867 and 1171; NA, E 315/233, fo. 338 (grant of the manors of Utlecote and Loxley), *LJ* (1767–1846), I, p. 112.

The two complementary indentures between Henry VIII, Mary Carey and her husband, William Stafford, and between Henry VIII, and Sir James Boleyn, are taken from C 54/418, entries numbered 14 and 18, belonging to 22 March 1539. As the result of a clerical error, entry no. 18 is misdated to the regnal year '31 Henry VIII' instead of '30 Henry VIII'. However, its position on the roll makes clear this is a slip, and the entry belongs to 30 Henry VIII.

28, A Question of Trust: pp. 255–66

Marillac's report on Henry's demeanour is taken from *LP*, XIV, i, no. 1092. Charles's comment on his leave-taking from Francis is in *CSP Sp*, V, ii, no. 102. For information on George Rochford's involvement with the Schmalkaldic League, see McEntegart (2002), pp. 27–9. Of the many references to the so-called Exeter or Pole conspiracy, I have chosen to use *LP*, XIII, ii, nos. 695, 702, 765, 955, 979 and 986. The appearance and personal qualities of Anne of Cleves are from *LP*, XIV, i, no. 552, and *LP*, XIV, ii, no. 719. I have also relied upon Starkey (2004), pp. 618–22, and Warnicke (2000), pp. 77 and 88–93. The references to Anne's ladies are from *LP*, XIV, ii, nos. 572 and 719, and *LP*, XV, nos. 21 and 776. The extracts from Cromwell's 'Remembrances' are from *LP*, XIV, ii, no. 573. D. R. Starkey gives a succinct but highly readable account of Henry's first meeting with Anne: see Starkey (2004), pp. 627–9. Retha Warnicke gives a similar account, but also analyses the protocol required for the meeting of a foreign bride: see Warnicke (2000), pp. 130–7. Another version can be found in Wriothesley (1875–7), I, pp. 109–10. The procession after the marriage is from ibid., I, p. 111; the voyage from Greenwich to Westminster is from ibid., p. 112; the May Day Jousts are from ibid., pp. 117–18.

The most usual interpretation of Cromwell's fall bases it upon factional struggles. This is very clearly described in *ODNB*, under the heading 'Cromwell, Thomas'. Alternative explanations can be found in Warnicke (2000), pp. 187–228, and Bernard (2005), pp. 556–79. The extracts from Cranmer's letters, including those from his letter to Henry VIII, are from Cox (1846), pp. 399–401. Cromwell's plea for mercy is from *LP*, XV, no. 776.

Of the plethora of references to Henry's distaste for Anne of Cleves and its consequences, including the divorce proceedings and Anne's response, I have relied on *LP*, XV, nos. 776, 822, 823, 845, 850, 861, 872, 899 and 925. Covos's comment on the divorce is from *CSP Sp*, VI, i, no. 115. However, I also relied heavily upon the analysis in Starkey (2004), pp. 632–5, for details on the lack of consummation and the ladies' evidence, and pp. 639–43 for the divorce proceedings. See also Warnicke (2000), pp. 162–5 and 204–5, for an opinion concerning non-consummation of the marriage and further discussion of Henry's impotence.

Warnicke distrusts the evidence of Jane and the other ladies because of Anne's language difficulties (ibid., pp. 233–5). It is indeed true that the councillors specifically mention taking an interpreter with them when

visiting Anne (*LP,* XV, no. 845) but that may have been in order to avoid
error in the future. This was, after all, a highly complex legal matter
with potentially massive international implications. Starkey raises no
objections to the usual interpretation: see Starkey (2004), pp. 633–5.
Neither does Bernard (2005), p. 549, a rare point of agreement between
these historians. Indeed, Bernard points out that if Henry wanted to
suggest that Anne was no virgin before she came to England, the ladies'
testimony points to the opposite, so there would be no reason for the
government to fabricate such testimony, although the women do, of
course, confirm Henry's statement that he did not have sexual relations
with Anne himself. In the absence of further evidence, it is impossible
to be certain about how much knowledge of English Anne had picked
up in the six months or so since her arrival but, since the predominant
language spoken around her would have been English, she must have
absorbed at least the rudiments. Anne still had a handful of German
attendants, including the influential Mrs Loew, so it is possible that some
simultaneous translation could also have taken place. Whatever the truth
of the episode, Jane Rochford's testimony places her firmly on the side
of the king, the very place where she has to be if she is to remain at court,
which is crucial to her story.

29, The King's Jewel: pp. 269–79

A basic biography of Catherine Howard can be found in *ODNB.* For a
fuller picture, which also sets her within the context of her world, see
Smith (1961). The most recent assessment is Starkey (2004), pp. 644–84.
The chronicler Edward Hall provides an excellent account of Cromwell's
final speech and his unpleasant death: see Hall (1904), II, pp. 306–7. The
Council's request to Henry to marry Catherine, with his comment upon
her as a 'jewel for womanhood', is from *LP,* XVI, no. 1334. Dorothy
Josselyn's opinion of Catherine is from *LP, Addenda,* I, ii, no. 1513. Mary's
disagreement with her is from Chapuys *LP,* XVI, no. 314. Chapuys also
reports Mary's present to Catherine and the visit of Anne of Cleves:
ibid., no. 436. Catherine's agreement to Mary's residence at court is
from ibid., no. 835. Marillac's account of Henry's devotion to Catherine
is from ibid., no. 12, which is also the source for the reintroduction of
French fashions. Information on some of Henry's gifts to Catherine is
from ibid., no. 1389. Marillac's report of rumours concerning her pregnancy and possible coronation is from ibid., no. 712.

The abstracts of Jane's possessions, from *LP*, XVI, no. 1340, and *LP*, XVII, no. 267 (p. 147), are too brief. I have used the fuller, handwritten lists from NA, SP 1/167, fo. 163–4 (which begins at stamped fo. 147) and E 315/160, fos. 104r–v and 106.

Opinions of Henry's health are from *LP*, XIII, i, no. 995 and *LP*, XVI, no. 589. The new building at Chenies was discovered by excavations at the site in 2004. The fact that Henry was accommodated in a 'lower chamber', together with the state bed specially prepared for him, which would have had to be constructed within the room as it was far too big, heavy and cumbersome to be moved, is from Sir John Russell's will: NA, PROB 11/69. Henry's method of hunting is from *LP*, XVI, no. 1089. For my account of Henry's size and ailments, I relied upon Starkey (1991a), pp. 125 and 144–5. See also Chamberlin (1932), pp. 278–82. The river pageant is from *CSP Sp*, VI, i, no. 155, and *LP*, XVI, no. 650. Information on the northern progress is from ibid., nos. 1011, 1088 and 1089. Chapuys is the main source for Catherine's fears of a possible reconciliation with Anne of Cleves and rumoured divorce plans: see *CSP Sp*, VI i, no. 163, and *LP*, XVI, no. 1328. Henry's joy at his marriage is from *LP*, XVI, no. 1334, and my account of his early reactions to news of Catherine's betrayal is taken from ibid., nos. 1328, 1332 and 1334.

30, In the Maidens' Chamber: pp. 280–90

The reasons for Jane's decision to support Catherine in her doomed affair with Culpepper are crucial to her story and to an understanding of her life. I cannot agree with Retha Warnicke's suggestion (*ODNB*, under the heading 'Howard, Catherine') that Jane chose this course because she was 'financially straitened'. Since she had just obtained her jointure settlement and was richer than ever before in her own right, Jane did not need to endanger her life for money. In any case, although Henry was generous to his young wife, it is hard to believe that constant payments from Catherine to Jane would have gone unnoticed for long. D. R. Starkey compares Jane to Juliet's nurse in *Romeo and Juliet*, indulging and pandering to her charge: see Starkey (2004), pp. 673–4.

Whilst Jane and Catherine do appear to have rubbed along happily together, as the queen's reliance upon her proves, Jane's earlier experiences of Anne's fall would surely have deterred her from an altruism that came accompanied by such a degree of risk. I think Jane had come through too hard a school to deliberately jeopardise her own position even if she did feel some sympathy for the young queen. Lacey Baldwin Smith suggests that, since Jane 'went mad under the strain of disclosure and ceaseless interrogation', it might be 'charitable to believe that she was insane from the start': see Smith (1961), p. 156. Apart from the obvious non sequitur, this does not fit with the considerable acumen that Jane had displayed in obtaining her jointure settlement. There is no hint in the sources of any unbalanced behaviour until she was sent to the Tower. The Culpepper affair lasted from April 1541 until the exposure of Catherine's early conduct in November of that year. If Jane was 'insane' for six months, it seems odd that there is no mention of it. Her confession (see the notes to chapter 31) is completely lucid. I think the most plausible explanation for Jane's foolish behaviour is simply that she became involved because Catherine gave her a direct order. She was the queen's pawn, rather than the other way round. Then, once she was embroiled, and with no male protector in whom she could confide and upon whom she could rely, her dangerous situation spiralled out of control.

Catherine's childhood is discussed in Smith (1961), pp. 42–3, 47–9 and 194–6, and in Starkey (2004), pp. 645–6. Marillac's report on the outbreak of the scandal is from *LP*, XVI, no. 1332. As to the affair and the events leading to the fall of Catherine, the calendared abstracts – from *LP*, XVI, nos. 1317, 1320–1, 1325, 1337–9, 1348, 1385, 1400, 1407, 1409, 1415–16, 1423–4, 1442, 1461 and 1469 – are useful, but no more than a starting point; they have been heavily abridged and any sexual innuendo has been censored to match the editor's opinion of what might properly appear in print in 1898. The letters from and between members of the Council are fully transcribed and printed in *State Papers* (1830–52), I, pp. 691–728. Catherine Howard's examinations by Cranmer are from Longleat, Portland Papers PO/1, fos. 51–53v, fully printed in HMC Bath (1907), II, pp. 8–10, and in Burnet (1820), III, ii, pp. 226–9 (no. 71). Cranmer's letter to Henry VIII, describing Catherine and her state of mind is from NA, SP 1/167, fos. 139–40 (stamped fos. 121–2), and *State Papers* (1830–52), I, pp. 689–91. Further reports of her mental state are from Paget's letter to Henry printed in *State Papers* (1830–52), VIII, p. 636.

This leaves the most important evidence: the interrogatories and signed (and sworn) depositions, which are difficult to read and are therefore still almost untouched in the National Archives. D. R. Starkey was the first to decipher some of them: see Starkey (2004), pp. 667–81. My account is substantially based on these handwritten depositions, which are as follows: Mary Hall's (born Lascelles) deposition from SP

1/167, fos. 128–31 (stamped fos. 110–13); Henry Manox's depositions from SP 1/167, fos. 135–8v (stamped fos. 117–20v) and 161 (stamped fo. 144); Margaret (also known as Mary) Morton's depositions from SP 1/167, fos. 153–4 (stamped fos. 133–4) and 162 (stamped fo. 146); Katherine Tylney's depositions from SP 1/167, fos. 149 (stamped fo. 131) and 157 (stamped fo. 140); Alice Wilkes's deposition from SP 1/167, fos. 155 and 157 (stamped fos. 136 and 140); Margaret, Lady Howard's deposition from SP 1/167, fo. 155 (stamped fo. 136); Anne Howard's deposition from SP 1/167, fo. 155 (stamped fo. 136); Margaret Benet's deposition from SP 1/167, fos. 155–6 (stamped fos. 136–8); Malyn Tylney's deposition from SP 1/167, fo. 156 (stamped fo. 138); Edward Waldegrave's deposition from SP 1/167, fo. 156 (stamped fo. 138); Francis Dereham's deposition from SP 1/167, fo. 157 (stamped fo. 140); Thomas Culpepper's deposition from SP 1/167, fo. 157–9 (stamped fos. 140–2); Jane Rochford's deposition from SP 1/167, fos. 159–60 (stamped fos. 142–3); John Lascelles's deposition from SP 1/167, fo. 162 (stamped fo. 146); Joan Bulmer's deposition from SP 1/167, fo. 162 (stamped fo. 146); Robert Davenport's deposition from SP 1/167, fo. 161 (stamped fo. 144); the Council's list of examinates from SP 1/167, fo. 151 (stamped fo. 132).

Further background on Henry Manox is from NA, DL25/1031, DL25/1032/(1), NA, C 1/1076/4–7, C 1/1304/19–26, C 1/1308/6–8, and C 1/1313/23–6. Although Manox is listed in the index to *LP*, XVI (p. 889) as executed in December 1541, a view apparently endorsed by Smith (1961), there are no trial or execution records for him. In fact, he escaped scot-free, living at Streatham, before moving to Hemingford in Huntingdonshire, where he died in his bed in 1564: see NA, PROB 11/47 (his will).

Further background on Robert Davenport and Francis Dereham is from *State Papers* (1830–52), I, p. 698. D. R. Starkey provides a succinct analysis of the incident involving Mr Johns: see Starkey (2004) pp. 661–2. The reference to Culpepper's involvement in a rape and murder, for which he received a royal pardon, is from *LP*, XVII, Appendix, no. 10, although his brother, another Thomas, might possibly have committed these offences. Catherine's letter to Culpepper is printed in full in *LP*, XVI, no. 1134. Her gifts to him are from NA, SP 1/167, fo. 157 (stamped fo. 140). Her comments to Jane about Culpepper are taken from Jane's confession (see above). Andrew Maunsay's statement is from *LP*, XVI, no. 1348. Jane Bulmer's letter is from *LP*, XV, no. 875. Catherine's warning to Dereham is from NA, SP 1/167, fo. 157 (stamped fo. 140). The Duchess of Norfolk's remark that neither Catherine nor Dereham would die for actions committed before Catherine's marriage is from *LP*, XVI, no. 1400. The enrolment of Lord Morley's purchase of Markhall from Thomas Shaa is from NA, C 54/420.

31, 'That bawd, the lady Jane Rochford': pp. 291–303

Just as there is debate about Jane's part in the Culpepper episode, so there is about whether or not it really was a full-blown affair or nothing more than talk. Inevitably, we can but speculate. D. R. Starkey believes that Culpepper's story rings true: see Starkey (2004), p. 675. Lacey Baldwin Smith also tends to exonerate Catherine. I remain sceptical that a woman as sexually experienced as Catherine could spend so long, and at such risk, with an equally experienced young man just talking. She could have talked to him, although admittedly not for such long periods, within the normal confines of the court if that was all she wanted. Since marriages in Tudor times were primarily business contracts, it was not unknown for a woman to take a lover, although the practice was certainly not condoned. It was Catherine's tragedy that marrying the king made this not only socially and morally unacceptable, but fatal. Retha Warnicke (*ODNB*, under the heading 'Howard, Catherine') believes that, far from wanting to sleep with Culpepper, Catherine was in fact trying to buy his silence on the Dereham episode. She sees Catherine's romantic letter to Culpepper as innocent, merely indicating her need to see him as 'a misguided attempt at appeasement'. If so, it took the queen a great many attempts, and Culpepper's confession does not even mention Dereham. I remain unconvinced by this theory, interesting as it is.

My sources for this chapter are those also used for chapter 30, in particular the signed (and sworn) depositions of Culpepper, Jane Rochford, Margaret Morton and Katherine Tylney (for full references, see notes above). Marillac's accusation of Dereham as Culpepper's betrayer is from *LP*, XVI, no. 1366. Henry's determination to discover everything is taken from *State Papers* (1830–52), I, p. 703. The list of what Catherine was to be allowed at Syon, and who was to accompany her, is from ibid., pp. 691–2 and 695, and *LP*, XVI, no. 1331. Catherine's attempt to shift all the blame on to Jane, insisting it was she who had pushed her into encouraging Culpepper, is from her so-called 'confession' to Cranmer, dated 12 November 1541: see Longleat, Portland Papers, PO/i, fos. 51–3v, printed in full in HMC Bath (1907), II, pp. 8–10. The seizure of Culpepper's possessions on 14 November is from *LP,* XVI, no. 1343. The Knyvett affair is from *LP,* XVI, no. 760, and Wriothesley (1875–7), I, p. 125. Henry's reaction to Catherine's betrayal is from *LP,* XVI, no. 1426. The trial and executions of Dereham and Culpepper, and subsequent parliamentary attainders, are from NA, KB 8/13/1; *LP,* XVI, nos. 1395, 1426, 1430, 1432 and 1434; *LP,* XVII, nos. 28 (p. 13) and 63; Parliament (1542) [*Anno tricesimo tertio Henrici Octavi*], sigs. f.ii–f.v (*STC*, no. 9405.5); *State Papers* (1830–52), I, pp. 701, 704 and 707. Mary Lascelles's narrow escape is from *State Papers* (1830–52), I, pp. 704–5, and *LP,* XVI, no. 1433. The Duchess of Norfolk's opening of the coffers is from *LP,* XVI, nos. 1409, 1416, 1422, 1423, 1424, 1425, 1467, 1469 and 1470, and *State Papers* (1830–52), I, pp. 696–702. Dereham's visit to Ireland is from *LP,* XVI, nos. 1409 and 1416.

Walsingham's problem concerning the secure custody of his many prisoners is from *LP,* XVI, nos. 1433, 1437 and 1489 (pp. 706 and 708). The prisoners' repentance is from ibid., no. 1471, and *State Papers* (1830–52), I, p. 726. Norfolk's letter to Henry is from *State Papers* (1830–52), I, p. 721 and *LP,* XVI, no. 1454. Marillac's reference to Catherine's brothers riding through the streets is from *LP,* XVI, no. 1426. The Morley land transaction is from *LP,* XVII, no. 54. James Boleyn's securing of Jane Rochford's 'stuff' is from *LP,* XVII, no. 119. Gage's breaking up of Catherine's household at Syon is from *LP,* XVII, no. 92. Her behaviour at Syon is from *CSP Sp*, VI, i, no. 228. Her journey to the Tower and her request to practise with the block are from ibid., no. 232, and *LP,* XVII, no. 124.

Jane's removal from the Tower to regain her sanity in the more congenial surroundings of Russell House is from *LP,* XVI, no. 1401. This interpretation is further documented by Charles Wriothesley, who mentions Jane being taken to the Tower on two separate occasions: see Wriothesley (1875–7), I, pp. 131 and 133. Since Henry wanted justice to be seen to be done, it makes perfect sense that he would ensure that Jane was fit enough to acquiesce rather than collapse completely on the scaffold or, worse, to die from fright inside the Tower. This had also been his policy prior to the execution of Bishop John Fisher, to whom Henry sent his finest doctor and whose bills he paid.

32, Royal Justice: pp. 304–14

The only genuine eyewitness account of the executions is from Ottwell Johnson: see *LP,* XVII, no. 106, transcribed and printed in full in Ellis

(1824–46), 1st series, II, pp. 128–9. Marillac's account is from *LP,* XVII, no. 100. That of Chapuys is from *LP,* XVII, no. 124, and *CSP Sp,* VI, i, no. 232. The Privy Council meeting attended by both Norfolk and Suffolk is from *LP,* XVII, no. 103. Henry's reaction is from *LP,* XVII, nos. 124 and 178, and ibid., Appendix B, no. 13.

I am indebted to James Simpson for considering *De claris mulieribus* in relation to Jane's death. His superb analysis is from his essay in Axton and Carley (2000), pp. 153–69. His interpretation of Polyxena's death forms the basis of my ideas on Morley's response to Jane's execution, although I tend to go slightly further in seeing Morley's translation as a veiled obituary for his daughter. I am deeply indebted to Jessica Sharkey of Clare College, Cambridge, for her incisive comparison of Boccaccio's original text with Morley's translation of the Polyxena passage. She has pointed out that Morley turned 'throat' into 'neck', a far more significant word in the context of decapitation. The Latin version may conveniently be compared with Morley's English translation: see Wright (1943), pp. 105–6.

Lady Morley's contribution to the new bells at St Giles is from ERO, MS DP/27/5/1, fo. 31. This is the only known reference to either of the Morleys contributing to the village church before Jane's death, although the bells were often in need of repair or replacement. For reference to the bell today, see Cocks and Hardie (1994), p. 14.

My account of the geography of the Tower of London is from Keay (2001), pp. 25–49. Cf. Ives (2004), p. 357.

EPILOGUE: pp. 315–26

The first references to the eighteenth-century works are from Stone (1766), p. 247, Carte (1752), III, p. 163, Granville [undated], I, p. 104, Coote (1791), V, p. 79, and Birch (1747), p. 26. It is true that Marillac wrote to Francis that 'all her life' Jane 'had the name to esteem her honour little', but had Marillac been correct it is quite improbable that Henry would have allowed such a woman unrestricted access into his wives' privy chambers. Since Marillac also said in this despatch that Jane was now 'in her old age', whereas she was actually less than forty, his information is suspect: see *LP,* XVI no. 1366. In my investigation of John Foxe's *Actes and Monuments* I examined the following editions: Foxe (1563) [*STC,* no. 11222], Foxe (1576) [*STC,* no. 11224], II, p. 1181, and Foxe (1583) [*STC,* no. 11225], II, p. 1210. The account by Chapuys of the trials is from *CSP Sp*, V, ii, no. 55. John Spelman's reference in his notebook to Lady Wingfield is from Spelman (1976–7), I, p. 71. The references to Cromwell and Husee are from *LP*, X, nos. 873 and 953; see also the notes to chapter 21.

Discussion of Wyatt's 'Memoir of Anne Boleyn' is from the text printed as an appendix to Cavendish (1825), II, pp. 182, 207 and 212. Constantine's 'Memorial' is from Amyot (1831), pp. 50–78. The crucial reference to a letter is on p. 66. For details on John Payne Collier, see *ODNB*. Alexander Ales's letter to Elizabeth is from NA, SP 1/70, fos. 1–10 (stamped fos. 3–13), and *CSPF, Elizabeth*, I, 1558–9, no. 1303. John Day's career and links to Cecil are from Evenden (2004a), pp. 383–94, Evenden (2004b), and Evenden and Freeman (2004), pp. 1288–1307. Day as Cecil's 'tame printer' is from Guy (2004), pp. 467–8. Lord Herbert of Cherbury's denunciation of Jane is from p. 36 of the 1649 edition (Wing H-1504), and from p. 583 of the 1672 edition (Wing H-1701). For Heylin's references to Jane, see Heylin (1660), pp. 91 and 93. Burnet's opinions are from Burnet (1820), I, i, pp. 306 and 484–5. His later comment, stating that the only evidence that could be brought against Anne was Smeaton's confession, is from Burnet (1820), III, i, p. 174. John Stow lists his sources in Stow (1592), the table of authors after 'Preface to the Reader', and *STC*, no. 23334. His accounts of the deaths of Anne and of Catherine appear on pp. 966–7 and 982–3. Neither Stow nor Burnet accuses Jane of being the key informant who brought down the Boleyns. William Camden's account of Anne's fall, which again makes no mention of Jane, is from Camden (1635), Introduction, sigs. d2^v–d3^v, and *STC*, no. 4501.

To eliminate Anthony Anthony as a source of Jane's traducement, it is essential to consult Thomas Turner's notes on Anthony's lost 'Chronicle', bound into his mispaginated copy of the 1649 edition of Herbert's *Life and Raigne of King Henry the Eighth*: see Bodleian, Folio Delta 624 [*sic*], pp. 381–5 (pages out of sequence; new numbering beginning after p. 404), and (on Catherine Howard and Culpepper) pp. 473–4. For Turner's unique system of annotation, see especially the interpolations facing pp. 384, 385, 392, 394, 462, 473–4 and 565. Ives (2004), p. 131, cites Anthony's lost journal as referring to Jane, stating that the words he used probably included the 'particular instrument' phrase. In fact, as I have shown, this is Turner, not Anthony at all, and Turner's reference to '*postea* 474' is to the printed text of Herbert. Quotations in the eighteenth century deploring the alleged 'iniquities' of Jane are from Smollett (1759), VI, p. 35, *Book of Martyrs* (1765), IV, p. 117, Cavendish (1825), II, p. 74, Helme (1798), I, p. 63, and Hume (1796), III, p. 64.

APPENDIX: pp. 327–9

For general details on Holbein's life and work, see Foister (1981), Foister (2004), and Foister (2006). The drawing of Lady Parker is from Parker (1983), no. 73. Discussion of her identity relies on ibid., p. 56. The identification of the woman as Grace Parker is not disputed by Susan Foister, ibid., p. 158. G. S. Davies is the one dissenting voice, maintaining that Lady Parker is indeed Jane Rochford, a woman for whom he has no sympathy whatsoever. See Davies (1903), p. 182. He also states that the drawing is on white, not pink-primed paper, but in this also he is alone in his view. For information on Holbein identifications in general, and John Cheke's role in particular, see Foister (2004), pp. 24–9. Of the many references to Holbein's use of white and pink-primed paper, see Parker (1983), pp. 24–8, and Foister (2004), pp. 51–2.

While it is true that Holbein produced no definitely authenticated likenesses of Anne Boleyn, two of his drawings have been alleged to depict her. For an interesting analysis, see Rowlands and Starkey (1983), pp. 88 and 90–2. Susan Foister discusses the costume drawing in Foister (2004), p. 56, and Foister (2006), p. 110. For further information on the table fountain designed for Anne as a present for Henry, see ibid., p. 86, no. 93.

Bibliography

The printed works cited in the Bibliography are intended to provide a checklist of full references to the works cited in the notes, and also to include books and articles that were extensively consulted in researching this book.

Amyot, T. (1831). 'Transcript from an Original Manuscript, containing a Memorial from George Constantyne to Thomas Lord Cromwell', *Archaeologia*, 23, 50–78

Anglo, S. (1969). *Spectacle, Pageantry, and Early Tudor Policy*, Oxford

Anglo, S. (1992). *Images of Tudor Kingship*, London

Annenberg School (1972). *Westminster Abbey*, ed. Annenberg School of Communications with the co-operation of Weidenfeld & Nicolson, London

Anon. (1532a). *The maner of the tryumphe at Caleys and Bulleyn*, London

Anon. (1532b). *The maner of the tryumphe at Caleys [and] Bulleyn. The second pryntyng, with mo addicio[n]s as it was done in dede*, 2nd edn, London

Anon. (1533). *The noble tryumphaunt coronacyon of quene Anne wyfe vnto the moost noble kynge Henry the viij*, London

Anon. (1761). *Adultery Anatomized: in a Select Collection of Tryals, for Criminal Conversation. Brought down from the Infant Ages of Cuckoldom in England, to its Full Growth in the Present Times*, 2 vols., London

Arnold, Janet (1988). *Queen Elizabeth's Wardrobe Unlock'd: The Inventories of the Wardrobe of Robes prepared in July 1600, edited from Stowe MS 557 in the British Library, MS LR 2/121 in the Public Record Office, London, and MS V.b. 72 in the Folger Shakespeare Library, Washington DC*, Leeds

Atkinson, A. G. (1896). 'Reformation Changes in a City Parish', *English Historical Review*, 11, 522–7

Axton M. and Carley, J. P. (2000). *Triumphs of English: Henry Parker, Lord Morley, Translator to the Tudor Court, New Essays in Interpretation*, London

Baker, J. H. (2003). *The Oxford History of the Laws of England*, VI, *1483–1558*, Oxford

Baker, Richard (1670). *A Chronicle of the Kings of England from the Time of the Romans' Government unto the Death of King James*, London

Bätschmann, O. and Griener, P. (1997). *Hans Holbein*, London

Bayley, J. (1821). *The History and Antiquities of the Tower of London, with Memoirs of Royal and Distinguished Persons, deduced from Records, State Papers and Manuscripts*, 2 vols., London

Bayne, C. J. (1907). 'The Coronation of Queen Elizabeth', *English Historical Review*, 22, 650–73

Bayne, C. J. (1910). 'The Coronation of Queen Elizabeth', *English Historical Review*, 25, 550–3

Bell, D. C. (1877). *Notices of the Historic Persons buried in the Chapel of St Peter ad Vincula in the Tower of London*, London

Bernard, G. W. (1991). 'The Fall of Anne Boleyn', *English Historical Review*, 106, 584–610

Bernard, G. W. (1992). 'The Fall of Anne Boleyn: A Rejoinder', *English Historical Review*, 107, 665–74

Bernard, G. W. (1993). 'Anne Boleyn's Religion', *Historical Journal*, 36, 1–20

Bernard, G. W. (1996). 'The Fall of Wolsey Reconsidered', *Journal of British Studies*, 35, 277–310

Bernard, G. W. (1998). 'The Making of Religious Policy: Henry VIII and the Search for the Middle Way', *Historical Journal*, 41, 321–49

Bernard, G. W. (2005). *The King's Reformation: Henry VIII and the Remaking of the English Church*, New Haven and London

Bindoff, S. T. (1982). *The House of Commons, 1509–1558*, 3 vols., History of Parliament, London

Birch, T. (1747). *The Heads of Illustrious Persons of Great Britain*, London

Blomefield, F. (1739–75). *An Essay towards a Topographical History of the County of Norfolk, containing a Description of the Towns, Villages, and Hamlets*, 5 vols., London

Book of Martyrs (1765). *The Book of Martyrs: or, Compleat History of Martyrdom, from the Crucifixion of our Blessed Saviour, to the Present Times*, 5 vols., London

Boorde, Andrew (1547). *The Breuiary of helthe for all maner of syckenesses and diseases the whiche may be in man, or woman doth folowe, expressynge the obscure termes of Greke, Araby, Latyn, and Barbary in to Englysh concerning phisicke and chierurgye / compyled by Andrewe Boord of phisicke Doctour an englysh man*, London

Brigden, S. (1989). *London and the Reformation*, Oxford

Brooke, Ralph (1619). *A catalogue and succession of the kings, princes, dukes, marquesses, earles, and viscounts of this realme of England, since the Norman Conquest, to this present yeare, 1619 Together, with their armes, wiues, and children: the times of their deaths and burials, with many their memorable actions. Collected by Raphe Brooke Esquire, Yorke Herauld: discouering, and reforming many errors committed, by men of other profession, and lately published in print*, London

Brown, R. (1854). *Four Years at the Court of Henry VIII: Selection of Despatches Written by the Venetian Ambassador, Sebastian Giustinian, and Addressed to the Signory of Venice, January 12th 1515 to July 26th 1519*, 2 vols., London

Burnet, Gilbert (1679–1714). *History of the Reformation of the Church of England*, 3 vols., London

Burnet, Gilbert (1820). *History of the Reformation of the Church of England*, new edn, 6 vols., London

Caius, John (1552). *A boke, or counseill against the disease commonly called the sweate, or sweatyng sicknesse*, London

Calais Chronicle (1846). *The Chronicle of Calais in the Reigns of Henry VII and Henry VIII to the Year 1540*, ed. J. G. Nicholls (Camden Society, 1st series, vol. 35), London

Camden, William (1635). *Annals, or The historie of the most renovvned and victorious princesse Elizabeth, late Queen of England Containing all the important and remarkable passages of state both at home and abroad, during her long and prosperous reigne. Written in Latin by the learned Mr William Camden. Translated into English by R. N. Gent. Together with divers additions of the authors never before published*, London

Campbell, T. P. (2007). *The Art of Majesty: Henry VIII's Tapestry Collection*, New Haven and London

Carley, J. P. (1989). 'John Leland and the Foundations of the Royal Library: the Westminster Inventory of 1542', *Bulletin of the Society for Renaissance Studies*, 7, 13–22

Carley, J. P. (1998). '"Her moost lovying and fryndely brother sendeth gretyng": Anne Boleyn's Manuscripts and their Sources', in

Illuminating the Book: Makers and Interpreters, ed. Michelle P. Brown and Scot McKendrick, London and Toronto, pp. 261–80

Carley, J. P. (2000). *The Libraries of King Henry VIII*, London

Carley, J. P. (2004). *The Books of King Henry VIII and his Wives*, London

Carte, T. (1747–55). *A General History of England*, 4 vols., London

Caryll, John (1999–2000). *Reports of Cases by John Caryll*, ed. J. H. Baker, 2 vols., Selden Society, London

Cavendish, George (1825). *The Life of Cardinal Wolsey* and *Metrical Visions*, ed. Samuel Weller Singer, 2 vols., London

Chamberlin, F. (1932). *The Private Character of Henry the Eighth*, London

Cocks, H. (1997). *The Great House of Hallingbury, its Place in History*, Great Hallingbury Local History Society, Great Hallingbury

Cocks, H. and Hardie, C. (1994). *St Giles, Great Hallingbury, A Brief History and Description to Commemorate its Restoration in 1874*, Great Hallingbury Local History Society, Great Hallingbury

Colvin, H. M. (1982). *The History of the King's Works*, IV, *1485–1625 (Part 2)*, London

Complete Peerage (1987). *The Complete Peerage of England, Scotland, Ireland, Great Britain and the United Kingdom by G.E.C[okayne].*, 6 vols., Gloucester

Coote, C. (1791–8). *The History of England, from the Earliest Dawn of Record to the Peace of MDCCLXXXIII*, 9 vols., London

Cox, J. E. (1846). *Miscellaneous Writings and Letters of Thomas Cranmer*, Parker Society, Cambridge

CPR (1914–16). *Calendar of Patent Rolls, 1485–1509*, 2 vols., London

Cressy, D. (1997). *Birth, Marriage and Death: Ritual, Religion and the Life-Cycle in Tudor and Stuart England*, Oxford

CSPF, Elizabeth (1863–1950). *Calendar of State Papers, Foreign: Elizabeth*, 23 vols., London

CSP Spanish (1862–1954). *Calendar of Letters, Despatches, and State Papers Relating to the Negotiations between England and Spain, Preserved in the Archives at Vienna, Brussels, Simancas and Elsewhere*, 13 vols., London

CSP Spanish Supplementary (1940). *Further Supplement to Letters, Despatches and State Papers Relating to the Negotiations between England and Spain*, ed. G. Mattingly, London

CSP Venice (1864–1947). *Calendar of State Papers and Manuscripts Relating to English Affairs, Existing in the Archives and Collections of Venice and in Other Libraries of Northern Italy*, 38 vols., London

Davies, G. S. (1903). *Hans Holbein the Younger*, London

Day, Angel (1586). *The English secretorie Wherin is contayned, a perfect method, for the inditing of all manner of epistles and familiar letters, together with their diuersities, enlarged by examples vnder their seuerall tytles. In which is layd forth a path-waye, so apt, plaine and easie, to any learners capacity, as the like wherof hath not at any time heretofore beene deliuered. Nowe first deuized, and newly published by Angel Daye*, London

Dewhurst, J. (1984). 'The Alleged Miscarriages of Catherine of Aragon and Anne Boleyn', *Medical History*, 28, 49–56

Dowling, M. (1984). 'Anne Boleyn and Reform', *Journal of Ecclesiastical History*, 35, 30–46

Dowling, M. (1986). *Humanism in the Age of Henry VIII*, Beckenham

Dowling, M. (1990). 'William Latymer's Chronickille of Anne Bulleyne', *Camden Miscellany*, 30 (Camden Society, 4th series, vol. 39), 23-65, 501–3

Duffy, E. (1992). *The Stripping of the Altars: Traditional Religion in England, 1400–1580*, New Haven and London

Dyer, A. (1997). 'The English Sweating Sickness of 1551: An Epidemic Anatomized', *Medical History*, 41, 362–84

Ellis, H. (1824–46). *Original Letters, Illustrative of British History*, 3 series, 11 vols, London

Elton, G. R. (1972). *Policy and Police: The Enforcement of the Reformation in the Age of Thomas Cromwell*, Cambridge

Elton, G. R. (1973). *Reform and Renewal: Thomas Cromwell and the Common Weal*, Cambridge

Elton, G. R. (1974–92). *Studies in Tudor and Stuart Politics and Government*, 4 vols., Cambridge

Elton, G. R. (1977). *Reform and Reformation: England, 1509–1558*, London

Elton, G. R. (1982). *The Tudor Constitution*, 2nd edn, Cambridge

Evenden, E. (2004a). 'The Michael Wood Mystery: William Cecil and the Lincolnshire Printing of John Day', *Sixteenth Century Journal*, 35, 383–94

Evenden, E. (2004b). 'Biography of John Day', in *Actes and Monuments of Matters Most Speciall and Memorable*, Foxe's 'Book of Martyrs' Variorum Edition Online (v.1.0) (electronic publication) at www.hrionline.ac.uk/foxe/apparatus/evendenbiogjdayessay.html

Evenden, E. and Freeman, T. S. (2004). 'Print, Profit and Propaganda: The Elizabethan Privy Council and the 1570 Edition of Foxe's "Book of Martyrs"', *English Historical Review*, 119, 1288–1307

Fiddes, R. (1724). *The Life of Cardinal Wolsey*, London

Flood, J. L. (2003). '"Safer on the Battlefield than in the City": England, the "Sweating Sickness", and the Continent', *Renaissance Studies*, 17, 147–76

Foister, S. (2006). *Holbein in England*, London

Foister, S. (1981). 'Holbein and his English Patrons', unpublished London Ph.D. thesis, London University

Foister, S. (2004). *Holbein and England*, New Haven and London

Fox, A. and Guy, J. A. (1986). *Reassessing the Henrician Age: Humanism, Politics, and Reform*, Oxford

Foxe, John (1563). *Actes and monuments of these latter and perillous dayes touching matters of the Church, wherein are comprehended and decribed the great persecutions [and] horrible troubles, that haue bene wrought and practised by the Romishe prelates, speciallye in this realme of England and Scotlande . . .*, London

Foxe, John (1576). *The first volume of the ecclesiasticall history contayning the actes [and] monumentes of thinges passed in euery kinges time, in this realme, especially in the Churche of England principally to be noted . . . Newly recognised and inlarged by the author*, 2 vols., London

Foxe, John (1583). *Actes and monuments of matters most speciall and memorable, happenyng in the Church with an vniuersall history of the same, wherein is set forth at large the whole race and course of the Church, from the primitiue age to these latter tymes of ours . . . Newly reuised and recognised, partly also augmented, and now the fourth time agayne published . . .*, 2 vols., London.

Foxe, John (1843–9). *The Acts and Monuments of John Foxe*, ed. G. Townsend, 8 vols., London

Friedmann, P. (1884). *Anne Boleyn: A Chapter of English History, 1527–1536*, 2 vols., London

Gairdner, J. (1983). 'Mary and Anne Boleyn', *English Historical Review*, 30, 53–60, 299–300

Granville, C. (1747?). *A Synopsis of the Troubles and Miseries of England, during the Space of 1800 Years*, 4 vols., London

Gunn, S. J. (1988). *Charles Brandon, Duke of Suffolk, 1484–1545*, Oxford

Guy, J. A. (1980). *The Public Career of Sir Thomas More*, New Haven and Brighton

Guy, J. A. (1982). 'Henry VIII and the *Praemunire* Manoeuvres of 1530–1531', *English Historical Review*, 97, 481–503

Guy, J. A. (1985). *Christopher St German on Chancery and Statute*, Selden Society, London

Guy, J. A. (1988). *Tudor England*, Oxford

Guy, J. A. (2000a). *Thomas More*, London

Guy, J. A. (2000b). *Politics, Law and Counsel in Tudor and Early Stuart England*, Aldershot

Guy, J. A. (2004). '*My Heart is My Own': The Life of Mary Queen of Scots*, London

Haigh, C. A. (1993). *English Reformations: Religion, Politics, and Society under the Tudors*, Oxford

Hall, Edward (1904). *Henry VIII* [an edition of Hall's Chronicle], ed. C. Whibley, 2 vols., London

Halliwell, J. O. (1848). *Letters of the Kings of England*, 2 vols., London

Harpsfield, N. (1932). *The life and death of Sir Thomas Moore, knight, sometymes Lord high Chancellor of England, written in the tyme of Queene Marie*, ed. E. V. Hitchcock (Early English Text Society, original series, no. 186), London

Harris, B. (1986). *Edward Stafford, Third Duke of Buckingham, 1478–1521*, Stanford, Ca.

Harris, B. (2002). *English Aristocratic Women 1450–1550: Marriage and Family, Property and Careers*, Oxford

Harrison, K. (1953). *An Illustrated Guide to the Windows of King's College Chapel Cambridge*, Cambridge

Hayward, M. (2004). *The 1542 Inventory of Whitehall: The Palace and its Keeper*, 2 vols., Society of Antiquaries, London

Helme, E. (1798). *Instructive Rambles in London, and the Adjacent Villages. Designed to Amuse the Mind, and Improve the Understanding of Youth*, 2 vols., London

Herbert of Cherbury, Edward (1649). *The Life and Raigne of King Henry the Eighth*, London

Herman, P. C. (1994). *Rethinking the Henrician Era: Essays on Early Tudor Texts and Contexts*, Urbana and Chicago, Il.

Heylin, P. (1660). *Affairs of Church and State in England during the Life and Reign of Queen Mary*, London

HMC Bath (1907). *Calendar of the Manuscripts of the Marquis of Bath preserved at Longleat, Wiltshire*, vol. II, Historical Manuscripts Commission, London

Howard, M. and Wilson, E. (2003). *The Vyne: A Tudor House Revealed*, London

Hume, D. (1796). *The History of England, from the Invasion of Julius Cæsar to the Revolution in 1688*, 5 vols., Montrose

Ives, E. W. (1972). 'Faction at the Court of Henry VIII: the Fall of Anne Boleyn', *History*, 57, 169–88

Ives, E. W. (1983). *The Common Lawyers of Pre-Reformation England*, Cambridge

Ives, E. W. (1992). 'The Fall of Anne Boleyn Reconsidered', *English Historical Review*, 107, 651–64

Ives, E. W. (1994a). 'Anne Boleyn and the Early Reformation in England: the Contemporary Evidence', *Historical Journal*, 37, 389–400

Ives, E. W. (1994b). 'The Queen and the Painters: Anne Boleyn, Holbein and Tudor Royal Portraits', *Apollo*, 140, 36–45

Ives, E. W. (1996). 'Anne Boleyn and the "Entente Évangélique"', ed. C. Giry-Deloison, Centre d'Histoire de la Région du Nord et de l'Europe du Nord-Ouest and Institut Français, Collection 'Histoire et Littérature Régionales', 13, Lille and London, pp. 83–102

Ives, E. W. (1998). 'A Frenchman at the Court of Anne Boleyn', *History Today*, 48:8, 21–6

Ives, E. W. (2004). *The Life and Death of Anne Boleyn*, 2nd edn, Oxford

Keay, A. (2001). *The Elizabethan Tower of London: The Haiward and Gascoyne Plan of 1597*, London

Kelly, H. A. (1976). *The Matrimonial Trials of Henry VIII*, Stanford, Ca.

Kingsford, C. L. (1905). *Chronicles of London*, Oxford

Knecht, R. J. (1994). *Renaissance Warrior and Patron: The Reign of Francis I*, Cambridge

Knighton, C. S. and Mortimer, R. (2003). *Westminster Abbey Reformed, 1540–1640*, Aldershot

Knowles, D. (1959). *The Religious Orders in England*, III, *The Tudor Age*, Cambridge

Lehmberg, S. E. (1970). *The Reformation Parliament, 1529–1536*, Cambridge

Lehmberg, S. E. (1977). *The Later Parliaments of Henry VIII, 1536–1547*, Cambridge

Levine, M. (1973). *Tudor Dynastic Problems, 1460–1571*, London

Lisle Letters (1981). *The Lisle Letters*, ed. M. St Clare Byrne, 6 vols., Chicago and London

LJ (1767–1846). *Journals of the House of Lords*, 61 vols., London

Lloyd, C. and Thurley, S. (1990). *Henry VIII: Images of a Tudor King*, London

Lloyd Jones, G. (1983). *The Discovery of Hebrew in Tudor England: A Third Language*, Manchester

Lloyd Jones, G. (1989). *Robert Wakefield: On the Three Languages (1524)*, ed. and trans. with introduction and notes, New York

Loach, J. (1994). 'The Function of Ceremonial in the Reign of Henry VIII', *Past and Present*, 143, 43–68

Loach, J. (1999). *Edward VI*, New Haven and London

Loades, D. M. (1968). *The Papers of George Wyatt, Esquire, of Boxley Abbey in the County of Kent* (Camden Society, 4th series, vol. 5), London

Loades, D. M. (1986). *The Tudor Court*, London

Loades, D. M. (1989). *Mary Tudor: A Life*, Oxford

Loades, D. M. (1991). *The Reign of Mary Tudor: Politics, Government and Religion in England, 1553–1558*, 2nd edn, London

LP (1862–1932). *Letters and Papers, Foreign and Domestic, of the Reign of Henry VIII*, ed. J. S. Brewer, J. Gairdner, and R. H. Brodie, 21 vols. in 32 parts, and *Addenda*, with revised edition of vol. 1 in 3 parts, London

MacCulloch, D. (1995). 'Henry VIII and the Reform of the Church', in *The Reign of Henry VIII: Politics, Policy and Piety*, ed. D. MacCulloch, London, pp. 159–80

MacCulloch, D. (1996). *Thomas Cranmer: A Life*, New Haven and London

McEntegart, R. (2002). *Henry VIII, the League of Schmalkalden and the English Reformation*, Rochester, NY

Madden, F. (1831). *Privy Purse Expenses of the Princess Mary, Daughter of King Henry the Eighth, afterwards Queen Mary*, London

Manuale (1875). *Manuale et Processionale ad Usum Insignis Ecclesiae Eboracensis* [with appendix 1: *Manuale ad Usum Insignis Ecclesiae Sarum*], Surtees Society, York

Mendelson, S. and Crawford, P. (1998). *Women in Early-Modern England, 1550–1720*, Oxford

Merriman, R. B. (1902). *Life and Letters of Thomas Cromwell*, 2 vols., Oxford

Monumenta Westmonasteriensia (1683). *Monumenta Westmonasteriensia. Or an Historical Account of the Original, Increase, and Present State of St Peter's, or the Abbey Church of Westminster, with all the Epitaphs, Inscriptions, Coats of Arms and Achievements of Honour Belonging to the Tombs and Gravestones*, London

Morant, P. (1768). *The History and Antiquities of the County of Essex. Compiled from the Best and Most Ancient Historians*, 2 vols., London

Mottley, J. (1733–5). *A Survey of the Cities of London and Westminster, Borough of Southwark, and Parts Adjacent*, ed. Robert Seymour, 2 vols., London

Murphy, B. A. (2003). *Bastard Prince: Henry VIII's Lost Son*, Stroud

Murphy, V. M. (1984). 'The Debate over Henry VIII's First Divorce: an Analysis of the Contemporary Treatises', unpublished Ph.D. dissertation, Cambridge University

Murphy, V. M. (1995). 'The Literature and Propaganda of Henry VIII's First Divorce', in *The Reign of Henry VIII: Politics, Policy and Piety*, ed. D. MacCulloch, London, pp. 135–58

Murphy, V. M. and Surtz, E. (1988). *The Divorce Tracts of Henry VIII*, Angers

Newcourt, R. (1708–10). *Repertorium ecclesiasticum parochiale Londinense: An Ecclesiastical Parochial History of the Diocese of London*, 2 vols., London

Nicholson, G. D. (1988). 'The Act of Appeals and the English Reformation', in *Law and Government under the Tudors*, ed. Claire Cross, D. M. Loades, and J. J. Scarisbrick, Cambridge, pp. 19–30

Nicolas, N. H. (1834–7). *Proceedings and Ordinances of the Privy Council of England*, 7 vols., London

Norris, Herbert (1997). *Tudor Fashion and Costume*, New York

Paget, H. (1981). 'The Youth of Anne Boleyn', *Bulletin of the Institute of Historical Research*, 54, 162–70

Parker, K. T. (1983). *The Drawings of Hans Holbein in the Collection of Her Majesty the Queen at Windsor Castle*, with an appendix by Susan Foister, London and New York

Parliament (1542). *Anno tricesimo tertio Henrici Octaui Henry the VIII by the grace of God Kyng of Englande ... helde his moste hygh courte of Parlyamente begun at Westm[inster] the XVI. daye of Janyuer, and there contynued tyll the fyrste day of Apryll, the XXXIII. yere of his moste noble and vyctoryouse reygne wherin were establysshed these actes folowinge*, London

Perkins, Jocelyn (1938–40). *Westminster Abbey: Its Worship and Ornaments*, 2 vols, Alcuin Club, Oxford

Peters, C. (2000). 'Gender, Sacrament and Ritual: the Making and Meaning of Marriage in Late-Medieval and Early-Modern England', *Past and Present*, 169, 63–96

Pollard, A. F. (1902). *Henry VIII*, London

Pollard, A. F. (1903). *Tudor Tracts, 1532–1588*, London

Pollard, A. F. (1929). *Wolsey*, London

Prockter, A. and Taylor, R. (1979). *The A to Z of Elizabethan London*, London

Puttenham, R. (1589). *The Arte of English Poesie*, London

Rapin de Thoyras, P. (1727). *The History of England, as well Ecclesiastical as Civil*, 15 vols., London

Reformation Narratives (1859). *Narratives of the Days of the Reformation*, ed. J. G. Nicholls (Camden Society, 1st series, vol. 77), London

Reformation Records (1870). *Records of the Reformation: The Divorce, 1527–1533*, ed. Nicholas Pocock, 2 vols., Oxford

Rex, Richard (1993). *Henry VIII and the English Reformation*, London

Rex, Richard (1996). 'The Crisis of Obedience: God's Word and Henry's Reformation', *Historical Journal*, 39, 863–94

Rogers, E. F. (1961). *St Thomas More: Selected Letters*, New Haven and London

Roper, W. (1935). *The Lyfe of Sir Thomas Moore knighte, written by William Roper, Esquire, whiche married Margaret, daughter of the sayed Thomas Moore*, ed. E. V. Hitchcock (Early English Text Society, original series, no. 197), London

Round, J. H. (1886). *The Early Life of Anne Boleyn: A Critical Essay*, London

Rowlands, J. and Starkey, D. (1983). 'An Old Tradition Reasserted: Holbein's Portrait of Queen Anne Boleyn, *Burlington Magazine*, 125, 88, 90–2

Royal Book (1790). *A Collection of Ordinances and Regulations for the Government of the Royal Household*, Society of Antiquaries, London, pp. 109–33

Royal Collection (1978). *Holbein and the Court of Henry VIII*, London

Rutland Papers (1842). *Original Documents illustrative of the Courts and Times of Henry VII and Henry VIII . . . from the Private Archives of His Grace the Duke of Rutland*, ed. W. Jerdan (Camden Society, 1st series, vol. 21), London

Sarum Missal (1913). *The Sarum Missal in English*, ed. and trans. F. E. Warren, 2 vols., Alcuin Club, Oxford

Scarisbrick, J. J. (1956). 'The Pardon of the Clergy, 1531', *Cambridge Historical Journal*, 12, 22–39

Scarisbrick, J. J. (1968). *Henry VIII*, London

Scarisbrick, J. J. (1984). *The Reformation and the English People*, Oxford

Schofield, R. S. (1986). 'Did the Mothers Really Die? Three Centuries of Maternal Mortality in "The World We Have Lost"', in *The World We Have Gained: Histories of Population and Social Structure: Essays presented to Peter Laslett on his Seventieth Birthday*, ed. L. Bonfield et al., Oxford, pp. 231–60

Schofield, R. S. (2005). '"Monday's Child is Fair of Face": Favoured Days for Baptism, Marriage and Burial in Pre-Industrial England', *Continuity and Change*, 20, 93–109

Seymour, R. (1734). *A Survey of the Cities of London and Westminster*

Smith, L. B. (1961). *A Tudor Tragedy: The Life and Times of Catherine Howard*, London

Smith, L. B. (1971). *Henry VIII: The Mask of Royalty*, London

Smollett, T. G. (1758–60). *A Complete History of England, from the Descent of Julius Cæsar, to the Treaty of Aix la Chapelle, 1748*, 11 vols., London

Spelman, John (1976–7). *The Reports of Sir John Spelman*, ed. J. H. Baker, 2 vols., Selden Society, London

Starkey, D. R. (1987a). 'Court History in Perspective', in *The English Court from the Wars of the Roses to the Civil War*, ed. D. R. Starkey et al., London, pp. 1–24

Starkey, D. R. (1987b). 'Intimacy and Innovation: the Rise of the Privy Chamber', in *The English Court from the Wars of the Roses to the Civil War*, ed. D. R. Starkey et al., London, pp. 71–118

Starkey, D. R. (1991a). *The Reign of Henry VIII: Personalities and Politics*, London

Starkey, D. R. (1991b). *Henry VIII: A European Court in England*, London

Starkey, D. R. (2004). *Six Wives: The Queens of Henry VIII*, London

Starkey, D. R., Ward, P. and Hawkyard, A. (1998). *The Inventory of King Henry VIII. I, The Transcript*, Society of Antiquaries, London

State Papers (1830-52). *State Papers during the Reign of Henry VIII*, 11 vols., Record Commission, London

Statutes of the Realm (1810–28). *Statutes of the Realm*, ed. A. Luders, T. E. Tomlins, J. Raithby et al., 11 vols., London

STC (1976–91). *A Short-Title Catalogue of Books Printed in England, Scotland and Ireland, and of English Books Printed Abroad*, ed. W. A. Jackson, F. S. Ferguson and K. F. Pantzer, 2nd edn, 3 vols., London

Sterry, Wasey (1943). *The Eton College Register, 1441–1698*, Eton

Stone, E. (1766). *Remarks upon the History of the Life of Reginald Pole*, 2nd edn, Oxford

Stone. L. (1961). 'Marriage among the English Nobility in the 16th and

17th Centuries', *Comparative Studies in Society and History*, 3, 182–206

Stow, John (1592). *The Annales of England faithfully collected out of the most autenticall authors, records, and other monuments of antiquitie, from the first inhabitation vntill this present yeere 1592*, London

Stow, John (1956). *Stow's Survey of London*, ed. H. B. Wheatley, London

Strype, John (1721). *Ecclesiastical Memorials relating chiefly to Religion and the Reformation . . . under King Henry VIII, King Edward VI and Queen Mary I*, 3 vols., London

Strype, John (1840). *Memorials of Thomas Cranmer*, 2 vols., Oxford

Thurley, S. (1993). *The Royal Palaces of Tudor England Architecture and Court Life, 1460–1547*, New Haven and London

Thurley, S. (1999). *Whitehall Palace. An Architectural History of the Royal Apartments, 1240–1698*, New Haven and London

Thwaites, G., Taviner, M. and Gant, V. (1997). 'The English Sweating Sickness, 1485–1551', *New England Journal of Medicine*, 336, 580–2

Thwaites, G., Taviner M. and Gant, V. (1998). The English Sweating Sickness, 1485–1551: A Viral Pulmonary Disease?', *Medical History*, 42, 96–8

Wakefield, Robert (1528). *Roberti Wakfeldi sacrarum literaru[m] professoris eximij oratio de laudibus & vtilitate triu[m] linguar[um] Arabicae Chaldaicae & Hebraicae atq[ue] idiomatibus hebraicis quae in vtroq[ue] testame[n]to i[n]ueniu[n]tur*, London

Wakefield, Robert [n.d.]. *Kotser codicis R. Wakfeldi, quo praeter ecclesiae sacrosanctae decretum, probatur coniugium cum fratria carnaliter cognita, illicitum omnin, inhibitum, interdictumq[ue] effetum naturae iure, rum iure diuino, legeq[ue] euangelica atq[ue] consuetudi[n]e catholica ecclesiae orthodoxe*, London

Walker, G. (2002). 'Rethinking the Fall of Anne Boleyn', *Historical Journal*, 45, 1–29

Warnicke, R. M. (1985a). 'Anne Boleyn's Childhood and Adolescence', *Historical Journal*, 28, 939–52

Warnicke, R. M. (1985b). 'The Fall of Anne Boleyn: a Reassessment', *History*, 70, 1–15

Warnicke, R. M. (1986). 'The Eternal Triangle and Court Politics: Henry VIII, Anne Boleyn, and Sir Thomas Wyatt', *Albion*, 18, 565–79

Warnicke, R. M. (1987). 'Sexual Heresy at the Court of Henry VIII', *Historical Journal*, 30, 247–68

Warnicke, R. M. (1989). *The Rise and Fall of Anne Boleyn*, Cambridge

Warnicke, R. M. (1993). 'The Fall of Anne Boleyn Revisited', *English Historical Review*, 108, 653–65

Warnicke, R. M. (1998). 'The Conventions of Courtly Love and Anne Boleyn', in *State Sovereigns and Society in Early-Modern England: Essays in Honour of A. J. Slavin*, ed. C. H. Carlton et al., Stroud, pp. 103–18

Warnicke, R. M. (2000). *The Marrying of Anne of Cleves: Royal Protocol in Tudor England*, Cambridge

Wedgwood, J. C. and Holt, A. D. (1936). *Biographies of the Members of the Commons House, 1439–1509*, History of Parliament, London

Weever, John (1630). *Ancient funerall monuments within the vnited monarchie of Great Britaine, Ireland, and the islands adiacent with the dissolued monasteries therein contained: their founders, and what eminent persons haue beene in the same interred*, London

Wilkins, D. (1737). *Concilia Magnae Britanniae et Hiberniae*, 4 vols., London

Wood, M. A. (1846). *Letters of Royal and Illustrious Ladies of Great Britain*, 3 vols., London

Wright, H. G. (1943). *Forty Six Lives, Translated from Boccaccio's De Claris Mulieribus by Henry Parker, Lord Morley* (Early English Text Society, original series, no. 214), London

Wriothesely, Charles (1875–7). *A Chronicle of England during the Reigns of the Tudors, from AD 1485 to 1559*, 2 vols. (Camden Society, new series, vols. 11, 20), London

Wyatt, T. (1963). *Life and Letters of Sir Thomas Wyatt*, ed. K. Muir, Liverpool

Wyatt, T. (1969). *Collected Poems of Sir Thomas Wyatt*, ed. K. Muir and P. Thomson, Liverpool

Index

affair with Culpepper,
  287–90, 291, 292–9
taken to Syon, 291–2
Henry's despair and anger
  at behaviour of, 299–300
at Syon, 301, 302–3
found guilty, 302
taken to Tower, 303
preparations for execution
  of, 304–8
execution, 308–9, 311
burial, 312
brief references, 313, 315, 317,
  319, 320, 322, 325, 326
Howard, Lord Edmund, 269,
  280
Howard, Sir Edward, 9–10,
  214
Howard, Elizabeth *see*
  Boleyn (*née* Howard),
  Lady Elizabeth
Howard, Joyce, 280
Howard, Lady Mary, 106,
  126, 160
Howard, Thomas, second
  Duke of Norfolk *see*
  Norfolk, Thomas
  Howard, second Duke of
Howard, Thomas, third
  Duke of Norfolk *see*
  Norfolk, Thomas
  Howard, third Duke of
Howard, Lord William, 105,
  113, 236–7, 282
Hundred Years War, 9
Hungary, Queen of, 276
Hunsdon, 48, 223
Hunsdon, Henry Carey,
  Lord *see* Carey, Henry,
  later Lord Hunsdon
Huntingdon, Earl of, 133
Husee, John, 189, 198, 316
Hussey, Lord, 232

Ingham, 10
Ireland, 56, 276, 286, 301
Italy, 67, 69

James V, King of Scotland,
  256, 274, 275, 276
Jeanne of France, 66
Jenet, Ralph, 1
Jennings, Margaret (later
  Margaret Manox), 283
Jennings, Nicholas, 283
Johns, Mr, 286–7
Johnson, Ottwell, 307–8, 309,
  310, 311, 313

Jordan, Isabel, 73
Josselyn, Mrs Dorothy, 270
Julius II, Pope, 64

Katharine of Aragon, Queen
  birth and death of son
    Henry, 3
  problems with
    childbearing, 4, 22–3
  birth of daughter Mary, 4,
    22
  sewing skills, 11
  at Field of Cloth of Gold,
    16, 18, 23
  Henry's attention not
    focused on, 21
  marriage to Arthur, 22
  marriage to Henry, 22
  enjoys personal contact
    with Charles V, 27
  and elevation of Henry
    Fitzroy, 49
  and Henry's extra-marital
    affairs, 59
  no further hope of
    producing heir for Henry,
    60
  Henry seeks to end
    marriage to, 64–9
  informed about Henry's
    doubts about marriage, 70
  refuses to retreat to
    convent, 76
  and court case, 78–80
  and fall of Wolsey, 80–1
  remains in place, 84
  banished from court and
    separated from Mary, 88
  ordered to return her
    jewels, 88
  evaluates her position, 89
  title stripped from 94
  refuses title of Princess
    Dowager, 94
  Cranmer pronounces that
    Henry was never married
    to, 95
  barge requisitioned for
    Anne, 100
  coronation compared with
    Anne's coronation, 111
  lands transferred to Anne,
    116
  defiance of, 117, 134, 164
  Chapuys fears Anne will
    harm, 117, 165
  fears Anne's vengeance on
    Mary, 117–18

grass-roots support for, 118
and Clement's verdict, 119,
  121, 134
and Jane Boleyn, 135
frequent moves, 135
poor treatment of, 164
and support of Chapuys,
  164–5, 174
not allowed to care for
  Mary, 166
Anne appropriates property
  of, 167–8
illness, 174–6
death, 176
Anne's anxieties following
  death of, 177
Funeral, 178–9, 242
Anne accused of poisoning,
  199
brief references, 15, 29, 40,
  41, 55, 86, 125, 128, 146, 148,
  149, 150, 187, 188, 196, 205,
  228, 262, 323
Kenilworth, 212
Kent, 33, 35, 191, 195, 196
Kimbolton, 174, 175, 176
'King's Books', 69
King's College, Cambridge,
  120, 161, 162
Chapel, 162–3
King's Hall, 199, 201
King's Hatfield, 212
Kingston, Lady, 205, 237, 244
Kingston, Sir William, 89,
  102, 147, 186, 192, 193, 195,
  196, 197, 198, 199, 200,
  203, 204, 206, 220
Knights of the Bath, 102–4,
  109, 110, 113
Knights of the Garter, 182,
  236, 244, 263
Knyvett, Charles, 27
Knyvett, Sir Edmond, 299

Lambeth, 247, 280, 290
Lancashire, 118
Lascelles, Mary *see* Hall (*née*
  Lascelles), Mary
Lathbury, Hugh, 146
Latimer, Bishop Hugh, 132,
  232
Launceston, 146
Lawrence, Robert, 148
Leadenhall, 107
Lee, Edward, Archbishop of
  York, 91, 105, 110, 112
Lefèvre d'Etaples, 132
Leicester Abbey, 87, 159

The DESCRIPTION of the TOWER of LONDON with all the Buildings and the Outermost Limits thereof together with all such places adjoyning as do confine and abound the said Liberties. made by the direction of Sr John Peyton Knt.

TOWER HIL

The Posts of the Scaffold

Barkin Church

TOWER STREET

The Houses betwext the Church Yard and the Hill are old Katherines Rents.

The Cage

AH

The Bulwark Gate

THAMES STREET

Petty Wales

A

AB

B   C

THE

SCALA PERTICARUM